FEMINISM'S EMPIRE

FEMINISM'S EMPIRE

CAROLYN J. EICHNER

CORNELL UNIVERSITY PRESS
Ithaca and London

First published 2022 by Cornell University Press

ISBN 978-1-5017-6380-9 (hardcover)
ISBN 978-1-5017-6381-6 (paperback)
ISBN 978-1-5017-6382-3 (pdf)
ISBN 978-1-5017-6383-0 (epub)

Library of Congress Control Number: 2022931182

For Kennan

Contents

Illustrations

Acknowledgments

This book and I have shared a long, complex journey from inception to completion. Feminisms and feminists, and imperialisms and anti-imperialisms, stayed consistently centered as the project evolved and grew through research on three continents over more than a dozen years. In this frequently fascinating, often exciting, and sometimes frustrating process, what became *Feminism's Empire* and I together benefited from the generous support of multiple institutions, colleagues, friends, and family.

I had the privilege of spending an academic year researching and writing in the School of Historical Studies at the Institute for Advanced Study, Princeton. At the IAS, the member-organized Law and Colonialism seminar provided superb feedback, support, and fun. I sincerely thank members Emmanuelle Saada, Meredith Terretta, Daniela Caglioti, Rozaliya Garipova, Bryna Goodman, and Judith Surkis. My year-long Global Studies Research Fellowship at the University of Wisconsin–Milwaukee's Center for International Education allowed me time and the opportunity to work with a wonderful group of scholars. Much appreciation goes to former Director Patrice Petro, and to my "fellow Fellows," Rachel Ida Buff, Ivan Ascher, Bernard Perley, and Scott Graham. Additional grants and awards from the University of Wisconsin–Milwaukee's Department of History, Graduate School, Office of Research, and Center for International Education supported this project. At the University of South Florida, grants from the Humanities Institute, the College of Arts and Science, the Department of Women's Studies, and the Office of Research also partially funded my early research.

I am fortunate in having a magnificent set of mentors, superb scholars and kind friends, on whom I have long relied, and continue to do so. My profound gratitude to Elinor Accampo, Karen Offen, Laura Levine Frader, Patricia Lorcin, Marilyn Boxer, and the late, much missed Rachel Fuchs. I am also indebted to Julia Clancy-Smith, John Merriman, Joan Scott, and Odile Krakovitch for their insights and their support; to Steven Hause for sharing his enormous expertise; and to Lisa Silverman for our exciting and fruitful discussions. Naomi

Andrews, Jennifer Boittin, and Courtney Booker each enthusiastically read and provided keen, valuable critiques of substantial portions of this book. Jennifer Sessions, Camille Robcis, Jennifer Popiel, Mona Siegel, Lisa Leff, Joel Berkowitz, Robert Ingalls, and China Miéville have all given me discerning, constructive comments and ideas that bettered my study. One of the lovely aspects of academia is that professional interactions and connections have provided contexts through which my marvelous colleagues have become my friends. For this, and for this spectacular group of people, I am intensely thankful.

Thoughtful feedback and critique from generous colleagues in workshops and seminars have deeply enriched this study. I am grateful to the participants in the Beyond France seminar at Columbia University (especially Emmanuelle Saada, once again). My thanks also to the members of the Workshop on Interdisciplinary Approaches to Modern France and the Francophone World at the University of Chicago (particularly Bastien Craipain); to Roxanne Panchasi, at Simon Fraser University, for the seminar she organized around my work; to Jennifer Sessions (again!) and the Iowa European Studies Group at the University of Iowa; to Nina Kushner and the valuable colloquium she brought together at Clark University; to Katharina Karcher and the Militant Feminisms in Art and Politics interdisciplinary symposium at the University of Warwick, England; and to Regina Kreide and the Reemerging Racism: Genealogy, Mediations, and Contestations workshop at Justus Liebig University in Giessen, Germany. At the University of Hawai'i, Manoa, my thanks to Jonathan Goldberg-Hiller and the Indigenous Politics Network; to Alexander Mawyer and the Center for Pacific Island Studies; to the Oceana Ensemble and the East-West Center; and to Kathy Ferguson and the Women's Studies Colloquium. Near the beginning of the project, the extraordinary Valérie Morignat's invitation to speak at the *Louise Michel, figure de la transversalité* conference at the Sorbonne not only influenced my scholarship but also launched our deep friendship.

I presented elements of this book at a broad range of conferences across disciplines, years, and continents. I appreciate the thoughtful and careful comments of panel discussants, including Cheryl Koos, Gary Wilder, Joshua Cole, Bettina Brandt, Sina Kramer, Nina Kushner, Kathi Weeks, Richard Sonn, David Troyansky, Ulla Wikander, Kristina Hodelin-ter Wal, Judith Zinsser, and here again Laura Levine Frader and Elinor Accampo.

Valérie Morignat later extended a remarkable welcome to her home in Nouméa, New Caledonia. I am exceedingly grateful for the doors she opened and the introductions she made, for allowing me to see Nouvelle-Calédonie through her eyes and those of her family. Valérie's generosity, along with her late father André Morignat's hospitality, and her cousin Frédéric Medevielle's conviviality and kindness, assured that my research trip exceeded my highest expectations.

The librarians at the Centre Culturel Tjibaou and the archivists and librarians at the Archives de la Nouvelle-Calédonie—Ingrid Utchaou, Roselyne Kromopawiro, Christophe Dervieux, and Jean Moé Léonidas—directed me through their collections expertly and enthusiastically. I truly appreciate their help.

I owe a debt of gratitude to librarians and archivists at Paris's Bibliothèque nationale de France, Archives nationale, Archives de la préfecture de police, as well as at the Archives nationale d'outre mer in Aix-en-Provence. Special thanks for their knowledgeable and patient guidance to the archivists and librarians at the Bibliothèque Marguerite Durand, particularly Annie Metz, and at the Bibliothèque Historique de la ville de Paris, especially Luc Passion and Geneviève Morlet. Starting with my early research, Mieke Ijzermans, former Information Director at the International Institute of Social History in Amsterdam, facilitated and furthered my scholarly investigations, while simultaneously sharing with me her delightful friendship and hospitality. I also acknowledge the other staff at the IISH, who have been consistently helpful over many years.

At Cornell University Press, Emily Andrew patiently and persistently championed this book, for which I am grateful. Many thanks to Bethany Wasik for ably and generously stepping in on Emily's departure, and to Allegra Martschenko for the care and attention she has given me and my project. I also want to recognize the three readers for their thoughtful and useful critiques. An earlier form of chapter 3 appeared as *"La citoyenne* in the World: Hubertine Auclert and Feminist Imperialism," *French Historical Studies* 32, no. 1 (Winter 2009): 63–84 (Copyright 2009, Duke University Press. All rights reserved. Republished by permission of the publisher). Portions of chapter 4 originally appeared as "Language of Imperialism, Language of Liberation: Louise Michel and the Kanak-French Colonial Encounter," *Feminist Studies* vol. 45, no. 2 (2019), 377–408, in a special issue on *Indigenous Feminisms in Settler Contexts*. I appreciate the editors and anonymous readers at both journals.

Sarah Miles deserves special recognition for her excellent research assistance and superbly conscientious and thorough bibliography work. To my niece, Tess Eichner Considine, another *mille mercis* and much love for her careful contributions. I also want to acknowledge the undergraduate and graduate students in my courses on gender, sexuality, and imperialism at both the University of South Florida and later the University of Wisconsin–Milwaukee, for their creative ideas and enthusiasm that helped inspire my project. Thanks also to colleagues who attended and participated in my Brown Bag presentations in both Departments of History and Women's and Gender Studies at UWM.

My sister, Susan Eichner, has read and edited a good deal of this book, as she has generously done for the previous two. I continue to rely on her as my unfailing long-term "grammar hotline" and deeply value her outstanding editing skills and English language prowess. In these and many other ways, she is a marvelous sister and pal. My parents, Corrine Bochan Eichner and Norman Eichner, provided me near endless, enthusiastic, and loving support. My mother's commitment to feminism and love of history, my father's support of her choices, and both parents' social justice activism inspired and shaped my intellectual, personal, professional, and political trajectories. Both of my parents passed away during the writing of this book, leaving beautiful legacies and enormous absences.

Kennan Ferguson's contribution to this project is incalculable. Our ongoing discussions and debates, his incisive analyses and insights, and his near-boundless patience in reading, editing, and rereading my work, have fundamentally influenced the form and content of this book. I dedicate *Feminism's Empire* to Kennan in resounding appreciation for our magnificent partnership and the myriad ways he has enriched both this study and my life.

FEMINISM'S EMPIRE

Introduction

On June 25, 1878, an alliance of indigenous Kanak tribes undertook coordinated attacks on French colonial settlements in New Caledonia, France's South Pacific penal colony. The Kanak rose up against the imperial power that had maintained an oppressive regime in the archipelago for decades, one that had appropriated property, exploited people, undermined cultural practices, and disrupted ways of living. Struggling to drive out the French, the Kanak employed guerilla terror tactics. In planned simultaneous incursions, they slaughtered colonists and livestock and destroyed villages and crops. The colonial authority refused to recognize the raids as military strategies. Identifying the acts instead as mere savagery, the French responded with massive, brutal retaliatory force.

This Kanak revolt exploded as French political prisoners filled New Caledonia's colonial penitentiaries. Veterans of France's 1871 revolutionary civil war known as the Paris Commune, these insurgents had been exiled to the South Pacific penal colony in the wake of France's bloody repression of their insurrection. Yet when the Kanak rebelled, nearly all of the four thousand Communards incarcerated in New Caledonia sided with the imperial power. Despite France's ferociously violent suppression of the Paris Commune, including the military's slaughter of nearly twenty thousand insurgents in Paris's streets, the surviving defeated veterans now stood on the side of their vanquisher and jailer.

Louise Michel did not. Alone among the Communards, she allied with the Kanak. The revolutionary anarchist feminist, in dramatic contrast to her fellow French exiles, ripped in half the red revolutionary scarf she had successfully hidden during her arrest, incarceration, and deportation. Presenting the halves to two Kanak men, who, she later explained in her memoir *La Commune*, "had wanted to say *adieu* to me, they said, before joining their compatriots to battle the evil whites," she symbolically demonstrated her support for their anti-imperial uprising.[1] Michel's commitment to the Kanak raises questions as to why she prioritized an association based on rejecting the French state over the racial and civilizational solidarity chosen by the thousands of other French prisoners. What led her to a radicalism and identification that the others lacked? Why did only she resist French colonialism? What set this anarchist feminist apart from the other Communards and ultimately led her to both cross-racial alliances and an anti-imperialist stance?[2]

Feminists' Empire

Michel was one of five French feminists whose politics emerged as precursors to Third Republic (1873–1940) anti-imperialism. During a two-decade period of imperial expansion and rising metropolitan awareness of empire—a period that included the deportation of thousands of Parisians to the New Caledonian penal colony and uprisings against French colonization in both New Caledonia and Algeria—the vast majority of French feminists (and socialists) remained focused solely on European France. In sharp contrast, these five feminists separately and independently not only turned their attentions to empire, but also traveled into it either physically or fictionally. Modeling what would become French activists' and thinkers' censures of colonialism at the century's end, Olympe Audouard, Hubertine Auclert, Léonie Rouzade, Paule Mink, and Michel brought multiple feminist critiques against imperial power.[3]

The five activists espoused divergent feminist stances. Indicative of the era's diversity of feminisms, their positions ranged (along a right to left spectrum) from the liberal monarchist Olympe Audouard, to the republican socialists Hubertine Auclert and Léonie Rouzade, to the revolutionary socialist Paule Mink, and finally to the revolutionary anarchist socialist Michel.[4] Their politics fell distinctively along the era's feminist ideological continuum. The coincidence that the era's first feminists involved with empire stretched so neatly along the span of feminist politics presents a vivid array of the early intersections of feminisms and imperialisms. Despite espousing dissimilar ideologies, each of these feminists developed critiques of empire. What was it about feminism that fostered anti-imperialism? Given their differing politics, what role did ideology play in shaping both their feminisms and their individual attitudes toward empire? Tracing these activists' political engagements and interrelationships creates an ideological cartography that maps onto the emergence of the period's anti-imperialisms.

Each of the five feminists contested the French imperial project in specific ways. None of their anti-imperialisms, however, was absolute: they did not all reject imperialism *per se*, but instead sought to transform it for their own goals. Suffragist Auclert and novelist Rouzade, for example, saw in empire the potential for positive sociopolitical change, while revolutionaries Mink and Michel overtly opposed the practices and justifications of empire. The feminists' five diverse political stances established the intricacies and contradictions of subsequent French anti-imperialisms, a range of positions that would evolve and expand, convulsing the Francophone world for the next century.

Opposition to empire had long existed among certain French thinkers, reaching back to Enlightenment philosophers Voltaire and Diderot, through the French Revolution to Maximilien Robespierre, and the post-revolutionary Benjamin Constant, but it had essentially disappeared by 1830.[5] Socialists, like feminists, almost universally remained mute on the topic until the mid-1880s.[6] When Michel, Mink, Rouzade, Auclert, and Audouard engaged with empire between the mid-1860s and mid-1880s, they inaugurated an array of anti-imperial perspectives.

With gender as a shared central analytic, these five feminists' writings and orations dramatize the race, class, religious, and sexual politics of the epoch's imperial worlds. The political bound closely with the experiential, as these activists traveled and lived in places including Algeria, New Caledonia, Egypt, and the North American "Kingdom of the Mormons." Colonial encounters shaped their politics. Just as their interventions had varied levels of impact on colonial spaces, the activists' outlooks and ideas altered the metropolitan ideological landscape.

Jews held a distinct position in empire, as they dwelled both in France and in many imperial locales. Associated with the Orient, they retained a foreignness at home; when encountered in empire, they appeared simultaneously recognizable and distant: what could be called a "familiar stranger." Jews spanned, but remained separate from, both worlds. Of the five women, Audouard, Auclert, and Michel each wrote of encounters with Jews—either impressionistically, as in Michel's poem denouncing Algerian antisemitism; instrumentally, as in Auclert's political use of the threat of the foreign male Jew; or intimately, as in Audouard's stereotypically antisemitic description of the stench arising from a Constantinople Jewish neighborhood. Audouard, Auclert, and Michel all used the figure of "The Jew," a widely recognized trope wrapped in gendered, sexualized, and racialized stereotypes, as a straw-person around and against whom they could promote profoundly divergent political goals.

Tracing the topography of nineteenth-century French feminisms and their interconnections with the era's broader politics involves navigating interlaced ideological and experiential paths. Crucially, these feminists based their anti-imperialisms in opposition to exploitation. Among the five women, resistance to empire ranged from the anarchist Michel's professed complete opposition to imperial power to Rouzade's feminist literary appropriation of colonial undertakings. Imperialism presented for feminists a possible political framework through which to critique state power. It also appeared as a potential tool for advancing their own politics. Despite ideological and positional differences and despite advocating what they considered the liberatory capacities of empire, all of these activists opposed forms of existing imperialisms.

The Activists

Why and how did Audouard, Auclert, Rouzade, Mink, and Michel become involved in empire so much earlier than other French feminists and socialists of their era? Delving into the five women's histories and their personal and public trajectories helps to clarify the diverse life courses that brought them all into the contested realms of global empire. Analyzing and contextualizing aspects of each woman's history show what led them to reframe and reproach imperialisms—even while advocating and participating in some of its forms. Their experiences and politics provide entrées into the gendered, racialized, and sexualized imperial milieux and demonstrate both the breadth and centrality of feminisms in the evolution of French imperial politics. Each woman exemplified a strain of the era's feminisms. Exploring their positions not only illuminates the period's range of French feminisms, but also asks what these differing politics meant as each feminist engaged with empire.

The farthest to the political right of the activists was the monarchist Olympe de Jouval Audouard. Born in 1830, she was a prolific and well-known travel writer, a journalist and editor, a novelist, and a charismatic public speaker. Rooted in liberal feminism, royalism, and Catholicism (although she later turned to Spiritism), Audouard had begun her public push for women's political rights and marriage reform in the 1860s.[7] In 1867, she established the journal La revue cosmopolite. When she requested to register it as a political publication—a necessary step under the Second Empire's press restrictions—the government refused, stating that such a privilege was due only to citizens, not to women. This gender-based denial intensified Audouard's existing hostility toward the regime. Participating in Paris's widely attended and controversial public meetings movement in the final months of the Second Empire, she lectured on "Marriage, Separation, and Divorce."[8] This speech numbered among her numerous attacks on women's subordinated legal status during the Second Empire and into the Third Republic. Audouard published over thirty books and pamphlets between 1862 and 1886 on topics ranging from the history of women over millennia, to travel across the American West, to the Turkish harem.

Audouard maintained a fairly high profile in the world of moderate, rights-based feminism. As a liberal, she accepted the era's socioeconomic status quo; as a monarchist, she supported hierarchies of rank; as an observant Catholic, she embraced the teachings of the church. Although critical of republicans (but not republican ideals), free-thinkers (whom she suggested be more properly termed "tyrannical thinkers"), and the working class (whom she called "la canaille," the rabble), when she did challenge power relations, it was those of gender.[9]

Personal experiences clearly influenced Audouard's developing politics. As a young woman, she married a cousin she had known only briefly. Her husband proved feckless and deceitful—she described him as a "Don Juan"—and he ran away with her inherited wealth shortly after the birth of their children. France's Napoleonic Code of Law gave husbands complete control over the wealth and property a wife brought to marriage and forbade legal divorce. The personal impact of this deeply gendered legal system profoundly shaped Audouard's worldview and politics. Long a traveler and a writer, Audouard combined the two to meet her sudden economic need. As she journeyed across Russia, the United States, North Africa, and the Middle East, Audouard focused especially on the gendering of law and custom as it affected women's lives. Her narratives went beyond the descriptive in analyzing the gendered nature of formal and informal structures.

Audouard approached the cultures she encountered with a combination of curiosity and prejudice. For example, as an elite European in the Ottoman Empire, she had entrée into wealthy Turkish homes, and on her first trip to Constantinople, she marveled at the comfort and luxury in which women lived, as well as expressing surprise at the contrast with the image that she held previously from reading the tales of Scheherezade in *One Thousand and One Nights*.[10] She accepted this rarefied realm as the norm and did not engage in a class-based critique—in contrast to the four other feminists examined here. Audouard valued wealth and luxury; her writing expressed a relative ease and a kind of solidarity with other elites. For her, class alliance often superseded racial and religious differences. Correspondingly, class dissimilarity intensified those differences, as exemplified by her antisemitic remarks on the filth and squalor in which Constantinople's Jews lived.

The suffragist Hubertine Auclert's politics contrasted notably with those of Audouard (although she, too, wielded prejudicial Jewish stereotypes).[11] Auclert's interest in Algerian women grew from her feminist, socialist, and republican commitments. Born in 1848, Auclert spent her teenage years living and studying in a Catholic convent, following the death of her father. Deeply unhappy in this world, she became intensely anticlerical and anti-Catholic. By the age of twenty-five, Auclert decamped from her provincial home in the *département* of Alliers for Paris, where she quickly emerged as one of the first and foremost of the era's advocates of French women's suffrage.

Though she initially joined liberal feminists Léon Richer and Maria Deraismes in the nascent moderate women's rights movement, Auclert subsequently broke with both because their advocacy of civil, but not full political, rights for women conflicted with her more radical goals.[12] Espousing a rights-based republican socialist feminism, she worked with a number of burgeoning socialist groups in the late 1870s, attempting to integrate women's political equality into their programs. Briefly successful in gaining the backing of the socialist Parti Ouvrier Français in 1879, she faced expulsion the following year in the aftermath of internecine battles.

Auclert stood alone at the head of the suffrage campaign in these years, garnering minimal support from other feminists and attracting enormous opposition from detractors across the political spectrum. Never a proponent of violent revolutionary change, she nonetheless gained widespread notoriety for her electoral activism, which reached a crescendo in 1880–1881. That year she undertook public civil disobedience by organizing women in a property-tax boycott (against taxation without representation), heading a campaign to (illegally) register women to vote, coordinating a strike against the national census, and—famously—publicly overturning a ballot box.[13] Auclert contended that women, denied the right of full citizenship, had no obligation to pay taxes, and that the disenfranchisement of 50 percent of the population rendered both elections and the census illegitimate. Flamboyantly expressing her resistance to the Napoleonic Code of Law, at its one-hundredth anniversary celebration, she attempted to set a copy on fire.[14] As a profound believer in the liberatory potential of republicanism, Auclert condemned the existing republic for perpetuating women's marginalization. Sustained by her family wealth, she (through what her biographer Steven C. Hause has termed her "indefatigable dedication") inserted the idea of women's suffrage into the French political landscape, where she persisted as its champion for the remaining three and a half decades of her life.[15]

Her 1881 establishment of *La citoyenne*, France's first suffragist newspaper, epitomized this project. It also became the platform for her developing feminist imperialism. Insisting on the Third Republic's illegitimacy, she likewise attacked its imperial undertakings. She promoted, instead, a feminist imperialism, asserting the power of feminist principles to better fulfill what she considered France's true civilizing mission. Arguing that feminist imperialism would improve women's condition in both metropole and colony, Auclert advanced the politics as ultimately moving France closer to becoming a true republic. Focusing especially on Algeria, she assumed that the indigenous populations, particularly women, universally desired assimilation in the French regime. Ignoring their particular interests or wishes, she held that Algerian women could reach their full potential under a feminist-influenced French republic.

As a novelist, Léonie Rouzade also saw feminists as leaders in radical reform. Born Louise-Léonie Camusat in Paris in 1839, she was a daughter of a republican and a granddaughter of a deputy of the 1789 Third Estate (at the dawn of the French Revolution). Deeply invested in the republican ideal, her vision of the "true republic"—like that of Auclert—was a social republic imbued with gender equity. Rouzade came to working-class activism via feminism. After attending the Feminist Congress of 1878, she joined the organization Le Droit des Femmes, in which she encountered socialist activists. Increasingly involved in the French Socialist Party, her oratory talents resulted in her speaking widely, sharing the podium with party leaders such as Jules Guesde and Auguste Blanqui. Guesde's ultimate resistance to women's rights led socialist feminists to leave the party in 1882. Led by Rouzade, they formed L'Union des Femmes Socialistes, France's first socialist women's organization since the Revolution of 1848, which held a high profile and drew substantial membership.[16]

Before her affiliation with feminist or socialist organizations, Rouzade had published three novels in the early 1870s.[17] All inspired by the utopian socialism of Étienne Cabet, the novels served as critiques of the patriarchal inequities of the Napoleonic Code of Law. In one of these books, *Le monde renversé* (*The World Turned Upside Down*), Rouzade examines imperialism making one of the earliest such assessments by any of the era's French feminists or socialists. Setting the book in a fictional sultanate, Rouzade uses tropes of a patriarchal Muslim world, into which she inserts a beautiful European feminist who—via beguilement and intrigue—manages to completely invert gender hierarchies. Rouzade intended her "World Turned Upside Down" to illuminate the absurdity of one sex ruling the other. In the novel, the feminist Célestine ultimately rebalances this topsy-turvy world, leaving it as an egalitarian republic. Presaging Auclert's feminist imperialism by a decade, Rouzade employed an amalgam of utopian ideals and republican feminism to envision a "true" republic in an exoticized space on the eve of the Third Republic.

The revolutionary socialist feminist Paule Mink joined Rouzade's Union des Femmes Socialistes in the 1880s—despite the two women's differing politics. A writer, orator, and agitator, Mink had played a prominent and radical role in the 1871 Paris Commune, after which she escaped to Switzerland to avoid arrest and deportation. Born Adèle Paulina Mekarska in the French city Clermont-Ferrand in 1839, Mink undertook her first political action at the age of seventeen, when she disrupted a Catholic religious procession. It prefaced a life of anticlerical, anti-state, and antipatriarchal agitation.

Mink grew up in a politicized realm of activism and liberatory ideology, the daughter of exiled Polish revolutionaries who had fled to France after participating in the failed 1830 Polish uprising against Russian rule. Mink's father was an aristocratic military officer and her mother a Polish-born daughter of minor French nobles, but Mink rejected her elite lineage and instead embraced and identified with her revolutionary heritage. Leaving her provincial home and moving to Paris in the early 1860s, she immersed herself in the radical wing of the city's nascent socialist and feminist movements, which ultimately led to her central role in the 1871 Paris Commune. Following the 1880 General Amnesty for Communards, Mink returned to France and resumed a program of revolutionary socialist feminist agitation. Speaking and protesting throughout the country—often with Michel and occasionally with Rouzade—Mink faced frequent arrest and imprisonment and lived on the edge of penury while raising her children.

A flamboyant and charismatic polemicist, she focused her analyses on three issues: class, gender, and religion. Mink vociferously promoted an equitable reorganization of social and economic relations, while consistently invoking the heritage of France's revolutionary past. Contesting contemporary gender norms, she attacked the existence of civil, commercial, and penal codes that institutionalized women's subservience. This, too, she historically contextualized, lecturing on the roles and experiences of "Woman across the Ages." An advocate of free thought, she assailed the Catholic Church for the economic and intellectual exploitation of both French women and men.

Mink's three broad topics intermeshed as a larger critique of inequity and oppression, which she also applied to colonialism. A one-year gap in Mink's file in the Paris Prefecture of Police—which closely tracked her from 1871 to her May Day, 1901, funeral—marks her one extended trip abroad.[18] Although she had previously expressed limited interest in questions of empire, in 1884 she voyaged to Algeria, intending to instigate both anticlerical and anti-imperial unrest. Her experience in the colony, particularly her observations of Algerian gender relations, had a long-term impact on her feminist politics. Incensed by her perceptions of Algerian women's status, Mink seriously considered the value of ameliorative imperial intervention—a stance antithetical to her revolutionary, anti-state, and anti-imperial positions. Although she wrote little specifically about this voyage, it ultimately altered her politics.

Louise Michel also traveled to Algeria to agitate against empire, two decades after her friend and comrade Mink. However, Michel's formative imperial experience was her exile to France's penal colony in New Caledonia as punishment for her major role in the Paris Commune.[19] A much-mythologized revolutionary hero, Michel was born in 1830 in the village of Vroncourt and raised by her mother, an unmarried domestic servant, and her paternal grandparents, provincial bourgeois who acknowledged and supported Louise as their grandchild. At once marginalized as "illegitimate" and privileged in terms of education and resources, Michel's position allowed her a particular "insider/outsider" perspective on issues including social relations and stratification.

Trained as a teacher, Michel opened a small provincial girls' school in 1852. She moved to Paris in 1856 and continued teaching while becoming increasingly involved in radical politics. Her pedagogy and her activism rooted in gender and class, enmeshed, briefly coming to fruition in the Paris Commune. This manifested through her plan for mandatory, egalitarian, secular education. During her New Caledonian exile, Michel extended her radical educational theory and practice to include the indigenous Kanak. Her efforts to undermine French colonial racial oppressions and exclusions did not, however, fully escape the era's racially and culturally rooted civilizational assumptions. Michel demonstrated a deep respect for Kanak life and culture, yet she simultaneously advanced the value of aspects of Western education. This apparent contradiction permeated even the most progressive of the period's thought and presents a tension throughout her work.

Despite her status as a prisoner, Michel experienced New Caledonia as a site of cultural engagement and political, linguistic, pedagogical, and narrative exploration. Her work and interactions there illuminate alternative perspectives on the particulars of New Caledonian life, including the penal colony, contextualized concepts of civilization, and Kanak oral culture. Michel's involvement in New Caledonia also reveals indigenous links to universal concepts of language, education, and revolution.

In the three decades separating Michel's experiences as a political prisoner in New Caledonia in the 1870s and as a political agitator in Algeria in 1904, her visibility and notoriety effloresced. Despite the French government's efforts to repatriate Michel earlier, she refused freedom until all other Communard prisoners received it as well. When Michel subsequently returned to Paris after the 1880 General Amnesty, thousands of supporters and well-wishers welcomed her train at the Gare St. Lazare.

Pedagogical, theoretical, ethnographic, and literary work punctuated Michel's manifold feminist, anarchist, and revolutionary engagements. Her activism overlapped with that of numerous political organizations, but she allied herself with none. Internationally recognized, repeatedly imprisoned, shot by an adversary, vilified by the Right, exalted by the radical Left, and honored in poems by both Victor Hugo and Paul Verlaine, she became a legend during her lifetime.

Feminisms and Imperialisms

Each of these five feminists—the monarchist, the suffragist, the novelist, the polemicist, and the anarchist—took on empire as a central part of her project. But why did feminists precede other Third Republic progressive thinkers in critiquing imperialism? What can this development reveal about the relationships between feminism and imperialism? Feminisms and imperialisms (both plural) both grew rapidly and became increasingly intertwined during this period. These two markedly different political frameworks played essentially opposite roles within the era's social, cultural, and political contexts. While feminisms emerged as responses to gender inequities and oppressions, imperialisms (by definition) actively established racialized hierarchies rooted in subjugation: colonizer over colonized. French feminisms and imperialisms reflected and refracted each other. Metropolitan feminists from across the political spectrum faced marginalization—of themselves as embodied women and of their gender politics.[20] Those activists who engaged with empire recognized in imperialism a similar structure of internality and externality. French colonialism instituted gendered and sexualized racial hierarchies that created categories of inclusion versus exclusion.

These classifications rested on ideas of universalism and rhetorics of "nature," which presented colonized people theoretical (yet impossible) paths to integration: the route to "becoming French" ultimately required possessing the characteristics of already-being-French, a state by definition antithetical to being non-European and to being colonized. French feminists faced similar barriers to political, civic, and economic incorporation. The universalist ideals undergirding French citizenship promised full inclusion, but universalism's default maleness fixed women as outsiders. As Carole Pateman argued, and as Joan Scott has traced within the French context, the "rights of man" belonged to men; France had established the rights-bearing individual as male, as the exclusion of the female.[21] Questions of control—of indigenous populations under colonialism and of women in patriarchal metropolitan politics—permeated and exacerbated the inequities within both sets of relationships.

Feminists' peripheral stances beyond the bounds of political power and patriarchal privilege, combined with their deep interest in and distrust of this power and privilege, encouraged their critical perspectives. As citizens and activists, they needed to navigate these pathways of power. Continuous reminders that they were trespassers on those pathways sharpened feminists' interrogations of those landscapes in both metropole and colony. Leaving France, they carried with them the inquisitorial and analytical tools they had honed in metropolitan political worlds. As outsiders, feminists approached colonial realms attuned to structures of control and exploitation—as exemplified by Louise Michel's New Caledonian encounter. Feminist politics proved key to their ability to analyze the injustices of colonial structures.

The late nineteenth century served as an incubator for the commingling of these analytics. When French feminists encountered colonialism, both were transformed. Scrutinizing these junctures and their outcomes through the ideas and experiences of Audouard, Auclert, Rouzade, Mink, and Michel elucidates the intersections of the era's gender- and race-based politics, which emerged as precursors to Third Republic anti-imperialism. Scholars generally recognize the 1890s as the decade of Third Republican anti-imperialism's flowering.[22] In the preceding decades, liberal and conservative economists had denounced empire as financially wasteful, and conservatives had asserted the unworthiness of potential colonial subjects. By the *fin de siècle*, the idea of anti-imperialism meant opposing empire because of its oppressions.[23] Feminist anti-imperialisms prefigured these latter politics, whether critiquing gender, race, or class hierarchies in colonial contexts.

As these activists interacted with various forms of empire, their ambit reached beyond the limits of imperial France. The Ottoman Empire and Turkish metropole, the Russian Empire, the American West, the realm of fiction, as well as the French colonies New Caledonia and Algeria: the locations of this book conceptualize empire beyond its geopolitical definition to include spaces of the imperial imaginary. French feminists experienced empire in these milieux—literal colonies such as New Caledonia and Egypt, a colonized realm such as the "Kingdom of the Mormons," an Orientalized metropole such as Turkey, or an invented, nameless sultanate such as the fictional land Rouzade created in her novel *Le monde renversé*.

In traversing imperial worlds, feminists marshaled modes of global emancipation. Ann Laura Stoler contends that French agents of empire sought colonial models in multiple metropolitan and colonial contexts across the globe.

They mixed and matched examples and ideas to piece together imperial realms, collectively rooted in what she terms "a cross-imperial genealogy for a 'carceral archipelago of empire,' where penalty, reform, cultivation of the body, and cordoned-off space were rolled into one."[24] Using Stoler's language, but inverting the focus, this book argues that the five feminists' activisms also formed a cross-imperial genealogy; alongside Stoler's "carceral archipelago of empire," they created a "liberatory expanse of empire" in their quests for emancipatory models. They formed this expanse at the junctions of global examples of freedoms and justice, with legacies of French history and a range of feminist ideals. Built in opposition to extant imperial practices and as eclectic in construction as colonialisms, this "liberatory expanse of empire" simultaneously—and in apparent contradiction—comprised multiple feminist forms of imperialism. The desire to dissolve gender hierarchy often masked the use and reinforcement of geographical and racialized oppressions.

As feminists left France and traveled into empire, they experienced a hierarchical shift.[25] Their racial and national statuses as white Europeans gave them new power, creating uneasy linkages between themselves and the colonial authorities. In the relatively fluid context of empire, some feminists turned to and appropriated imperial concepts—including racialization, sexualization, and ethnographic categorization—to advance their particular political goals. As colonial experiences influenced the French women's perspectives and politics, their subsequent writings and militant actions carried these issues and concerns back to the metropole, in differing ways that in turn affected both the functioning and metropolitan comprehension of France and its empire.

French feminisms had developed from two different French revolutionary sources: the liberalism of 1789 and the radicalism of 1793. Liberal, or republican, feminism emerged from Enlightenment roots. Liberal French Revolutionary thinkers such as Olympe de Gouges (1748–1793) and the Marquis de Condorcet (1743–1794), who asserted women's individual and civic rights, provided the intellectual seeds for feminisms that focused on suffrage and equality under the law. Republican socialist and liberal feminists, including Auclert and Audouard, descended from this rights-based tradition. They sought change under existing political structures. The more radical thread, in contrast, traced its legacy to the revolutionary women of 1793, including Pauline Léon and Claire Lacombe; the utopian socialist feminists of the 1830s and 1840s, such as Suzanne Voilquin and Flora Tristan; the female insurrectionists of 1848, such as Pauline Roland and Jeanne Deroin; and the women of the 1871 Paris Commune, including anarchists such as Michel and revolutionary socialists such as Mink.[26] They sought systemic overthrow. Some republican socialists including Rouzade, who rejected both capitalism and violence, drew influence from both traditions to build new gender and class critiques.

France's strong and multifaceted field of feminisms intersected with the early Third Republican expansion of empire in the context of an emerging metropolitan imperial culture. Why did French feminisms develop foundational anti-imperialisms in France, while neither US nor British feminisms did so in their respective nations? North American and British feminists began to challenge empire in the 1890s—the same decade that the wider French anti-imperialist movement fluoresced. The Anglophone world drew upon existing (male) anti-imperialisms.[27] In France, in contrast, these five feminists became among the earliest critics of the injustices of French imperialism. Was this due to complexities of French culture, or politics, and/or religion? Did it emerge from the plurality of approaches of feminisms rising from the wreckage of the Paris Commune? Its cause could not have been a unity of feminist purpose. Not all of these feminists fought for the vote (although Auclert did), not all of them pursued revolution (although Mink and Michel did), and not all of them sought legal change (although Audouard, Auclert, and Rouzade did). These five feminists did all oppose the sexual and gendered inequalities imposed by the state, but so did feminists in the United States and Britain. While the French feminists' travel, politics, and histories differed, each attempted to remake or remove the power of empire.

The History of the History

Despite the salience of both nineteenth-century French feminisms and imperialisms, few scholars have investigated their conjunctions.[28] Why have the historiographies of nineteenth-century French feminism, of French imperialism, and even of the intersection of women, gender, and French empire, ignored the rich connections between feminisms and empire? While scholarship on women and gender in France began engaging empire more than twenty years ago, research on the histories of French feminisms in the later nineteenth-century has remained (with notable exceptions) tightly focused on the metropole. Conceptualizing nineteenth-century feminisms' concerns as primarily metropolitan has created a delimited version of feminisms' histories.[29] This exclusion exemplifies the long-dominating nation-state paradigm in French historical scholarship. Regarding the metropole and colonies as binary, with only the former shaping the latter, this approach has ignored the multiple ways in which these geographies constituted each other.[30] The persistence of the nation-state model in histories of French feminisms long resulted in a partial picture of the era's gender-based movements for change. Notably, it overlooked feminist writings about, engagements with, and reciprocal influences on and by empire. It thus also missed significant aspects of extra-national and international feminist concerns, including race, language, comparative law, transnational and colonial Judaism, and Islam. More broadly, it obscured the interrelated development of both feminisms and empire. These omissions led, in turn, to the erasure of feminisms' role in the emergence of French anti-imperialism. This book aims to fill these gaps.

The existing historiography began with Yvonne Knibiehler and Régine Goutalier's 1985 *Les femmes aux temps de colonie*, which brought together the fields of women's history and French colonial history for the first time. Addressing the sheer absence of women in histories of French empire, this groundbreaking text stood alone for many years. During the same period, British historians began to address the paucity of women in their imperial histories (as well as the lack of scholarship critiquing Britain's imperial project). Unlike in the French context, this became a significant movement among British women's historians, who "recuperated" historically erased women and wrote them into narratives that also contested the imperial project. Like the early stages of most women's history, this "add-women-and-stir" approach provided a first historiographical step.[31] Although problematically Eurocentric and insufficiently critical, it revealed documentary evidence of British women's imperial engagements, shone a light on their existence, and provided empirical fodder for future studies.[32] It also countered the pro-imperial dominance of British imperial history. Beyond the research of Knibiehler and Goutalier, virtually no such work exists for France.[33]

While scholarship on the nineteenth-century British Empire and gender burgeoned, that concerning the French context stagnated. Feminist scholars of Britain deepened and expanded their investigations to examine not only women and empire, but also the gendered nature of imperialism.[34] As British historian Philippa Levine stipulated, "The very idea as well as the building of empires themselves cannot be understood without employing a gendered perspective."[35] This constituted a fundamental reconceptualization of historical approaches to imperialism, one that would deeply affect feminist scholars of French empire. Yet, from the 1990s into the early 2000s, only Julia Clancy-Smith grappled with these questions in the French imperial context.[36]

French scholars have long resisted first women's, and later gender, history. In the American context, where the fields initially emerged, women's and gender historians of France only slowly abandoned the nation-state model and expanded their vision beyond the metropole—nearly a decade after those studying Britain did so.[37] The French academy's politicized opposition to women's and gender history, combined with Anglophone French historians' adherence to the national model, delayed the appearance of scholarship on French women, gender, and empire. The particular absence of attention to feminisms in these contexts—radical, gender-based ideologies deployed in racially charged colonial milieux—reflects the political and intellectual disregard for these movements and ideas. Despite the presence and visibility of multiple feminisms during the imperial expansion of the Third Republic, scholars have paid scant attention to their junctures. Recognizing and exploring one of the era's significant sets of political entanglements further clarifies understandings of feminisms and imperialisms (both separately and intersectionally), while also illuminating a cradle of Third Republican anti-imperialism.

Scholarship concerning feminisms and imperialisms earlier in the nineteenth century focuses nearly exclusively on Utopian socialist women's travel narratives and their advocacy of empire.[38] Only this small body of scholarship traces feminists who traveled into empire.[39] The authors demonstrate how these few feminists—in many ways, the forerunners of the subjects of this study—became part of the colonial project. Scrutinizing the gendered nature of this era's colonialisms, as well as their interrelationship with French feminists and feminisms, this historiography moves beyond the metropolitan focus of most histories of French feminisms. These feminist subjects, however, unlike their Third Republic–era successors, did not challenge imperialism.

Few scholars have considered late nineteenth-century feminists' engagements with empire, and of those who have—including Julia Clancy-Smith, Bénédicte Monicat, Isabelle Ernot, and Rachel Nuñez—none has focused on feminists' anti-imperialisms.[40] Clancy-Smith, in her influential 1998 essay, began exploring Auclert's intertwined arguments for Algerian Arab women's assimilation and French women's enfranchisement. Literary scholar Monicat analyzes Audouard's travel writing. Ernot posits women travelers' roles, including those of Auclert and Audouard, in establishing the era's dominant colonial discourse. Nuñez, in both her 2012 article, and especially her unpublished 2006 dissertation, argues that both Auclert and Audouard, in differing ways, appropriated France's civilizing mission and utilized cosmopolitanism as strategies both to critique French women's status and to assert themselves as political actors worthy of full citizenship.[41] Building on this work and interrogating the myriad rhetorical and embodied interrelationships between feminists, feminisms, and imperialisms, this book finds within them nascent challenges to the inequities of empire.[42]

In investigating these convergences of feminisms and imperialisms, this text examines both discourse and the lived experiences of subjects within their larger socioeconomic frameworks. It follows Gary Wilder's challenge to the absolutism of the linguistic, or cultural, "turn," which embraced discourse analysis while rejecting the investigation of the material and the social.[43] Rather than throwing out the socioeconomic baby to make way for the discursive bathwater, I, like Wilder, reject the conceptualization of these two scholarly approaches as antithetical binaries. Centering feminists' lived, contextualized experiences, this book simultaneously recognizes the importance of language in the creation of power and thus drills into discourses of class, patriarchy, and empire.[44] This approach enables a gendered questioning of empire that interrogates power as well as the construction and perpetuation of regimes of knowledge in specific colonial contexts through an interrogation of the lives, intellectual productions, and ideologies of historical actors. These, in turn, reveal feminist roots of French anti-imperialisms. Feminists' experiences with empire and their ideas and rhetorics of empire emerged from and formed one another. They thus share mutual historical importance. While experience and discourse hold equal significance, so, too, does situating them within the larger socioeconomic, political, and ideological milieux from which they emerged, as part of the developing French imperial nation-state.[45]

Feminisms' Empires

The French feminist cases against imperialisms began with investigations of intimate, gendered relationships and structures shaping women's lives across multiple empires. From their origins in the attempt to make Frenchness more capacious (mainly but not exclusively for metropolitan women), to their particular anthropological and civilizational claims, to their use of the troubled and evocative figure of the Jew as both inside and external to the empire, these feminists participated in complex and sometimes contradictory political projects to promote equity. The anti-imperialisms that emerged and grew from these projects carried within them the intricacies and incongruities of these struggles.

Each of the following chapters examines a different relationship between feminisms, empire, and France; each analyzes aspects of the feminists' engagements with questions of imperialisms and equity, interrogating their experiences of traveling into empire both to understand these activists' emerging attitudes toward colonialism and to illuminate the overall co-constitution of France and empire.

The book begins by sketching the networks of later nineteenth-century French feminisms as they evolved in a period of imperial expansion. Feminists proved central actors in nineteenth-century imperial history. Reconstructing the crucible of gender and class politics that shaped the era's range of French feminisms shows how each feminist's developing approach to imperialism was mediated by both her class-based ideologies and her embodied experiences in imperial spaces. As they moved into imperial milieux, the five feminists observed and assessed the institutions and structures shaping women's lives. They frequently found France lacking in comparison. In contrast, when assessing women's social and sexual standings, some feminists used racial and sexual imperial tropes to judge France superior to Algeria, Egypt, and Native North America. Their feminist critiques remained enmeshed with white domination.

Seeking to transform France, feminists found inspiration for redefined Frenchness in imperial realms. In their deliberate explorations of empire (both literal and literary) Audouard, Auclert, Rouzade, and Mink focused on marriage, women's legal status, and polygamy as sites central to women's lives, comparing such gendered rights and positions in imperial milieux to those in France. Each activist strove, in distinct and often opposing ways, to illuminate and to ameliorate women's conditions in metropole, colony, and broader imperial spaces. Working to reimagine a more gender equitable Frenchness, these women exposed the hypocrisies of France's colonial project. Their emerging anti-imperial stances did not, however, preclude advocating other imperialist forms.

Hubertine Auclert and her fellow journalists at *La citoyenne* exemplified such complexities. France's first suffragist newspaper, *La citoyenne* was also the first feminist periodical to address imperialisms. The publication presaged not only the broader French press's increasing attention to empire, but also its emergent criticism of it. Engaging issues of religion, race, and gender, the newspaper reported on related global events and concerns. Living in Algeria altered Auclert's understanding of suffrage politics, as well as her perspective on empire. In turn, through her newspaper, she and her fellow journalists influenced their metropolitan public's perceptions of imperialism. *La citoyenne* created a feminist imperialism that challenged women's oppression in both metropole and colony. At the same time, it castigated existing approaches to empire, particularly that of France. Advocating a different sort of empire, and envisioning an alternative type of France, Auclert and *La citoyenne* both critiqued and appropriated the imperial model, adapting it to new objectives. This kind of feminist imperialism, paradoxically, both relied on empire and contested it.

Occasionally imperial projects overlapped. Two of this book's chapters turn to one feminist and her experience at the intersections of multiple French imperial projects. In the New Caledonian penal colony, three revolutionary forces mixed: deported Communards, exiled Algerian anti-imperial insurgents, and an Indigenous uprising. Louise Michel arrived there with her fellow convicted Commune veterans. Enmeshed in this settler colonial context, she forged a politics grounded in quotidian encounters. She examined the French colonial prison system, translated and transcribed indigenous Kanak oral tales, and theorized the logic of French civilizational rankings. Interrogating the gendered and racialized nature of these everyday engagement points, Michel developed a feminist anti-imperialism. Yet despite her anti-imperialism and advocacy of Kanak culture, she imposed aspects of her feminist politics and of Western norms on the Kanak and on their cultural productions.

Michel also had a deep interest in universal questions of language, education, and revolution as sites of imperial engagement and potential opposition. Michel's anarchist feminism, wrought in the colony, led her to re-envision these institutions as part of her global goals. Promoting an organic universal language modeled on a Kanak pidgin, an anarchist feminist pedagogy that recognized and valued indigenous ways of knowing, and the Kanak's violent overthrow of French imperial authority, Michel fostered what could be termed "decolonized" means of communication, education, epistemology, and political power. However, despite articulating a profoundly anti-imperial stance, Michel asserted elements of Western, anarchist education for advancing Kanak culture—a position she would not have recognized as imperialist. Her experience in supporting and learning from an Indigenous population, combined with race-based and civilizational assumptions regarding their needs and desires, makes clear the impossibility of a clear pro-imperial versus anti-imperial binary.

In encountering new people and cultures in empire, some feminists drew on ideas and images of a historically and perennially othered metropolitan group: the racialized, sexualized, and Orientalized figure of "The Jew." Both French and foreign, familiar and alien, Jews inhabited the metropole and multiple imperial locations, yet belonged in none of them. The trope of "The Jew," and of "The Jewess," however, had a widespread legibility. Audouard, Auclert, and Michel each used this image to advance a broad range of often clashing political goals, in contexts ranging across the French, Ottoman, and Russian Empires. They wielded it to advance seemingly unrelated positions and programs, including both pro- and anti-imperialism. Audouard's unabashed antisemitism, Auclert's instrumentalism, and Michel's relative philosemitism illustrate the ways the figure of the Jew influenced the era's gendered and racialized political thought and its attitudes toward empire in metropole and colony.

Feminists' divergent politics mediated their colonial experiences, while their varied imperial encounters shaped their politics. Investigating the institutions and experiences of women's lives reveals divergent paths to a variety of imperial critiques. Examining these activists' engagements with empire through the optic of ideological relationships reveals a correlation between class politics and a self-identified anti-imperialism. All five of the women opposed France's imperial undertakings, yet the more leftist the feminist, the more likely she was to reject the broader legitimacy of empire. Ideology also correlated with an openness to difference and to a resistance to stereotypes of Orientalized antisemitism. Those most opposed to existing hierarchical structures and power relations tended to be more receptive to other ways of knowing, creating, and living. Yet even the most critical feminist anti-imperialisms remained imbricated in the rhetorics and practices of empire.

Feminists developed their oppositions to empire earlier than, and differently from, the majority of their contemporaries. Whether contesting a specific imperial power or challenging imperialism more broadly, feminists undertook gendered analyses of empire. Their condemnations arose from their focus on equity at everyday and embodied levels, their gender-based ideologies, and the likelihood that as women traveling into empire, they identified with women as women. Despite its multiplicity, feminist politics constituted the shared and central factor in these activists' anti-imperialisms. Feminisms set them apart from other female and male thinkers, activists, and travelers.

CHAPTER 1

Ideologies and Intimacies of Imperialism

In 1890, Hubertine Auclert declared: "Arab women raised the banner of emancipation well before European and American women. Five hundred years ago the women of Miliana, Algeria, rose up against masculinism."[1] Proclaiming "Bravo to our ancestors!" Auclert contended that their revolt demonstrated how "thirteenth-century feminists" who lived under male oppression had carried on the legacy of their less-subjugated ancient progenitors. Enacting "their foremothers' love of independence," the thirteenth-century Arab women recalled the centuries earlier "epoch of idolatry, before Mohammad proclaimed man's superiority to his companion, [when] the woman of the Arab race enjoyed the same rights as her spouse. . . . The Arab woman has not always been treated like an animal."[2]

To Auclert, contemporary Algerian society existed as the degenerate remnant of a once-great culture. Lauding Arab women of the distant past in her book *Les femmes arabes*, Auclert simultaneously disparaged the status of their descendants in her contemporary Algeria. She pointed to the pre-Islamic period (pre–seventh century) as one of gender equity and acclaimed the "thirteenth-century feminists" who harkened back to that era in their uprising against male domination. Auclert lamented what she considered the interlinked decline of both Arab culture and Arab women's status. Alleging Algerian women's subhuman social standing—each woman was "treated like an animal"—Auclert asserted that the once glorious Arab culture had devolved to the point that it had displaced women from civilization into the realm of beasts. Auclert thus appropriated a popular racist trope and updated it into feminist critique.

Auclert wrote *Les femmes arabes* while living in Algeria, France's premier colony, considered part of "Greater France." Yet her interest in empire had developed nearly a decade earlier. Along with Olympe Audouard, Louise Michel, Léonie Rouzade, and Paule Mink, Auclert was among the first of the era's French feminists to travel into empire, either literally or literarily. These women came from a broad span of feminisms, left the metropole for varied reasons, visited or dwelled in distant places, were personally and intellectually influenced by their experiences, and brought their newly shaped politics back to the metropole. Investigating colonial milieux from feminist perspectives, they often adopted imperial concepts—including racialization, sexualization, ethnographic categorization, and civilization. In this way, they became agents of imperial ideologies. These same women, however, opposed nearly all existing empires or colonial projects as inequitable. Embracing a range of complicated politics in the 1860s and 1870s, they were among the era's first French critics to condemn empire as an oppressive force.

Observing and evaluating imperial worlds, the five feminists compared gender orders and women's lives with those in France. They frequently found the French context inferior, especially in terms of legal equity.[3] In contrast, as this chapter shows, they often judged women's social value in France to be superior to that of women in other milieux. They held varied ideological positions and contested French institutions, structures, and traditions in differing ways. Witnessing particular social and sexual orders and customs—practices they often found illegible—these women turned to racialized and sexualized imperial tropes for explanations. Their observations resulted in both embraces and contestations of empire, complex and contradictory responses that grew from intimate encounters. Forged in the crucible of radical midcentury Paris, their divergent class- and gender-based politics and embodied experiences shaped their emerging critiques of empire.

As Ann Stoler has shown, the regulation of racialized and sexualized intimacies underpinned the practices and imaginaries of empire.[4] Intimacy encompasses not merely the sexual but also a broad range of other affective interpersonal engagements, including regimes of control, physical violence, and bodily threats, as well as quotidian domestic, commercial, and social interactions.[5] Traveling and dwelling internationally in the mid- to late-nineteenth-century world, these five feminists lived the embodied intimacies of empire. From Audouard's attendance at a Coptic Christian wedding in Egypt, to Auclert's interviews with women in an Algerian harem, to Michel's interactions with both prison guards and local Kanak in the New Caledonian penal colony, these close interpersonal encounters both informed and fashioned the French women's understandings and experiences of gender in empire.

Hierarchies

Feminisms and imperialisms surged in the later nineteenth century, both political projects rooted in contestations for power. Motivated by apparently oppositional goals—while feminisms strove to dismantle hierarchies, imperialisms expanded and reinforced them—their intersections altered both movements. Feminists fought from the periphery, disenfranchised and othered, pressing to dislodge extant powers, but also to claim authority of their own. In imperialism, they confronted a force to be both employed and opposed. As Jennifer Pitts notes regarding the apparent contradictions of liberals supporting empire, feminist adoption of aspects of imperialism also involved uneasy "theoretical justifications."[6] Questions of race, religion, and class, as well as gender and sexuality mediated different feminist responses, while being in empire shaped the activists' politics and understandings of power.

As feminists, the five women began from positions of marginalization, excluded from dominant ideologies and power structures by both their politics and their gender. As elite white women entering colonial and Orientalized spaces, they had even greater distance from those around them.[7] In differing ways, each of these feminists used her othered perspective to imagine and articulate a new kind of Frenchness, one that integrated dominant and peripheral ideas of gender and race in both metropole and colonies.[8] These oppositions informed one another: the opposition of feminism to dominant French society affected their interpretations of empire, but so, too, did their encounters with empire and colony inform their feminisms. As Isabelle Ernot writes, female European imperial travelers "between two worlds . . . have incontestably lived a singular experience: a distancing and a liberation from their own gendered culture, while never really escaping it."[9] Physically removed from France, the feminists left behind the constraints of its gender roles and hierarchies. Yet the pervasiveness of such structures meant that these European women unavoidably internalized and reproduced elements of them. Despite feminists' attention to inequities and oppressions (in terms of gender, but also class and race), they too, remained imbricated in these power relations.

Audouard, Auclert, Rouzade, Mink, and Michel thus simultaneously contested and reified the period's dominant constructions of alterity. The term "alterity" refers not only to absolute otherness, but also to the processes that form the otherness. It denotes the historically and culturally specific creation of hierarchical realms of inclusion and exclusion. French scholars often use "alterity" in place of race—the latter a concept deeply contested, and frequently avoided, in French intellectual and political contexts. In the latter half of the nineteenth century, the metaphorical walls dividing the included "us" versus the excluded "them" established the parameters of Frenchness. Race, specifically whiteness, formed its base. So, too, did religion, gender, and class. Frenchness was defined not merely by what it was—white, Catholic, male (for full citizenship), and elite (to be civilized and thus truly French)—but fundamentally also by what it was not: indigenous, non-Catholic, female, and working class (equated with savagery).[10] The imperial state shaped and shifted these barriers in its colonizing efforts, assuring the reinforcement of the line between French and other.[11]

The European model that marked marginalized groups as fundamentally different and inferior has roots in the late Middle Ages, with the racialization of Jews as a group inherently and irrevocably separate from Christians. By the sixteenth century, Europeans relegated Africans and Amerindians, with whom they had come into contact via "discovery" and imperialism, to this othered racial category. In the post-Revolutionary period, French republicanism promised inclusion in Frenchness to all on French soil. While enshrined in law, the universal republic failed in practice to eradicate the marginalization of racial and racialized religious peoples (Jews and Muslims) in either metropole or colonies.[12] In the mid-nineteenth century, Arthur de Gobineau's profoundly influential, multivolume *Essai sur l'inégalité des races humaines* established a "scientific" justification for European racial superiority rooted in whiteness, one that shaped dominant French conceptions of race well into the twentieth century.[13] As Herrick Chapman and Laura Frader argue, French understandings of race have long operated at the intersection of the myth of the universal republic and "entrenched habits of bigotry."[14] Biological race undergirded late-nineteenth-century Frenchness, even as republican universalizing rhetoric claimed to overcome it. In France's empire, these allegedly opposed conceptualizations interacted to justify political oppression, land theft, and deadly force.

The Imperial Presence

Each form of anti-imperialism arose from specificities within the practices of empire. Comprehending these entanglements involves analyses of the nineteenth-century political, ideological, and social contexts within which these multiple feminisms and imperialisms emerged and intersected.

European imperialism expanded dramatically in the latter third of the nineteenth century, temporally overlapping with and intersecting feminisms' growth.

Europe's empires covered 35 percent of the globe in 1800, but by 1914 Europe ruled 84 percent of the Earth.[15] During this dawn of "new imperialism," France's imperial holdings eclipsed those of all European nations except Britain's. The serious expansion of what became France's second colonial empire (the first extending from the seventeenth century through the fall of Napoleon) started with the collapse of the Second Empire and the establishment of the Third Republic. No longer an empire in name, the state increasingly intensified its position as one in fact. Beginning with Algeria and then expanding to West and equatorial Africa, Mexico (briefly), Southeast Asia, and Oceana, it grew by the early twentieth century to include even more territories in North Africa, East Africa, and the Middle East, as well as smaller claims on parts of China and Antarctica.

Several factors motivated European competition for colonies. Economically, France sought raw materials, labor, and markets. Politically, it pursued international power and prestige, as well as a way to counter domestic social unrest and socialist agitation (the empire created opportunities for jobs and land to placate workers in the wake of the Paris Commune). Imperial conquest was seen as a demonstration of the nation's masculine virility following the humiliating loss of the Franco-Prussian War, the cataclysm of the Commune, and declining birth rates.[16] Finally, the *mission civilisatrice*, the "civilizing mission," motivated many imperial supporters who believed (or rationalized) that it was their moral duty to spread Western education, Christianity, and modern medicine.[17]

France's imperial project emerged from its republican tradition and from the centuries-long belief in European superiority, a fiction reaching back to the ancient Greek myth of Zeus selecting and honoring Europe.[18] In the 1870s the new, fragile, and tenuous Third Republic embraced the colonial idea in an effort to transcend deep political rifts, erase the shame of the Franco-Prussian War and the crisis of the Paris Commune, and solidify governmental authority and legitimacy. The *mission civilisatrice* represented the idealized potential of what France could become. It cast imperialism in a republican light: France would bring the civilized, highly evolved characteristics of its republic to its colonies as an act of benevolence.[19]

In metropolitan Britain, the empire and its related concerns garnered significant popular attention and were actively promoted in the latter half of the nineteenth century, including in school curricula and ultimately through a national holiday.[20] In the French metropole, popular interest in empire developed more slowly. A nascent colonial culture arose with the dawn of the Third Republic but did not concretize until near the century's end. Blanchard, Lemaire, Bancel, and Thomas have termed the initial decades of the 1870s and

1880s as "a time of impregnation" of colonial culture, when pro-colonial publications, images, conferences, and organizations emerged, but were not fully embraced until the 1890s.[21] During the impregnation decades of the 1870s and 1880s, the lag in substantial organized colonial promotion created a space for alternative, nongovernmental, noncommercial, and nonreligious voices. Feminists stepped into this space. Part of a vanguard of French people engaging empire, these activist women presented critical gendered visions of empire to audiences in Europe and in colonies, through journalism, literature, public lectures, political agitation, and education. Many provided imperial counternarratives. While some promoted imperialism and some condemned it, none supported the government's position.

Feminist representations of colonial worlds illuminated intersections of gender, race, class, and religious strata in the ongoing power struggles between metropolitan authorities and Indigenous, colonized peoples. In various imperial milieux, including Algeria, New Caledonia, Egypt, and Turkey, feminists critiqued the gendered and racialized nature of legal structures, reported on women's subjugated status, commented on the place and prevalence of Jews, sometimes lauded and sometimes castigated the impact of Islam on women, championed Indigenous anti-imperialist uprisings, and challenged the existence and operation of the penal colony. They brought their audiences combinations of complicities and resistances, filtered through feminist lenses.

As counternarratives, the five feminists' assessments exemplify the multidirectional flows of influence between metropole and colonies. These currents moved within broader processes of national and imperial development, the fundamentally interwoven, co-constituent growth of the modern imperial nation-state.[22] The ideas and circumstances of empire shaped feminists' intellectual productions and lived experiences—they fashioned the critical tools they brought to their analyses of not only empire, but also metropoles. In disparate ways, the colonial encounter infused their ensuing work. The resultant colonially permeated feminisms infiltrated the French political landscape. Their lecturing, writing, publishing, organizing, and agitating reveal the ways in which empire affected them and simultaneously illuminate how they altered the terrain of French politics. This circulation of ideas and bodies exemplified the ways in which metropole and colonies together created each other.

Audouard, Auclert, Rouzade, Mink, and Michel were among their era's earliest voices to criticize imperialism as an unjust institution. Before them, in the late eighteenth century, the abolition of slavery motivated most contestations of colonialism. In the same era, liberal economists challenged empire as financially unsound, while also philosophically and morally condemning its relationship with slavery. With the 1848 termination of slavery in the French

Empire, some liberal economists continued to resist imperialism due to its associated anticompetitive fiscal practices, including protectionism and interventionism, which contradicted economic liberalism and the free market.[23] The period's conservative nationalists, monarchists, and Bonapartists rejected colonialism as a waste of resources on unworthy recipients.[24]

Socialist anti-imperialism flowered only in the 1890s but had begun to emerge slowly in the early 1880s, a period of intensified French imperial expansion (Tunisia in 1881; Annam in 1883; Tonkin in 1885). Apart from these five feminists, few other French expressed egalitarian anti-imperialist sentiments before the mid-1880s. One of the earliest leftists to turn against empire, the renowned geographer and former Communard Elisée Reclus, decried imperialism in the late 1870s. An anarchist, male feminist, and friend of Michel's, Reclus collaborated in Geneva with other Commune exiles and published the newspaper *Le travailleur* (1877–1878), to which he contributed essays denouncing the ethics and challenging the legality of imperialism.[25] Reclus's feminism differentiated his politics from those of his contemporaries, as did his anti-imperialism.

Another friend of Michel's, the socialist legislator Georges Clemenceau, also developed an early form of egalitarian anti-imperialism. In 1885, he joined with conservatives, liberal economists, and socialists to force pro-colonial politician Jules Ferry from office in what Claude Liauzu has termed "the false victory of anti-colonialists."[26] While Clemenceau's allies countered Ferry's colonial program for economic reasons, Clemenceau, with fellow member of the Chamber of Deputies Camille Pelletan, stood nearly alone in the government in contesting colonialism as an exploitative undertaking.[27] As a long-time associate of Louise Michel, Clemenceau was familiar with and likely influenced by the anti-imperialism she had by then promoted for over a decade. The 1885 event, as Liauzu suggests, constituted a brief anticolonial moment in the years before the 1890s.[28]

The Feminist Foundation

Recognizing the presence, significance, and power of feminisms during this period constitutes a vital step toward comprehending the depth and intricacies of gender politics. Understanding gender politics, in turn, is fundamental to apprehending an era's hierarchies and relations of power—including imperialisms and anti-imperialisms. Multiple forms of feminisms operated in France during this period. The common presumption that feminism constituted a unitary and fixed ideology reductively simplifies and flattens multifaceted, varied, and evolving politics. In imperial realms, feminisms emerged as both historically specific responses to the gendered status quo and ideologically particular gendered positions on a broad range of issues, institutions, and practices. They therefore provide portals into the manifold gendered relations of power in both metropole and colonies. Reexamining mid- to late-nineteenth-century imperial history with the inclusion of these multiple feminisms and with the knowledge that understanding their respective constitutions brings, allows a more thorough comprehension of the era's intricate matrices of power. Identifying and analyzing those various French feminisms and their interactions with empire both elucidates these gender politics and connects them to larger ideas and themes, thereby revealing a deeper and more expansive understanding of empire.

Hubertine Auclert coined the term *feminisme* and was the first person to self-identify as a *feministe*, beginning in 1882 in her newspaper *La citoyenne*. As Karen Offen has shown, before the end of the 1890s the word spread to publications in eleven different countries, including England, Spain, Russia, Argentina, and the United States.[29] While the label did not exist prior to the 1880s, the politics it signified clearly did. Reaching back to the eighteenth century, movements that can be termed "feminist" (as well as people who can properly be called "feminists") engaged in efforts to alter male-dominated gender hierarchies. From the Enlightenment through the French Revolution and into the nineteenth century, feminisms and feminists emerged in response to inequities in politics, society, economics, and culture. The feminisms examined here did not arise in response to imperialisms, nor did these feminists come to their gender politics through an opposition to, or embrace of, empire. Rather, these activist women espoused a range of feminist positions emerging from a combination of gender and class politics, from revolutionary anarchism on the Left to liberal monarchism on the Right. These intersecting politics developed from their intellectual influences and their lived, embodied experiences. Each of them came to empire with a particular feminism, one that would both form and be formed by their time in imperial worlds.

The five women intersected in Parisian feminist circles, with four of them—all but Audouard—overlapping in the activist Left. Michel and Mink shared the strongest and longest connection, reaching back to their involvement in the political public meeting movement in the final years of France's Second Empire and their deep involvement in the 1871 Paris Commune. When they returned to Paris following France's issuance of the 1880 General Amnesty to Communards—Mink from Swiss exile, Michel from New Caledonian prison—the two allies commenced an extensive national lecture and propaganda tour, in which Rouzade periodically participated.[30] Through the rest of their lives (Mink died in 1900, Michel in 1905), the two women frequently undertook well-attended joint speaking tours of France, advocating feminism, anticleri-calism, and revolution.[31] Their perceived threat to the status quo was such that police spies followed and observed both of them for the rest of their lives, and thus ironically provided a detailed (although hostile) historical memorializa-tion of the specifics of their travels and speeches. As an 1880 police report noted about Michel's orations, "This woman has the effect of a great theater artist on stage."[32] Michel and Mink endured multiple arrests and imprison-ments for their activism over the decades; police harassment of Michel esca-lated to such an extent in the 1890s that she fled France for London.[33] The two militants maintained their political and personal alliances throughout, despite supporting divergent politics.[34] Their years of association frequently linked them in the public eye. Because Michel was the more widely known of the two, observers such as a Le matin journalist writing in 1889 periodically mistook Mink for a "follower of Louise Michel."[35]

During the Commune, Michel had espoused a top-down revolutionary so-cialist feminism, while Mink had promoted a grassroots revolutionary anar-chist feminism. The profound experience of the insurrection and its suppression led both women to reject their respective politics after the Commune's fall. Michel abandoned revolutionary socialism because of her disillusionment with the insurgency's leadership; she turned instead to revolutionary anarchism, advocating a bottom-up approach to radical change. Mink, in contrast, con-cluded that the Commune had suffered from lack of strong leadership and forsook revolutionary anarchism in favor of the centralized revolutionary so-cialism of Auguste Blanqui. Now closer to one another's previous political positions, both women also adapted their feminist stances to their respective new ideological outlooks. These differing politics subsequently shaped their responses to empire. Michel and Mink each extended their opposition to the state to actively contest imperialism in divergent ways.

Michel decried empire in itself. She defended the right of all peoples to govern themselves and to remain free of oppressive internal or external authority. She promoted anti-imperialism as part of a cohesive set of claims of human equality. For her, resisting empire dovetailed with rejecting both capitalism and patriarchal authority. Michel revealed little ambiguity in her articulation of imperial oppo-sition. A strong promoter of New Caledonian independence, she nonetheless contended that the indigenous Kanak would benefit from radical Western edu-cation. Understanding egalitarian education as emancipating, Michel would not have considered her advocacy as contradicting her anti-imperialism.

Mink held a less consistent position concerning empire. An anti-statist com-mitted to liberatory and revolutionary politics, she condemned colonialism as she traveled and spoke, including on her 1884 anti-imperial, anticapitalist,

1.1.   Paule Mink, ca. 1870. Bibliothèque National de France.

and anticlerical propaganda tour of Algeria. During that trip, Mink's observation and interpretation of Algerian gender roles led her to consider the possibility of France's civilizational superiority and, with that, an imaginable and limited legitimacy for empire. She never backpedaled on her professed anti-imperialism. Yet in the immediate aftermath of her time in North Africa, she began to consider the potential that targeted imperialism could hold for ameliorating Algerian women's conditions. Though discrepant with her otherwise consistent denunciations of state power, including over non-French peoples, this conflict reflects the intensity with which Mink's colonial encounter disrupted her thought.

Auclert arrived in Paris in 1873, after the fall of the Second Empire and within two years of the Commune's defeat. During her subsequent few tumultuous years of frustrated political alliances with liberal feminists and the French Workers' Party (Parti Ouvrier Français), she emerged as one of the prime advocates for exiled Communard women, especially Michel.[36] In a widely reported March 1880 speech, Auclert defended Michel's role in the 1871 civil war, lauded her for teaching the New Caledonian Kanak while in exile, and called for amnesty for the female insurgents.[37] Simultaneously, Auclert began arguing that women's participation in the Commune demonstrated that their sex was deserving of suffrage, appropriating revolutionary women's militancy to promote a reformist tool: the vote. Her enthusiasm extended to symbolically naming Michel honorary president of her organization Droits des Femmes (Women's Rights) and declaring that "Michel would be quite worthy of being a president of the Republic."[38]

Later that year, Léonie Rouzade founded the Union des Femmes Socialistes. Auclert joined—as did Mink, Michel, and many other feminist Commune veterans who had just returned to France that July, following the General Amnesty.[39] Finally meeting the woman she had lionized, Auclert discovered that she and Michel held profoundly opposing ideologies. At an early Union des Femmes Socialistes meeting, Michel directly criticized the fight for women's political rights, Auclert's primary goal. The revolutionary socialist women, particularly Mink and Michel, roundly rejected Auclert and her brand of reformist republican socialism (although they did not force her from the Union des Femmes Socialistes), in spite of Auclert's dogged advocacy for Communard women. Mink and Michel considered the pursuit of suffrage and parliamentary participation in the existing government to be both useless for most women's concerns and counterproductive to larger revolutionary goals. As Michel later asked, "How would the triumphal entry into legislative palaces aid the unhappy women dying of hunger?"[40] This shared stance placed Michel and Mink directly at odds with Auclert's objective of changing, rather than overturning, the republic. In the wake of these failed alliances, Auclert began her intense push for women's suffrage. None of the other four feminists supported her campaign.[41]

Due to her focus on political reform, Auclert's politics and goals diverged from those of the revolutionaries. Yet their paths crossed even in opposition. In an April 1884 speech, Mink challenged Auclert's women's suffrage advocacy, maintaining that women were too far under the sway of the Catholic Church to be trusted with the vote.[42] The following year Auclert's newspaper, *La citoyenne*, published a letter Mink wrote from Algeria, further elaborating on her opposition to women's enfranchisement.[43] Journalists compared and contrasted the women, referring to them as the "three great modern speakers," while describing Auclert as having "neither the originality nor grand phrases of Madame Paule Mink."[44] In a 1901 response to a letter from the Director of the monthly review, *L'intermédiare des chercheurs et des curieux*, Auclert—a year after Mink's death—stated adamantly, "I have never shared the ideas of Madames Paule Mink and Louise Michel."[45] Their ideological divisions ultimately superseded any feminist alliance.

Auclert did maintain her positive connection with Rouzade. Despite the radical nature of her organization, the Union des Femmes Socialistes, Rouzade never advocated revolution. Like Auclert, she championed parliamentary, republican socialism. Their overlapping ideologies led Auclert and Rouzade to respond similarly to empire, with each ultimately seeing in it a possible means to deliver feminist change.

Like Michel and Mink, both Auclert and Rouzade opposed existing imperialisms. Unlike them, however, Rouzade and Auclert both promoted aspects of the colonial relationship as potentially liberatory. Their feminist imperialisms aimed to take advantage of France's colonial projects. Just as neither woman rejected the state nor the republican form, neither considered empire to be inherently subjugating. For Rouzade, it provided a structure through which to imagine a means to recalibrate gender and class relations. Her novel *Le monde renversé* exemplified her conceptualization of a republican socialist feminist civilizing mission. Through colonialism, she envisioned the establishment of an egalitarian republic, one that would also reflect back and shape the gendered social and political texture of the metropole.

Like Rouzade, Auclert saw empire as a route to achieve the true republic. She also saw it as a responsibility. Intensely critical of French and other imperial programs, she developed and promoted a feminist alternative, a politics that intertwined with her fight for women's suffrage, and evolved through her years in Algeria. While Rouzade addressed empire a decade earlier than Auclert, the latter embraced it more fully and extensively. She developed a republican socialist feminist imperialism with which to oppose extant imperial relations and practices. As Alice Conklin has shown, French imperialism reflected faith in republican government.[46] While Auclert and Rouzade's denunciation of aspects of French empire exemplified their mistrust of the current republic, their advocacy of imperialist undertakings reflected their confidence that the republican form held the potential to be wrought into an egalitarian legal and political structure.

Over the decades, Rouzade and Auclert buoyed each other's projects and sustained a personal friendship, as illustrated by a December 26, 1901, note from Rouzade to Auclert, thanking the latter "with all my heart" for an empathetic condolence letter following the death of Rouzade's husband, Auguste. Rouzade expressed warm gratitude, promising to "kiss you as soon as I am strong enough to walk and not shed too many tears."[47]

Yet despite their long friendship and ideological agreements, the two women diverged in terms of the centrality of class politics. Although both espoused republican socialist feminism, their specific iterations of it contrasted. Auclert strongly prioritized women's suffrage, especially after her 1880 split with organized socialisms. She remained concerned with class inequality, but held it secondary to that of gender, or even tertiary as her focus on empire grew, and with it her interest in questions of race. Rouzade, in contrast, understood working-class and women's emancipation as not only on a par with each other, but also as fundamentally interlinked. Like Michel and Mink, and unlike Auclert, Rouzade promoted class conflict as a means to sociopolitical change. She never championed Michel or Mink's violent forms of struggle. Rather, given that "the proletariat and women" were seen to be "the last pariahs of modern society," she contended that "the only way for them to work successfully for their common emancipation is to march together against the dominant class."[48] Rouzade's politics pushed the limits of reform but did not preclude parliamentary change. In 1881, she stood as a candidate for the Municipal Council elections in Paris's twelfth *arrondisement*.[49] Her candidacy was contentious and ultimately unsuccessful. Nominated by the Union des Femmes Socialistes, Rouzade received backing from the quarter's working class; Jules Guesde and his socialist followers gave her lip service but no actual support, and anarchists cynically promoted her, hoping to reveal what they considered the sham of the republic if she were elected but barred, as a woman, from taking her seat. This all played out in the context of a larger ongoing conflict: socialist reform versus revolution. As the founder and head of the relatively "big tent" Union des Femmes Socialistes and as an activist with socialist feminist politics that bridged the reform versus revolution divide, Rouzade showed her optimism and adaptability in her willingness to run for office in this fraught milieu. These characteristics suggest how she managed to remain allied with feminists on both sides of an increasingly deep rift. They also emerged in Rouzade's literary creation of a utopian imperial republic, one formed by feminist actions at the collision of gender and class.

Audouard took a complicated stance concerning empire. It arose at the intersection of her reproach of French authority and her experiences across multiple empires. She contested French state power due to her opposition to the deep gender biases that permeated the Napoleonic Code of Law. As a liberal monarchist and exponent of the status quo in hierarchies outside of gender, however, Audouard espoused few radical positions. She supported imperialism, but not that of France: she considered its inherent sexism a disqualifier for colonial leadership. This paralleled her position on republicanism: she viewed it as acceptable in theory, but not in practice in France, because of France's radical tradition.

While Audouard avoided much of the evolving world of early Third Republican feminist socialists, she did overlap with Mink and Michel in the years immediately preceding the Commune, during the denouement of the Second Empire. All three women had participated in the public meeting movement.[50] The lecture topics ranged widely, but those related to women and gender included women's labor, legal marriage versus "free unions," and marriage and divorce. Audouard and Mink each spoke publicly on the latter theme. Already known as a writer and feminist, Audouard lectured in 1870 attacking French marriage law for subjugating women and denying divorce. In 1869 Mink led a public meeting decrying marital law and the absence of legal divorce. While it is unclear if either woman attended the other's presentation, their interests clearly crossed. Indeed, during this pre-Commune period, Audouard and Mink (and Michel) advocated rights-based feminism. Both Audouard and Mink continued to condemn France's conjugal law in subsequent decades and to extend their respective attentions to marriage law and custom beyond the metropole.

In the wake of the cataclysmic 1871 revolutionary experience, Mink and Michel both abandoned their belief that equal rights, enshrined in law, could emancipate women. Audouard, in sharp contrast, considered the Commune an episode of savage mob rule, proof of the impossibility of French republicanism, and the need for a liberal monarch. Despite their extreme political differences, all three women continued to contest France's legal and customary treatment of women. Auclert and Rouzade also shared this opposition. This critique constituted the essence of their otherwise divergent feminisms. Such a common element led each of these activists to oppose the French state in varied ways, and, when each engaged with empire, it birthed their developing, albeit differing, anti-imperialisms.

Although each woman opposed existing empires, they all simultaneously championed distinct aspects of imperialism. Audouard, Auclert, and Rouzade saw theoretical value in colonial forms as means to elevate women's status and to promote aspects of their own particular political programs—they promoted feminist imperialisms. Mink and Michel more specifically condemned empire, rejecting the imposition of external political, cultural, and economic structures, as well as the assumptions of superiority underlying those endeavors. Yet none of their positions were purely either pro- or anti-imperialist. No clear dichotomy existed between pro- and anti-imperialist stances. Even anti-imperial activists such as Michel and Mink remained enmeshed in elements of the era's civilizational hierarchies, underscoring the pervasiveness of those social and racial constructs. The resultant complexities and contradictions within pro- and anti-imperial allegiances reflected the ways in which differing feminist politics intersected with evolving imperial contexts and relationships.

Empire Abroad

A wide range of politicians and thinkers, reaching back to the Scottish Enlightenment, have argued that women's status reflects a society's level of civilization.[51] This judgment or measure either denigrates or elevates, alleging barbarity or praising progress. As Julia Clancy-Smith has demonstrated, by 1900, both European and Indigenous communities in Algeria assessed one another based on women's status.[52] Audouard, Auclert, Rouzade, Mink, and Michel prefigured this trend by decades. Analyzing women's embodied experiences across the lifecycle, their sexuality, education, and their relative acceptance in the public sphere, these feminists interrogated alternative practices and ideologies of femaleness. Using gendered and racialized imperial metrics to examine women's societal status and value, they found both models and foils for their reconceptualizations of Frenchness. While often critical of women's status in France, especially in terms of law, these feminists frequently judged French women's social standing preferable to that of women elsewhere.

These lands included the United States. In her 1869 *À travers l'Amérique: Le Far-West*, Audouard described and evaluated Native Americans, whom she encountered while traveling across the American West. "The Indians," she wrote, "are truly mysterious beings; they appear to be somewhere between monkey and man."[53] Her depiction continued by likening their noses to "muzzles," their expressions to "the dull look of a hyena," and their "long, rough hair," to "a horse's mane."[54] Using the era's imperial language of civilization versus savagery, Audouard constructed Indians as the antithesis of civilization: as animals. "One feels that these beings are ferocious," she continued, "and of an absolutely bestial ferocity. . . . The soul is absent."[55] Characterizing them as soulless creatures, Audouard placed Native Americans on the lowest rung of the civilizational hierarchy, among nonhuman beings.

This system of ranking emerged as part of the period's conceptualizations of evolutionary race and civilization. It held that different racial groups progressed at varied rates, with fully developed white Europeans at the peak of civilization, and black Africans, Melanesians, and North American Indians at the bottom. Addressing the evolutionary trajectory of the latter, Audouard suggested, "One asks oneself, if they [the Indians] are the degenerate products of a great extinguished race, or the debris of an exhausted civilization, returned to its starting point—savagery."[56] Reflecting her embrace of civilizational evolution, Audouard's rhetorical query also exemplified an extinction narrative, the nineteenth-century Western understanding that savage peoples stood on the precipice of disappearance, over which they would inevitably fall, pushed by the progress of colonization.[57] By this point in the nineteenth century, Native populations seemed (to Europeans) to be vanishing. This assumed disappearance, not coincidentally, helped rationalize European claims to land.

This theorization—locating Indians as part of an "extinguished race" or "exhausted civilization"—temporally displaced them, denying them coevalness or what anthropologist Johannes Fabian terms the "sharing of present time." It relegated Native Americans to a bygone time beyond which Europeans had moved.[58] This dislocation presented their very existence as anachronistic. Correspondingly, the "extinction discourse" portrayed the diminution or disappearance of Indigenous groups deemed particularly undeveloped to be evolutionarily natural, rather than colonially caused. Together, the denial of coevalness and the extinction narrative justified both past and future repressions, dislocations, and erasures of North American Indians.

Audouard interacted with an extensive variety of informants in the Western United States. She likely encountered multiple expressions of "anti-Indianism," the race-based and ultimately genocidal set of denigrations, distortions, and exploitations of Native North Americans that permeated white American culture.[59] Her intensely negative and racialized portrayals of Indians reflect her observations of Native people filtered through her racialized white European understanding of the vanishing Native, which was influenced by the region's and era's pervasive, de-humanizing, American anti-Indian discourse.

Audouard's resultant narrative emerged as place-specific and gendered, supporting Indian alterity while simultaneously rationalizing their ultimate erasure. This gendered analysis folded racialized assumptions into sex and sexual relations. Emphasizing and generalizing Native men's characteristics, Audouard stressed the value placed on stoicism and pain tolerance. She saw this lack of physical and emotional feeling and expression extending to their "complete indifference to the joys of love."[60] All Indian men, Audouard stated, had "a profound contempt for women."[61] Providing evidence for the extinction argument, she stated that "this instinctive dissociation from women explains the progressive diminution of the Indian population."[62] She denied Native men's possession of some of the most fundamental—and human—of instincts in the realm of sexuality and love, resting her claim on the cultural absence of European-type marriage.

Asserting that Native men chose women solely based on their labor potential, Audouard maintained that the men regarded women "only as a type of beast of burden, destined to arduous labor, and to carrying the heaviest loads."[63] In a continuation of her animal analogies, she purported a lack of human passion between the sexes while alleging women's subjugation. Audouard's accusations regarding women's exploitation emerged at least in part in response to Indian women's agricultural work.[64] Like Europeans and Euro-Americans across North America, Audouard mistook Native women's labor in, and control of, agriculture as an unnatural type of forced toil. Rather than recognizing it as a realm of skill, authority, and status, she could only see Indian women as forced into men's proper work, pressed into unwomanly, aberrant duties.

Disparaging Indian women's "debased" social status, Audouard contrasted it with that of white American women. "Yankees," she declared, "more than any other people in the world, understand the respect that one must give to a woman."[65] Audouard explained this respectful treatment as the absence of gallantry, "because gallantry borders very closely on impertinence." Yankee practicality and groundedness presented a contrast with French men, who, Audouard contended, are "the most gallant of all, but also, the least respectful toward women. . . . In a word, the French only judge women from the point of gallantry."[66] She avowed that "Yankee" esteem for women created a society in which women "could come and go without the least fear, they travel alone all across America, and they go out alone in the evening without any apprehension."[67] Audouard painted an idealized white America in which men held women in such high regard that women enjoyed an exceptional level of bodily safety, mobility, and independence. Men's attitudes toward women, from her perspective, shaped the female experience.

Audouard's fantasy of white American women's freedom and social status reflected her conceptualization of a culture spared the masculine flaws at both ends of the civilizational spectrum. Her fantastically gendered United States emerged as sheltered from both the impudent disrespect masculine gallantry imposed on French women and the brutish male disregard she believed that Indian women suffered.

Paule Mink's perceptions of Algerian Muslim men and women shared commonalities with Audouard's assessments of Native Americans. After nearly a year traveling and speaking across France's preeminent North African colony, Mink wrote, "Under the tent or in the slum, women's situation is the same: they are . . . resigned to the state of a domestic animal."[68] While the liberal monarchist Audouard undertook literary reportage-motivated voyages, the revolutionary socialist Mink journeyed to Algeria to foment anti-imperial and anticlerical activism.[69] Both women observed and critiqued women's status by examining gender relations and roles, although they did so through contrasting political lenses, while traveling for dissimilar reasons. They both wielded animal metaphors to derogate those relations and roles they perceived among the two colonized peoples. Audouard and Mink each developed racialized gendered criticisms of the occupied culture they observed, and each blamed women's abasement on what they considered the populations' gendered animality.

Mink sustained the metaphor to underline the ways in which Algerian women's status—always denigrated, in her eyes—degenerated with age. Assessing the female lifecycle, Mink summarized that "women are in their youths beasts of pleasure, and in their old age beasts of burden, nothing more . . . dragging the plow harnessed side by side with an undernourished donkey and the husband's whip."[70] Her analysis denied Muslim women's human status and agency. Incensed at what she saw, Mink presented women as sexually objectified creatures in their youths, and desexualized, yoked brutes "in their old age." Writing in her mid-forties, she emphasized "at 45, Arab women are old."[71]

Abhorring Algerian Muslim women's position led Mink to liken them not only to animals but also to things. A woman, Mink declared, "does not exist as a human being, she is an object, she is a thing, a household tool. . . . A woman is literally sold . . . by her father to her husband."[72] Pushing the non-human metaphor beyond the animal and into the realm of the object, Mink's reference to women as things to be sold alluded to the Arab practice of men bringing a dowry to marriage. (Auclert had held this custom responsible—at least partially—for child marriage, alleging that fathers sought profits from selling young daughters to willing husbands.) Deeply disturbed by her Algerian experience, Mink expressed frustration as she attempted to bridge cultural chasms she found to be as profound as the gap between people and animals, or even people and things.

Mink thus perceived Algerian women as devoid of agency. She blamed their subjugation on Algerian men and censured women for accepting their degradation. "The saddest aspect of Algerian women's situation," Mink lamented, "is that they surrender themselves to their slavery and make no attempt to escape it. . . . They think that it will be this way for all of eternity, and to speak to them of their enfranchisement would, in their eyes, be blasphemous, a religious crime."[73] Noting the absence of Arab women from her public lectures, she suggested that their patriarchal religion and culture prevented them from even hearing of an expansion of their own rights.

Following her post-Commune political exile, Mink returned to France in 1880. Subsequently traveling, speaking, and agitating in the metropole, she saw in many French people a readiness for change. Influenced by the dialogue on imperialism and colonization emerging on both the Left and Right, Mink increasingly turned her attention to these issues. In June of 1884, she participated in a conference titled "The Infamies of Government," in which she decried France's imperialist actions, "in Cochinchine, in Tunisie, in Tonkin," where "without compensation the government sacrificed the nation's money and the blood of its children." Mink concluded that "from every point of view—political, financial, commercial, industrial, and colonial—the situation in France is that a revolution is imminent."[74] Solidifying her anti-imperialism, she linked it to her insurrectionary project. Colonialism fit among the exploitative factors that she understood as pushing France's population to once again rise up—as they did in the 1871 Paris Commune, in which Mink had played a significant role.

In innumerable political speeches and writings throughout the 1870s and 1880s, Mink typically employed incendiary rhetoric to advocate radical change. She contested women's suffrage as insufficiently emancipatory. Considering it a slight bandage on a gaping socioeconomic and political wound, she called instead for violent socialist revolution as the only sure means to liberate both workers and women. Although ideologically opposed to rights-based feminism, because it strove to ameliorate conditions without attacking larger structural problems, she modified her stance in the Algerian context. Comparing European and Algerian women's status, Mink explained that

> the women of France, of England, of America, are right to be pursuing their emancipation and the conquest of their rights, which are none other than those of the equality of all human beings, without distinction of sex, of race, of class, and of nationality. Certainly, the situation of women in countries called civilized is still quite precarious, and we understand very well that they fight to make it better. But how different it is from that of women in the countries not yet pulled from the violent and brutal primordial ages, in which strength was all, where liberty only existed for those who earned respect by the fist.[75]

Relative to her perceptions of Arab women's debased status within a society she saw as mired in a savage and prehistoric age, European women's plight appeared less dire to Mink—to the point that she acknowledged the value of reformist activism, at least under Algeria's distinct circumstances.[76]

Just as her Algerian experience led Mink to contextually amend her ideological position regarding rights-based feminist activism, so, too, did it lead her to a place-based shift in her opposition to the state. Suggesting the possibility of France's imperial project ameliorating Algerian life, Mink asked, "Why have ideas of liberty and of dignity been introduced to these men who have perhaps never dreamed them?"[77] Considering the possible validity of France's civilizing role, Mink suggested the political and cultural superiority of the colonizing power—or at least the potential superiority of that power. By deeming Algerians a population mired in entrenched inequities, she constructed them as foreign to "ideas of liberty and of dignity." As a committed antiimperialist, she had traveled to Algeria to foment anticolonial activism. Yet her perception of the direness of Algeria's social relations led her, despite her radicalism, to presume that France's imperialism might improve its colony. Experiencing the colonial world disturbed Mink's political framework: for this single context, she moderated her anti-imperialism.

In the wake of her Maghrebian trip, Mink penned two articles about Algerian women for the French newspaper *Le coup de feu*, in which she brutally critiqued Arab gender relations. Her only published writings on her Algerian trip—Mink spoke much more than she wrote overall—the articles reveal a shift away from her usual anticlerical and anti-imperial agenda.

A vocal freethinker, Mink had long opposed the Catholic Church, challenging particularly its control over women's lives and arguing that "as long as the church has dominated, woman has been subservient."[78] In 1885, she extended her feminist anti-religiosity to Islamic patriarchy. Having traveled to Algeria as part of her propaganda efforts against the church, capitalism, and imperialism, Mink expressed frustration at what she perceived to be the entrenched nature of traditional gender relations there. An article in the socialist newspaper *Le Cri du peuple* described her as "the valiant, well-known socialist orator . . . who has ardently propagandized for the principles of socialism and freethought in all of France and in Algeria."[79] Mink agitated for and encouraged the multiple Algerian populations' moves toward free thought and liberation, finding responsive audiences across the colony.

Two Catholic missionaries from France, A. Beguin and Peigneaux, crossed paths with Mink in the Algerian city of Oran. Recounting their Mediterranean proselytizing in *En zizag du Maroc à Malte. À travers l'Algèrie, la Tunisie, et les États Barbaresque*, the missionaries positively described the malleability of the indigenous populations they encountered in Algeria, but they complained that French colonists' immoral behavior negatively influenced their potential converts and counteracted their holy work. In the midst of this, they lamented, "We learned with sadness the presence of the too-famous Paule Mink."[80]

Mink embodied the antithesis of Beguin and Peigneaux's goals. They described their book as a travel narrative intended "to make [the reader] better appreciate the efforts of those compatriots who work to propagate in these countries the knowledge and love of God with the love of France."[81] Promoting both colonization and Christianity, they bemoaned Mink's success as an "interesting speaker, pedaling unhealthy and insane theories from tavern to tavern," and doing so with great charisma and publicity.[82] Mink's speeches, weaving together anticlerical, anti-imperial, and antipatriarchal rhetorics, attracted large crowds. Somewhat apologetic for sullying their text by discussing Mink and her influence, the missionaries articulated her threat, explaining that "it was impossible for us to remain silent about something so profoundly humiliating to our patriotism."[83]

Continuing to speak against imperialism once she returned to France, Mink now folded those concerns into her larger political aims. Maintaining her opposition to religions in both metropole and colony, she attempted to establish a new newspaper, *Qui vive!*, which she hoped would "be the organ of diverse socialist and free-thinking groups from the *région méridionale*, from Bordeaux to Nice, and from Algeria . . . to Tunis."[84] She also published essays rebuking Algerian men and gendered Muslim traditions for Algerian women's debased social status. But despite France's fifty-five-year colonial presence in Algeria by the time of Mink's 1884–1885 sojourn, she did not link French imperialism to women's subjugation. In fact, she suggested the opposite.

Mink condemned Algerian patriarchal culture and Islam as the forces undergirding women's oppression and denying their agency. (Auclert, in contrast, saw the imperial and colonial authorities as contributing to Algerian women's repression, denying girls' education, and supporting traditional practices including child marriage and polygamy.[85]) Although actively opposed to imperialisms and colonialism, Mink nonetheless overlooked how these political structures could shape the lives of women of the colonies, possibly underestimating the specifically gendered nature of both of these forces. While she simultaneously reviled both empire as an extension of exploitative state and capitalist power and patriarchal culture as subjugating women and perverting society, she did not link the two. Instead, she constructed a racialized—or at least "culturized"—gender analysis that neglected the role of imperialism in shaping Algerian women's subjection.

Her Algerian experience also led Mink to acknowledge some value in rights-based feminism as a way to improve women's conditions and elevate their status. In 1893, after decades of opposing women's civil and political rights as distractions from revolutionary goals, Mink agreed to accept a symbolic candidacy and run in Parisian municipal elections. Making clear that she saw women's political participation as transitional and ameliorative, she stood as a revolutionary socialist candidate. Putting forth several reasons for agreeing to this candidacy, Mink did not mention Algeria.[86] Yet in writing about her North African journey a decade earlier, she had dramatically broken with her public and vociferous opposition to rights-based feminism. Her severe comparisons of Algerian women's lives with those of European women had led her to rethink the possibilities of a new, transitional Frenchness, one that could advance women's status.

Like Mink, Audouard perceived the Orientalized Algerian world as oppressing Indigenous women more profoundly than the French subjugated metropolitan women. While Audouard had focused on men in her gendered and racialized critique of Native American culture, she focused primarily on women in Algeria. In an 1863 issue of the literary review *Le papillon*, which she published, Audouard wrote of how "our [French] domination of Algeria . . . has civilized them a bit . . . [but] they will have a lot of trouble forcing the Arabs to treat their women suitably."[87] Countering what she claimed were Arab men's assertions that "their wives are very happy," Audouard insisted that it was "impossible to make them understand that women, like themselves, need air, sun, and exercise to live . . . the men respond *MACACHE* [impossible]!"[88] Elaborating on the limitations placed on women's mobility and independence, Audouard claimed that the poorest women, in her estimation are "the least unhappy, because they have to cook and take care of their house: this distracts them a little."[89] In contrast, wealthier women have servants to do their work. Illiterate and "nearly task-free, crouched on their cushions, they have no other distractions beyond painting their nails diverse colors (which, parenthetically, are frightfully ugly), tinting their eyelashes and eyebrows." Shifting from a somewhat sympathetic stance, she continued by denigrating their aesthetic choices and beauty standards. "They have a habit . . . of dying their children's hair, some with red ox blood, some with black soot; these children, with their hair tinted like this, are simply frightful."[90] Continuing to address the attention Algerian women paid to their appearance, despite living in gender-segregated reclusion, Audouard stated, "This proves that men are wrong when they think that women only make themselves beautiful for them."[91] Rather, she contended, the women "love their husbands because of the fineness of the clothing they give them."[92]

While emphasizing Algerian women's subjugation, Audouard simultaneously recognized that they possessed some agency, an unmistakable dissimilarity with Mink's assessments. Audouard argued that Algerian Arab women,

1.2. Olympe Audouard dressed "à la Egyptienne," ca. 1860. Bibliothèque National de France.

particularly those from families with some resources, "use marriage as specula-
tion. They marry a man with some money; the man must give the wife a dowry
and gifts. . . . A month later, or sometimes several days after their marriage,
these women make efforts to irritate their husbands."[93] This escalates to the
point of divorce—which Audouard explained was easily attained, unlike in
France where it was barred. The women then "marry another who again gives
them gifts and money."[94] In clear distinction from Mink's portrayal of Algerian
women as powerless, Audouard saw them—at least those with some wealth—
as manipulatively utilizing the power to which they had access as embodied females. Noting their restricted mobility—"Their marriage decrees stipulate the
number of times per month they have the right to go out, usually between two
and four; they go out accompanied by an elderly female relative or a négresse"—
Audouard acknowledged that they nonetheless managed to extract value and
pleasure, while exercising some control over their lives. She presented a distorted picture of Algerian women's experience, in which she condescended and
passed moral judgements. Yet Audouard did assert that they found power
through the tradition of men bringing dowries to marriage, the legal existence
of divorce, and the cultural acceptance of remarriage—all factors absent from
France.

Writing three years later, in her 1866 Les mystères de l'Égypte dévoilés (The
mysteries of Egypt unveiled), Audouard also presented Egyptian women as
more deeply subjugated than either Turkish or French women. Subjecting
Egypt to a scrutiny harsher than she did most other contexts, Audouard's gendered and racialized critique focused on women's bodies and sexuality. Referring to Turkey—which she idealized both in terms of law and some aspects
of social relations—she compared those Muslim women's lives with the lives
of Egyptian Muslim women and determined that "Muslim women in Egypt
are kept more severely restricted than in Constantinople. . . . They enjoy less
liberty."[95] She described the Egyptian harem as "generally filled with slaves,"
unlike the "good Turkish houses," where women could "claim a bit more
liberty for themselves."[96] Women's lack of domestic liberty reflected, for Audouard, the broader, restrictive Egyptian milieu in which, she stated, "justice
is something unknown." Audouard exemplified the gendered injustice by relating an account of a father grabbing and strangling his daughter as she attempted to slip undetected back into her home, following a clandestine visit
to her lover. The narrative underscored masculine power and authority—
they buried the daughter the next day, with no questions asked—as it played
out on women's bodies.[97] Audouard characterized Egyptian gender hierarchy as controlling women's bodies and sexualities through fear, violence, and
pain.

1.3. "Arab Woman," photographed by Felix Nadar, 1878–1879. Rijksmuseum, Amsterdam.

She portrayed these embodied repressions as occurring across the many ethnic and religious groups she encountered in Egypt. In a detailed recounting
of her attendance at a Coptic Christian wedding, Audouard wrote of the mix
of "a hundred women, *negresses*, slaves, grand dames . . . sitting on divans or
on the floor . . . everyone pell-mell, without distinction, without hierarchy."[98]
The undifferentiated physical promiscuity of women of different classes and
races unsettled Audouard. A creature of hierarchy and elite European conceptions of personal space, she became increasingly uncomfortable as the evening progressed. "Little by little," she complained, "all of the women moved
closer to us. One examined the fabric of my dress, another lifted it to see what
was underneath. . . . They all treated us as like old friends."[99] This level of familiarity, occurring relatively early in her journeying, clashed with Audouard's European standards of social interaction, privacy, and personal space.
As an observer and critic of peoples and cultures, Audouard—who titled her
book "The Mysteries of Egypt Unveiled"—underwent a type of corporal un-
veiling at the hands of these women. They physically subjected her to the kind
of psychic, cultural, and literary examination to which she subjected them.
Although friendly and nonaggressive, her fellow wedding guests' actions presumed a level of intimacy that left Audouard uneasy, as she could not control
access to her own body in this milieu.

A woman then asked Audouard if she would like to see the bride. Completely shrouded and immobile, the young woman was literally nearly invisible. "Unveiled," Audouard affirmed, "I saw a skinny child . . . who appeared to
be at most eight years old. I was unable to retain an exclamation of surprise.
'How can this child be marrying!' I said."[100] The other women laughed and informed her that the bride was eleven years old. Stunned, Audouard continued,
"But she has not yet grown, her chest is not yet developed."[101] Wrapped in veils,
which were lifted for the European woman, the child bride (and the women
assured Audouard that, rather than live with her parents for another year or
two, as Audouard assumed, the girl would immediately be "the true wife of
her husband."[102]) symbolized Audouard's perception of Egyptian womanhood,
waiting for their bodies to be acted upon.

Ultimately, the wedding festivities, swirling around the swathed and station-
ary young woman, led to the actual nuptials. Following the ceremony, Audouard asked her host, the male owner of the house, if the young bride would
now go home with her new husband. "No!" she reported his reply, "Not for
seven days. But now . . .' He then bluntly explained to me what was about to
happen. . . . Seeing my embarrassment and astonishment, he questioned, 'Is
this not done in France, Madame?'"[103] The host described to Audouard a virginity test, undertaken following the wedding, and from which the bride was given

a week to recover. Relating the way in which she learned of this tradition, Audouard described not only her shock at the act itself, but also her discomfort at an elite man's ease in openly discussing something of such a sexual and bodily nature with an elite woman such as herself.

The Coptic woman who served as Audouard's guide invited her to attend the virginity test, and she accepted. Waiting for "the operation," Audouard explained that she "was stupefied, all the women laughing and talking. . . . They gave me the details of the technique."[104] All of the men and most of the women left the salon, in which many had gathered after the nuptials. Next, "Four women took the bride by force and dragged her to a side room."[105] Following with her companion, Audouard reported that the four women held down the young girl on the divan, and her husband, "took a fine cloth handkerchief in his hand . . . and made the operation; the unhappy girl cried out in pain. Nothing could equal the brutality of this operation! Yet the women began to shout with joy. The famous handkerchief, stained with blood, passed from hand to hand, ending up in the yard, where the men welcomed it with hurrahs!"[106] For Audouard, Egyptian Coptic women's complicity in perpetuating sanctioned, public violence against their own daughters revealed a profound debasement. She did not question the expectation of a bride's virginity, or the gendering of virginity, but rather the social demand of its ritualistic proof, and what those rituals reflected about women's status. In her long discussion about Coptic Christians, Audouard characterized them as living secluded lives that led them to remain "attached to ancient ways."[107] Although she wrote her Egypt narrative a few years earlier than her sweeping history, *Gynécologie; La femme depuis six mille ans* (*Gynecology: six thousand years of woman*), Audouard likely recognized virginity tests as having existed in Europe centuries earlier, as part of customs left in the past—where, she argued, the Egyptian Copts still dwelled.[108]

Among the other Egyptian populations she examined in *Les mystères de l'Égypte dévoilés*, Audouard treated the Bedouins in an overall positive and enthusiastic manner, with one strong caveat. Countering the warnings of "all of the French travelers," who, she wrote, characterized Bedouins as "barbarous, cruel," and dangerous, Audouard spent a dozen pages effusively lauding their generosity, graciousness, and warmth. She then qualified: "Now, the love of truth forces me to admit that the Bedouins, so hospitable, so gallant, are sometimes also barbaric."[109] "I would now like to tell you," she confided to her readers, "of one of their customs which has a barbarity beyond compare. But it is extremely difficult to articulate, so difficult that I truly do not know what paraphrases will allow you to understand."[110] She alluded to "that famous belt, found in the Hotel de Cluny, invented during the Crusades"—a medieval chastity belt; in French a *ceinture de confiance*, literally a "belt of trust"—but noted that the Bedouin custom to which she referred "could not be called a *ceinture de confiance*, because the most atrocious distrust had created it."[111] She went on to portray female genital mutilation—a topic discussed with extreme rarity by female travel writers in this period, according to Dúnlaith Bird.[112] "The Bedouins make something similar for their young girls," Audouard explained. "I say make because a needle and thread is all they need to make it. On the eve of marriage it is cut. This operation is incomparably painful and of an incomparable barbarity. Those leaving for a long excursion in the desert re-make the belt or padlock on their wives."[113] For Audouard, this literally unspeakable procedure exemplified Bedouin women's extreme objectification. They were denied corporal autonomy through the imposition of a physical violence, undertaken on the basis of the cultural assumption (which Audouard termed "the most atrocious distrust") that women could not be entrusted with the control of their own bodies. Women were acted upon, sewn up to protect the asset that determined their worth. This was the extreme literalization of valuing women based only on chastity. Audouard did value chastity as one element of women's virtue, but it was the decision to guard her own chastity that made a woman virtuous. The *ceinture de confiance* removed the decision from the individual women.

Empire at Home

As feminists ventured beyond France, traveling to colonies or to metropoles such as Turkey and Egypt that anchored the imperial imaginary, they took a deep interest in each context's gender order. As the next chapter will show, when these feminists compared women's status under law, France often came up short. This contrasted with feminist assessments of women's societal place and value, in which they critiqued their social and sexual standings. Audouard and Mink both exemplified European feminists' incomprehension of unfamiliar social and sexual practices in imperial spaces. The women's resultant anger at or revulsion from these customs led them to support an imperial presence in those places, in contrast to their contestation of nearly all extant imperialisms. Sexualized gender injustice trumped their other political concerns.

When she journeyed through the American West, Audouard judged Native American intimacies as the antithesis of civilized, as savage to the point of animalistic. Her encounters also supported her perception that highly evolved "Yankees" had the right to colonize lands held by soon-to-be-extinct Natives. She exemplified and prefigured racialized white feminisms' support for imperialism.

Audouard was not a feminist imperialist. She did not advocate the imperial promotion of feminist ideas or programs. Rather, her liberal feminism supported American colonial expansion because the United States met her criteria of gender equity. Audouard's fantasy vision of a nation of respectful men and respected women stood as an imperial ideal. France absolutely did not meet that standard—a failure that formed the basis of Audouard's opposition to France's imperial program. Yet she did consider French women's social and sexual statuses superior to those of Native Americans.

Social and sexual intimacies in Algeria and Egypt also discomfited Audouard. Judging gender relations across Egyptian religions and cultures as especially unjust, Audouard expressed particular abhorrence of Egyptian Coptic Christians' virginity tests and Bedouin female genital mutilation. Labeling Coptic Christians as anachronistically engaging in "ancient ways" and Bedouins as undertaking a "barbarous" version of a medieval European practice, she located them in the remnants of a dying distant past, denying them coevalness as she had done Native Americans.

Like Audouard's classification of Indian intimacies as unnatural and animalistic, Mink's descriptions of Algerian women as beasts and things were dehumanizing. And, like Audouard, she blamed Indigenous women's social and sexual statuses on men of their culture. Again, like Audouard, but uncharacteristically for her, Mink advocated imperial action. Their commonalities as feminists motived these assertions, driven by outrage at sexualized gender oppression.

The similarities ended there. Audouard traveled to report; Mink journeyed to agitate. Audouard observed and assessed, often comparing gender hierarchies in global imperial milieux to those in France and pushing for alterations in the French gender order. Mink's primary motivation was inciting anti-imperial uprising. Audouard expressed outrage at the sexual, physical, and social abuses women suffered, hoping to both expose those exploitations and to gain readership. Mink saw sexual and labor practices she considered beyond the pale, and these led her to consider the viability (short term and exacting) of the very system that she otherwise militantly challenged. Their differences emerged from divergent feminisms and disparate relationships to empire.

CHAPTER 2

Sex, Love, and the Law

Transforming Frenchness

"Crossing the Rocky Mountains," Olympe Audouard reported in 1871,

> one finds oneself in Utah, a state colonized by the followers of Brigham Young. Frenchmen, unhappily for French women, also support polygamy. For those tempted to join the Latter Day Saints in order to benefit from this institution, I give a little charitable advice: in Salt Lake City, a man must feed all of the women he marries; wives have the right of divorce, but the husband does not; he must give his name and bread to all of his children. . . . Frenchmen, so accustomed to taking pleasures without any inconveniences, would undoubtedly miss the Napoleonic Code which grants men complete impunity for all their bad passions.[1]

In this passage from her account À travers l'Amérique: North-America, Audouard likened French men's lack of fidelity to a kind of polygamy, while mocking their absence of responsibility for their sexual behavior. Her stark set of comparisons catalogued the marital obligations that Mormon men had and French men did not, and the rights that Mormon women held but that French women lacked. She stressed that, in terms of marriage and sexual relations, the French state required of men distinctly fewer responsibilities than did the polygamous Mormon society. Similarly, it granted women fewer rights than did the Latter Day Saints. In certain ways, Audouard contended, the Napoleonic Code of

Law undercut monogamy, enabling a sort of French polygamy—at a time when France allowed literal polygamy in its colonies.

As Audouard voyaged to "America, the kingdom of the Mormons, the European Turkey and the Asian Turkey, Egypt, Syria, Palestine, Algeria, Italy, England, and Germany," she paid particular attention to women's status under law.[2] As a faithful Catholic and a liberal monarchist, Audouard did not resist existing hierarchies, except gender. She compared the structure and influence of gendered legal systems in imperial contexts with that of France, pointedly highlighting examples of France's greater gender inequality. Audouard was the only travel writer among the five feminists. Yet like her, Hubertine Auclert and Léonie Rouzade also came away from their imperial encounters with new perspectives on France and Frenchness. As revolutionaries, Paule Mink and Louise Michel rarely sought such nation-based reform. Michel and Mink stood apart in another way. Unlike the three others, they took little interest in law.

Feminists' focus on legal structures varied, generally increasing in correlation with the moderation of their class politics and with their adherence to the structural status quo. Those who worked for change within the current political order tended to focus on jurisprudence to a much greater extent than did revolutionaries or anarchists, who sought to overthrow or undermine entire existing systems. Promoting legal reform reflected confidence in a legal structure having sufficient flexibility and capaciousness to allow for serious change. Feminists concerned with legal codes recognized that the gendered nature of laws reflected the dominant gender ideology of the metropole or colony from which it emerged. Audouard, Auclert, and Rouzade evocatively and critically described the rights and legal statuses of women in these places, comparing them—most often positively—to those of women in France. These assessments became part of their efforts to rethink and transform Frenchness and to change France.[3]

Women held inferior political and civil status under France's Napoleonic Code of Law. Increasingly challenged about this inequity in the latter part of the nineteenth century, French and French colonial authorities consistently contrasted it with Algerian Muslim women's subjugation under Muslim and customary law, insisting the latter far outweighed the gender imbalances of the Napoleonic Code. As Judith Surkis shows, French officials focused especially on Muslim men's legal sexual privileges, deflecting attention from their own legal sexual prerogatives. They also disregarded the reality that Muslim law allowed married women greater legal and property rights than did the French.[4] Auclert, especially, saw this contradiction and challenged its hypocrisy.

Imagining and pursuing alternative versions of Frenchness, feminists who addressed empire often deployed imperial presumptions of racialization, sexualization, ethnographic categorization, and civilization, while simultaneously contesting existing imperial projects. Experiences in empire, interwoven with their feminist ideologies, had profound influences. These involvements shaped their politics, their critiques of Frenchness, and their understandings of imperialisms and colonialism. In a period in which empire became increasingly central in the definition of Frenchness, these activists developed distinct and complex imperial critiques.

Audouard, Auclert, Rouzade, and Mink each took differing routes to politicizing imperialism. Audouard opposed French imperialism because of the nation's inequitable gender hierarchies, yet she did not reject imperialism per se. Auclert focused primarily on Algeria, where she lived and worked from 1888 to 1892. Identifying women's status in France and in its Algerian colony as fundamentally interlinked, she advocated a feminist imperialism. A harsh critic of France's approach to empire, Auclert nonetheless promoted the export of French feminist-influenced egalitarian gender laws and customs from the metropole to Algeria. Rouzade, the republican socialist novelist and activist, took a fictional approach to women's subjugation in both France and the "Arab world." In her 1872 novel, Le monde renversé (The World Turned Upside Down), set in an unspecified fictional sultanate, a young European woman triumphs over a male Muslim ruler; she imposes the inversion of the entire realm's gender roles, thus turning the world "upside down." A satirical tale, the story nonetheless reflects a feminism complicit in the republican imperial system of racial and cultural superiority. Paule Mink traveled to Algeria in 1884–1885 to propagandize against imperialism and religion and to experience France's colonial domination firsthand. As a revolutionary socialist feminist, she did not focus specifically on law. Her condemnation of Algerian polygamous marriage, however, directly engaged gendered legal questions. Deeply censorious of the contexts she observed, Mink condemned Algerian and Islamic patriarchies as the powers undergirding women's oppression.

Pressing to redefine Frenchness while in empire, these four feminists grappled with its constitutive racial, gendered, religious, and class-based elements. In sharing public and private space, engaging in relations of exchange or service, making ethnographic observations, or attempting political persuasion, these French women operated within intimate matrices of inclusion and exclusion. Experiences such as Audouard's encounters with formerly enslaved African Americans in Wyoming, Auclert's probing into Algerian polygamous marital practices, Rouzade's imagining a Western woman taken captive by a Muslim sultan, and Mink's questioning the absence of Algerian Muslim women at her lectures intellectually and emotionally marked these women.

Voyageuses and Voyages

The era's first French feminists to engage, and ultimately to contest, empire were women who traveled into it, a fact that underscores the significance of first-hand experience and the notable role of travel.[5] Marginalized in the metropole first as women and doubly so as feminists, female travelers—*voyageuses*—became further othered, due to their abandonment of women's prescribed domestic sphere for the literal wider world.[6] A significant number of French women traveled into empire during this period, motivated by various reasons (leisure, adventure, spousal duty, politics, religion, employment). Merely by virtue of traveling, these women challenged restrictive parameters of female propriety. Journeying women possessed mobility, and those who wrote narratives, memoirs, or polemics had voice.[7] In telling their stories, sharing their perspectives, presenting their particular impressions of colonial spaces and Indigenous people, female voyagers played roles in the construction of colonial discourse and in the production of racial and social hierarchies.[8] They influenced both metropolitan understandings of empire and the forming of empire itself.

Scholarship on *voyageuses* (most from a feminist perspective) emphasizes the gendered nature not only of their writing, but also of their travel experience and encounters. Highlighting the potentially emancipatory and self-discovery aspects of travel, the historiography also underscores these European women's attention to the lives and experiences of Indigenous women. Many female travelers criticized or denigrated women's status in various colonial milieux, while others positively contrasted legal or cultural elements to those in France. Examining the often-intimate interactions involved in these observations and encounters makes clear the co-constitutive nature of such colonial relationships; women travelers both shaped and were shaped by their experiences. Importantly, current scholarship insists on the heterogeneous nature of the women travelers and on the specifically located nature of their imperial encounters.[9]

All of these recognitions apply to Audouard, Auclert, Rouzade, and Mink. But these four also differed from other *voyageuses*: as feminists, they pushed beyond observation, description, and critique to call for—even demand—change. As Nicolas Bourguignat notes, there was nothing intrinsically emancipatory or resistant to gender hierarchies in women's travel writing.[10] As each woman developed specific feminist ideologies in her metropolitan life, she subsequently experienced various global sites through these particular analytical frameworks. Colonial experiences, interactions with "new" peoples, cultures, ideas, and places, and the uniqueness of each colonial space, in turn, altered her analytical frame. In ensuing publications and orations, these feminists

introduced—or reintroduced—a plethora of gendered images and interpretations of imperial worlds to their audiences both within and outside of Europe.
Tracing these multidirectional pathways of influence illuminates the formations
and transmissions of politics between metropole and colony. French imperial
authorities continually adapted and bolstered the boundaries of Frenchness, and feminists doggedly worked at transgressing them.

In their travels, feminists interested in jurisprudence focused on the ways in
which legal systems shaped women's lives. Their concerns intersected at three
broad, gendered sites—marriage, women's legal status, and polygamy—where
patriarchal power relations played out in context-specific yet overlapping ways.
Feminists interrogated these sites in their wide-ranging and often divergent efforts to alter hierarchies and to ameliorate women's lived experiences—of sexualities, love, conjugal sexual politics, agency, and rights.[11] Analyzing marriage,
women's legal status, and polygamy invariably led the activists to contrast
France with colonized and non-European societies, as they intended to illuminate the hypocrisies of France and its civilizing mission and to undermine its
imperial endeavors. Promoting an array of feminist goals, these women drew
on imperial locales to create and advance new visions of Frenchness.

Marriage

In *Les femmes arabes en Algérie*, Hubertine Auclert explained the prenuptial economic exchange between a young Algerian Arab woman's fiancé and her father,
charging that "the sale of a young girl is accomplished with no more ceremony
than the sale of a heifer."[12] Four pages later, she contended that nonetheless,
"Muslim marriage is . . . more advantageous than French marriage, because far
from losing rights, the woman acquires some, and in lieu of giving a dowry, she
receives one."[13] Auclert's investigation exemplified the complexity of the marital
question. Having recognized legal and economic advantages of Muslim conjugality over French, in the very next sentence Auclert's appraisal again turned
unfavorable as she maintained that "however, this marriage is not consensual;
it nearly always occurs in spite of the young girl's opposition and it involves
polygamy."[14] Auclert's whipsaw assessment of conjugality reflected her—and
other feminists'—criticisms of both French and Algerian matrimony, and their
understandings of its economic ("The sale of a young girl"), rights-based ("far
from losing rights . . ."), and religio-social components ("it involves polygamy").[15] Marital customs and practices drew the attention and provoked the disputation of French feminists in multiple colonial and metropolitan contexts. A
fundamental transcultural social, sexual, economic, and legal institution and

HUBERTINE AUCLERT

LES

FEMMES ARABES
EN ALGÉRIE

Polygamie
Le Coût de l'adultère
Durée de la gestation chez les Musulmanes
Féministes au 13ᵉ siècle
Où la prostitution est un sacerdoce
Les Arabes sans représentant au Parlement

PARIS
SOCIETÉ D'ÉDITIONS LITTÉRAIRES
4, RUE ANTOINE-DUBOIS, 4
PLACE DE L'ÉCOLE-DE-MÉDECINE

1900

2.1. *Les femmes arabes en Algérie*, 1900. Title page of Hubertine Auclert's book. Bibliothèque National de France.

relationship, marriage structured women's lives in particularly gendered ways, thereby presenting a logical focus for feminist examination.

For French feminists, the question of marriage held particular salience. Across France's tumultuous long nineteenth century, marriage underwent significant change while remaining a central focus of multiple debates. An institution of everyday life and of social, economic, political, cultural, and symbolic importance, it became a principal site of contestation between those seeking transformation—not only feminists, but also socialists and liberal reformers—and those demanding continuity. The kinds of transformation, and the extents of continuity sought, shifted over the century as France moved through revolutions and reactions and reforms and resistances. As a core social formation, matrimony came to represent a period's dominant ideologies, standing as a measure of the political and cultural ascendency of those in power. Marriage policed intimacies and structured families, and those that governed used their authority to impose their political and ideological imprimatur on domestic institutions.[16] Gendered familial hierarchies reflected relations of power within the larger society.[17]

During the French Revolution, revolutionaries attacked the patriarchal family and religiously sanctioned conjugality, which they viewed as a microcosm of the monarchical Old Regime society, against which they rebelled. "Remaking the family and gender relationships," Suzanne Desan has shown, "was integral to forging the revolutionary state and politics."[18] Like the now contract-based state, marriage, the gendered relationship at the familial core, would also rest on a contract, one freely entered into by individuals.[19] This idea of contract grew from deeply gendered roots in Enlightenment origin stories. Carole Pateman argues that, while the original societal "contract" is most often discussed as a social contract, one among men, such a characterization ignores half of the population and the fundamental and integrally entwined sexual contract. Pateman elaborates: "The social contract is a story of freedom; the sexual contract is a story of domination. Men's freedom and women's subjection are created through the original contract. . . . The contract establishes men's political right over women—and also sexual, in establishing orderly access by men to women's bodies. . . . Contract is the means through which modern patriarchy is constituted."[20] As Pateman notes, this relationship played out most clearly in the literal marriage contract. Despite (somewhat) egalitarian reforms and alterations during the Revolution and reactionary emendations in its aftermath, this legal and social relationship persisted in granting men authority over and sexual access to women.

In the heady revolutionary context, however, questions regarding the meaning, structure, and practice of marriage engaged the French. Issues initially considered by Enlightenment thinkers—including matrimonial indissolubility, paternal power over spousal selection, dowries, and gendered hierarchies within marriage—became fodder for public discussion and debate. Women's clubs, as well as feminists such as Olympe de Gouges and Etta Palm d'Aelders, called for greater marital equity within the context of broader gender-based demands.[21] The 1791 Constitution made marriage a civil contract, and the following year the Legislative Assembly legalized divorce. Forever altered, matrimony dramatically moved from sacred and indissoluble to civil and terminable. Neither the significant limitations Napoleon's 1804 Civil Code placed on divorce nor the Restoration's 1816 termination of it could return matrimony to its former position of being holy and permanent.[22] Its significance, ubiquity, authority, and (now apparent) vulnerability centered conjugality as a long-term site of contention.

The code conceptualized marriage as different from "natural attraction," which it relegated to the realm of animals mating. Contractual conjugality instead rested in the social and legal, making it a matter of state. The code's authors asserted this as an exemplar of modern French civilization, setting it apart and above other societies with more "primitive" marital practices. Divorce, as Camille Robcis contends, would thus indicate a failure of not just an individual relationship, but rather of the entire social institution. They thus terminated divorce as a right.[23] The civil code did, however, allow a man access to divorce if his wife committed adultery. A woman held the same right only if her husband were to move his "concubine" into the connubial home. Napoleon's corresponding penal code went even further in establishing a new male conjugal prerogative: it gave a man the right to kill his wife if he caught her *in flagrante delicto* in the matrimonial residence. Women held no such right regarding husbands.[24]

Within a few years of Napoleon's ascension to power, his civil code reintroduced aspects of patriarchal spousal authority that the Revolution had lifted. As part of reestablishing post-Revolutionary order, the code backtracked on the rights and independence of wives and children, in some ways placing greater limitations on married women than had the Ancien Regime.[25] Repeatedly terming women "incompetent" and establishing them as on a par with minor children, the civil code prevented women from living apart from their husbands, from controlling their own wages or property (or the legal or financial affairs of their children), and from retaining their own nationality if different from their husband's. Article 213 of the civil code clarified this hierarchy: "The husband owes protection to his wife; the wife obedience to her husband."[26] With these reifications of patriarchal power, marriage continued as a site for political inscription, a realm for reappropriation and the demonstration of authority.

Defining and redefining conjugality remained part of claiming who and what was French. Napoleon had created France's first unified body of law as part of his larger universalizing project of clarifying and codifying Frenchness.[27] While in the wake of his abdication, Napoleon's governing structure was abandoned, the code itself endured (with modifications). The gendered legal, economic, and social relationships it institutionalized around marriage held as points of dispute throughout the century.

Following Napoleon's fall, the newly restored French monarchy terminated legal divorce in 1816, expurgating the remnants of what Theresa McBride has termed the social policy "most emblematic of republicanism."[28] That year, Louis Gabriel Ambroise Vicomte de Bonald, a counterrevolutionary politician and philosopher, analogized the state to the family, declaring that "to remove the Republic from the hands of the people, we must also remove the family from the hands of wives and children."[29] Just as a king, Louis XVIII, once again sat as father of the nation, so, too, would fathers' indissoluble familial reigns be restored. Wedded union, however, remained a civil contract. Therefore, for the next sixty-eight years, until the 1884 Naquet Law again legalized divorce, French marriages held the incongruous status that Rachel Mesch and Masha Belenky describe as "a contract that could not be broken."[30]

Feminists' focus on marriage made obvious sense, as these activists tried both to regain rights women held during the revolutionary era and to further expand those rights and redefine the union in egalitarian terms. In 1837, in the wake of the 1830 revolution that established a constitutional July Monarchy, the socialist feminist Flora Tristan petitioned the Chamber of Deputies for the restitution of divorce. Pointing to its 1816 prohibition by the reactionary Restoration monarchy, she attempted to shame the deputies, writing accusatorily, "Who would have thought . . . that this barbarous monument of the Gothic assembly would subsist in 1837?"[31] In 1848, during the short-lived Second Republic, Jeanne Deroin, Eugénie Niboyet, and the other publishers of France's first feminist newspaper, La voix des femmes, called for marital reform and the reintroduction of divorce;[32] and under the repressive Second Empire, feminist authors including Juliette Lamber and André Léo critiqued marriage in widely read novels and essays.[33]

Matrimony in the imperial world thus provided an alluring subject for feminist critique. During the final years of the Second Empire and the opening decades of the Third Republic, Olympe Audouard wrote extensively about marriage and divorce law and customs in her travel accounts and other publications, comparing those of France to those of the nations, colonies, and cultures she visited. In her first book, the 1866 Les mystères du sérail et des harems turcs (Mysteries of the seraglio and of Turkish harems), Audouard praised numerous features of what she understood as Turkish life and law—a world that countered many of the stereotypes and presuppositions with which she had arrived on her 1858 trip.[34] During this period when the Napoleonic Code barred divorce in France, Audouard lauded not only the existence of divorce in Turkish law, but also its availability and implementation.[35] She explained that in Turkey, a woman could obtain a divorce "immediately," if she "could prove that her husband had said a coarse word, had brutalized her, or had said to someone that he is bored, tired of her."[36] For less contentious relationships, she reported, couples could easily attain divorce by claiming incompatibility. If a woman did not subsequently want to remarry following divorce, her ex-husband was "forced to provide for her expenses."[37] Alternatively, if only the wife desired divorce, she presented her case to a tribunal. If it decided that she had insufficient reasons to terminate the relationship, Turkish law still allowed her to choose to live apart from her husband—something barred by the Napoleonic Code. Not only did a still-wedded woman have the right to move out of her husband's home, but her spouse was also "forced to give her a separate house, to largely meet her economic needs. If she did not want to receive him, he could not come to that home."[38] The husband still bore financial responsibility for his estranged wife, but—notably—he lost his guarantee of sexual access. In dramatic contrast with French law, the Turkish wife could choose to keep her husband from both her body and her home. "This law," Audouard enthusiastically proclaimed, "as all Turkish laws in general, is favorable to women."[39]

The relative expansiveness of Turkish women's conjugal rights clearly struck Audouard. Underscoring the contrast between France's restrictive marriage law and that of Turkey, she complained that one of the few ways French women could legally separate from their husbands was not when "a wife has been beaten by her husband"—which did not constitute cause—but only "if he has been clumsy enough to beat her before a witness."[40] Giving the lie to French assertions of superiority, Audouard continued, "This case does not exist in Turkey, a country that we call barbaric, because no man, not even a man of the people, would degrade himself to the point of lifting his hand against a woman. If he did, public opinion would condemn him, and the laws would punish him severely. A coarse, brutal word suffices to them; to us, civilized people, the law demands blows!"[41] Writing under the censorship constraints of France's repressive Second Empire, Audouard nonetheless denied Turkish barbarism and challenged French civilization, portraying Turkish society—across classes—as less violent and more respectful of women and Turkish marital law as more humane and just.[42] Her fervor extended to declaring, "There is not another country where women are more effectively legally protected than in Turkey."[43]

France, Audouard avowed, treated marriage more like bondage. In an 1870 speech titled "Woman in Marriage, Separation, and Divorce," she avowed that "while [French] woman's slavery is somewhat concealed, it is nonetheless real, and it is as rigorous as that to which Blacks submitted in the [American] South."[44] Having recently returned from a thirteen-month voyage through the immediate post–Civil War United States, where she had "seen everything and studied everything, with ardor, with curiosity, and with the firm desire to see well," she likened the type and quality of married French women's oppression to American chattel slavery.[45] Audouard elaborated the ways in which the Napoleonic Code gave a husband "all possible rights, he has authority without limit."[46] Under the code, the husband—with nearly boundless power—became the master and the wife his slave. Continuing her metaphors of unfreedom, Audouard spoke of how a young French girl, "when marrying, has no suspicion that she is actually delivering herself into perpetual serfdom. . . . One can call marriage, under these circumstances, an ambush."[47] Bursting any illusion of romantic, or even tolerable, wedded life, Audouard indicted French law for relegating women to the antitheses of citizenship—slavery and serfdom—in characterizing French nuptials as entrapment into female servitude.

In censuring French law and practice, Audouard simultaneously idealized enslaved women's physical and psychological circumstances. "The Southern slave has her hut," Audouard explained, "when her work is done, she can find a few moments of freedom there."[48] In contrast, "A wife has only the conjugal roof," Audouard declared, referring to the French code's mandate that a wife live wherever her husband chose, "under which the master can exercise his tyranny at any time, at any minute." Continuing in this vein, Audouard made deeply misinformed assumptions regarding enslaved women's control over their own bodies and sexuality. She argued that, since antiquity, female slaves have "had the right to refuse her favors to her master. It remains the last freedom of a *fille de couleur* [girl of color], that of the heart, her sentiments were respected, she was able to hate or love."[49] In comparison, Audouard wrote, "The French woman does not have this supreme freedom. . . . A wife must love her husband, or at least submit to his love!"[50]

Her suggestion that enslaved African American women possessed this bodily and sexual autonomy reflected her misunderstanding of antimiscegenation laws, nearly ubiquitous across the United States, which criminalized sex and barred marriage between races.[51] In reality, however, white male slave-owners were effectively and often statutorily exempt from these measures in their relations with enslaved Black women, given the women's legal status as human property and ubiquitous cultural assumptions regarding white men's right to bonded Black women's bodies.[52] French men's sexual access to their wives' bodies was guaranteed in patriarchal law; American white men's sexual access to enslaved Black women's bodies was guaranteed in a mesh of racialized patriarchal law and custom.

Audouard's assumptions regarding enslaved Southern Black women's "freedom . . . to hate or love" and their liberty relative to wedded French women likely emerged from an amalgamation of her reliance on legal codes, her frequent idealization of things American, and information from the informants she encountered on her travels. Deeply interested and invested in law, Audouard asserted, "When one wants to know the degree of civilization of a people, it is necessary to open its law code and read it attentively. One must examine the fate it assigns women."[53] While this was written specifically about her preparation before journeying to Russia, her recurrent comparisons of the Napoleonic Code with those in the myriad places to which she traveled make clear her concern with jurisprudence. In terms of the American South, Audouard presumed legal consistency and enforcement. Her understanding of law's profound influence dovetailed with her idealization of multiple aspects of the United States, as exemplified by her contention that "adultery is nearly unknown in America, in any case excessively rare. . . . The laws there are wise and excellent. . . . America is the wisest nation in the world."[54] These views underlay suppositions that antimiscegenation laws covered the South, that they thus shielded black women from white men, and that such protections effectively gave enslaved women greater sexual sovereignty than the Napoleonic Code allowed married French women.

Her underestimation of the brutal realities of US slavery was bolstered by her interpretation of encounters with former slaves. Audouard reported that she "was very surprised to see that all of the Negroes appear to miss their previous situation." Former bondsmen, she wrote, spoke of the "Yankees," asking, "Why did they get involved in our affairs? We were happy in the South, our position suited us, they could have just left us alone!"[55] This vision of a lawful and somewhat humane slavery was reinforced through accounts she heard, such as that of a hotel worker in the precarious world of Cheyenne, in the Wyoming Territory, who lamented his former enslaved life as a "domestic in a good house, where I was well-nourished and well-lodged . . . and my future was assured."[56] Such narratives enabled Audouard to construct and propound an American slavery that held bodily protections for bondswomen beyond those enjoyed by wedded French women. Marriage under the Napoleonic Code, Audouard argued, rested "on the despotic tyranny of the man, and the subjugation and complete annihilation of the woman's will."[57] Recognizing the central, constituent social role of marriage, and women's deprivation of autonomous selfhood under France's construction of the conjugal institution,

Audouard contended that the extant marital law not only dehumanized women, but also "threatens the inalienable rights of all human beings."[58] From her perspective, this fundamental legal inequity invalidated France's civilizational claims and its self-proclaimed right to empire.

While Audouard used an exaggeratedly ameliorated version of slavery to underscore married women's subjugation under French law, Léonie Rouzade, writing at the same time, created a fictional utopian tale to similarly attack the Napoleonic Code. In her 1872 *Le monde renversé*, Rouzade envisioned a beautiful slave, a young white French woman named Célestine Chopin, taken captive by pirates at sea and subsequently sold to a sultan. Célestine ultimately seizes control over the sultan's kingdom. Once in power, she inverts the laws governing women and men. Uproar and confusion ensue. Men express indignation and disbelief at the subservience and subjugation of their new position, and women voice stunned recognition of their suddenly acquired power and status. While the code's differential treatment of men and women surprised few, placing women under formerly male law and vice-versa illuminated the deep injustices inherent in France's profoundly gendered legal code.[59]

Célestine's decree specifically inverts the Napoleonic Code's spousal mandate by stating, "Man owes obedience to woman."[60] On acceding to the throne, the new empress immediately performs a mass wedding. Here Rouzade cuts to the code's patriarchal core. Célestine declares the usual marital vows irrelevant, because "their entire value could be summarized in the word 'obedience.'" The traditional nuptial pledge was thus replaced with an oath of obedience "of the man to his wife."[61]

As the story develops, the men and some women of the former sultanate express frustration with men's severe subjugation and the problems created by such obvious inequity.[62] Asked to "establish a balance" between men and women, Célestine replies by clarifying that she had merely, "inverted the roles, but had changed absolutely nothing" about the gendered laws. "I understand very well, gentlemen," she explains, "that women's role does not suit you, because it does not at all suit women either."[63] Rouzade illuminated the acute double standards in French law, relatively invisible when applied to women, but glaringly obvious when imposed on men. She wrote Célestine as an exceptionally self-assured and arrogant character, a stereotypical European male autocrat in the person of a stunningly beautiful French woman who does not hesitate to use her sexuality to extend her power.

Responding to popular demand, Célestine, in her role as enlightened despot, declares that "if tomorrow someone brings me a set of laws that recognize the equality of men and women, by tomorrow evening I will have abandoned the throne."[64] Presented with "the declaration of the equal rights of man and woman," Célestine, confident in her newly civilized peoples' embrace of social republicanism, abdicates. Before departing, however, she "designated an equal number of women and men as representatives to hold power for one year, decreeing that subsequently representatives, always in equal number, would be elected by the nation."[65] She institutionalizes a republic, mandating not only universal suffrage but also a representative governing body composed of an equal number of men and women.

Constructing this fictional "World Turned Upside Down," Rouzade laid bare the injustice and absurdity of one sex ruling over the other, a critique aimed specifically at the Napoleonic Code's subjugation of women in general and married women in particular. To do so, she created a relatively weak male other in the form of the "sultan" and his cadre of ruling men, seduced and manipulated by a stunning, overtly sexual, formerly enslaved woman. Without explicitly describing the sultanate as Muslim, Rouzade has Célestine address her subjects as "Dear children of Mohammed" in her first official speech, making clear both the religion and the "Oriental" nature of a state in which a white European woman could be enslaved, and in which that female slave could ultimately seize power.[66] Rouzade destabilized hierarchies of gender and class in creating Célestine not only as a royal usurper, but also as one who reversed gender laws and standards. Yet the work is imbued with a race-based French republican ideology of imperialism.

Rouzade wrote *Le monde renversé* during the early 1870s, a period of revolution and social conflict in France, which led to a decade of repression and struggle between republican and monarchist forces. The embattled conservative republican government promoted empire in hopes of constructing a new, strongly nationalist identity to unify disparate factions and counter an image of weakness and loss.[67] The idea of republic itself remained highly contested, conceptualized by those on the Left as social, and by centrists as political.[68] For republican socialist feminists such as Rouzade, the republican form held great liberatory potential, sufficiently capacious to allow universal representation, equality, and justice, if conceptualized and configured to do so. This vision of a social republic promised a reordering of economic, political, social, and gender hierarchies. It promised an egalitarian Frenchness. By placing a colonial encounter in a republican utopian tale, Rouzade embraced and appropriated the *mission civilisatrice*, the civilizing mission. A central concept in justifying France's imperial project, the *mission civilisatrice* propounded that France possessed a unique mission to bring "civilization" to less evolved peoples.[69] Adapting this politics to her socialist and feminist agenda, she depicted non-European peoples as civilizable, and correspondingly France under a reactionary republic and what she considered the barbaric Napoleonic Code

2.2. Léonie Rouzade, ca. 1870. Wikimedia Commons.

as also civilizable—but both only through elevation by a strong, guiding, and specifically female hand.

Rouzade sought an institutional and structural solution to married (and all) women's subjugation consistent with her republican socialist feminism. She situated an exaggerated version of the political and social struggle in a fictional Orient, but the metropolitan parallels were clear. Audouard sought only legal change—a goal in line with her broader politics. In *La femme dans le mariage, la separation et le divorce*, after articulating the injustices and horrors caused by French marriage law, Audouard argued that "the sole security that one can give to women . . . the one thing that will make marriage an association, calm, happy, and edifying, rather than making it a perpetual hell, would be divorce."[70]

A devout Catholic, Audouard insisted on divorce's compatibility with both France and the Church. Reaching back to the "Church Fathers," she explained that "their position on the subject was split: Saint Epiphanius of Cyprus supported it, Saint Augustine was opposed. They are both saints. . . . Saint Augustine's opinion prevailed."[71] Pointing to state precedent, Audouard presented divorce as unarguably French, reminding readers that divorce was legal in France from September 1792 to 1816. She charged that its outlawing had led to national moral degradation. Comparing France with other imperial powers allowing legal divorce, including Belgium, Germany, Russia, Britain, and the United States, she wrote, "Statistics prove that these countries have less than half the cases of divorce than France has separations. . . . There are only one-third the number of natural [born outside of marriage] children."[72] Turning the tables on conservative allegations of divorce as immoral, Audouard presented legal divorce as preventing both marital dissolution and unwed births. Because France's law barred separated individuals from marrying again, births outside of wedlock rose. Despite her critique, she defended her nation, insisting that "no one could say" that those countries with legal divorce "are more moral than France."[73]

Audouard's advocacy of divorce emerged from personal experience. Married at eighteen to her first cousin—whom she had known only three weeks—she sought a legal separation five years later. In her memoirs, *Voyage à travers mes souvenirs* (Travels through my memories), written during heated French legislative debates over the legalization of divorce, Audouard made clear the discrimination and hardship that women such as she suffered when legal separation provided the only possible official conjugal break.[74] Although the measure had permitted women to live apart from their spouses (something otherwise forbidden of wives under the code), it left them in legal limbo. Audouard explained that, following her "judicial odyssey . . . I obtained . . . a separation of bodies and property [*séparation des corps et biens*], custody of my children, restitution of my dowry, and a pension for my children." Nonetheless, she continued, "As a separated woman, I remained a minor."[75] Detailing the costly and complex legal and personal labyrinth she was forced to navigate, Audouard emphasized that although she had regained her dowry, magistrates controlled her access to the funds. Further, the law barred her from undertaking any business or investment without her husband's permission. The separated woman thus bore the guardianship not only of the courts, but also of her estranged husband—because marriage remained indissoluble. Impeded by being denied full autonomy and legal adulthood, Audouard asked her readers, "Was it not excusable for me to campaign for the past twenty years for reform of the code and for the reestablishment of divorce?"[76]

As a thoroughly gendered, social, sexual, economic, and legal construct, marriage drew extensive feminist attention in both metropole and colony. The deep inequity of conjugal law under the Napoleonic Code led feminists to compare it negatively to marital law and customs they encountered as they moved beyond France to various imperial and colonial contexts. In a sweeping condemnation in her 1904 book, *L'Argent des femmes* (Women's money), Auclert addressed the disastrous economic repercussions of French marriage for women, contending that "France, in terms of matrimonial arrangements, falls below those of Russia, Austria, England, Turkey, America, as well as Algerian Arabs."[77] These feminists' foci, and their disparate analyses and critiques, reveal a broad-based understanding of conjugal equity as a key step toward societal regeneration, as a means to ameliorating women's alterity, and as a fundamental element in establishing a new Frenchness and a better France.

Women's Legal Status

Marriage existed as a particularly fundamental social structure and set of legal parameters shaping women's lives, but it also intersected with broader questions of the gendered nature of law. Critical of women's status under the Napoleonic Code, nonrevolutionary feminists who engaged in French and other imperial contexts found multiple milieux with which to compare metropolitan women's legal standing. In most cases, France came up short—with the exception of child marriage, an institution barred in France but in few of these other places.

Audouard clearly lauded Turkish law, particularly for providing women the right not only to divorce but also to claim paternity suits. She explained that in Turkey, "unlike France, a man has no right to seduce a young girl, impregnate her, and then abandon child and mother. No, the girl deceived by a man has only to come before a court: the man will be condemned."[78] Audouard referred to the Napoleonic Code's bar on paternity suits, which left unmarried pregnant women (and their natural children) without legal or economic recourse. Her implication of simple resolution—"the girl deceived by a man has only to come before a court"—reflected another perceived difference in women's access to justice. Decrying the French system for requiring wealth or personal connections to access the courts, Audouard applauded Turkey, where, she contended, a woman could approach the tribune "without waiting the interminable delays that we have [in France] . . . and without any expense."[79] Her comparison highlighted the gendered and—unusually for Audouard—class barriers to justice in France.

As Rachel Fuchs has shown, the issue of paternity emerged as a site of contestation between women and men, the judiciary, and the law. During the first half of the nineteenth century, the prohibition of *recherche de paternité* (paternity searches), Article 340 of the Napoleonic Code, remained firm, as "magistrates tended to apply the letter of the law, especially adhering to Article 340."[80] This article and its enforcement protected men's individual right to accept or deny paternity outside of marriage (within marriage they had no choice); this decision was linked to their right to determine their heirs outside of marriage and thus to decide the disposition of their property. A shift began in the 1840s, however, as justices made high-profile decisions that held some men morally and financially responsible for the seduction and abandonment of young women. The magistrates made clear that these judgments were merely civil misdemeanors for not fulfilling legal agreements, and not about paternity. Such decisions, Fuchs argued, reflected the judiciary's acceptance of marital engagement as a contract between a man and a woman. This acknowledgment exemplified a notable judicial change: magistrates' "recognition of women's right to enter legal agreements" meant validating rights that did not exist in law.[81] During this period, particularly around the European-wide revolutions of 1848, women began exercising rights as citizens in the courtroom, as mothers and women, and increasingly as laborers, demanding the right to work. Some judges acknowledged these rights. After midcentury—when Audouard wrote—Fuchs explains, "The balance of power between the judiciary and the written law shifted, giving more weight to the magistrates."[82] Judicial actions reflected broader and relatively immediate cultural, economic, and political contexts. Along with women's legal and social efforts, they advanced the mounting opposition to patriarchal law.[83]

Audouard engaged in this developing French debate, reaching beyond both metropole and French empire to support her critique. Negatively comparing France's paternity laws and customs to those of both a deeply Orientalized

Turkey and an idealized United States, she pushed her readers to recognize what she considered France's untenable and embarrassing inferiority in gendered justice. In her 1866 *Les mystères du sérails et des harems turc*, Audouard told a cautionary tale of a French man who seduced and abandoned a young Turkish woman and was subsequently forced to pay an enormous indemnity. Audouard warned, "In the Orient, it is not nearly as easy as it is in France to seduce a girl, compromise her, and then, when his whim has passed, to abandon her without concern for what will become of her."[84] She reproached a society that enabled and protected men's deceptive behavior and women's exploitation, criticizing French legal and cultural morality relative not only to Turkey, but also to the entire "Orient." Promoting models of a remade and more equitable Frenchness, she pushed against a decreasingly rigid legal edifice.

Turning to the American context, in 1870 Audouard stressed the connection between cultural and national moral standards and law. Attesting that in the United States not only was a man who "committed the crime of adultery" (which she stressed occurred quite rarely) "called a dishonest man," but also "the law would punish them at the same time that they faced disrepute." She emphasized, "There, Don Juans are treated as they should be treated everywhere, as thieves of the worst sort."[85] Although again idealizing both American culture and law, Audouard points to a distinct difference in legal philosophy between the United States and France. Whereas the Napoleonic Code protected men's individual rights and property by outlawing paternity searches, such legal cases occurred frequently in the United States. The law and judiciary (generally at the state level) sought the resolution of paternity questions, prioritizing men's parental duties based on their paternal, rather than individual, rights. As Michael Grossberg has argued, "Despite growing maternal rights, paternity hearings (as the name implies) continued to rest on the assumption that support was a male obligation. . . . The preoccupation of these hearings with paternal support underscored the state's vital interest in fixing paternity upon some man and thus obtaining child support."[86] American law generally put the interest of the state and the child over that of the individual man. In a civil proceeding, Grossberg explains, "the woman merely had to establish a preponderance of the evidence in favor of paternity";[87] such a legal framework contrasted sharply with that of France, with its prioritization and shielding of men's individual rights. US paternity cases reflected a patriarchal legal system that denied women's right to authority over their children, yet, to Audouard, both the climate that demanded individual men's legal responsibility and the law that enforced it exemplified a more civilized and just system. Just as she had negatively compared France to Turkey in *Les mystères du sérails et les harems turc*, so too Audouard held the United States above France, charging the latter with having "codified laws that accord the most complete impunity to men for all of their passions; they are able to seduce, deceive, and abuse credulous young women, without facing any penalty. All responsibility for the act and its aftermath fall on the ignorant and unknowing person."[88] The law, created by men to protect men, facilitated the perpetuation of a misogynistic culture of deception.

Audouard's harsh critique reflected her opposition not only to the code's deep male bias and lack of protection for women, but also to the larger French culture that propagated these injustices in multiple ways—including raising young women to be ignorant and thus particularly susceptible to exploitation. She attacked the practice of "protecting" young women from sexual and social knowledge. Explaining that in France, young women "know absolutely nothing of real life . . . [and] have no suspicions regarding the dangers of certain immoral men," she saw them as being effectively denied the tools to defend themselves. The responsibility for guarding a sheltered and ignorant young woman's honor rested completely with her parents. In contradistinction, Audouard contended, the United States—which allowed women legal recourse if impregnated and betrayed by a man—educated young women about these realities. "Thus warned," Audouard attested, "she zealously watches over her own virtue, she works to preserve her own honor."[89] Audouard saw American culture as empowering young women, allowing them agency over their own person, and in many ways, their future; legal paternity searches supported such agency. She highlighted the absurdity and inequity of French society denying young women the knowledge with which to defend themselves—knowledge with which American mothers supplied their daughters—while it "has instituted no legal protection for these same young girls."[90] Audouard emphasized the symbiotic relationship between law and culture. As she had done with the Turkish example, she mined the American context for steps to developing a path to renewed Frenchness, contextualizing legal inequities in specific aspects of culture.

Audouard's trust in legal systems ran deep. In Les mystères du sérail, she had explained that in Turkey, slave girls—always Circassians brought to Constantinople from the northeast shores of the Black Sea—had the right to refuse a buyer's offer to purchase them as either wives (within a harem) or odalisques (harem concubines). She highlighted these young women's right to decline being purchased by a particular man but made no mention of their inability to avoid bondage. Audouard insisted on the importance of recognizing that "civilized" Turkey had ended the slave markets of "ancient barbaric Turkey," replacing them with a contemporary slave trade, "generally conducted by old women."[91] She thus elevated Turkey to a civilizational par with France. Emphasizing that "Turkish laws are very favorable to slaves," Audouard elaborated that "it goes without saying that a young girl must consent to becoming the wife or odalisque of this man, before one is able to sell her to him."[92] Audouard trusted in law and idealized Turkey to such an extent that she ignored the realities of slavery. Focusing on the progress made in the Turkish slave trade, and the ways in which Turkish law benefitted bondspeople—specifically the establishment of enslaved women's right to reject a particular buyer— Audouard discussed slavery as a legal relationship, neglecting the brutal human, gendered veracities of the affiliation. As in her presentation of American slavery in *À travers l'Amérique*, Audouard did not question the letter of the law. While she did recognize interconnections between law and culture, her focus on legal authority, to the exclusion of economic and social factors, occluded her comprehension of the lived experiences of those affected by the laws. Her liberalism and elite perspective bolstered her intense emphasis on the power of law to the extent that *de jure* obscured *de facto*.

Auclert also placed great value on jurisprudence, concentrating intently on women's relative legal positions and possession of rights, but—in contrast with Audouard—Auclert's assessments involved broader socioeconomic concerns, consistent with her republican socialist stance. Both women examined questions of paternity as part of larger critiques of patriarchal law and practice. For Auclert, "uncivilized" North African cultures, including the nomadic and matrilineal Touareg, provided foils against which to measure French women's lives. Writing on "Matriarchy" in 1897, in one of her weekly "Le féminisme" columns in the newspaper *Le radical*,[93] Auclert addressed the problem of women's inequality before the law. Although the effect of decades of women's legal claims and of magistrates' judicial activism in their favor had led, in 1878, to the first legislative proposal to allow paternity searches, they did not become legal until 1912.[94]

In one of her innumerable propositions for gender equity in law, Auclert's July 6, 1897, *Le radical* column on "Matriarchy" suggested "substituting matriarchy for patriarchy," explaining that "by recognizing women as equally fit to exercise authority over their children and to give them their names, matriarchy eradicates the distinction of 'natural' [unmarried] mothers and gives children an equal *état-civil* [civil status]."[95] Auclert addressed the concept of legal "illegitimacy," which had been condemned by nineteenth-century feminists ranging from the utopian Socialist Saint-Simonians in the 1830s to the 1871 Communards. An inequitable byproduct of patriarchy made more socially and economically problematic by the law barring paternity claims, illegitimacy marked not only the mother but also the child in profound and disadvantageous ways. Auclert argued that what she termed "matriarchy" would eradicate these problems by allowing women full legal authority over their children, including the right to the matronym—Auclert's intention when arguing for women's right "to give them [their children] their names."[96]

Supporting her proposal, Auclert explained that "matriarchy has existed and still exists in certain human communities. The Touareg, who inhabit the central Sahara . . . are matriarchal. . . . Because of this, they call themselves Beni-oummia, 'children of the mother.' Although nomadic, Touareg women are educated and everywhere hold primacy of place. . . . The civilized French have much to learn, from a feminist perspective, from the Touareg, considered barbarian by those who do not know them."[97] Auclert wrote this in an era when the developing field of anthropology widely embraced the idea that "primitive society" was primarily matriarchal, and this contention became publicly accepted. The theory—or theories—initially proposed by Victorian British anthropologists had envisioned the matriarchal era as savage and wildly sexual.[98] By the fin-de-siècle, feminists such as Auclert had appropriated and adapted matriarchy to provide historical evidence of women's competence and governing abilities. Auclert held up the Touareg—a nomadic, matrilineal society in which men, and not women, veiled their faces—as an exemplar of civilization and as a model from which the French should learn. She explained that a Touareg woman "speaks in tribal councils. She administers inheritance; only she owns the tents, houses, flocks, springs, and gardens . . . and she determines who has control over the serfs."[99] Negatively comparing France and its legal code, which not only subjugated, marginalized, and stigmatized women, but also, through the legal concept of illegitimacy, similarly marked certain children, Auclert belittled the nation's claim of cultural and legal superiority. While undoubtedly not expecting France to abandon patriarchy, or even patrilineality, she underlined French inequities by contrasting them critically to an allegedly "barbaric," matriarchal society, one that lived under French colonial control. For Auclert, these French legal and traditional inequities nullified the nation's civilizational claims and disqualified it from the right to imperialize.

Auclert understood gender equity as resting in law and rights, and most especially in the vote. She worked tirelessly and doggedly for women's suffrage throughout her adult life, this goal underlying and permeating nearly all of her myriad projects.[100] Auclert initiated France's women's suffrage movement, which remained small compared to those of Britain and the United States, and she led it until her 1914 death. In her 1908, 218-page text, *Le vote des femmes*, she opened by arguing that "women's suffrage . . . alone will enable reason to triumph over folly, thus giving the entire nation guarantees of security and well-being. . . . It will be able to modify society and to allow the realization of the Republic."[101] As a republican socialist feminist, Auclert regarded France's

Third Republic as flawed in multiple ways, but particularly in its ongoing disenfranchisement and political marginalization of women. This demonstrated
for her a hypocritical betrayal of true republicanism. Writing on "Des femmes
maires" (Women mayors) in her January 2, 1900, *Le radical* column, Auclert
used France's Polynesian colony Tahiti to underscore the republic's inconsis-
tencies and failings. Explaining that French colonial authorities recognized
Tahitian women as municipal government heads, Auclert exclaimed, "The
feminine sex is not . . . ex-communicated in our Oceanic possessions as it is in
France. What a nation of contradiction we are! Every government in the past
century has denied French women accession to political life. While in the
metropole, the Republic prevents women from participating in municipal elections, in Tahiti it permits them to be named Mayors! What an anomaly!"[102]
Again pointing to empire, Auclert illuminated discrepancies in Republican justice, while simultaneously promoting the republic's capacity for change. As
she argued, metropolitan governments had long denied women representation and participation but had allowed both (on the municipal level) in Tahiti
beginning in 1889. In Polynesia and in other colonies including Algeria, France
either permitted or established particular laws that granted greater gender equity than existed in the metropole. Auclert saw these legal variations as exemplary of both republican potential and of French male politicians' ongoing
sexism and duplicity.

She extended the enfranchisement argument to questions of race. In an 1899
Le radical column titled "Les femmes sont les négres" (Women are the negroes),
Auclert stated that "for the French, the true Negroes are not the blacks, they are
the women." Directly addressing the fact that Black men possessed the right to
vote in French colonies such as Senegal, while white French women remained
disenfranchised in metropole and empire, Auclert employed strong racial language and imagery to illuminate her point. Her contention recognized the mu-
tability of the category "Negro." Delinking it from its racial definition, Auclert
clarified that "Negro" referred to the most debased and most marginalized
group: for her that meant women. In these colonial contexts, she explained,
Black men enjoyed the franchise and the legal right to representation, which no
metropolitan women, and few women in colonies possessed. The legal capaciousness of the imperial republic, for Auclert, demonstrated France's capacity
for an expanded franchise and for broader legal reform.

French colonial law, as Emmanuelle Saada shows, was replete with contradictions. Legal structures and judicial systems varied across the empire, shaped
largely by race in the late nineteenth century.[103] Saada explains that colonial
law "relied on a juridical relativism heavily shaded with racist evolutionism,
while maintaining the principal of the superiority of the Civil Code."[104] The

imperial authorities shaped law based on particular contexts, on populations' preexisting institutions, and on French judgments of a group's civilizational level. Investigating women's legal status across French colonies, Auclert recognized the racial component in legal variation. In attempting to deracialize the word "Negro" and redefine it as "woman," she insisted that recognizing race-based legal manipulation—while demonstrating the presence of flexibility within the French legal structure—simultaneously masked women's relegation to the ranks of the least civilized.

Rouzade's *Le monde renversé* pushed the bounds of the republican possible, albeit fictionally. Her narrative relied on the initial weaknesses of men, and specifically Arab men—the Célestine character, described as brilliant, beautiful, and wily, would clearly not have attempted a political coup in a European state. Portraying the white European woman as triumphing over the "Oriental" male demonstrated a feminism complicit in the perpetuation of dominant French conceptions of racial hierarchies and cultural superiority. However, feminist rules turned into laws, rather than racial hierarchy, perfected Rouzade's utopia. The fictional coup d'état demonstrated the absurdity of one sex ruling over the other, a system so "natural" in most societies that its absolute inversion was necessary to illuminate its inherent problems. Under Célestine's tutelage, the former sultanate rose to a level of "civilization" greater even than that of France.

At the culmination of *Le monde renversé*, Rouzade presented her newly created democratic republic with a final challenge: the appearance of the sultan's nephew Djamil, raising an army to lay claim to his royal title. Dramatically, Célestine seduces the heir-apparent and convinces him to commit double suicide with her. "'Come with me,' said Célestine . . . 'into death.' . . . Djamil stared at her. All at once, in a feverish movement he uncorked the flask . . . deliriously pouring the poison into the wine . . . with his eyes fixed on her he swallowed like a madman."[105] In removing both the former ruler (Célestine) and the "pretender to the throne" (Djamil), Rouzade literarily killed off any threat to the society's newly independent and democratic status. The previously enslaved white French woman elevated the "Oriental" population, by fiat, to a position where "man and woman are equal, by mutual agreement!"[106] By subsequently imposing universal suffrage and egalitarian representation, Célestine established the social and governmental order that Rouzade sought for France. Written at the dawn of the Third Republic, Rouzade's utopian tale plotted an exoticized, supra-legal route to an egalitarian republic. Her fictitious Orient provided a canvas for redrawing hierarchies and power relations, illuminating the absurdity of the legal and cultural marginalization of half of the population.

When each of these authors compared France with colonial and non-European contexts, the metropole came up short in terms of women's legal status in nearly all areas except one: the protection of girls. As Auclert charged in *Les femmes arabes en Algérie*, "Arab marriage is child rape." She elaborated: "If consummating a marriage with a prepubescent little girl is a crime in France, it is a custom among the Arabs; young Arab girls marry at an age where young French girls are only playing at marriage."[107] Auclert explained that in contrast to France, where a woman must bring a dowry to her marriage, Arab nuptials required that "the husband provides the dowry as the price of buying his wife."[108] This arrangement, according to Auclert, led to the brutal exploitation of young girls, as essentially monetized daughters. "Fathers," she elaborated, "in a hurry to profit from their daughters, do not wait for their nubility to marry them. To mask this attack on nature, the husband is told that he cannot exercise his spousal right until four or five years after the marriage."[109] Husbands often ignored this stipulation, and in some cases "criminal parents and the man who had inflicted not marriage but rape on a child," were charged and brought to court, but most often acquitted.[110]

Attacking the absence of legal protection for young girls, Auclert demanded that "in order to end these spousal rapes, we must apply, on all French territories, the law forbidding girls to marry before the age of fifteen."[111] In diverging markedly from most of her legal comparisons, Auclert touted the Napoleonic Code as exemplary. Here she echoed official French colonial discourse. Pointing to child marriage as evidence of Algerian barbarity, as Surkis explains, France had made legal interventions to block such unions beginning in the 1850s. Colonial authorities used this profession of French civilizational superiority as part of their attempts to legitimize their colonization and subsequent juridical interventions.[112] While Auclert asserted that the French marital age law should extend beyond the metropole and across the empire, her position diverged from that of the government in insisting on an alteration in those laws. She contended that the situation would be remedied by the enfranchisement of metropolitan women, as "they would not permit a law allowing child rape to persist on Frenchified soil." "Men," she reproached, "tolerate this crime, because they are in solidarity with those who profit from it."[113] Auclert relied on essentialist gendered assumptions regarding men's and women's respective attitudes toward child protection. She painted French men as doubly complicit in Algerian child rape: first, due to their unwillingness to transgress boundaries of gender solidarity by extending the martial age statute to the colony, and second, by denying French women the vote. To end girls' legal exploitation, as well as other gender inequities in law across metropole and colonies, Auclert posited a two-step solution: grant women suffrage, then terminate France's existing imperial program and replace it with one generated by (newly enfranchised) French feminists.

Polygamy

Audouard also mitigated her anti-imperialism. Although she frequently lauded Turkish connubial law and custom, her praise had a distinct limit: the legality and practice of polygamy. Terming it "the plague of the Orient," she blamed the tradition for "having prevented and continuing to prevent Turkey from taking its place among the first nations of the world."[114] Audouard contended that despite being a "rich, fertile country, [with] intelligent, courageous, even brave inhabitants," Turkish "arts, industry, and civilization" lag because powerful and wealthy men—the leaders of society—have harems. Making no specific claims of immorality, Audouard instead argued that "the softness, the voluptuousness of their harem causes them to lose all of their energy and often their intelligence; they end up brutalized."[115] Essentially enveloped in the feminine, elite Turkish men lost their vital masculine power.

For Audouard, plural marriage deformed Turkish femininity and masculinity. "How can a woman love a man who treats her as a toy," Audouard asks, "a piece of luxury furniture? No, she does not love him, or if she does . . . she loves him *en femelle* [like a female animal] and not *en femme* [like a woman]." Polygamy thus deprived Turkish men of the sort of love—a Western, or French love—that would support and motivate them, that would allow them to "feel themselves sustained by an invisible force. He [the Western man] becomes great . . . because he wants to place his glory at the feet of the one who loves him."[116] This love, supported by law, exemplified Frenchness. In *Empire of Love,* Matt Matsuda explains that "individual sentiment was the presumptive basis of morality and the historical development of civilization."[117] Audouard considered this idealized, deeply gendered relationship as representing the proper and natural human sexual affiliation, as indicative of civilization, and as rooted in Catholicism and the French nation. In sharp contrast, polygamy meant that "the Turk thus only loves women with a sensual passion, one far from rendering man strong, energetic, brave."[118] The acceptance and practice of polygamous marriage damaged not only Turkish women and men, from Audouard's perspective, but also the global success and status of the Turkish nation.

But she carefully qualified her denigration of Turkey's sanctioning of polygamy, clarifying that "in Turkey, as in France, there are good and bad laws and customs. We, Europeans, are shocked by polygamy, it is true; but Orientals visiting Europe are also shocked, and no less rightfully, by the cloud of courtesans who congest our streets, our promenades, our theaters, and by the foul *maisons* tolerated by our police. . . . This proves that in all nations, even the most civilized, there is still much to be done."[119] Representing the proliferation and legality of prostitution in France as comparably, and rightfully, "shocking," Audouard placed France and Turkey on par. She considered the practices equally abhorrent: polygamy detracted from Turkey's otherwise impressive legal treatment of women, and prostitution undercut France's civilizational claims.

Paule Mink advanced similar sentiments regarding polygamy in Algeria in the 1880s. Unlike Audouard's otherwise positive perceptions of Turkish life and law, however, Mink presented a deeply negative portrayal of Algerian Muslims' lives and of Algerian peoples more generally. She insisted that "among the people in a state of infancy—or of senility—the Algerian tribes hold pride of place."[120] The practice of polygamy played a significant role in Mink's derision. Like Audouard, Mink interrogated plural marriage's effect on both love and femininity. She questioned the romantic legends of "des amours arabes," saying "we do not believe it; the Arab woman does not love in the sense that we give the word in Europe. . . . Polygamy . . . kills the flower of delicacy in her, the infinite tenderness that is the complement of love. . . . The man has a female animal [*femelle*] who gives herself to all of his desires."[121] Assuming the existence of one single and unchanging type of romantic love, Mink asserted a position consistent with Western conceptions. Modern, Western romantic love emerged from Romanticism as inextricably linked to monogamy. From this perspective, polygamous conjugality established conditions that made "real" love—European love—impossible.[122] It also deformed femininity, according to Mink, in dehumanizing women to the point of animality.

Writing a decade later, Hubertine Auclert, too, linked the public and the private in her condemnation of polygamy. She insisted that it perverted nuptial love and created "a perpetual state of war in the house of a man with multiple wives," creating the antithesis of a peaceful and loving domestic sphere.[123] Describing the conflicts, resentments, and jealousies she saw (and those she presumed) in polygamous Algerian families, Auclert found it impossible to imagine harmony in such a milieu. She claimed, "There is no love in this household of four or eight, only a ferocious jealousy which engenders crime. . . . Children do not escape this jealous furor."[124] For her, this lack of love created an unnatural family. Auclert described anecdotal incidences of women "crippling or blinding" or even murdering their rival wives' children.[125] She sought to expose the barbarous conditions she felt polygamy created—a literalized version of the "state of war" in the domestic sphere, in which women were pushed into violent insanity.

2.3.   Paule Mink (top row center), her daughter Héna Négro (lower right), and Héna's spouse Henri Julien (others unknown). 1894. Courtesy of Pierre Nourrisier.

It destroyed the individual, the family, and by extension the larger society. Simultaneously, Auclert felt it necessary to inform her readers that "the French must know that polygamy revolts the Arab woman."[126] Auclert believed that plural marriage transformed decent young Arab women into competitive and conniving vicious criminals. She feared that metropolitan citizens, unaware of the social realities of this conjugal form and holding anti-Muslim prejudices, would assume that these characteristics and behaviors were "natural" to Arab women and that they were satisfied with such domestic relations.[127]

Auclert reported "what Arab women say about love," trying to deepen her understanding of their intimate lives, and particularly the impact of polygamy.

She explained, "Ask them about love, they will respond: 'Love! It is a quick look, it is the embrace of arms and hands, it is a kiss! But . . . once a man is married, it is finished! Finished!' . . . Loved though they may be, Muslim women do not get attached to a polygamous husband who wounds their pride by sharing his heart and his favors."[128] She described plural marriage as the death knell of love. Like Audouard and Mink, Auclert asserted the impossibility of love in polygamous relationships.[129] Here she attempted to give voice to Algerian Arab women, to demonstrate the human—not only feminine—universality of their emotion.

Adding to her condemnation of plural marriage, Auclert maintained that it led to homosexuality and even bestiality because it created a shortage of women. Concerned with the enforcement of heterosexual gender norms as a central element of Frenchness and troubled by the aberrant possibilities of imagined Arab sexualities, Auclert argued that because wealthy men married multiple women, poor men were left "to take men for wives" or were found "in criminal conversation with a goat . . . or a sheep!"[130] Auclert saw this as another example of polygamy pushing Algerian Arabs—both women and men—into what she understood as "unnatural" relationships, which, she contended, undermined the social and familial fabric and thus the colony's civilizational evolution.

By allowing the perpetuation of legal polygamy, Auclert charged, the French government not only shirked its responsibilities to its colonized population, but also simultaneously undermined its own interests.

The Arab race, so beautiful and gifted, is absolutely scorned by the Europeans, who are rarely as beautiful or possess as many natural aptitudes as the Arabs. And here's the contradiction: the French vanquisher says to the Muslim: "I scorn your race, but I abase my law before yours." . . . The Republic—unless it contradicts its own principles—cannot continue to encourage polygamy and child marriage on one side of the Mediterranean and punish it on the other.[131]

Accusing the French republic of a contradictory set of resentments, repressions, and exceptions, Auclert attacked France for maintaining separate and inconsistent sets of legal codes in Algeria. Implying that at least part of French colonial repression arose from politics of resentment—in her characterization of Arabs as both more beautiful and able—she pointed to the incongruity of France dominating and denigrating Algerian Muslims, while simultaneously allowing the perpetuation of particular aspects of their legal codes—specifically in the area of personal status, which included allowing polygamy. As a republican socialist feminist, Auclert had great faith in the French republic's capacity for justice and equity. Understanding the republic as evolving and changeable, she had long pushed for political and legal alterations toward such ends. Arguing that the Republic held the right and the power to supersede the Algerian legal structure allowing polygamy, Auclert maintained that such an act would both liberate the Muslim population and end this aspect of republican hypocrisy.

Universalism seemed to be the answer. In an April 1891 essay in *La citoyenne* titled "Polygamie en France," Auclert wrote, "To unify itself, France must apply the same law on all of its colonial and metropolitan territories. Claiming that race and sex are the reason for two sets of law is as ridiculous as claiming that race and sex are the reason for applying two sets of morals. We have forbidden human sacrifice on all French territory, we must also forbid sacrificing love to the debauchery that is polygamy."

Algeria's conflicting legal codes were a legacy of Ottoman rule, which ended when France took military control in 1830.[132] The French inherited and modified the Turkish *millet* system, in which minority religions (in the Ottoman context, Jews and Christians) had independent legal authority over their own communities for matters of personal law, including marriage. Under French rule, Muslims and Jews constituted minoritarian groups, subject, respectively, to Qur'anic and rabbinic law and courts. In 1830, the newly established French military authority (civilian rule would not begin until 1870) made a dramatic promise to respect religion, property, and trade in the colony. The pledge held no legal authority, but for decades it influenced the debate over how to rule the new colony. It also directly contradicted the ideals of French universalism and the unifying concept behind the Napoleonic Code.[133]

A philosophical and political struggle ensued between those seeking to minimize cultural differences between Algeria and France—often, according to Judith Surkis, military officers—and those who sought to emphasize them; the latter ultimately prevailed. While France extended its penal code to all of Algeria in 1841, the next year it confirmed the perpetuation of Islamic and rabbinic courts' authority over civil issues in each of those communities, both of which permitted polygamy. By 1850 the military colonial government had abolished rabbinic courts, while further institutionalizing the Qur'anic.[134]

As Surkis has shown, some of Algeria's French military rulers viewed Qur'anic law pragmatically. Contending that it could be used to promote France's agenda of "moralization and domination," the officials argued that by revealing to Muslim women the extent of rights they had under the Qur'an, they could spark social reform.[135] Surkis quotes Charles Richard, an officer of the Bureaux Arabe and prolific chronicler of Arab Algeria, who in 1850 maintained that women, "astonished that they have these rights, might consider asking for all of them . . . and she will be quite surprised to learn again from us that . . . she can suppress polygamy, which is her cruelest enemy."[136] Quashing polygamy, along with other "old barbaric customs," Richard declared, "woman, liberated, will especially elevate the dignity of man."[137] He referred to women's relatively extensive rights under the Qur'an, while relying on Western assumptions of women's "natural" position of moral superiority vis-à-vis men. Nineteenth-century European imperialists often claimed that exposing non-European women to Western ideas could elevate that entire culture's civilizational plane. Patricia Lorcin points out that Richard, in contrast, underscored Arab men's sexual immorality and women's resultant degradation, while nonetheless asserting that Algerian Muslim women could find freedom from *within* their existing Qur'anic rights, if informed of those rights by the colonizers.[138] In turn, Arab women could lift the developmental level of their culture.

Richard promoted an associationist vision of imperialism in which the colonizer allowed indigenous institutions, including marital law and custom, to persist. In these early decades of Algerian colonization, assimilationist rather than associationist goals predominated. In France's traditional colonial theory, assimilation sought the subsumption of indigenous institutions and their ultimate replacement by those of the metropole. Correspondingly, the colonized people would concurrently be civilized and made French.[139]

Near the century's end, an increasing number of politicians and thinkers abandoned assimilationist policies, recognizing their failure, and began promoting associationism.[140] Auclert, however, continued to advocate an assimilatory convergence of France and Algeria. Covering the 1891 French Senate debates on Algerian Arab assimilation in her feminist newspaper, *La citoyenne*, in a March 15 article titled "Arabophobe, Arabophile," Auclert criticized Senator Remy Jacques, representative of Oran, Algeria, for terming the Arab woman "an obstacle to assimilation even greater than the Qur'an." She reported that Senator Jacques continued by insisting that "we must change this situation and elevate *la femme arabe*." Auclert responded by saying "That is what we ask. The question of *la femme arabe* is clearly, as we have seen, the core of the Algerian question. . . . When one ends arranged marriage, sequestration, and polygamy for the Arab woman, assimilation will be possible and France will have more than 3 million children who will love it with a passion."[141] Auclert saw assimilation as key not only to Algerian Arab happiness, but also to France's stability and legal and moral consistency. She placed marriage at the center of this problem. While most assimilationists considered both Muslim women and religion as the primary barriers to assimilation, Auclert instead saw patriarchal traditions as the problem. She believed that once French colonial authorities recognized the deleterious effect the Arab personal status laws had on Algerian Arab women and acted to terminate the inequitable marital practices allowed under those laws, Muslim women would become assimilable, and through them, so too would their entire culture. She understood the legal perpetuation of discriminatory gender and racial practices as the true bar to assimilation and colonial success, as well as to France's progress toward its universal ideal.

Auclert's view on assimilation contrasted with Mink's implied essentialism in terms of what they both saw as the grave problem of polygamy in Algeria. Legal reform seemed to Audouard both the cause of and the remedy for polygamy. All three women interrogated legal structures shaping women's lives in colonial milieux, approaching them from multiple perspectives, with differing yet intersecting goals. Deeply concerned with marital laws and customs, they all focused on plural marriage, reviling its influence on love, sexuality, and femininity. These critiques reflected back on France and its allowance of polygamy in its colonies, as part of its maintenance of separate religiously based personal status law codes. Simultaneously, the feminists' analyses alluded—directly or indirectly—to the overarching presence of France's profoundly patriarchal marital law, one enabling a French polygamy, or at least nonmonogamy. Addressing law, tradition, and imperialism from multiple feminist perspectives, each author combined them in different ways to reconceptualize Frenchness in the hexagon and its empire.

Laws of Empire

Moderate left and liberal feminists looked to legal structures as significant causes of gender inequities because they—like other liberals and moderate leftists—sought reform, rather than revolution. Audouard, Auclert, and Rouzade all saw changes in law as a means to advancing their feminist goals by ameliorating multiple aspects of French gender inequities. As they traveled to colonies and Orientalized metropoles, they encountered a range of legally enforced gender hierarchies which they more often than not found superior to those under France's Napoleonic Code.

These activists chose to journey into empire, either literally or imaginatively, for varied reasons. Audouard wrote travel literature to support herself and her children; Rouzade used Oriental and imperial tropes to shape her antipatriarchal fiction for maximal literary and political efficacy; and Auclert followed her longtime lover to his Algerian post in the wake of his diagnosis with a terminal illness. Although they carried divergent politics, concerns, and goals with them, their attentions converged in law and in the judicial regulation of intimacies, at the relationship between the state, patriarchal tradition, and women's lives. These intersections manifested themselves in marriage, women's legal status, and polygamy, three distinct yet overlapping categories and institutions that shaped female lives in metropole and colonies. Writing and speaking on these subjects for a primarily French audience, each author expressed distinct oppositions to existing empires. Their adoption of imperial categorizations (including civilization versus barbarism) as well as colonial rhetorics of racialization and sexualization demonstrates the complexities and incongruities involved in working toward their respective goals.

Mink considered legal change to be a superficial amelioration of an irreparable system. Like Audouard and Auclert, she intensely castigated the practice of polygamy, blaming it for warping femininity and dehumanizing women. She identified polygamy as part of the inequities in the larger Algerian Muslim culture and gender order. Having suggested the possibility that the French colonial authority could somewhat mitigate Algerian women's condition, she nonetheless remained committed to her long-term solution: anti-imperial uprising against that colonial power. Although Mink blamed Algerian men, rather than France or colonialism, for Algerian Muslim women's subjugation, as a revolutionary socialist feminist she saw revolutionary change as key to constructing a just social order.

Feminists found in empire aspects of women's embodied experience that inspired them, that challenged them, and that repelled them. Analyzing these contexts, these activists revealed gendered contradictions that they saw as openings to contestations in empire, leading to a mix of positive and cautionary examples for France.[142] Their interrogations of sexualities, love, conjugal sexual politics, agency, and rights suggested a range of evolutionary to revolutionary changes, ideas and arguments that pressed for new understandings of a gendered, and in some cases racialized, Frenchness. As Hubertine Auclert wrote, "When one sees the prejudice of race dominate everything in Algeria, one clearly understands the absurdity of the prejudice of sex."[143] Likening the destructive and pervasive nature of racism to that of sexism, Auclert made clear that the French state maintained oppressive and counterproductive structures based not on rational measures, but on baseless prejudices. Her contention that the state could—and should—correct these measures with the intent of elevating the level of civilization in both France and its colony typified the reconceptualized Frenchness, and appropriated imperialisms, that emerged from feminists in empire.

Chapter 3

La Citoyenne

Alternate Empires

Hubertine Auclert founded the feminist newspaper *La citoyenne* with the "single goal of bringing about the equality of woman and man."[1] Established in 1881 primarily to advocate French women's suffrage and full citizenship, the influential, controversial, and groundbreaking publication also looked beyond national borders. Its male and female journalists examined the lives of women across Europe and around the world, while focusing most frequently on France and its colonies, especially on Algeria. *La citoyenne* emerged not only as France's first suffragist newspaper but also as its first feminist periodical to address imperialism.

Auclert's publication presaged the French periodical press's fin-de-siècle interest in empire, just as the five feminists' developing imperial critiques foreshadowed that era's efflorescence of anti-imperialisms. Challenging the period's assumptions of civilization versus savagery, *La citoyenne* articles contrasted the circumstances of French women with those of women in Niger, Tonkin, and Tunisia, as well as in countries such as Italy, Ireland, Russia, and Turkey. While they most frequently concluded that French women held a preferable position, Auclert and her fellow writers also emphasized aspects of "uncivilized" women's lives and status that compared positively with those of women in the metropole, such as Algerian women receiving dowries and keeping their family name at marriage. Although *La citoyenne* journalists confronted issues of imperial domination and indigenous gender inequities, they simultaneously recognized that women in nations beyond Europe were not merely victims of patriarchal laws and traditions but rather also possessed some agency. Like Audouard and Rouzade, these feminist writers questioned France's level of civilization under a code of laws that disenfranchised and subjugated its entire female population. Guided by Auclert, *La citoyenne* strove to disrupt the absolutes of civilized France and uncivilized colonies. Its writers decried the French imperial project as illegitimate. Simultaneously, they embraced and amended the era's anthropological hierarchies of civilization and race. Auclert and her contributors developed a feminist imperialism that challenged women's oppression in both metropole and colonies by subsuming cultural differences into a universalized French identity. Advocating an alternative sort of empire, they appropriated the imperial model and adapted it to feminist objectives.

La citoyenne articles reveal particular French republican, socialist, and feminist conceptions of race and female agency, both in- and outside Europe. The journalists developed a set of feminist arguments from the widely accepted idea that women's status marked a society's level of civilization. They interrogated and compared gender roles and relations in France and other societies, agitating for the expansion of women's rights and the amelioration of their oppressions. The journalists' ascriptions of agency to Indigenous women, in particular, rested on a feminist adaptation of the period's dominant scientific and anthropological idea of races and peoples evolving at differing rates along a singular historical trajectory. Challenging France's presumed position at the evolutionary apex of civilization, they contended that while France had, indeed, advanced more than most on the developmental ladder, it was not yet fully civilized. Comparing women's lives in France with those in other European nations and in Indigenous societies under colonization, *La citoyenne* produced multiple and varied critiques of oppressions and argued for republican, egalitarian, and universalist solutions.

Beginning in the 1880s, Auclert herself developed and promoted a feminist imperialism, an explicitly racialized politics that emerged at the intersection of her republicanism, socialism, and feminism. Although scholars have long recognized her pivotal role in the suffrage struggle, only recently have many paid attention to Auclert's investigations and analyses of empire, which constituted a central aspect of her work.[2] Auclert recognized the permeable lines and multidirectional influences between metropole and colony.[3] Shaped by her understandings of civilization, history, and race, Auclert's republican universalism and Franco-assimilationism ultimately undervalued Arab women's experiences, eclipsed their voices, and marginalized their culture. Although she strove to improve their conditions, she nonetheless appropriated their subjugation to further her primary goal of French women's enfranchisement.

La citoyenne developed at the junction of Auclert's suffragism and her expanding interest in questions of empire. The newspaper became a laboratory for a nascent feminist critique of imperialisms, one that also promoted a new vision of the potential of feminist imperial power. It thus provided its readers with an alternative to government propaganda and images of empire and with new conceptions of imperialism.

Creating *La Citoyenne*

Between 1881 and 1891, in a context of expanding empire and a growing awareness of life in the colonies, *La citoyenne* examined the social, political, cultural, and economic conditions of women in France's empire and beyond. The newspaper, for example, published protests against militarism and imperial wars of conquest, stating that "the Republic has means other than the cannon to employ for civilizing the barbarians."[4] Auclert opposed neither imperialism nor the idea of the *mission civilisatrice*, France's professed "civilizing mission." Rather, she promoted the introduction of feminist-influenced ideals and laws into France's colonies, which she also advocated for the metropole.

Auclert launched *La citoyenne* in the immediate wake of the 1881 law liberalizing France's press. The new legislation removed nearly all restrictions on who could publish a newspaper. It also decriminalized the printing of governmental criticism—a key factor for many, including Auclert.[5] Between 1881 and the eve of World War I newspapers flourished in France, with a near tripling of the mass press, significantly expanding the range of opinions and voices available to readers.[6]

Auclert provided the heart, brain, and muscle of *La citoyenne*. As its editor, primary writer, fundraiser, and promoter, she sustained the publication through years of low circulation, tight finances, internal conflicts, and low morale.[7] Despite Auclert's tireless efforts to promote the newspaper and her willingness and ability to cover much of its expenses, the frequency of the paper's publication decreased over its decade-long run. Beginning as a weekly in February 1881, *La citoyenne* became monthly in April 1882, then bimonthly from December 1890 until its final issue in November 1891. Almost one-third of its 187 issues were published during its first year.[8] At peak, the newspaper had a circulation of one thousand copies. Auclert's biographer, Steven Hause, termed this number one on which "only a labor of love could survive."[9] In addition to seeking financial donations, she attempted to sell shares in the paper, and she offered premiums both underscoring and undermining gender norms: a

3.1. Front page of the newspaper *La citoyenne*, April 15, 1891. Ville de Paris/Bibliothèque Marguerite Durand.

six-month subscription received a discount on a bottle of Pinaud perfume, and a one-year commitment earned the reader an excellent price on a "superb revolver."[10]

While *La citoyenne*'s perpetuation remained an ongoing struggle, the periodical nonetheless persisted and garnered attention for a decade. It drew support beyond France, including from American feminists Susan B. Anthony and Elizabeth Cady Stanton, and generated sufficient attention to attract vitriol and insults. Criticisms extended to comments and cartoons denigrating Auclert's appearance and questioning her femaleness and her sanity.[11] The intensity and magnitude of these attacks indicated the extent to which Auclert—and her newspaper—threatened the metropolitan status quo.[12]

Auclert and *La citoyenne* also faced intense antifeminist disparagement from Algerian newspapers, particularly regarding her condemnation of polygamy and child marriage. Lys de Pac, a journalist from Oran, aggressively reproached Auclert, "Never in any epoch has anyone written more inaccuracies about Algeria. Madame Lévrier, née Auclert, has read nothing, seen nothing, retained nothing."[13] Sweepingly dismissing Auclert's journalistic abilities, the deriding male journalist also referred to Auclert by her husband's name—a surname she never took because she opposed France's patriarchal patronymic tradition. Undercutting the independence she displayed in retaining her birth surname, Lys du Pac made clear his intention to put her in her proper wifely place. He thus added an extra element of denigration to this wholesale dismissal of both woman and newspaper. Auclert, in turn, consistently defended her positions by responding to such attacks in the pages of *La citoyenne*.[14] While she fervently believed in the periodical's role as a forum "open to everything that interests women," suffrage clearly held primacy throughout the run of the paper.[15] Questions of women's rights and status dominated the columns, which focused mainly on France, but also extended beyond the metropole in investigations of individual countries or in comparative analyses of different nations or peoples. Auclert wrote the majority of the articles examining women outside of France. Antonin Levrier, her long-time collaborator, companion, and (later) husband, followed in frequency, along with Léon Giraud, a writer, financial backer, and unwavering ally. Levrier generally signed his pieces with his own name, while Giraud wrote under a variety of identities: his true name, the pseudonymous anagram "Draigu," and the unisex pseudonym "Camille."[16] Although the newspaper's contributors included a number of well-known female feminists, such as Eugenie Potonié-Pierre, Maria Martin (who would take over as the paper's editor in its final years), and Blanche D. Mon, the articles on non-European women were written almost exclusively by Auclert and her male allies and benefactors.

Having refused to follow Levrier to his posts in either central France in 1882 or Tahiti in 1886, she did join him in Algeria two years later. Now unwell, Levrier accepted a post as justice of the peace in the city of Frenda. They subsequently married there. Her one-time secretary at *La citoyenne* and in the Société pour la Revendication des Droits Politiques et Sociaux des Femmes, as well as a member since its 1876 founding of her organization Droit des Femmes (later to become Suffrage des Femmes), Levrier continued to contribute to *La citoyenne* during their years in Algeria, for him a period of failing health that ended in his death in 1892 (which led to Auclert's return to Paris).[17] Auclert had long resisted marrying Levrier, unwilling to enter into an institution that she contested as oppressive to women. Under France's Napoleonic Code, marriage necessitated that a woman surrender her economic and civil independence. Following him to Algeria, she ultimately acquiesced to legal matrimony in the face of his ill health, as well as the likely pressure Levrier likely faced as a colonial civil servant—a public face of France—to maintain what were considered to be the highest standards of morality and propriety.[18]

Living in the colony gave Auclert a new and distinct perspective. She spent much time investigating its social and cultural contexts, interviewing women and men about their customs and practices, and examining their perceptions of the colonial authority; she studied women's traditional arts and industries, pored over official government documents in libraries, and attended legal proceedings.[19] Through the specific vantage point of Levrier's role in the justice system and consistent with her deep interest in law and gender, Auclert also examined and critiqued the coexisting legal structures of French and Islamic law and their effects on Algerian women. Auclert's extensive publications on the Algerian context relate her thoughts, impressions, and analyses, yet Algerian women's voices, their experiences and their desires, remain virtually absent from her writings. Although Auclert undoubtedly sought to ameliorate the conditions of Algerian women's lives, her investigations served primarily as an intellectual workshop for her feminist ideas and projects.

Colonialism and Anthropology

When civil authority replaced military rule in Algeria in 1870, it confronted a highly masculinist and patriarchal culture.[20] With the governmental shift, France became increasingly concerned with the status of Muslim women, which colonial authorities viewed as a reflection of Algerian culture's level of civilization.[21] Faced with questions of Algerians' assimilation and rights under the French Republic, the colonial authority pointed to women's subjugation as evidence of all Arabs' fundamental and irreconcilable differences from Frenchmen and from French colonial settlers. This provided a rationalization for the local peoples' continued disenfranchisement.[22] Judith Surkis has shown that from its initial Algerian conquest, French authorities used ideas about Muslim families and Muslim sex to demonstrate the need for colonial domination.[23] Issues of gender and sexuality permeated the official imperial political and legal discourses.

The anthropological ideology of the period supported the government's rhetoric in asserting fundamental, hierarchical racial differences between the colonizers and the colonized. French anthropologists termed Algerian Arabs an aggressive "conquering race, with mores opposed to our civilization, and with an essential character resistant to "adaptation" to Western culture.[24] This conceptualization of an Arab race, imbued with values antithetical to those of the French, supported the dominant imperial argument against extending rights and equality to Algerians. Accordingly, Algerians would remain subjects, rather than becoming citizens, of the republic, because by their nature they could never be French.

France insisted that only one historical trajectory existed and that all peoples fell somewhere on this linear chronology, with France at the apex. Denying Indigenous peoples coevalness, in Fabian's conceptualization, situated them as lagging behind on the singular civilizational path.[25] In projecting this theoretical similarity, France could ignore or profoundly trivialize any differences between itself and the colonized—when convenient and beneficial for their imperial power. This justified the forced "improvement" of those cultures.[26]

Auclert's Feminist Imperialism

Auclert espoused certain aspects of the assimilationist evolutionary conceptualization of race. The discourse of cultural and racial hierarchies so permeated nineteenth-century thought that even those opposed to the imperial
project could not fully escape its hegemony.[27] Auclert's anti-imperialism—like
those of Audouard, Rouzade, Mink, and Michel—emerged in this context. As
a republican socialist feminist, Auclert considered republicanism an ideal governmental form. Although deeply critical of the French state, particularly for
its disenfranchisement and subjugation of women, as well as for its misappli-
cation of imperial power, she saw in republican France the potential to bring
justice and equality to its colonies. Her vision of a social republic, a government in which the social question remained fully intertwined with the political, was supported by most republican socialists, including Rouzade. Yet it
remained a much-contested concept under the Third Republic.

As Joan Wallach Scott argues, Auclert contended that the accepted symbolic
equation of women with the social (the private or domestic, in contrast to the
public or political), demonstrated the link between women's disenfranchisement and the ongoing depoliticization of the social question. In a true republic, the social would be constitutive of the political; it would holistically engage
issues of social, economic, and political equality. Such a republic would inclu-
sively embrace a diverse array of citizens, regardless of sex.[28] For Auclert, republicanism therefore held the seeds of emancipation for French women (and
workers) and, correspondingly, for other subjugated groups under France's
purview: namely, its colonial subjects. Although she was a socialist, her republicanism allied her with liberals of her era, who believed that the French republican model of secular education and representative government could
liberate the oppressed Arabs. Auclert specifically viewed imperialism as the vehicle for introducing social, cultural, and legal changes to improve the lives
and status of women in the colonies. "The Arab people," she wrote from Algeria in 1891, "have . . . everything to gain from becoming French."[29]

Based on her experiences in the colony, Auclert asserted both the similarities between the races and the desire for Frenchification held by Arab women
in particular, but also Arab men. Auclert sought the virtually complete assimilation of Algerians into French society.[30] Her contention that the "dream of
Arab women is to be assimilated and to become French" arose from her assumptions regarding the importance and appeal of French republicanism; she
projected her own values and desires on Arab women.[31] Auclert minimized
existing cultural and legal differences between the French and Algerians by,
for example, comparing Charlemagne's eight wives to the contemporary Arab

practice of polygamy. Attributing the extant differences to the progress of time, she thus placed Algerians on a historical trajectory, appropriating an imperial concept that located them in France's past, but doing so for her own political goals.[32] Auclert claimed that as Algerians became increasingly civilized under a feminist-influenced imperialism, they would reject antiquated practices such as polygamy.

As chapter 2 explored, Auclert considered the colonial authority responsible for expediting this process, an obligation that she and her fellow feminist journalists accused France of shirking. Calling for the legal curtailment of polygamy in Algeria, Auclert wrote that France did not deserve "the magnificent colony . . . if we do not know how to use our right to civilize the Arabs. . . . To morally annex Algeria, it is necessary to suppress polygamy."[33] Auclert presented this "right to civilize the Arabs" as contingent on proper moral application. She used the pages of *La citoyenne* to critique and challenge both the metropolitan and the colonial authorities, promoting feminist imperialism and demanding a legal end to what she termed the Arabs' "vulgar and perverse instincts."[34] She contended that French feminists could influence the introduction of egalitarian feminist principles, including those not yet extant in the metropole, to eradicate "base" Arab "instincts." Consistent with her idea of racial evolution, these "instincts" could be erased not only through a long-term historical process, but also, and more expediently, through a feminist-influenced French intervention in the legal code. In Auclert's conceptualization, instincts appear more cultural than essential; lacking permanence, they allow room for transformation. A feminist imperial intercession could thus lead to the legal and cultural end of polygamy, effectively elevating Indigenous women and thereby the conditions of the entire colony and of France as a whole.

Directly linking women's suffrage to the polygamy question, Auclert argued, "If the women of France had their due power, this monstrosity [polygamy] would have, for the common good, long ago ceased to exist on *our* territory."[35] She assumed female solidarity against polygamy. Auclert embraced and relied on the era's widespread essentialist assumption of women's "natural" moral superiority, which, in her eyes, would undoubtedly decry polygamy. Referring to a "greater France," she maintained that French women's disenfranchisement clearly delayed legal and sociocultural progress, and thus "the common good," on all French territory.[36]

Auclert faced detractors from across the political spectrum: from socialist men who opposed female suffrage because they feared women's traditional connection to the Catholic Church; from the conservative wing of liberal feminism, including her former allies Deraismes and Richer, who advocated civil rights only; and, most intently and aggressively, from the Right. Responding to Auclert's attacks on polygamy, an unnamed male detractor published a sarcastic reply: "We will accommodate our traditional system of hypocritical monogamy, but leave the fecund and virtuous polygamy to the Arabs, and also leave Algeria to the Algerians and the ladies of the feminine emancipation to their raving."[37] A conservative, an anti-imperialist, and an anti-feminist, this writer belittled La citoyenne's condemnation of Frenchmen's marital infidelities, played on the sexualized racial stereotypes of Arabs, advocated France's abandonment of the colony, and denigrated feminists. Opponents of imperialism came from both the Left and the Right, and this right-wing commentator considered Algeria and its Arabs to be base and unworthy of French intervention and "assistance."

As Antoinette Burton has argued regarding British feminists and as Leila Rupp has asserted regarding European and American feminists in international women's organizations, white feminists used a language of sisterhood while simultaneously envisioning themselves in the vanguard, leading their colonized "sisters" to emancipation.[38] Auclert's position differed from these assumptions in two significant ways. First, she recognized that French imperialism negatively affected the colonized and contended that "their political exclusion socially debases them and economically crushes them."[39] Second, as a republican socialist, she went beyond gender-based oppressions in her critique by recognizing that religion, race, and class also played central roles in the intellectual justification of French empire. She articulated a strong anti-imperialism, based on the ways that she understood empire to operate, while simultaneously promoting a feminist imperialism, based on the ways that she understood Algerian women to be oppressed. Appropriating imperial concepts and aspects of the imperial form, Auclert hoped to establish feminist imperialism as an expansive liberatory vehicle.

Auclert castigated existing colonial rule based on her observations of the interrelated prejudices and subjugations of women; of Muslims, Berbers, and other indigenous groups; and of the poor. Of these categories, class played the smallest role in Auclert's analyses of colonized women. Although she recognized differences between groups of Indigenous Algerians and called attention to women's poverty, she often discussed "Arab women" as a homogenous whole. As Clancy-Smith has noted, the title of Auclert's book, Les femmes arabes, reduced all Arab women to one type, erasing complexities and differences.[40] While not oblivious to class in the colonial context, her analysis focused most heavily on gender and race. Auclert's racialized othering of Arab women minimized differences.

Auclert saw the imperial project as a humanitarian mission. She asserted that "in taking possession of Algeria, France had assumed responsibility for the happiness of the Arabs . . . [and for] bringing them the advantages of civilization."⁴¹ Auclert saw France as completely failing in this duty. Both Arab men and women remained politically, socially, and economically disenfranchised; they lived under a regime in which, Auclert contended, "there is only a small French elite who consider the Arab race as human."⁴² Algerian Jews had gained French citizenship in 1870, benefiting from the new republic's emancipatory wave, its shift from military to civilian rule, and pressure from the French Jewish community. While European immigrants also had access to full citizenship by this period, Muslims did not.⁴³ Decrying this discrimination, Auclert wrote in an unpublished essay entitled "Prejuge de race et de sexe" (Prejudice of race and sex) that "Europeans have the same prejudices toward the Arabs that men have towards women."⁴⁴ Race- and sex-based disenfranchisements, she argued, were equivalent: colonial control and the oppression of women (including sequestration, child marriage, and polygamy) demonstrated the interlinked nature of imperial France's sexism and racism.

Feminist Precursors

A forerunner of Auclert's feminist imperialism developed a half century earlier. In the 1830s, a substantial feminist movement emerged in concert with the rise of utopian (or romantic) socialisms. Opposed to the violence of the French Revolution (and formed in the wake of the Revolution of 1830), these feminists also rejected its emphasis on Enlightenment rationalism, individualism, and the nation.⁴⁵ They adopted the label "socialist" to reflect their focus on "the social"—human networks, community, family, intimacies.⁴⁶ This included attention to class- and gender-based hierarchies. As Naomi Andrews explains, their focus was "on the moral and spiritual dimension of human existence."⁴⁷ Disinterested in political rights and disdainful of republicanism and links to the nation, these utopian socialist feminists rejected formal politics, but not the political.⁴⁸ They embraced a romanticism that strove to unite the era's accepted dichotomies: theory and practice, woman and man, and East and West. A few of these activists, most notably the journalist Suzanne Voilquin, pursued these ideals while traveling and living in empire.⁴⁹

Voilquin and Auclert shared similarities and comparable experiences. Each edited and wrote for a feminist newspaper, credentials rare in the nineteenth century.⁵⁰ Each woman developed her socialist feminist politics within male-dominated socialist movements, with which she ultimately broke, but retained contacts with individual male socialists. Each opposed women taking men's names at marriage, and the resultant perpetuation of the patronym at the expense of the matronym.[51] Each chose to not just visit a colonial location, but also to live there for years. Each envisioned her work as a humanitarian mission. And each saw women's enfranchisement as a means to liberate women in both metropole and colonies. Voilquin's life and writings thus foreshadow some of the major issues motivating Auclert's approach to imperialism, at least in attenuated form. The drive to cultural "improvement" based in feminist ideals, linked to a desire to aid North African women, and combined with an Orientalist, racialized outlook led each to seek the transformation of colonial society in her own image.

Despite the women's similarities, acute contrasts existed between Voilquin and Auclert. Engaging in profoundly different historical moments a half-century apart, Voilquin and the utopian socialist feminists embraced a politics nearly antithetical to that of Auclert. Disregarding the legal and national structures through which Auclert would later seek emancipation, they instead embraced a religiosity which she disdained. Although both socialist and feminist, their differences reflect not only the capaciousness and range of both class- and gender-based emancipatory movements, but also their historical evolution.

Voilquin became politicized in the romantic socialist Saint-Simonian movement, which attracted a significant number of women who, in the wake of the 1830 Revolution, saw possibilities for change and liberation in its doctrine. Led by Prosper Enfantin, male Saint-Simonian leaders developed a feminism rooted in idealized, essentialist female characteristics, rejecting the "tyranny of marriage" in favor of "free love," and asserting a "natural," dichotomous complementarity between the sexes. An embrace of the feminine typified the romantic socialist rejection of the masculinized Enlightenment ideal. However, this paternalist feminism never evolved to either theorize or promote women's actual emancipation, and within two years a group of women, including Voilquin and Pauline Roland, developed a distinct utopian socialist feminism.[52] One radical step was establishing France's first woman-only newspaper, ultimately named *Tribune des femmes*, around which they centered their militancy. They prioritized motherhood and the maternal, which, they contended, Enlightenment paternalism and republicanism had unnaturally subsumed. They also addressed issues of class and morality.[53]

The journalists published using only their first names. Abjuring the patronym—not only husbands' surnames, but also fathers'—they attacked this onomastic tradition as representing, confirming, and perpetuating the social valuation of the paternal over the maternal, which they considered an unnatural usurpation.[54] Voilquin, publishing as "Suzanne," edited the periodical for most of its nearly two-year life. In the wake of the 1834 governmental reaction against rising socialist and workers' movements, she shut down the *Tri-*

bune des femmes, undertook a socialist propaganda *tour de France* from Paris to Marseilles, and then sailed to Egypt to join the Saint-Simonian colony.[55]

Escaping French political repression, the Saint-Simonians envisioned Egypt as a potential utopia. They saw in Egypt a possible site for the emergence of the "Woman Messiah," a mystical Mother for whom they searched globally, to pair with Enfantin and lead what they called their "new religion."[56] Saint-Simonian ideas of Egypt emerged from the era's romantic, Orientalist conceptions of North Africa and its populations, combined with concrete research they had conducted into the possibilities Egypt held for attaining their goals. It particularly drew the Saint-Simonians because, although still under nominal Ottoman rule, Egypt's viceroy Mehemet-Ali welcomed them. Mehemet-Ali sought modernization, but not Westernization. He took advantage of European Orientalism to extract knowledge and skill.[57]

In Voilquin's memoir of her time in Egypt, *Souvenirs d'une fille du peuple, ou, La saint-simonienne en Egypte* (Memories of a daughter of the people, or, the Saint-Simonian woman in Egypt), she described how she and her comrades had planned their departure from France: "Colonize, colonize, colonize had become the watchword of the moment, and the theme that motivated all of us every day."[58] They imagined colonization as a way to expand and strengthen their political sphere and to aid and advance an Oriental population. Voilquin had hoped to study medicine in Egypt, which she did in a European-run school and then ultimately worked as a midwife in Alexandria and Cairo. In the spring of 1835 plague hit Cairo, killing some Saint-Simonians and leading the rest to flee the city. Voilquin chose to stay. When Enfantin tried to convince her to leave, she explained that after his departure she would remain with Dr. Dussap, with whom she studied medicine. "My choice is made, Father; you know that my goal is to study the women of this country. I thus could not be better placed than here." Elaborating, Voilquin continued: "The services will be reciprocal; I will work as moral tutor to the children who, in their turn, will be thrilled to be my Arab language teachers."[59]

For Voilquin, Egypt meant an opportunity to both learn from and teach Egyptian women. She investigated them first-hand—treating them medically, interacting with them socially (she visited public baths and harems), and observing them throughout the cities.[60] Unlike Auclert and other later nineteenth-century feminists, Voilquin learned Arabic to better understand women's lives and experiences first hand. Writing of Dr. Dussap's children, Voilquin referred not only to studying Arabic with them, but also to acting as their "moral tutor." While their father was a French doctor, their mother was a formerly enslaved Black Egyptian woman. The idea that these children needed a "moral tutor" reflected Voilquin's assessment of a deficiency; their Egyptian mother, from Voilquin's perspective, lacked European women's moral fortitude. As Auclert would later contend regarding Algerian women, Voilquin saw Egyptian women as needing guidance and uplift not just from European women, but more specifically from feminists.

Meeting with Coptic Christian women, Voilquin took the opportunity to act as an "agent provocateur," to push the women to question their status in their society. Voilquin relied on "the spirit of our common mother" to make the Coptic women feel connected to her and to hear her story—one of a France with idealized gender roles.[61] Voilquin's Egyptian experience, Renée Champion argues, led her to identify a "transcultural women's solidarity" that altered her feminism.[62] She also used that perceived connection to advance her own politics.

Like Auclert, Voilquin and the Saint-Simonians believed in European supremacy over the "Orient." And, like Auclert, Voilquin understood European women as possessing a particularly gendered ascendency, with which they could and should help elevate less civilized peoples.[63] A half-century later, Auclert would advocate feminist-influenced egalitarian gender laws and customs, rooted in the French republican tradition; she advanced a feminist socialist version of the *mission civilisatrice*. Voilquin, in contrast, promoted French women's moral superiority. This sense of moral preeminence arose at the intersection of liberty and religion. As Susan Foley notes, although Voilquin decried multiple aspects of French women's status within France, that status became burnished when measured against the broader imperial world. Relatedly, she understood religion of any sort to have a negative influence on less civilized women.[64] Perceiving her movement as one that could elevate and advance less-developed societies, Voilquin advocated a form of civilizing mission before it became an accepted and articulated doctrine during the Third Republic.[65] Unlike the later *mission civilisatrice*, however, neither the Saint-Simonians nor Voilquin asserted a national imperialism. In contrast, they promoted their own community-based, antinationalist, utopian socialist visions. The male leadership, which included many engineers and technocrats, intermeshed technological advances with social and spiritual regeneration.[66] Voilquin supported these programs, but her own politics and work centered on women's lives and health—especially those of nonelite women.

Another precursor of Auclert—and one who specifically inspired her—was Eugénie Berlau Allix Luce, a French woman who had established and run a school for Muslim girls in Algiers.[67] Born in 1804, Allix Luce escaped an abusive husband in 1832 and fled to Algeria, leaving behind her young daughter. Madame Luce (as she became known) opened her school in 1845. She subsequently obtained government funding for the institution, having promoted it as part of a civilizing, assimilating project. In a letter to the prefect of Algiers, Luce argued, "How else to achieve this goal but through the education of women, the touchstone of the family . . . to either inspire love or hate of the French?"[68] The colonial government continued to support her institution until 1861, when both Arab and French authorities terminated girls' schooling, alleging that Western education only made Muslim girls social pariahs. Shifting focus, Luce turned her school into an embroidery workshop for Muslim girls, teaching them this traditional, and marketable, skill.[69]

Luce came to Auclert's attention because influential British feminist Barbara Leigh Smith Bodichon had encountered—and became fascinated with—Luce during one of Bodichon's annual visits to Algeria, where her French army surgeon husband lived. The British feminist wrote extensively and enthusiastically about the French woman, her school, and the beautiful textiles her atelier produced. Bodichon's widely read publications brought Luce renown and admiration in Britain, and her school/workshop became an important stop on English women travelers' itineraries. Luce had no such recognition in France.[70] For Auclert, Luce's story provided support for her ongoing advocacy for Algerian girls' education. Over a period of decades, Auclert wrote letters, petitions, and articles advocating the reestablishment of girls' schools. In these, she not only argued for the importance of female education in and of itself,

3.2.   Hubertine Auclert. 1910. Bibliothèque Nationale de France.

but also contended (as Luce had) that such schools would be valuable tools for assimilation.[71]

Auclert advocated Western-based instruction as a way to combat both gendered and racial oppressions in Algeria, using her journalistic podium to promote girls' schooling as part of a multi-pronged route to assimilation.[72] Her push to elevate Algerian women's status and lived conditions remained entangled with, and often subordinated to, her drive toward French women's enfranchisement—which she envisioned as the ideal remedy to multiple gender- and race-based subjugations in both metropole and colony.

Three Feminist Polemics

La citoyenne, under Auclert's editorship, adapted the era's dominant hierarchical anthropological conceptions of civilizations and race to fit imperial feminist goals. La citoyenne critiques took three major approaches. First, it unfavorably compared French women's social and legal status with that of women in less developed, "uncivilized" cultures; second, it contested accepted Western hierarchies of civilization and race in societies that oppressed women; and third, it maintained that the golden age of Arab culture had collapsed due to the denigration of women. While the French government used women's status as a metric of civilization for its colonies, pointing to women's subjugated position as justification for denying rights to Indigenous people, Audouard, Rouzade, Mink, and Auclert each used aspects of women's legal and social status to promote new feminist articulations of Frenchness. La citoyenne's feminist journalists, under Auclert's editorial leadership, employed the same measure to condemn women's oppression in France and its colonies. Judging women's status appeared as a useful tool across the political spectrum.

Polemic I: Barbaric France

La citoyenne's most frequently employed polemical device was to invert dominant hierarchies of civilization to demonstrate France's need to emancipate women further. Auclert repeatedly employed the pages of La citoyenne to attack the French imperial project. She pointed out the French government's unacknowledged double standard in judging colonized peoples uncivilized and therefore unworthy of rights, based on their subjugation of women, while simultaneously disenfranchising French women. In a May 1881 issue, the newspaper carried a front-page statement from Auclert's organization Droit des Femmes denouncing France's imperialist invasion of Tunisia. Entitled "Protestation des femmes contre toutes guerres de conquète" ("Women's protest against all wars of conquest"), it declared: "When the French cease to crush women with their despotism . . . when the voters and the legislators cease to impose on women laws to which they have not consented; and finally, when the French treat women more humanely than the Arabs do, then they can speak of civilizing the savages."[73]

Establishing the amelioration of French women's condition as a prerequisite to the nation's civilizing mission, Auclert undercut France's imperialist rationale: its cultural superiority and advanced evolutionary position. The *Droit des femmes* statement addressed the nation's weakness in both political and social realms, reflecting Auclert's vision of the "true" social republic. Censuring the violence of the imperial project, it confronted the republic regarding its supposedly universal principles. The "Women's Protest" specifically assailed France's brutal "repression of the Kroumirs," a confederation of North African Berber tribes; in its extensive coverage of the Tunisian conflict, *La citoyenne* exposed French violence against the Indigenous peoples. The *Droit des Femmes* statement reprovingly claimed that "the Republic that seeks to eliminate borders would outlaw killing as a means of extending its frontiers"[74] and condemned what it considered France's perversion of the republican ideal: a universal republic ought not seek the violent expansion of its borders but rather the peaceful and beneficent spread of its purview, and with that expansion, its rights and freedoms. Auclert's feminist imperialism constituted an alternative approach to empire, one that called for the establishment and augmentation of a more just and civilized republic.

Using metropolitan women's legal and social status, *La citoyenne* endeavored to expose France's political hypocrisy and the ongoing disenfranchisement of French women. A June 1881 article, written by Léon Giraud and signed with his anagramic pseudonym "Draigu," again addressed the issue of polygamy. "The Turk found that polygamy was, for his concerns, a good thing and made polygamy a social institution. The French proclaimed monogamy in principle, without renouncing polygamy in practice. . . . I prefer the first system: it is less shady [*louche*]."[75] In a newspaper that consistently attacked the immorality of polygamy, this article lauded the honesty involved in embracing polygamy—just as Audouard had done regarding the Mormons—intending to highlight the duplicity of France's monogamy claims. Directly attacking France's superiority as a civilized nation, Draigu continued: "What difference do you see between these two countries? . . . [The Turk] has the courage of his convictions and less of his instincts and his appetites."[76] Equating France with "instincts and appetites" and Eastern Turkey with moral courage strategically inverted the dominant hierarchy of civilization.

Indicative of her acute attention to jurisprudence, Auclert also challenged France's civilized status by comparing Algerian women's legal position to that of French women under the Napoleonic Code. She maintained that under French law "the superiority of the man is strongly analogous to that established by Muhammad" and that "we have an extreme need to civilize ourselves. We must first abolish the slavery of half of our nation . . . Algeria will be a precious conquest if she forces us to a *mea culpa*, and to come to know ourselves."[77] Auclert intended to hold Muslim Algeria up to France as a mirror of itself, likening women's oppression in the colony to that in the metropole, in measure, if not in kind. In marriage, a French woman gave up her family name, paid a dowry, and surrendered rights to her person and property as she entered a union only recently made dissoluble, whereas an Arab woman kept her name, received a dowry, legally controlled her personal property, and held the right to appear in court, including in case of divorce.[78] As Audouard had positively compared Turkish marriage law to French, so, too, did Auclert favorably contrast Algerian Muslim marriage to that of the metropole. While unequivocally reviling the Muslim practices of polygamy and child marriage (which she called "child rape"), Auclert argued that for women, ultimately, "Arab marriage is . . . more advantageous than French marriage."[79] Dramatizing her point, Auclert wrote: "The Arabs say, 'We take the woman by force; we pay for her and we take her, like buying a horse.' These words are shocking; the French, refined by civilization, nonetheless impose on the woman a heavier yoke than the barbarian who speaks this way."[80] Auclert explained this inflammatory statement: "In marrying, the Muslim woman keeps her family name, and in a context where the French woman loses part of her liberty, the Muslim woman, in contrast, acquires a sort of civil and economic emancipation. . . . Moreover, she receives from her husband a dowry proportional to his fortune."[81] Auclert recognized that these differences involved complexities and limitations. Yet, highlighting and publicizing this contrast worked toward undermining France's colonial project. It also served as a propaganda tool to underline her condemnation of women's status under the Napoleonic Code and to support her campaign for legal and cultural change on both sides of the Mediterranean.

Polemic II: Who Is Truly Civilized?

In a second approach to challenging existing imperial authority, *La citoyenne* worked to undermine the assumption of Europe as fully civilized. Exposing a case where "the English counsel in Morocco ordered eight Jewish women publicly whipped in his presence," an unsigned article stated, "The English are not excluded from barbarism."[82] The author of this short item noted not only the viciousness of such punishment but also the gender and religion of the victims. Decrying the action as beyond the realm of the civilized, the journalist laid bare the anti-Semitism and misogyny in British culture. Such a whipping involved the public degradation of the recipient and embodied a sadistic, sexualized intent. By underscoring the English counsel's attendance at the punishment, the author addressed the perversion, and thus barbarism, present among Englishmen. In doing so, the newspaper subverted European categories of historical evolution in accusing an English man of the sort of base sexuality and brutality with which Europeans typically linked Arab men.

A March 1884 piece signed by "Une Voyageuse" similarly developed the theme of savagery versus civilization. The pseudonymous journalist explained how the recently crowned queen of Madagascar had, at her coronation, "demonstrated her interest in education by replacing a military guard with a guard of students, made up of five hundred boys and four hundred girls" and then the following day "gave audience to all the school masters . . . exhorting them to continue to educate well."[83] Une Voyageuse ended with a note of exasperation: "And to think that the kings and queens of Europe, as well as the presidents of republics, are going to consider this queen a barbarian!"[84] This female monarch, who the author assumed the European power elite considered to be a savage, glorified education over arms and ceremoniously surrounded herself with a nearly gender-balanced student guard. Challenging the presumptive tie between Africans and savagery and between militarism and civilization, Une Voyageuse made clear where she believed the true barbarism lay.

The French imposed a complex web of racial, religious, and gender hierarchies in the colonial context. The indigenous Algerian peoples were mainly, but not exclusively, Berbers and Arabs. The French considered the Kabyles, the largest Berber group, more highly evolved than (and thus superior to) the Arabs, perpetuating the cultural and race-based "Kabyle Myth."[85] An unsigned article in the May 16, 1881 edition of *La citoyenne* countered this idealization of Kabyles, arguing that they "are not to be praised at all for their conduct toward women. . . . The Kabyle, like the Arab, buys his wife. . . . The Kabyle has the right to repudiate his wife, even without cause. . . . The Kabyle wives are virtually pack animals."[86] This feminist journalist typified *La citoyenne*'s ongoing argument that the mark of true civilization lay in the lives and position of women. The article likened Kabyle women's situation to that of female Arabs: both suffered socially, economically, and politically. In presenting this degraded position, *La citoyenne* challenged France's dominant imperial image of Kabyle superiority. This exposé supported the feminist imperial assertion that France needed to allow feminist, or feminist-influenced, intervention throughout Algeria to raise the status of Arab and Kabyle women and therefore of the society as a whole.

Continuing to publish on this topic long after *La citoyenne* folded, Auclert wrote in 1899 in her weekly *Le radical* column "Le féminisme" that the "prejudice that ranks humans by sex and by race makes no sense."[87] For her, France was merely more intellectually and culturally advanced than Muslim society, and feminist imperialism could aid in elevating the Arabs to the French level of civilization. Likening aspects of Arab culture to those of the Greeks, Romans, and Gauls, Auclert emphasized parallels between the Arabs and ancient Western societies, arguing that races evolved along a path of historical development. Rather than having fixed, essential characters, "backward" peoples could mature and ultimately become "civilized."[88]

Auclert's conceptualization of race harked back to that of sixteenth-century French theorists who understood race as mutable. Having entered French usage less than a century earlier, the term *race* referred to biological as well as social traits. The sixteenth-century theoretical use referred specifically to noble lineages: it addressed the ways in which breeding, education, and other social factors could bring either the elevation or the degeneration of a "race."[89] Auclert's advocacy of education and assimilation, as well as her warnings of France's potential degeneration, reflected these early theorizations, rather than the fixed racial conceptualizations of the two subsequent centuries.

This approach differed distinctly from the British imperial feminism of the era. Burton has shown that British imperial feminists, most of whom were liberals, constructed women in colonial India as fully subjugated and passive. They intended to demonstrate how Indian women needed uplift by the more emancipated and civilized British women. According to Burton, British feminists believed that by creating and enacting this benevolent role for themselves, they demonstrated their devotion and importance to Great Britain. Engaging in the support and solidification of empire by aiding downtrodden and objectified Indian women, British imperial feminists sought to prove themselves "worthy of" fully enfranchised citizenship. Rather than condemn Britain's approach to empire, they sought to cement their role in the existing imperial project.[90] This idea contrasts with Auclert's feminist imperialism and her censure of France's approach to empire. Like the British feminists, Auclert emphasized women's oppression under colonialism, but, unlike them, she attacked the extant form of imperialism. As a socialist feminist, she opposed the established hierarchy rather than attempting to infiltrate it as the liberal British feminists did. Auclert also acknowledged and valorized the positive aspects of indigenous laws and culture and recognized Algerian women's possession of agency. She perceived and portrayed these women living not in a state of passive degradation but with varied levels of rights and freedoms, some of which

French women did not possess. Auclert denounced France's colonial approach, with its sweeping denigration of the populations under its control.

Auclert operated in a milieu markedly different from that of British feminists. Where the British suffrage movement was expansive and strong, suffrage played a marginal role in French feminism; where imperialism stood central to British feminism, it remained peripheral to the French movement during this period.[91] Burton, Clare Midgley, and others have made clear that the British women's movement can be understood only in the context of empire, a complex set of institutions and relationships whose dominance both shaped and was influenced by feminism.[92] This dynamic also applies in the French context, where an ascendant colonial culture infused the metropole. Consciousness of France's overseas possessions and their peoples became increasingly unavoidable for female activists concerned with issues of justice and rights. These divergent sets of ideologies—feminist, racist, and imperial—underscore the importance of analyzing ideas of gender, race, and empire (and class and sexuality) in their evolving historical contexts.[93] Over the subsequent decades, questions of empire and of suffrage increased in significance in French feminism. Auclert's politics and those of Audouard, Rouzade, Mink, and Michel, anticipated the centrality and import of these issues.

Auclert promoted the power of republican feminism to advance women in both France and its colonies. She argued that French women's enfranchisement would not only improve their own position but also bring ameliorative programs to women under colonial rule. Embracing what can be termed a "difference feminism," Auclert believed that women *qua* women possessed essential traits of morality and justice and that they had a natural connection to the social. (This, notably, stands in distinct contrast to her anti-essentialist conceptions of race.) Women would therefore naturally vote away customs, traditions, and laws adverse to women. Female enfranchisement would join the social to the political, shaping Auclert's true republic.

Polemic III: Signs of Degradation

Finally, *La citoyenne* not only pointed out how women's subjugation reflected a group's lack of civilization but also warned that it could cause cultural degeneration. Rhetorically inquiring as to the historical decline of Arab society, an 1884 article signed only "X," but almost certainly written by Auclert, asked how a culture that once led in "science . . . agriculture, algebra, and chemistry . . . has now been relegated outside the sphere of thinking nations and finds itself behind his younger brothers on the road to progress?"[94] Restating one of the publication's central themes, the author answered that "a truth that one cannot overemphasize" was that "to judge the extent of a peoples' advancement, it is necessary above all to investigate the social condition of women."[95] Moreover, "in the *beaux temps* of the Arab race . . . we find women poets, women educators, occupying chairs in schools as they did in Italy in the fifteenth and sixteenth centuries. The female musicians of this era, singers and composers . . . are still celebrated. . . . But this is the same nation that today closes women away from the light of day. . . . The ignorance of the *mauresque* [Moorish woman] is complete. There are no schools for her; public life is absolutely forbidden."[96] Pointing specifically to women's sequestration and to the complete absence of girls' schools in Algiers, Auclert directly linked the subjugation of women to historical decline.[97] Making a contention to which she would return repeatedly, she argued that no matter how highly evolved and sophisticated a society, if it increased the marginalization and oppression of women, the entire cultural and intellectual level would fall. Women's condition, therefore, served not only as a metric of a society's advancement but also as a determining factor. Auclert undoubtedly intended this contention as a warning for France and for its European contemporaries.

During this period, French political and social discourse rang with fears of decay and degeneration, following the loss of the Franco-Prussian War and the enormous upheaval of the Paris Commune and in a context of falling birth rates and stagnant population numbers.[98] *La citoyenne* played on these fears, suggesting the potential for France to slip from its international perch atop the world's cultures. Giraud, employing his pseudonym "Camille," reiterated this point in an article anticipating a voyage to Algeria by a delegation of French deputies and senators. He wrote that in their travels they would "have a close look at" what he called "a decrepit civilization. . . . They will be able to ask how the Arab race, which had such a brilliant past, has descended so low. . . . They will see that the Muslim tribes had increasingly become victims of a false principle . . . the subjugation of women."[99] Arguing that women's oppression led directly to cultural decline and debility, *La citoyenne* reminded its readers of the dangers of France's subjection and marginalization of women. Logically, if societies could ascend the historical ladder of civilization over time, they could descend it too.

Conclusion

Auclert established *La citoyenne* primarily to promote women's suffrage. She and the other feminist journalists writing for the newspaper approached this goal with the belief that female enfranchisement would bring about a wide range of political, economic, and social changes. They also expanded their perspective, and that of their readers, beyond the borders of France and of Europe. By exposing gender relations in and between contemporary nations and cultures, they attempted to expose contradictions in the era's accepted hierarchies of civilization. The French colonial authority maintained that societies such as Algeria that severely oppressed women were too barbaric to be granted rights, effectively doubly oppressing the victims. *La citoyenne* instead called for feminist intervention in extending colonized peoples' rights and freedoms to bring about progressive change and to enable the culture to ascend the ranks of civilization. Much of this analysis presupposed non-French peoples', especially Algerians', desire to be assimilated into French culture, as well as their willingness to abandon their own traditions and practices. Auclert's and *La citoyenne*'s feminist imperialism appropriated aspects of France's imperial program, particularly its *mission civilisatrice*, and worked, in turn, to influence that program with feminist actions and ideals. The newspaper's journalist activists did this by engaging in an international and historical discourse that placed women's status as the central marker of civilization.

Auclert attempted to improve the lives and status of French and Algerian women by pushing French authorities to live up to what she envisioned as the promise of the republic. In the metropolitan context, Auclert viewed political rights, and thus women's full participatory citizenship, as her goal.[100] She asserted that armed with the vote, women would eradicate legal inequities in metropolitan France and what she considered "barbaric" customs in the colonies, including polygamy and child marriage.[101] Espousing the essentialist understandings of a feminism of female moral superiority, Auclert believed that, given the choice, women would universally and naturally oppose these practices. Her goal for Algerian women differed, however. Rather than arguing for their immediate enfranchisement, Auclert advocated for Algerian women's assimilation into French culture. She argued that Algerian women either did or soon would recognize that nothing could benefit them more than "becoming French." Ultimately, following a process of cultural, religious, and political absorption, they, too, as "French women," would become enfranchised citizens of a true French republic.

Building on the feminist imperialism of Suzanne Voilquin and the Saint-Simonian women, and the feminist educational advocacy of Eugénie Allix Luce (Madame Luce), Auclert developed a historically rooted yet original politics. *La citoyenne*'s international focus stood out among feminist publications of the period in bringing the lives and experiences of "other" women to its metropolitan readers.[102] While Auclert's interests in Arab women and gender issues predated her 1888 move to Algeria, living in the colony influenced her understanding of political and racial hierarchies while intensifying her long-held gender ideology. By introducing these topics in her newspaper, she brought the politics of empire and race into the French feminist vista, challenging the dominant presumption of women's universal whiteness. *La citoyenne* presented its readers with women of different races and cultures, with lives unlike their own or those of other European metropolitan women they might have encountered. These journalists emphasized the commonality of women across borders and overseas. Auclert's gendered imperial critique provided her readers with an alternative to governmental imperial propaganda and the "benign" influence of the expanding colonial culture in the metropole. In an era of emerging consciousness of empire, Auclert thus shaped her audience's understandings of and potential responses to imperialism. She introduced the possibilities of alternative visions of, or even clear opposition to, imperialism.

Auclert also complicated issues of religion and gender by offering these readers her perceptions of Islam and of *Les femmes arabes*, effectively expanding the feminist religious debate beyond the dichotomy of secularism versus Catholic clericalism. She extended anticlericalism, so prevalent among French socialist feminists, to include a castigation of Islam, which she often conflated with Arab culture.[103] Auclert, like Mink, decried marriage practices and gender roles enforced by religion, culture, and law on both sides of the Mediterranean.

Recognizing the multilayered and interwoven reciprocal influences between metropole and colony, Auclert saw women's rights and positions in France and the colonies as entwined with each other and with questions of race, religion, and sexuality. Her imperial politics held two seemingly contradictory positions in tension, as she both supported and critiqued empire. In addressing issues including suffrage, polygamy, marriage, and fidelity, Auclert aggressively opposed France's imperial and colonial undertakings. Simultaneously, she promoted a dualistic feminist imperialism, an activist politics through which she sought French women's immediate political equality and the ultimate assimilation of native Algerian women into the equitable French republic of the near future. For her, women in France—both the France of Europe and the France of Algeria—would bring about equality through the flourishing of the socialist republic.

CHAPTER 4

Imprisoned, Colonized
Civilization and Translation in New Caledonia

The experience of exile in France's New Caledonia penal colony led Louise Michel to her own form of anti-imperialism.[1] Deported to the South Pacific archipelago as punishment for her participation in the Paris Commune, Michel had become disillusioned with the Commune's revolutionary leadership and the cataclysmic, brutal repression that followed in its wake. During her four-month sea voyage on the prison ship *Virginie*, Michel turned to anarchism through shipboard discussions with her fellow deportee, the anarchist feminist Nathalie Lemel.[2] Michel's anarchism, deeply committed to transformative political and social change, dovetailed well with her feminism. It manifested a politics intent on surmounting the barriers between peoples and nations, privileging community over individualism, and breaking down hierarchies and their underlying power inequities. Michel's time in the New Caledonian prison colony and her interactions with the Indigenous Kanak expanded her anarchist feminist politics to include anti-imperialism—a logical extension of her antihierarchical worldview.

With her typical optimism and curiosity, Michel recognized her punishment as an opportunity to see parts of the world she might otherwise never experience, to encounter people she might otherwise never meet, and to effect some change in a new context. (Her primary concern was being away from her aged mother, with whom she was quite close. Michel carried substantial guilt regarding her mother's fears and worries for her revolutionary and often-incarcerated daughter's safety.) Monsieur de Fleurville, the Montmarte inspector of schools who acted as Michel's agent during her imprisonment and exile, wrote on August 2, 1873, "Perhaps I will be the only one, but I congratulate you on your departure because you have wanted this so much and for such a long time, convinced that you will be useful in this new country."[3] Awaiting deportation in a prison cell in Auberive, France, Michel had arranged, via de Fleurville, to undertake research for France's Société d'Acclimatation (Botanical Society) during her time in New Caledonia. The society's president, Édouard Drouyn de Lhuys, asked Michel (again through de Fleurville) to plant various seeds and report on their growth on the South Pacific island and to investigate the indigenous flora, sending back "the names or descriptions of those you have judged useful in France or Algeria."[4] Facilitating the advance of botanical and agronomic knowledge—particularly of the sort that might benefit and link diverse populations—fit with Michel's pedagogical and political interests. As she wrote to Victor Hugo on July 14, 1876, "I have not traveled six thousand leagues to see nothing and to do nothing useful."[5]

Michel had also arranged with France's Geographic Society to investigate Indigenous Kanak communities. Writing from the *Virginie* during her voyage to the penal colony, Michel hoped "in my excursions for the Geographic Society, to teach the Kanak to equal us, which will not be as difficult as one would believe."[6] Interested in the Kanak even before her arrival in the archipelago, she expressed the mix of condescension and boosterism that became typical of her assessments of these New Caledonians. She continued, "This dying race, instead of being dispossessed and crushed by the cannon, would be able to form alliances with ours which would produce an intelligent and strong race. One at least a little more [intelligent and strong] than ours, which is stupid and cowardly."[7] Denigrating "our" race, the "French race," Michel simultaneously proposed it as the potential savior of the Kanak. Assumptions of the inevitable vanishing of "savages" permeated the nineteenth-century Western world in what Patrick Brantlinger has termed the "extinction discourse," a supposition exemplified by Audouard's observations about "disappearing" Native Americans.[8] Michel, who had clearly researched the Kanak before her exile, reiterated the discourse, yet challenged its inevitability.

Intrigued by the Indigenous New Caledonians, Michel studied their languages, oral traditions, and culture during her seven years of incarceration in the archipelago. Although, as a prisoner, she initially had only limited contact with Kanak, Michel ultimately made personal, intellectual, and literary connections with them. She found—or created—bridges that she understood as spanning cultures as well as space and time. Rejecting the era's prevalent civilized/savage dichotomy between Europeans and Pacific Islanders, she challenged assertions not only of Kanak "savagery," but also of French civilization. She did, however, repeat the common conceptualization of the Kanak as child-like and dwelling in the Stone Age. Michel's efforts to reach across oceans and millennia reflected her desire to both advance her own political agenda and to aid the Kanak, aims that intertwined and reinforced one another the fur-ther she delved into the Kanak world. In learning their legends and languages, she found inspiration and connections among her unifying, global goals. She discovered mutualism in Kanak conceptions of self and community and tran-scendence in their interconnectedness within both the natural and spirit world—while also encountering misogyny in their gender roles and relations. A committed poet and novelist, Michel employed her literary skills to shape and transform Kanak tales and Kanak history. She both advocated for, and ap-propriated from, Kanak culture. By amending tales and abating inequities, Michel advanced both the Kanak image and her own political aims while simultaneously assailing the French imperial project.

Michel was rare among the era's feminists in self-identifying as anti-imperialist. The specifics of her colonial experience illuminate the develop-ment of her imperial critique, what it looked like, and what it meant to her. Michel came to recognize, appreciate, and work with aspects of the particu-lar in Kanak life through her involvement with the New Caledonian every day. Living under the colonial prison authority and engaging with local Kanak, Mi-chel both experienced and observed the collisions of imperial and Indigenous powers and cultures. Interrogating the quotidian gendered and raced encoun-ters in this settler colonial context helps illuminate the development of her feminist anti-imperialist politics. Michel spoke about New Caledonia in the af-termath of her deportation, but she also voiced opposition to France's ex-panding imperial undertakings, particularly decrying the 1881 Tunisian con-quest and French and British aggressions in the Egyptian War the following year. She accused the two imperial powers of "wanting the Nile to flow with blood like the Seine had in 1871," referring to France's brutal "Bloody Week" repression of the Paris Commune.[9]

Opposed to both France's carceral and its colonial projects, Michel con-demned the state's civilizational presumptions and imperial practices. Draw-ing on Kanak tales, Michel interwove the promotion of Kanak culture and independence with her broader political goals, developing a language of lib-eration. Concurrently, however, Michel's ethnographic project immersed her in the inherently hierarchical power relations of empire. Her self-described anti-imperialism used Indigenous Kanak tales and histories to develop and pro-mote her own European-facing political project. One spatial, one traditional, and one conceptual realm—all based in daily life—provide contexts through which to understand core aspects of Michel's evolving politics: the colonial prison; Kanak oral culture; and ideas and practices of civilizational rankings. Publishing, and changing, Kanak narratives for a French audience served more than one purpose. Michel's engagements in these penal, linguistic, and civilizational realms illuminate intersections between the colonial and the Indigenous spheres as well as their gendered and racialized natures and the impossibility of their disaggregation. Her language of liberation proved inseparable from the legacies and circulations of French imperial power.

Deportation

After four months at sea, Michel arrived in New Caledonia on December 8, 1873.[10] Aboard the ship *Virginie*, the Communard deportees lived in four large cages, constructed to allow some light, air, and movement. Michel and the twenty-four other women prisoners (and one woman's two children) shared a single enclosure, a space which had removable panels to provide minimal privacy and a degree of warmth. The prisoners' circumscribed, regimented, and monitored days included at least one free hour on deck, affording a brief escape from the confinement and mustiness of their cells. Contact between men and women was technically prohibited, but the unusually sympathetic ship's commander established an environment that allowed discussions as well as book and letter exchanges.[11] The ship's doctor, proud that every passenger survived the trip, explained in his report the importance of air and decent food and drink, as well as of "reading, games, and song, allowed at specified times. The moral influence of these liberties influenced the general health."[12] Comparing the surprisingly humane shipboard conditions to the harsh jailers the Communards had endured in the two-and-one-half years since the uprising, the deportee Henri Messager later asserted, "We were far from the police mob we had faced for so long."[13]

The carceral shipboard climate limited the movement of bodies, but not of ideas. Michel communicated regularly with her fellow Communard veterans on the passage, including the well-known polemicist Henri Rochefort (who became her life-long friend and benefactor) and the anarchist Nathalie Lemel, whose politics Michel adopted during the voyage. Describing her profound disenchantment following the French government's brutal repression of the uprising and slaughter of the Communards, she recounted, "I shared with Madame Lemel my thought on the impossibility of any powerful men doing anything other than committing crimes if they are weak and egotistical, or being annihilated if they are devoted and energetic." In response, Lemel convinced her this

4.1. Louise Michel, photographed by Boissonas. ca. 1880. Emma Goldman Papers, International Institute of Social History, Amsterdam.

outlook was properly called "anarchism."[14] This constituted a critical intellectual moment for Michel. Recognizing a politics in harmony with her own philosophy, she embraced anarchism; she both practiced and theorized its tenets and possibilities through the end of her life.

Even as an imprisoned political deportee, Michel welcomed the opportunity to travel and encounter new worlds. Ernest Girault, with whom she later gave a lecture series in Algeria in 1904, reported that Michel spoke of her great fortune in "being able to see . . . the Cape, the edges of the polar regions, Australia, and New Caledonia. Many people would voluntarily give ten years of their life to make such a voyage."[15] She loved the sea. In her *Mémoires*, Michel wrote, "The sun created facets on the waves, as though two rivers of diamonds shone on the sides of the ship."[16] She penned her experiences and impressions of the voyage and of the ports where they stopped for supplies. At La Palma, in the Canary Islands, with its white houses that "seemed to emerge from the sea," Michel encountered islanders who rowed out to the anchored *Virginie* on small boats, selling "enormous raisins." (The prisoners could not leave the ship.) Michel held that "The most interesting thing was the appearance of the people, two of whom were magnificent. Science will pardon me, but . . . these are the Guanches and their ancestors inhabited Atlantis."[17] Michel identified the Guanches, the indigenous population of these coastal African islands, forcibly colonized by Spain. Simultaneously, she romantically connected them to the mythical Atlantis. This evocation of science, history, power, aesthetic, and fable exemplifies Michel's references and interests, as well as her approach to encountering and engaging new people and worlds.

Prisoners or Prostitutes?

Michel's arrival in New Caledonia resulted from a tumultuous set of circumstances. In an effort to rid the metropole of revolutionaries in the aftermath of the Commune and to simultaneously expand the colonial presence, France deported 4,500 Communards, of whom only twenty-five were women. All the women were sent together on the *Virginie*.[18] Their particularly gendered experience in the penal colony began from the moment they arrived. While New Caledonia had become a prison colony in 1863 (ten years after France "took possession" of the archipelago), women convicts arrived only in 1870, delivered into a profoundly masculinized colonial world.[19] The first two to land were married to fellow deportees; both husband and wife had been convicted of the same crime. Three months later, the ship *Sybille* brought six widows and *célibataires* (single women), and with them the "problem" of housing and handling these women without men. A ministerial dispatch directed colonial authorities to send the six women to the nuns at the Convent St. Joseph de Cluny "to wait until the women are able to marry."[20] All six of the female *Sybille* passengers wed by 1874. Beginning in 1870, French authorities recruited selected metropolitan female prisoners for emigration to New Caledonia. Placed initially with the sisters of St. Joseph de Cluny at Burail, they remained there until they found spouses. As Odile Krakovitch contended in *Les femmes bagnardes*, female prisoners, as "fundamental elements of colonization, were sent to distant lands as punishment, but, like livestock, particularly to be married, procreate and populate the colony."[21] The prison administration held complex motivations: deportation not only rid the metropole of "undesirable" women, but also advanced the forced colonization of the archipelago. The female prisoners, although miniscule in number relative to the men, facilitated the European peopling of the South Pacific colony.

The introduction of women required alteration of, and thus created disruption to, the intensely male penal context. Notified of the imminent arrival of twenty-five female Communards on the *Virginie* in late 1873, New Caledonia's governor general, Gaultier de la Richerie, expressed his opposition to the "complicated regulations and considerable expenses required to establish Feminine Penitentiaries."[22] The penal colony operated as a masculine space, into which women could be integrated only under the control of individual men. Although the female deportees, as convicts, were already subsumed to the patriarchal prison authority, their embodied presence introduced a particular set of complexities and perceived dangers.

When the *Virginie* arrived in Nouméa harbor, the colonial authorities directed the ship's captain to deliver the eight women condemned "in the first degree" to the prison camp at Bourail, rather than the Presqu'île Ducos (Ducos Peninsula), the location where, under law, all "first degree" convicts were to be jailed. At Bourail, a day's travel from the peninsula, the women would have been under the control and monitoring of the nuns of St. Joseph de Cluny. Michel explained the directive, "As they always foolishly endeavor to make women's lot different from men's, they wanted to send us to [the prison camp at] Bourail, under the pretext that the situation is better there. But we energetically protested this, and with success. If our men are unhappier on the Ducos peninsula, we want to be with them!"[23]

The male and female prisoners of the "first degree"—political prisoners receiving the harshest possible sentence, deportation to an *enceinte fortifiée*, a stockade—had been destined for the Ducos Peninsula, which would serve as an open-air prison, a fortress without actual walls.[24] Michel described it as a "narrow tongue of land closed at the throat by soldiers, without fresh water, without greenery, crisscrossed by two little arid hills . . . a dead territory" on the otherwise lush New Caledonian archipelago's primary island, the Grand Terre.[25] Convicts could live with a degree of freedom on the small peninsula, as prison guards fully blocked and fortified its narrow connection to the rest of the island.[26] Yet at the last moment, the correctional authorities endeavored to separate the women from the men. The attempt to provide Michel and the other women with the "better" conditions at Burail would have meant less freedom and greater isolation under the punitive eye of the St. Joseph de Cluny sisters—described by a French observer, Madame Hagen, as "subject to a severe regime."[27] As unmarried women living in the female-only, religiously dominated context, the deportees would have faced ongoing pressure to marry male colonists or freed convicts as part of governmental efforts to colonize the archipelago. The French government and colonial authorities envisioned particularly gendered roles for the female deportees.

"The law that prescribed putting men and women on the Ducos peninsula is outside of typical penal laws," the colony's governor wrote. "Condemned men and women have never been held together."[28] Yet the edict did specify the location of their deportation. Michel recalled her remonstration when faced with the gendered separation: "Because we were condemned like the men, is it not just that we undergo the same punishment as them?" To which, Michel contin-

4.2. Presqu'île Ducos (Ducos Penninsula), "prison without walls" where Michel and many other Communards were incarcerated. 1870–1871. Bibliothèque Nationale de France.

ued, a "large man in a colonial uniform" responded, "what I heard about all these *pétroleuses* [Communards accused of burning Paris during the revolution's repression] being hot-heads was right."[29] According to fellow deportee Joannès Caton, Michel and Nathalie Lemel "protested so energetically against this exile within their deportation, the governor decided to leave them at the *presqu'île* in accord with the law."[30] Word of their successful resistance reverberated widely, and, like Caton, many deportees ultimately mentioned it in their letters and memoirs.[31]

The chaplain at the Ducos Peninsula, Père Jean Xavier Hyacinthe Montrouzier, reacted against the decision. Vigorously opposed to a mixed sex population, he expressed his outrage that "eight unmarried *pétroleuses* . . . have been sent to the Ducos Peninsula, in the middle of the camp . . . across from my lodgings, at most one hundred meters away, without separation, without surveillance, and with the complete liberty to make and receive visits."[32] Infuriated at this "revolting" situation, he abhorred these adult women living unsupervised among a large number of adult men. The chaplain iterated the era's gendered, anti-Communard stereotypes that assumed working-class women to be incapable of considered political decisions, attributing their revolutionary participation to irrational and unfettered sexuality.[33] Père Montrouzier understood this as the placement of eight wildly sexualized female insurgents among his "flock" (although the vast majority of Communard deportees remained anticlerical throughout their imprisonment). Even more specifically, he contended, "By law they have changed the purpose of the Ducos Peninsula. It was a place of deportation, but they have made it a place of prostitution."[34] For Montrouzier, the mere presence of these women fundamentally altered the nature of the site. The insertion of eight female political prisoners sufficiently infected the masculinized penal colony to effectively destroy its character and function, transforming it instead to a place of immoral, "revolting" feminized sin. Montrouzier soon moved his own lodgings off the *presqu'île*, fearing his continued presence would imply his implicit approval of what he termed the "brothel." Accused by the governor of deserting his post, he did continue his chaplain duties, but left Ducos each night for his new quarters in the prison camp on the Ile Nou. He felt more comfortable living among murderers and thieves than among revolutionary women.[35]

Montrouzier believed the colonial authorities were shirking their duty to moralize and reform the female political prisoners. As participants in the recent revolutionary civil war, the Communard women had transgressed gender and class boundaries intended to maintain the hierarchical status quo. Attempting to explain women's motivations and actions in the Commune's wake, governmental reports and analyses argued that the women were "seduced by socialist theories. . . . [Their] laziness, envy, [and] thirst for enjoyments unknown and ardently desired contributed to their blindness, and they threw themselves, without thinking, into the revolutionary movement which engulfed them."[36] Denying women's conscious political and ideological intentions or actions, the report portrayed the Communards as impressionable, petty, and blind. It reinscribed their engagement as sexual rather than political, likening them to naïve and vulnerable innocents duped into an illicit encounter.[37] Neither French, nor colonial, nor church authorities could conceive of women as deliberate political actors. Their revolutionary participation demonstrated an abandonment of gendered propriety indicative of defective morality.

French authorities envisioned the remote penal colony as a moralizing space.[38] As Alice Bullard has explained, moralization entails a deeply gendered, patriarchal, and profoundly intimate approach to civilizing.[39] Female prisoners faced presumptions of licentious and reactive behavior that denied their agency and intentionality. Attributing women's political action to sexualized immorality, the colonial authorities intended to moralize—and thus properly civilize—female prisoners through matrimonial domestication.

Male convicts' experiences of the gendered, patriarchal, and intimate moralization played out in a masculinized, predominantly homosocial context of physical labor and deprivation intended to repair their improperly civilized selves. As Stephen Toth asserts, "The penal colonies were founded on the fantasy of regenerative work and labor in faraway, unoccupied (devoid of French citizens, if not Indigenous peoples) lands."[40] In this idealized scenario, the deportation of political prisoners and the transportation of common criminals simultaneously rid the metropole of "undesirables" and transformed such people into productive citizens through labor, while also establishing French colonial settlements. To encourage colonization, the government allowed the wives and families of prisoners to join them in New Caledonia. The authorities also saw this as advancing moralization (via the "natural" moralization of family life), while additionally ameliorating the profound emotional difficulties resulting from exile.[41] French colonial administrator Charles Lemire's statement regarding the New Caledonia penal colony reflected the government's perspective on transformative colonization: "Our maxim will be thus: to moralize in order to govern. To moralize the people *ignorant* of civilization; to moralize the men corrupted by the *abuse* of civilization; there is no better means to attain these results than through colonization."[42]

Efforts to civilize the criminalized French citizen paralleled efforts to civilize the colonized Kanak. Imperial powers often used similar methods to coerce or integrate "internal others"—racial, cultural, or political—as they did colonial subjects.[43] In New Caledonia, France pursued its most typical colonial objective in attempting to transform a racialized "savage" people, the Kanak, by bringing them French civilization. As Lemire claimed, this would "moralize the people ignorant of civilization."[44] But New Caledonia's particular circumstance as a penal colony added a second objective: to *correctly* civilize the convicts sentenced to its charge. Gaps, cracks, or flaws in France's civilizational façade allowed the emergence of malefactors, most clearly demonstrated in the 1871 Paris Commune. French authorities considered these French insurgents to be literal savages in need of proper civilization.[45] Characterized as examples of racial degeneration, these white Europeans threatened and debased what was understood as the French race. Racial theorists of the era, such as Count Arthur de Gobineau, judged the Communards and working classes to be a degraded race on par with people of color rather than with whites. The colonial prison thus had the task to "moralize the men [and women] corrupted by the abuse of civilization." Explaining that "we want to give the recidivists a new and beautiful country on the virgin lands, with the means of beginning a new life, of making new skin," Lemire erased the Kanak ("virgin lands") to assert the penal colony as a pristine site to re-form and re-birth degraded criminals.[46]

Lemire's desire to give convicts "new skin" echoes Franz Kafka's short story "In the Penal Colony." Set on a distant, fictionalized, French-held island, it centers on a torture apparatus that engraves convicts' sentences into their skin using knife-like needles, cutting deeper and deeper until, after approximately twelve hours of torment, the prisoner dies. But before death, its proponents contended, in the sixth hour, the condemned man would attain enlightenment.[47] As the prison Commandant explains, in the sixth hour, "Enlightenment comes to the most dull-witted. . . . You have seen how difficult it is to decipher the script with one's eyes; but our man deciphers it with his wounds."[48] As Lemire articulated the penal colony's goal of giving criminals the means to "mak[e] new skin,"[49] Kafka literalized it. He underscored the absurdity and viciousness of colonial and penal practices in the embodiment of creating a "new skin" for the offender—a skin ripped through with the words of his judgment.[50] The moralizing and civilizing process of reforming criminals, already replete with brutal physicality, became elevated to the complete "re-forming" of the condemned man from living body to mutilated corpse.

As Margaret Kohn argues, "In the Penal Colony" critiques Western assertions of justice which "insist upon a link between punishment, enlightenment, and moral reform; it exposes the way that this legitimizing function can obscure the reality of punishment."[51] Kafka's brutal denunciation of penal injustice confronted the French colonial assumption of their righteousness and right to discipline in order to reform. Contesting (in Kohn's terms) both the

Commandant's authoritarian understanding of justice and the Explorer's liberal conception of justice (the Explorer is the more enlightened European traveler who, although shocked and repulsed by the apparatus and its application, does nothing to interfere), Kafka delegitimizes the bases of Western colonial and carceral authority.[52] Philosopher and sociologist Michael Lowy writes that Kafka may have modeled his prison colony after that of New Caledonia, as he had attended anarchist meetings on topics including the Paris Commune in the years just prior to writing "In the Penal Colony" in 1914.[53]

Influenced by Octave Mirbeau's *Le jardin des supplices* (*The Torture Garden*), an allegorical novel deeply critical of Western justice, punishment, capitalism, and imperialism (often termed pornographic because of its graphic descriptions of sexually explicit torture), Kafka evokes a different form of the obscenity inherent in manifestations of these power relations.[54] The purification promised by Kafka's literary machine and by France's punitive institution underscored the interwoven physical and psychological elements of punishment. Rehabilitation was to be inscribed throughout the prisoner's body. The deportees lived this physical deprivation—through the relocation of exile, through prison routines, and through denial not just of comfort but basic needs. (In 1876 Michel wrote to the prison administrators on behalf of her fellow convicts, protesting their "iniquitous laws that condemn the deportation [sic] to die of hunger."[55]) Bodies, in their material, fleshy and gendered existence, became objects of the moralizing machines of the French state.

In the French imperial imaginary, New Caledonia constituted a literal version of what Michel Foucault would later term the "carceral archipelago." In the case of the New Caledonian archipelago, the prison and the colonial project overlapped and reinforced each other in the work of creating docile and obedient subjects. The "carceral continuum" existed where "prison continues . . . a work begun elsewhere, which the whole of society pursues on each individual through innumerable mechanisms of discipline. By means of the carceral continuum, the authority that sentences infiltrates all those other authorities that supervise, transform, correct, improve."[56] The offer of land incentives to emancipated (male) prisoners exemplified state efforts to move these potential settlers on a continuum from prisoner to colonizer, civilizable and civilizer in turn. By this argument, the former convicts, assumed to have been moralized and reformed as individuals, would bring their now-internalized discipline to their encounters with the Kanak. This would then expose the Kanak to civilizing forces not just from the French colonial authority, but also from the newly remade settlers. The eventuality of deliverance from imprisonment for the French inmates and the potentiality of emancipation from the Stone Age for the Kanak, together formed an ostensible model of freedom and improvement that was a key piece of the colonial project. If successful, the penal colony would—as Foucault argued for metropolitan prisons—"render individuals docile and useful."[57]

In New Caledonia, colonial authorities therefore focused their moralizing efforts simultaneously on the Kanak, seen as lacking civilization, and on the condemned criminals and revolutionaries, considered improperly civilized. Michel inverted these categorizations—as did Audouard, Auclert, and Rouzade in other colonial locations. Invited in 1881 (the year after the General Amnesty of Communards) to testify before the Investigative Commission on the Disciplinary Regime in New Caledonia, Michel refused to appear. While she "approved of the light that our friends are shedding on our distant tormentors," Michel denied the legitimacy of the Investigative Commission because it operated under a government that still included those who slaughtered the Communards. This especially applied to General Galliffet, whom she labeled the "true savage."[58] Michel continued to recognize an alliance with the subjected Kanak. Unlike any of her fellow deportees, she engaged with and studied their life and culture. Her efforts reflected a combination of motivations, both opposed to and supportive of the civilizing project of the archipelago. Even subjected to its practices and power, she introduced to the state, to anthropologists, and to her popular readers a set of alternative stories that resisted the location of the Kanak as backward and uncivilized. Interested in advancing the understanding and valuation of the Kanak, she worked to re-present them to a European audience, while simultaneously furthering her own political goals.

Encountering Kanak

In the 1885 version of her *Légendes et chants de gestes canaque*, a collection of Indigenous New Caledonian narratives, Louise Michel wrote, "The Kanak storyteller, if he is in high spirits, if he is not hungry, and if the night is beautiful, adds to a tale, and others add more after him, and the same legend passes through various mouths and various tribes, sometimes becoming something completely different from what it was at first."[59] Explaining this oral tradition as a transmission of unwritten histories, legends, and myths, Michel also described her role in the translation, transcription, and publication of Kanak tales. Like the Kanak storytellers of whom she spoke, Michel added to and altered the stories she heard. Respecting the tales and the tellers, she nonetheless presented a particular version of Kanak narratives to her European readers.

The name "Kanak" originally came from *kānaka maoli*, the Hawaiian term for "people." Used initially by eighteenth-century European sailors, the appellation took on a French spelling—"Canaque"—and emerged as a broad derogatory label for the people of Oceania. Coinciding with the region's colonization in the mid-nineteenth century, the name came to signify the "uncivilized" Melanesians, in contrast to the more "advanced" Polynesians. Associated with savagery and cannibalism in both French and English worlds, the label "Canaque" became the degrading and widely employed epithet for the Indigenous New Caledonians. Easily rhyming "Canaque" with "macaque" (a familiar North African monkey genus), the idea of Kanak as primate, as nonhuman, as primitive, as savage, and as cannibalistic took hold in the French popular imaginary.[60]

When the mostly urban French political prisoners arrived in the remote tropical penal colony following their 120-day sea voyage, they faced harsh rural living conditions and severe isolation.[61] While the majority remained aloof from the Kanak population, Michel engaged with them. Of her seven-year deportation, Michel spent the first five imprisoned on the Ducos Peninsula, where she first encountered Kanak men operating concessions or working for the colonial authority and where she initially visited a Kanak camp.[62] Despite fellow prisoners' efforts to discourage her—"Don't you know that the Kanak are capable of killing you. . . . They have already assassinated many whites"—two months after her arrival she set out alone to the camp.[63] Following the Kanak's initial suspicion and confusion at the appearance of a white woman, Michel's minimal knowledge of their language and the chief's rudimentary French allowed her to convey her solidarity with them. Within a year, she began a weekly school for Kanak. In one of her many letters to Victor Hugo, on June 18, 1876, Michel expressed her desire to live with a more distant Kanak tribe "for a sufficient time to understand their language and its uses" and to "open a school."[64] She sought a reciprocal exchange. After five years of living on the peninsula, she gained permission to live in the capital, Nouméa, and to open a school. Because of administrative delays (waiting for her "certificates and diplomas" to arrive from France), she became the under-mistress of Mademoiselle Penaud's school, where she instructed the daughters of deportees and colonial administrators. On Sundays, she held classes for the Kanak.[65]

On the Ducos Peninsula, Michel befriended a Kanak man named Daoumi; he became Michel's first conduit to Kanak history, lore, and language. In her *Mémoires*, Michel noted that Daoumi "is nearly European because of living among the whites. He knows how to read perfectly, he writes no worse than many others."[66] Daoumi introduced Michel to the linguistic and cultural traditions of both Grand Terre, New Caledonia's primary island, which included the capital and the main prison colony, and his birthplace Lifou, one of the neighboring Loyalty Islands within the New Caledonian archipelago. Michel wrote of their relationship: "He told me tribal legends and taught me his vocabulary, and I tried to reciprocate by telling him things that I believed were the most necessary for him to know."[67] She looked to him as a trusted resource, but also as an example of how Europeans and Kanak could develop mutually enriching associations.

Political Time

Like many of her contemporaries, Michel considered the Kanak a prehistoric culture. In the introduction to her 1875 ethnographic and linguistic study, *Légendes et chansons de gestes canaques*, published during her second year in New Caledonia, Michel explained "To European friends": "You are there in the 19th century; we are here in the Stone Age and we have *chansons de geste* [epic tales] for literature. Not the *chansons de geste* of the Middle Ages, but those of an entirely primitive time, with limited vocabularies and child-like works."[68] Placing the Kanak "in the Stone Age," Michel accepted the era's predominant anthropological premise of an evolutionary, race-based scale of civilization. She situated the Kanak as culturally coterminous with Europeans of millennia past.

While in the 1875 version of the tales Michel located the Kanak and their epics in the Stone Age, she later suggested a more historically recent, but still distant, temporality for them. Her significantly edited and reissued 1885 version included an additional section titled "Customs of the Middle Ages in Calédonie." Retaining the Kanak's temporal distance, she simultaneously relocated their culture millennia forward. In contrast to her earlier publication, she suggested an unusual level of cultural development. Michel wrote: "One is more than a little surprised to find, in the midst of the Stone Age, customs and manners of the Middle Ages. . . . The fortunes told, spells cast in cemeteries, are like those seen in France at the time of Urbain Grandier."[69] Following five additional years in the South Pacific archipelago, the experience of the Kanak's 1878 anticolonial uprising, and five years back in the metropole, Michel recast Kanak culture as both coterminous with and similar to the relatively recent European past. She wove the Kanak into world history.[70] For her, these "Stone Age" people did not fundamentally differ from the French; rather, they merely lagged behind in terms of historical development. The juxtaposition of a Stone Age culture displaying medieval manners and customs, therefore, exemplified the Kanak's progress; they were rapidly advancing through the historical stages of humanity—something Michel lauded to her readers.

Despite Michel's assertion of the Kanak's rapid cultural and historical progression, by situating them in an alternate timeframe, she defined them as anachronistic.[71] Michel thus participated in the epoch's typical colonial practice of constructing Indigenous people as temporally dislocated from the civilized world, just as Audouard discursively relocated the Native Americans she encountered in western North America and Auclert temporalized Algerians. In relegating the Kanak to a historical past, Michel exercised the inequitable power relations inherent in the nineteenth-century ethnographic process. Although a prisoner and an avowed anti-imperialist, as a white European, Michel held the power to temporally locate and represent the Kanak. This denial of coevalness went beyond the discursive; it was, as Fabian has maintained, a political act.[72]

Michel's conception of civilizational evolution allowed that peoples' historical progression could be expedited. Suggesting European intellectual development as more advanced than Kanak (but still quite limited), she contended that if the Kanak were "taught everything (that is to say, the little that we know). . . . Who knows . . . how far these people could go? The leap from the Stone Age to ours would be interesting to study."[73] Michel, the pedagogue, saw education as key: "Their curiosity of the unknown will bring them to our level, or even beyond."[74] As Michel's biographer Xavière Gauthier has pointed out, in many ways Michel questioned whether the whites or the Kanak were civilized, and which was of the Stone Age.[75] Juxtaposing stereotypes and generalizations about peoples and time, Michel established characterizations reflective of her social, political, and anthropological observations.

Although she supported a theory of civilizational evolution, Michel disallowed the widely held claim of Europe's absolute supremacy, contending instead that each culture embodied both virtues and weaknesses. Arguing that Europeans and the Kanak could, and should, learn from each other, Michel worked to establish cross-cultural exchanges that she believed would facilitate the advancement of both groups. Considering France and Europe more intellectually developed than the Kanak, she employed her radical pedagogy—which she had been developing over the previous decade—to instruct them in what she regarded as the most positive aspects of European thought and science.[76] Yet she also wrote of Europe's "poor, narrow civilization."[77] Long critical of the hierarchical character of European socioeconomic and political cultures, Michel rejected imperial assertions of European superiority. In comparing the democratic nature of the two societies, she found France lacking, explaining that while French governmental ministers disregard the peoples' interests, Kanak chiefs consistently consult their tribes.[78] "Under the Republic to which we submit," Michel argued, "we see only infamies. We do not want more Tonkins or Tunisias."[79] Despite her efforts to present pros and cons for both European and Kanak culture, and her intentions to portray the Indigenous population positively, Michel's status as a white European gave her the privilege of presenting her own version of both cultures. Her cultural mediation of the Kanak world rested on imperial and racial hierarchies.[80]

Michel experienced and observed ruthless colonial conditions and policies that contributed to her developing anti-imperialism. France had "taken possession" of New Caledonia in 1853, and begun undermining Kanak lifeways two years later with the appropriation of Indigenous lands. In 1855, the colonial Governor Joseph Fidèle Eugène du Bouzet officially "recognized" indigenous property rights, but only to land that they occupied at that moment.[81] This disregarded local practices of land rotation, which made substantial portions of their property appear untended and unowned. Having determined the Kanak to be among the least civilized groups of peoples, the French colonizers demonstrated no interest in understanding either Kanak hierarchies or property relationships, and they misconstrued both. Incorrectly assuming that chiefs held complete authority over a "primitive" people, who the French considered incapable of conceptualizing or managing private ownership, they erroneously presumed a system of collective property tenure. In actuality, the Kanak had a complex property system, involving clear divisions between individual and communal proprietorship.[82]

In spite of "recognizing" native land ownership, that same year the Governor General claimed a natural, colonial right to all property. He declared, "Considering that the principle exists that when a maritime power makes itself sovereign over a land unoccupied by a civilized nation, and possessed only by savage tribes, the taking possession annuls all previous contracts made by anyone with the naturals of this land; in consequence, the chiefs and the indigenes of New Caledonia and its dependences have never had, nor will ever be able to have, the right to dispose of all or part of the ground occupied by them in common, or as individual proprietors, either by sale, exchange, or voluntary gift, or any other mode of transmission, in favor of any individuals outside of their tribe, or who are not aboriginals from this territory."[83] This all-encompassing claim erased any Kanak right to sell, exchange, or give any land to any non-Kanak person, in the past, present, or future, effectively denying them a fundamental right of property ownership: its alienation. This legal, political, and economic maneuver initiated not only the expropriation of indigenous land, but also the undermining, denigration, and destruction of the Kanak world. Taking it a step further, in 1867 the French created "tribes" as a legal category, imposing a non-local concept and structure, and with it collective legal and administrative accountability. The following year, the colonial authority defined Indigenous property as collective (forcing upon the Kanak the only form of ownership the French could conceive of them having) and inalienable (consistent with Governor Bouzet's 1855 property decree).[84] They also introduced reservations. Effectively appropriating still more Kanak soil, uprooting clans, and forcing them into French-created tribes—often mixing together groups of traditional enemies—the Indigenous people found themselves on earth less fertile, less hospitable, and less familiar than their ancestral homes.[85]

Yet, the Kanak demonstrated contentment and satisfaction with their lives. As the Naval surgeon and ethnographer Victor Rochas wrote in 1862, "One would be seriously wrong to think that the New Caledonian was unhappy with his condition, however miserable it appears to us, or that he looks at ours with admiration and envy. Far from that, [he is] attached to his country, his customs, his prejudices, in sum satisfied with his fate."[86] The French colonizers nonetheless demanded Kanak submission and recognition of French superiority, both of which the Kanak resisted. Rochas continued, "We find the savage's presumption, his deep appreciation of himself and his race, sorely ridiculous."[87] Refusing to acknowledge Kanak culture and society, the French worked to devastate them.

These French colonial undertakings dislocated and undermined Kanak life. As Mohawk scholar Taiaiake Alfred states, the settler colonial state must disparage and undermine Indigenous culture and knowledge to legitimate their entire colonial project.[88] France's strategy followed this logic, and Michel recognized both the colonizers' destruction and Kanak efforts to counter the imperial efforts. Echoing popular conceptions of "primitive" groups as dying races—and reiterating the anthropological "extinction discourse" she had articulated and challenged on her way to New Caledonia—Michel asked, "Is this an emergent or a disappearing race?"[89] The answer mirrored both Michel's understanding of the two cultures' often complementary strengths and weaknesses as well as her interest in overcoming human divisions: "Saving these people would be possible by mixing them with the European race; one will give their force, the other its intelligence, to a young generation."[90] In a period of French demographic decline and rhetorics of impotency, Michel saw the Kanak compensating for the absence of European racial "force."[91]

Michel considered the present as a point of contact, an initial meeting of temporally, spatially, and culturally distinct peoples. She thus proposed *métissage*—or more accurately *créolization*—as a means of preserving Kanak society. Mixing the two races, in Michel's view, could beneficially strengthen and temper both populations. In Édouard Glissant's definition, *métissage* means "crossbreeding." "*Créolization*," Glissant asserts, "adds something new to the components that participate in it. . . . Furthermore, *créolization* opens on a radically new dimension of reality, not on a mechanical combination of components, characterized by value percentages."[92] Creolization thus more appropriately characterizes

Michel's proposal, rooted in her belief that "race-mixing" would better both groups, creating a whole that was more than its constituent parts.[93]

Michel's proposition reflects the complexity of how she conceptualized race. Abjuring European ideas of racial superiority, Michel nonetheless attributed specific, innate characteristics and strengths to each race. Although she argued for the possibility of racial development and advancement, that meant something different from altering essential racial characteristics. Michel did put the two groups' strengths and weaknesses on a par, rejecting European-imposed hierarchy. Her argument on behalf of race mixing, however, undermines her self-described anti-imperialism. Contending that the Kanak needed saving, and that a European-generated plan such as race mixing might be the solution, suggests an intentional imperial effort. This mixture of advocacy and superiority, though not unique to Michel, typifies much of her complex relationship with imperialism.

Given France's destruction of Kanak lifeways and means of survival, Michel's assertion of Kanak precarity likely reflected her fear of impending cultural demise. Even before arriving in New Caledonia, Michel considered the Kanak as a potentially dying "race." Her subsequent first-hand knowledge and observation of colonial displacement and devastation confirmed for her the danger of Kanak extinction. The possibility that as an Indigenous group they might not survive the clash with "civilization," that they might not survive colonization, likely contributed to Michel fearing Kanak erasure as well as her efforts to "save" them.[94]

4.3. Postcard depicting Kanak men and boys in New Caledonia, 1870s. The Trustees of the British Museum.

Spoken Words

By translating and transcribing Kanak tales, Michel hoped to record, disseminate, and preserve the society's linguistic and cultural core. The stories she encountered resulted from generations of retelling and, as with any oral legacy,
ongoing revision. Narratives changed each time someone told them. In his introduction to a collection of spoken tales from the New Caledonian island of
Lifou, sociolinguist Weniko Ihage explains, "Because of the specificity of the
oral, that is to say its movement, much is left to subjectivity. The storyteller
never tells the exact same story twice, depending upon the situation and vary-
ing according to context; it is impossible to discover a truly "original" version."[95] As in translation, transcription thus becomes a question of attempting
to adhere to the sense, the feel, and the intent of the tale.[96] Linguist Raylene
Ramsay explains that Michel was not only among the first to transcribe and
translate Kanak stories into French, but she was also the first who understood
and sought to capture the feel and sense of their orality. The few previous translators had neither interest in, nor comprehension of, the ways in which an oral
tradition differs from a written one. For example, the Marist missionary le Père
Mathieu Gagnière sent a compilation of tales to his superiors in France in 1853,
after resisting earlier requests for translations, arguing that such work "would
have no interest to the French." A decade later, Jules Garnier (the French explorer who discovered nickel in New Caledonia, which serves to justify French
economic colonialism to the present day),[97] translated and transcribed the Kanak
Chief of Arama's farewell speech, replacing word repetitions and lists of
names with "etc.," effectively eradicating the sound and flow of the oration.[98]
As the literary scholar Virginie Soula maintains, Michel, in sharp contrast, "is
the first author to reveal the poetic dimension of oral Kanak literature."[99]
Indeed, Michel was likely the first French person to recognize that the Kanak's
spoken stories constituted an oral literature—what linguist Pio Zirimu would,
a century later, term "orature."[100]

Attention to sound and comprehension of its cultural significance set Michel apart from other Western colonial observers and ethnographers of her
era (as well as those of subsequent decades). The Western cultural bias toward
the visual, at the expense of the other senses, reaches back to Lockean em-
piricism.[101] Expanding one's focus beyond the visual allows an interpretation
and representation that moves closer to multidimensionality and that engages
the intersections of imagistic and aural. Michel composed and taught music,
drew, wrote poetry and fiction, and conducted ethnography. She paid intellectual and emotional attention to sound and vision. Recognizing the centrality of oral traditions to Kanak culture, Michel attempted to honor the resonance

and atmosphere of their tales in order to capture both the stories and their role in the wider Kanak world.[102]

Michel's fascination with and respect for this oral tradition led her to strive for preserving and conveying the tales' liquid flow and texture. Not only was she interested in the Kanak culture and language, but also in language itself. Her connection to the oral reached back to her youth in the Haute-Marne region of France, and to vivid memories of traditional village storytelling. Writing from New Caledonia in 1875, in the newspaper *Petites Affiches de la Nouvelle-Calédonie*, Michel explained, "There, like in the evening gatherings in European villages, the storyteller's suspended words raise ardent curiosity; tales of adventure send shivers running through the audience."[103] Although raised in a privileged milieu, Michel had regular interactions with local peasants, and felt a bond with their world and its spoken culture. Orality resonated deeply with her. In Michel's memoirs, she wrote of the social and linked nature of verbal tales, of the ways in which certain events passed historically through generations of storytellers.[104] She expressed a sense of embodying aspects of the past, of a transgenerational linkage manifested through stories. "I have spoken of atavism. There, at the very root of my life, are legendary stories, dead with those who told them to me. But today I still see these phantoms."[105] While lauding science and progress, Michel simultaneously criticized many facets of her contemporary European society.[106] She embraced the sensorial and social aspects of the oral traditions she had youthfully encountered in the local peasant community, and she considered herself a conduit, both of their form and their content.

In her memoirs, Michel recalled the local *écrègnes* of her childhood, winter evening meetings when women gathered "to spin, to knit, and especially to recount or listen to old stories of spirits dancing on the prairies in robes of flame, and new stories of what was going on in one house or another."[107] These female-only meetings served multiple purposes—work, socializing, news, and cultural transmission—the most important of which, for Michel, was story telling. Recalling the *écrègnes* in her village, led by Marie Verdet, a woman Michel remembered as nearly one hundred years old, Michel evoked both the sound and the feeling of the events, describing clicking knitting needles, a quaking voice, and trembling listeners.[108] Verdet's voice and power, her connection with the past, and the sense of female community, profoundly impressed Michel. The *écrègnes* provided an alternative social template, with a hierarchy based on age and experience, rather than wealth and birth, in a female realm of learning, production, and inclusion. For Michel, this contemporary link to the past remained a potent model.

Kanak spoken culture comported with this Haute-Marne framework, aesthetically, temporally, and politically. In recognizing and appreciating the tales' rootedness in place and in sound, she strove to translate authentically both meaning and feeling. Her acceptance of the Kanak as people co-terminus with the European past dovetailed with her sense of herself as a temporal bridge. Politically, Michel identified a female voice and power in the New Caledonian stories reminiscent of those of the Haute-Marne.

Like the oral stories of her youth, she noted, the Kanak tales passed from generation to generation, told as part of the fabric of daily life. They emerged from and engaged with the sights, sounds, smells, and sensations of the environment. In the first version of the tales published in 1875, Michel explained how, sitting under the coconut palm trees, "like in the old European villages, a suspenseful story awakens ardent curiosity and its adventures run a frisson through the audience. . . . They are able to be infinitely retold without boring the listeners."[109] Most audiences knew the tales, having heard them again and again throughout their lives, but each storyteller uniquely embellished the narratives, keeping them fluid and alive. As Raylene Ramsay explains, "The creative dimension of storytelling in Kanak oral tradition does not reside in the invention of a new or unique story, but rather arises from the skills of the orator and the way in which the story . . . is told."[110] Acts of translation and transcription, therefore, froze one version of an evolving story and extracted it from an otherwise performative context.[111] Michel, unlike other early transcribers of Kanak tales, understood and valued orality as well as the ways in which it differed from the written word. The Kanak, Michel wrote, "have the gift of speech. Their discourse, eloquent and concise . . . clearly renders their thought."[112] She attempted to represent this on the page.

Introducing Tales

In sharp contrast to the French colonial undertakings, Michel recognized and valued Kanak culture at a time when few Europeans believed that the Kanak had one, and she worked to record and disseminate it.[113] As a central part of this project, Michel, with the help of Daoumi, collected, translated, transcribed, and published these stories. Michel initially published her versions of Kanak oral legends and tales serially, and subsequently in two distinctly different editions.[114] The serial pieces appeared between September 29 and December 15, 1875, in the weekly newspaper *Petites affiches de la Nouvelle-Calédonie. Journal des intérêts maritimes, commerciaux & agricoles*. Unsigned, they began with the author's introduction, "Aux amis d'Europe," followed by fourteen tales. The first collected volume, titled *Légendes et chansons de gestes canaques*, appeared that same year, only twenty-one months after Michel arrived in New

Caledonia.[115] In 1885, five years after returning to France from New Caledonia, and seven years after supporting the Kanak in their quashed 1878 uprising against French rule, Michel published an expanded and significantly altered edition of the narratives. Introduced by a thoroughly revised version of "Aux amis d'Europe," the work included sixteen stories, plus sections of ethnolinguistic reflections and lists of Kanak vocabularies.[116]

This later version also carried a slightly changed title: *Légendes et chants de gestes canaques*. The titles of the two editions differed by only one word. In the 1885 version, "chanson de gestes" had become "chants de gestes." Replacing "chansons," which indicated literal songs that were usually ephemeral and often of rustic or peasant origin, with "chants" indicated a shift in Michel's representation of the Kanak legends. The new word "chants" denoted more lyrical and noble pieces.[117] Substituting "chants" for "chansons," Michel re-labeled the tales in a way that elevated and imparted greater legitimacy to them.

Michel's translation and transcription of Kanak lore manifested three of her interests: first, her desire to valorize and publicize Kanak culture; second, her hope to preserve evidence of a purely oral tradition that she feared to be at risk of extinction; and third, her political intentions to undermine European hegemony and to promote a feminist egalitarian global unity. The dissemination of Kanak stories to a French audience could operate in all three ways simultaneously.

Opening the tales with an appeal to her European audience (in both colony and metropole) in the 1875 version of "Aux amis d'Europe," Michel propounded the Kanak's similarities to Europe's historical past. Suggesting cross-cultural links, she asserted that Kanak tales and medieval legends employed similar linguistic approaches. They "are not the same," she wrote, but Kanak tales "may resemble them, due to their ability to frequently materialize the spoken word into symbols."[118] She created a temporal bridge, connecting Medieval European with contemporary Kanak orality and positioning Kanak development with that of Europe's past. Broadening the association, she continued, "These are the tales and songs that cradle all humanity in its infancy."[119] In theorizing bases for her emerging ideas regarding fundamental global human coherence, Michel allowed for such temporal differences, and established these nonsynchronous stories as part of a universal human developmental experience.

The introductory "Aux amis d'Europe" alternates between establishing transcultural, transtemporal connections and introducing Kanak difference—painting a verbal picture while blurring sharp or shocking contrasts. In one telling example, Michel pointed to the prevalence of cannibalism in the tales, while also explaining that cannibalism, while part of Kanak "national customs," had virtually disappeared, "except in some cases of revenge."[120] She recognized cannibalism as part of Kanak history—it appears in several of the tales she translated and transcribed—but she felt that Europeans over-emphasized the custom and mistakenly imagined it lurking within all "primitive" societies. As Roger Boulay, Alice Bullard, and others have shown, the French used allegations of cannibalism as part of their efforts to construct the Kanak as savages who occupied the lowest rung on the civilizational ladder.[121]

Discussing the Kanak school she established, in her memoirs Michel described the colonial authority's ongoing efforts to halt her pedagogical efforts, fearing the "pernicious doctrines" she might teach the Kanak. Declaiming the absurdity of being "forbidden to open their intelligence," Michel gibed sarcastically, "What a shame that they did not send Galliffet to give them cannibalism lessons!"[122] To Michel, the French general Gaston de Galliffet, infamous for his central role in the bloody repression of the Paris Commune, was the real cannibal—the human who brutally consumed other humans. Alluding to the indiscriminate slaughter of thousands of Communards in the final, "Bloody Week" Michel juxtaposed the categories of civilized and savage. She contended that the cannibalistic legacy was an objectionable practice that the Kanak had mostly evolved beyond, and it paled in comparison to contemporary nefarious practices carried out by France, barbarisms many Europeans refused to decry or disown. Describing Europeans' distorted sense of cannibalism as a spectral beast lurking within "primitive men," Michel immediately clarified that "The Kanak race is better than we think."

Choosing and Using Tales

For *Légendes et chansons de gestes canaques*, Michel selected tales she had heard primarily from her informant Daoumi and his brother, probably both in translation to French and in the original language.[123] Michel likely worked with Daoumi to comprehend the context, experience, and means of delivery as well as the audience and typical receptions.[124] As literary scholar François Bogliolo writes, Michel "interpreted the interpreter."[125] Daoumi's perspective and understanding of his culture's tales and legends mediated Michel's encounter with them. Her translations thus represent Michel's comprehension and interpretation of Daoumi's translations of particular versions of traditional stories. At that point, Bogliolo argues, "the legend becomes situated outside of the Kanak realm and outside of the French realm, in a literary space transformed by the encounter, becoming something separate yet part of both."[126] Raylene Ramsay has suggested that this third space, or place of hybridity, where

Kanak and French meet, is where the transcriber and translator makes their mark on the orature.[127] Michel chose to give voice to the Kanak, to use the first person, and to use the present tense. In this, she followed Kanak tradition, where even ancient stories are told using present language, reflecting a cultural understanding of the past as integral to and inseparable from the present. Unlike most translators, Michel—attuned to temporalities different from Western linearity and sympathetic to transtemporal connections—used the present tense in her versions of Kanak lore.[128]

Yet in the process of selecting, translating, and transcribing the oral tales, Michel participated in an imperial ethnographic project. As European travelers and colonizers had done for centuries, Michel collected and recorded evidence of an Indigenous society, and transmitted her results—presumed to be the truth of that world—to a European audience. Imperial expansion led to the development of ethnographic studies, as the colonizers/imperialists sought to "understand" Indigenous populations. Based on the personal encounter between the European ethnographer and people of other cultures, the resulting reports formed the bases of anthropology, which Johannes Fabian has argued, "contributed above all to the intellectual justification of the colonial enterprise."[129]

Though Michel, by contrast, used ethnography in order to undermine colonialism, she nonetheless presented a particular version of her understanding of Kanak culture. Hers became the public voice of the Kanak. She wrote and spoke for the other. "Ethnography is situated between powerful systems of meaning," James Clifford explains. "It poses questions at the boundaries of civilizations, cultures. . . . It decodes and recodes . . . and is itself part of these processes."[130] Michel's interventions occurred at the intersections of European and Kanak cultures, mediated by the Kanak's experience of colonization. The recorded versions of specifically chosen Kanak tales reflected Michel's presuppositions, prejudices, and goals—both conscious and unconscious. Her translations became part of the ethnographic process itself. "No ethnography," anthropologist Micaela di Leonardo clarifies, "is ever entirely nonevaluative."[131] Through selection, translation, interpretation, and transcription, Michel's resultant written versions of Kanak tales exemplify Clifford's assertion that "ethnographic truths are inherently partial."[132]

Michel used the tales to advance her own politics. Among the stories that she translated and transcribed were those in which women appear as strong, central characters. Kanak culture, Michel implied, celebrated the heroism of women as much as that of men. By printing narratives of women who fight like warriors, or of women who are incorruptible, brave, and always truthful, Michel held up a model of equality based in tradition, one that she intended her metropolitan and colonial French readers to see as an implicit criticism of French inequality.[133] She simultaneously appropriated aspects of Kanak culture and worked to advance Kanak status. This seemingly contradictory approach clearly emerged as a conscious political decision on her part.

Through her growing knowledge of Kanak language, culture, gender roles, and hierarchies, Michel recognized women's material and discursive oppression, explaining in *Légendes et chants* how the Kanak word for woman, *némo*, was synonymous with "nothing."[134] In a volume of her memoirs, published after her return from New Caledonia, Michel examined Kanak family and marriage structures, later explaining that "traditionally, marriages are contracted between parents when the future spouses are still young. The girl's parents receive gifts of food from the boy's parents, establishing an irrevocable purchase. . . . The unions are thus often badly matched . . . and the woman has no other choice than to run away from the village."[135] Michel clearly disapproved of Kanak marriage practices, terming the exchange between the parents of the girl and the boy an *achat*, a sale, and pointing to the irrevocable, and often ill-suited, nature of the relationship. Many Kanak tales transcribed by other anthropologists and ethnographers include casual references to giving a young woman to a man in marriage—with no discussion or implication of consent. Michel published no narratives making any such reference.

In both a portion of her memoirs only published serially in the revolutionary newspaper *L'égalité* during her life, and in her unpublished *Souvenirs de Calédonie* (Memories of Caledonia), she did address Kanak women's subjugation. Michel presented a starker, less varnished vision of their lives. Having chosen to keep this information from global view while presenting a consistently positive image of the New Caledonians through their stories, she later acknowledged it to select present and future audiences. Explaining Kanak women's status as "nothing, or an object of utility," Michel also decried the inequities of social practices surrounding Kanak marriage, including brutal, gender-based punishment.[136] "The men . . . are often very jealous of their women. It is said that they kill them if the women are found to be guilty. In cases of adultery, the cuckolded man's tribesmen carry out revenge by submitting the adulterous woman to the ultimate affronts [*les derniers outrages*]. The men can have as many wives as they are able to feed; they make them their slaves."[137] Michel recounted examples and customs of misogynist violence, including gang rape as revenge for adultery, as well as patriarchal dominance, and she described women's "degraded" status in her unpublished *Souvenirs de Calédonie*, but she did not pursue these issues in her published work.[138] Nor did she discuss speaking with Kanak women, or attempt to convey their perspectives on their own lives. While Michel's report on gender violence clearly goes well beyond the "childhood foolishness" to which she attributed other problems in Kanak culture, Michel preferred to look ahead to potential advances rather than confronting the existing, gender-based oppressions within the community.

Telling Tales

Michel interpreted the legends to emphasize women's value and strength, intending to present a more "civilized" vision of the Kanak.[139] For example, Michel tells the story of "Idara la prophetess" ("Idara the prophetess"), an elderly Kanak woman who sings "La chanson des blancs" ("The song of the whites"), an account of the white man's arrival and subsequent abuse and betrayal of the Kanak people.[140] Michel presented two different versions of this tale in the 1875 and 1885 volumes. In the first version "Idara is the daughter of tribes, she has fought with the brave against the pale men. Idara is the mother of heroes." Not only is she the mother of heroes and heroic herself, but Idara also gives voice to the epic. In the later edition, Idara elaborates on the whites' infamies, lamenting, "They forced the young boys and girls to serve them, they took everything that we had. The Whites promised us the sky and the earth, but they gave nothing but sadness." In the 1885 volume, Michel also added introductory paragraphs, explaining that "La chanson des blancs," as told by Idara—a warrior, mother, prophet, healer, storyteller, and sorcerer—was the oldest *chanson de geste* her informant Daoumi knew. Michel asserted the importance of this narrative in which a powerful woman played a central role in Kanak survival and told the tale of colonial betrayal and destruction. Idara embodied the voice of the people—even within a culture where "woman counts as nothing." Connecting Kanak inequities with those of Europe, Michel underscored that "human illogicality is everywhere."[141]

Women play powerful roles in the majority of narratives in both the 1875 and 1885 versions of Michel's *Légendes*. Both human and mythical, female characters display independence and bravery. They are strong, clever, and embody self-sacrifice. "La génie Ondoué" is a tale that Michel likened to the legend of Faust, "with the difference that Faust . . . is a woman: the sorcerer Keidée . . . and that Mephistopheles is the genie Ondoué."[142] Michel equated the Kanak legend with this European counterpart, but with a notable gender switch. This female Faustian character, the tale explains, demonstrates deep independence, "while still young, leaving her tribe and building her house near the Peak of the Dead; she never had a fiancé and she had refused so many that no young man would any longer dare to offer her the bamboo comb [traditional marital offering]. . . . They knew that she did not want to marry."[143] Similarly, in

"Le lit des aïeux" ("The bed of the ancestors"), the mythical Téi, "the daughter of the cemetery . . . no longer had parents and the dead had adopted her."[144] A winged figure who floats on the wind, Téi lives among the deceased on a high mountain, where she sings ceaselessly. The tale tells how Nahoa (The Morning), son of a Great Leader, proposes marriage to Téi. He boasts, "Our mothers and wives are heavy with fat; they eat the most beautiful fruits of the forest, the best fish from the big lake; they wear fringed belts and have tortoiseshell combs in their hair." Having presented this life of comfort and luxury, he proclaims, "I am the son of the Great Leader, king from birth. . . . Will you come live in my house, oh daughter of the cemetery?" In response, "Téi sweetly shakes her head and disappears into the funerary forest."[145]

In both stories, women reject marriage in favor of freedom. They demonstrate self-reliance and competence, living lives independent not just from husbands, but from human society as well. Literally transcending the earthly world and its limitations, Keidée constructs her home up high near the Peak of the Dead, and Téi flies among the mountains, also among the dead. Yet while each removes herself from human social bonds, neither rejects community—they choose the spirit world instead. In traditional Kanak culture, there exists no separation between the living and the dead.[146] These tales show capable, self-sufficient females who individually separate themselves from quotidian life and its concomitant gendered expectations to engage themselves in an available alternate realm. Although mythical, Keidée and Téi's rejections of the status quo represent both female and larger human possibilities.

Michel presented these stories as positive exemplars of Kanak culture and as evidence of the complexity and equity of Kanak civilization. Other tales also involve strong women and mothers, including "Déluge canaque" ("Kanak deluge"), an origin myth involving Paia, the brave daughter of warriors, who protects her children from a cataclysmic storm.[147] The tale not only lauds women's power and ability, but also suggests their cultural significance, in playing a central and heroic role in an origin narrative.

In "Les souffles" ("The winds"), one of several tales in which women commit suicide, three beautiful girls successively jump into a chasm, "going toward the winds that call them, pushed by the winds that pursue them."[148] Consistent with an indistinct line between life and death, suicide—according to ethnographer and missionary Maurice Leenhardt, who lived and worked in New Caledonia several decades after Michel—allowed a person to pass from living to "a state of invisibility and release from the body, where, liberated from the laws of this world, they can increase their strength tenfold."[149] It was an acceptable act. Leenhardt explained that women in particular used suicide to shame and punish unfaithful husbands, recognizing it as an ongoing revenge.

Suicide, in this understanding, allowed women a social power otherwise denied them.[150] The girls in "Les souffles" follow or are pushed by the wind, easily slipping from positions of passivity to ones of potential power. While Michel did not articulate this understanding of suicide, her inclusion of several tales involving women taking their own lives, as well as those featuring women who choose the world of the dead over that of the living, reflect her transmission of Kanak understandings of suicide and death, which she implicitly contrasted with those typical of European cultures.

Michel integrated death into her own writing and thought. She titled the second volume of her memoirs *À travers la mort* (Through death).[151] In the first volume, *À travers la vie* (Through life), published in 1886, she presented the work to the reader: "Here it is, laying on the table, the cadaver of my life: dissect it at your leisure."[152] Deeply marked by the loss of comrades and friends in the bloodbath that ended the Commune, subsequently by the high mortality of fellow deportees, and again by the death of her cherished mother the year before the first volume's publication, Michel lived with death. As exemplified by her self-conception as a temporal bridge, as one who could still "see the phantoms" of the female-centered Haute-Marne peasant culture, she challenged the binary between the living and the dead. In an undated poem titled "Aux morts" ("To the dead), she wrote, "In the great silence in the shadow, across space and time, oh dead taken back by the nightfall, you are there alive."[153] Michel's openness to fluidity and alternate ways of seeing contributed to her receptivity to and respect for Kanak culture.[154]

Another story relating women's abilities involved evoking the riches of the sea and women's roles in its harvest, "Les jeune filles d'Owie" ("The young girls of Owie") appeared in distinctly different versions in the 1875 and 1885 editions of the tales. These revisions reflect Michel's continual editorial efforts to make the stories portray women more positively. In the first rendering, the men are central, fishing and singing in their pirogues at sea and braving the "black devil-fish slipping between the red coral branches." The story tells how "the ocean blooms and is filled with riches for the tribe's sons. To take the riches, one must dare."[155] The women remain on the shore, playing a supportive, mystical role in hunting for fish, "hitting the ground with heavy bamboo sticks or rubbing palm fronds together, accompanying the songs."[156] In the second, 1885 edition, Michel minimized men's role and made the women primary and powerful. Rather than a blossoming sea filled with riches for "the tribe's sons," it now offers up "flowers for the tribes." The women no longer merely accompany the men's songs, as they summon the fish by beating bamboo and rubbing coconut branches—the women sing in their own right. And, Michel explains, "They are tall, they are strong, and they do not complain of their burden. . . . The daughters of Owié are brave, but they prefer to hear the rumbling of the wave than to see the blood of friends."[157] Maintaining the structure and central message of having women call the fish to the fishermen, Michel presented a story that retained distinct gender roles while shifting and thus balancing their significance in providing the tribe with sustenance through fishing. The 1885 version allowed the "daughters of Owié" greater agency in singing themselves rather than merely accompanying the singing men. It also glorified women's stature, strength, and bravery, as well as their preference for peace. The oral tales became reflections of Kanak culture, but one mediated by Michel's political interests.

Just as she had recontextualized Kanak tales from the Stone Age to the Middle Ages between the 1875 and 1885 editions of *Légendes* (while keeping the Kanak themselves situated in the earlier period), Michel altered and amended "Les filles d'Owié" to present a more egalitarian, idealized version of Kanak society. The process of selecting particular stories from among those she encountered, combined with her purposeful translation and adaptation of those tales, resulted in a distinct rendering of the Kanak world. Her ethnographic privilege allowed her to determine and shape this rendering. Michel created a hybrid literature, pulling oral legends from the Kanak realm, preserving these stories and respecting their orality, but imbuing them with egalitarian and in some cases feminist politics. She issued a package of edited tales intended to elevate the Kanak's global status and to weave them into the European historical narrative, while also demonstrating an alternative, valorized culture to France and the West.[158]

Tales Untold

What Michel omitted from her collections is also significant. As mentioned above, Michel avoided reference to women's lack of agency in Kanak marriages and society. While we cannot know precisely which stories Michel encountered, in her effort to present the Kanak in the best possible light, she did not recount narratives that could offend European sensibilities. By excising references to bodily functions, as Raylene Ramsay suggests, or rejecting tales involving sexuality or scatology, Michel presented accounts she deemed palatable to European readers.[159] In her examination of the body in Pacific Francophone literature, the literary scholar Titaua Porcher-Wiart discusses a transcription of a Polynesian myth, in which parts of the creator god Ta'aroa's body are used to construct the first house of god. "The backbone was the ridgepole, the ribs were the supporters," but, Porcher-Wiart notes, "as for the sex [organs] of God, it is surprising that no mention is made of it when one considers the important role of sexuality in Pacific societies."[160] Explaining that Christian missionaries, in translating and transcribing narratives, would omit elements they considered immodest, Porcher-Wiart suggests that they would have excluded any mention of the male god's genitals in this myth.[161] Although Michel approached oral stories from a profoundly antireligious stance, she nonetheless employed a filter similar to those used by missionaries—omitting details, or entire tales, that too closely linked to the body or its functions. Whether these stories reflected or exaggerated normal Kanak experiences, the physical and sexual stuff of life, Michel either considered them base and thus uncivilized or believed that her European audience would think the same.

Many tales directly engaged the human body. As Florence Klein explains, for the Kanak "a person's body did not have an individual existence."[162] They understood humans as intimately interlinked with each other. The Kanak "kamo"—or personage—was not conceptualized as isolated or individualized. It existed not just within a person's body, but also in relation with other human bodies, the land, or the plant and mineral world.[163] Michel recognized and admired the Kanak sense of interconnectedness; it meshed well with her anarchist worldview, which emphasized global human unity. In terms of the physicality of bodies, Michel undoubtedly understood the Kanak sense of the body as one profoundly different from that of Europeans'—a fact clearly manifested in each culture's attire. According to travel writer and colonial administrator Charles Lemire, Kanak men traditionally ornamented their hair with fronds and feathers and wore a bat-skin necklace, shell-embellished bands around their naked legs, shell or pearl bracelets, large earrings, a skin or cord belt, and penis wraps (an honored man could wear one that descended to the ground). Women wore bat-skin or seed necklaces, as well as a belt and skirt of palm.[164] Western images and representations of the Kanak circulated during this era supported exoticized misconceptions about their savagery and coarse sexuality, ideas based at least in part on European interpretations of Kanak self-presentation. Seeking to counter these notions, Michel completely omitted tales that might support them.

An example of the types of tales that Michel omitted include those with scatological references. In a widely known Kanak story, likely intended as a cautionary tale about work and proper feminine behavior, two sisters live together and share responsibility for finding food. The younger, named Mounhouda, says she will go out and catch some shrimp. Instead, when she arrives at the shore she removes her two eyes, places them on a rock, and dances. When she finishes dancing, Mounhouda calls to her eyes and they jump back into their sockets. Returning home, she tells her sister that she had encountered some boys exercising, and they had prevented her from fishing. The younger sister does this day after day, until finally the older secretly follows her, sees the eye removal and dancing, and vengefully steals her younger sister's eyes, which she brings home, cooks, and serves to her now-blind, unknowing sibling.[165] Life goes on, and at some point the older sister asks Mounhouda to fetch some water, saying it is her turn to work. Instead of looking for water, the younger sister urinates into the water gourd. When the elder sister realizes this, she angrily reveals to the younger that she had been made to eat her own eyes. The two women fall to fighting and kill each other.[166]

Michel also elided narratives involving scatology. In another story involving siblings, the elder Bèn "is a farmer; his brother is a sloth."[167] Shirking his work responsibilities, the younger sibling, Piwuwu, asks Bèn to prepare a meal for him, fabulating that a Great Chief in a nearby village had asked him to speak at his celebration. The older brother prepares a basket of food, and Piwuwu sets off, but subsequently stops along the road and "stuffs himself." Having eaten everything in the basket, "he balances himself on a tree and allows his excrements to fall, then he goes back to his brother's house." This repeats day after day, with the younger brother contending that the fête is continuing and the Great Chief requires his presence. Bèn grows suspicious, follows Piwuwu's route, and finds a pile of excrement "the height of a house." Recognizing that his brother had leaned on the tree while defecating, Bèn subtlety cuts into the tree. The next day, when his younger brother once again eats all the food and then props himself up on the tree to defecate, it breaks, and Piwuwu falls headfirst into his own excrement. Caught deceiving his brother and behaving slothfully, Piwuwu is punished and shamed.[168]

Another tale that engaged sibling relations, "Le frère et la soeur" ("The brother and sister"), addressed the Kanak's strong incest taboo; it too was not included in Michel's collections.[169] As related in a rather graphic tale translated by ethnographer Jean Guiart, one manifestation of the taboo prevented a younger sister and older brother seeing each other's naked bodies.[170] In "Le frère et la soeur," a blind, childless woman lives alone. She has a brother, "but tradition forbids her brother from caring for her and feeding her." Unable to search for food or to ask her brother's help and not knowing quite what to do, "she speaks to her vagina and tells it to search for food for the two of them. The vagina detaches from the woman and leaves with a basket. . . . It returns with a full basket, and they prepare food together." Warning her vagina to carefully avoid meeting her brother because of the taboo, the woman sends it out again the next day. Despite the vagina's efforts to hide in a stream, it encounters and speaks to her brother, although it refuses to admit its owner's identity. Upon learning that her brother has seen it, the extremely angry woman hangs herself in her house.[171]

None of these stories, widespread among Kanak tales of the time, appeared among Michel's publications. All three narratives provide cautionary tales in terms of acceptable behaviors within familial and social relations, and two involve women surviving without men's aid. Yet the use of scatology and sexuality represented a discourse that Michel chose to avoid. This was not merely a case of circumventing non-European sensibilities. Both suicide and the idea of interactions between the living and the dead fell outside of Western norms, but Michel nonetheless translated and transcribed stories engaging these topics. The scatological and the sexual, even when employed to bolster characteristics such as honesty, responsibility, and hard work, remained off-limits for her. Acutely aware of how such references would bolster European perceptions of the Kanak as base savages, Michel presented a desexualized, sanitized version of the Kanak to her readers.

Imperialist Anti-Imperialism?

Michel intended to introduce Kanak culture to France, in effect re-presenting a people the metropole had deemed savage, base, and devoid of culture. She did so primarily by translating, transcribing, and publishing Kanak tales. Michel augmented, edited, and transformed the narratives; pushing the boundaries of oral transmission and transcription, she shaped the stories for political ends. External to the culture, although sympathetic to and—within her milieu—respectful of it, Michel's imprint pulled the tales from their Kanak rootedness and created a European-infused Kanak hybrid mythology. Her published versions of their lore reflect Michel's feminist and anarchist politics, emphasizing gender equity and women's strength; the stories also appear with form and content she would have considered palatable to Europeans. As with most ethnographers of her era, the power differentials inherent in the colonial relationship enabled Michel to shape a version of the Indigenous people about whom she wrote. Her translations both distance and assimilate, exoticize and familiarize. But through her fealty to the stories, and by taking them seriously as literature and a kind of history, Michel ultimately insisted on the legitimacy of Kanak life, epistemology, and tradition.

European audiences recognized the published tales for both their ethnographic and linguistic contributions. Notably, Charles Letourneau, the secretary of France's Society of Anthropology from 1887 until his 1902 death, cited

Michel's *Légendes et chants de gestes canaques* as a legitimate scholarly work. In his *L'évolution littéraire dans les diverses races humaines* (Literary evolution in diverse human races), Letourneau extensively quoted Michel's translations of Kanak narratives, arguing, for example, that "Chanson des blancs is the work of a woman clearly expert in Kanak poetry, and this fact is not exceptional."[172] Given his position as a widely regarded anthropologist, Letourneau's recognition and use of Michel's work demonstrate the influence of her ethnography in scholarly anthropology.[173]

Other authors and journals accepted Michel's version of the tales as what *La revue socialiste* termed "faithfully translated" in an 1885 review of the second edition.[174] The *Revue française de l'étranger et des colonies* (The French foreign and colonial review) extensively discussed and reprinted several of Michel's Kanak tales, explaining—per Michel—that women play important roles in the legends, in spite of their inferior status. Further following Michel's lead, the journal stated that "the Kanak hardly lack intelligence" and that "perhaps by undergoing race-mixing, it will be possible to assimilate them to our civilization."[175] While undoubtedly imperialist, the journal reiterated Michel's suggestion that miscegenation could possibly save Kanak culture, something she had implied in a letter written on board the *Virginie*, on her voyage to New Caledonia. The *Revue française* added an assertion of Kanak intelligence and assimilability that echoed Michel's stance while clashing with the assumptions made by French colonial authorities.

The following year, in 1886, the *Revue de linguistique et de philologie comparée* (Comparative linguistic and philological review) included Michel's collection under "Bibliographie des traditions et de la literature populaire en orale de France d'Outremer" (Bibliography of French overseas oral popular traditions and literature).[176] A decade later, the multivolume collection *Les étapes de la chanson: Histoire pittoresque de la chanson à travers les ages* (The stages of song: Picturesque history of song across the ages) took Michel's telling of Kanak legends as proof that their tales emerged from the "dawn of humanity." The author, Henri Papin, commented on the surprising contrast between Kanak women's subjugation and the poetry that "blooms in their full hearts."[177] Michel had considerable success in her efforts to re-present the Kanak to a French audience, emphasizing their intelligence and minimizing their gender hierarchies.

Not all readers accepted Michel's authority or the veracity of her version of the legends. In the *Revue des traditions populaires* (Review of popular traditions), for example, folklorist Paul Sébillot questioned the value of the tales published by Michel, whom he termed "the celebrated agitator." His article, "Les femmes et des traditions populaire" (Women and popular traditions), contended that the narratives "must . . . be the object of strong reservations."[178] Skeptical of her ability to collect stories, Sébillot included her with other nineteenth-century female folklorists, who, he alleged, often "embroidered, elongated, or disturbed" the material they gathered.[179] His sweeping dismissal of women folklorists dovetailed with his suspicion regarding Michel's politics, resulting in his damning review. A German journal, *Englische studien: Organ für englische philologie unter mitberücksichtigung des englischen unterrichts auf höheren schulen* (English studies: Organ for English philology with special attention to the teaching of English in secondary schools), held a similar perspective, calling the work of "the famous Frenchwoman" untrustworthy, unscholarly, and confused.[180]

Michel's exposure to the Kanak and her experience in New Caledonia altered and expanded her politics. From her previously Eurocentric position, Michel integrated a non-European dynamic and internationalism. Seeing France's domination and denigration of the Kanak intensified her awareness of racialized oppression, leading Michel to broaden her class-and gender-based analysis, thus developing an anti-imperial and anticolonial politics that was feminist as well as anti-racist. Living as a convict within the prison colony, observing the French exploitation of the Kanak, and ultimately working with the Indigenous population, Michel constructed a profound critique of the French imperial project and its attack on Kanak sovereignty, economy, community, and life. This censure meshed easily with her long-term resistance to the French state. Michel negatively compared French political culture with that of the Kanak, intending to undermine European dominance and assumptions of civilizational superiority.

Michel viewed the Kanak as a "young," not-yet developed race of people; in the Rousseauian tradition, she argued that the French could learn from this "youthful" race. "Their curiosity of the unknown is as great as ours or possibly even greater; their perseverance is great, and it is common that—in the effort to understand something interesting—they will think about it for several days or even years."[181] Michel wrote repeatedly of the childlike nature of the New Caledonian people. In a chapter of *Légendes et chants de gestes* entitled "Aptitudes de Kanak" ("Kanak aptitudes"), she held that "after having discussed many things about the Kanak, one must return to the initial impression that they have the qualities and vices of childhood."[182] And yet, she continued, "Loving the unknown, taken by the epic poetry that frees them . . . they will question you for an hour, and if they have not understood immediately, they will ask you for weeks, months, years after (having long reflected), 'You know, I understand what you said the other day.'"[183] Suggesting that this condition can lead to a more engaged, more contemplative, and more egalitarian way of life, Michel lauded what she perceived as the Kanak's natural curiosity and persistence, qualities that made them open to historical advancement; they were akin to educable children. Here she viewed cultural development in terms of the individual body, growing from infancy to adulthood. This constituted a cultural version of the nineteenth-century concept of "ontogeny recapitulates phylogeny," in which the development of an individual reenacts the development of the species.[184] Employing this logic, Michel warned that if "enthused by their progress," one is suddenly "reminded of reality by some childishness, one should not be disillusioned by this; don't children become men? It is the same with peoples."[185]

Constructing the Kanak in the romantically anachronistic space of youth, Michel associated childhood with the Stone Age and correspondingly maturity with Western civilization. She believed the New Caledonians lagged behind developmentally, but through expedited growth and progress, they had the potential to progress rapidly through evolutionary history. Michel approached her ethnographic project with a sense of respect and a degree of responsibility, but lacking an acknowledgment of the power that the imperialist relationship granted her.[186]

Michel's self-definition as anti-imperialist thus proves incomplete. Suggesting the possibility of race-mixing to ensure Kanak cultural survival, locating the Kanak as coterminous with the European past, promoting a radical anarchist version of Western education to expedite Kanak civilizational evolution, and publishing versions of Kanak lore altered to align with her own political and cultural standards, all constituted imperial projects. In each case, Michel's actions differed dramatically from the French state's imperial undertakings—in terms of intention, application, and impact—but they were European interventions nonetheless.

Michel's language of liberation reflected the complexity of her politics. It involved using the tales both for her own ends and in support of Kanak culture. It also defied a binary between pro-imperial and anti-imperial positions. Although an avowed anti-imperialist and critic of existing empire, Michel held no absolute noninterventionist line. A revolutionary anarchist feminist and life-long radical, she was also a product of European education and culture, operating under particular historical understandings of what it meant to be pro- or anti-imperial. Opposition to empire emerged within the context of the era's racial and civilizational categories, hierarchies that could be rejected but not fully escaped.[187] Michel used the tools available to her, tools tinged with white imperial privilege, in order to undermine imperialism. She also pragmatically considered erstwhile imperial programs, which she appropriated and altered to advance Kanak survival and liberation, while simultaneously furthering her broader politics. The constitution of "anti-imperial" emerged, and still exists, as both socially constructed and historically specific—a shifting and subjective category.

Today New Caledonia uneasily remains a special collectivity of France, riven over the question of independence, which most Kanak support.[188] Many contemporary Kanak, themselves opposed to empire, hold Michel in high regard—both for her support of their 1878 uprising against French imperial rule and for her translation and transcription of their tales. To commemorate the one-hundredth anniversary of Michel's death in 2005, the Tjibaou Cultural Center, the dynamic heart of Kanak cultural and intellectual life in Nouméa, mounted an exhibition on the Communard deportees, giving Michel primacy of place.[189] The following year, Marie-Claude Tjibaou, a widely respected contemporary Kanak politician, activist, and widow of slain independence leader Jean-Marie Tjibaou, wrote that Michel "has captured the music of our languages, creating a kind of symphony which, if it does not constitute a formal linguistic work, nonetheless represents a beautiful homage to our language."[190] This acclamation of Michel's efforts to honor Kanak stories appears in the introduction that Marie-Claude Tjibaou wrote for a new edition of Michel's translated Kanak tales. Such an unmistakable tribute by one of today's most prominent Kanak is a fitting recognition of Michel's legacy. Both accommodating and resisting the intellectual milieu of her time, she laid the groundwork for later anticolonial projects. Michel's work illustrates the complex possibilities and limits of enacting an anarchist anti-imperial feminist vision.[191]

CHAPTER 5

Universal Language, Universal Education, Universal Revolution

Comparing New Caledonia's Kanak to the French in her *Mémoires*, Michel asked,

> Which is the superior being, the one who, through a thousand difficulties, assimilates foreign knowledge and makes it useful to his race, or the one who, well-armed, annihilates those more poorly equipped? If it is proof of superiority that the other races efface themselves before the whites, how many legions of tigers, elephants, and lions would seem superior to us if they suddenly covered Europe and attacked us! The primitive monsters, in their destructive triumph, would, terribly, be our masters![1]

Rejecting the equation of military might with any but the basest physical supremacy, Michel lauded the Kanak for their openness and adaptability, sharply contrasting these traits to France's mindless destructiveness. Inverting the stereotypes of savagery and civilization, she likened France's brutal takeover of New Caledonia—and by extension, all imperial undertakings—to rampaging wild beasts overrunning and overtaking Europe.

Michel's championing of the Kanak in their 1878 uprising against the French colonial authority affirmed her frequently articulated opposition to imperialism and colonialism. Among the French deportees to the New Caledonian penal colony—including the 4,500 Paris Commune veterans—only Michel consistently supported the indigenous insurgency. She engaged with the Kanak in ways that created connections, understandings, and empathies that her comrades lacked. Few of Michel's fellow former Communards, having been politicized in a radicalized metropolitan context focused on the nation and internationalism—but not particularly on imperialism—were concerned with issues of empire; their experiences in the penal colony did not alter this.

Michel's trajectory differed dramatically from her fellow political exiles, as it did from the other feminists engaged in empire. Just as her interactions with the Kanak exposed her to their culture and tales, which led to her translation, transformation, transcription, and publication of the narratives, her contact with Kanak languages also had intellectual and political results. Michel ultimately strove to universalize what she had learned from the Kanak, arguing for its global pertinence, linguistically, educationally, even epistemologically. First, in the era of Esperanto, amid the promotion of multiple other proposed universal tongues, Michel advocated the Kanak Bichelamar—a pidgin used for both external and internal trade among the Indigenous people, speakers of twenty-eight different languages—as an extant, functioning universal vernacular.[2] Second, in New Caledonia, Michel's encounters with the Kanak transformed her pedagogical theory, encouraging and sharpening instructional philosophy and methods she had begun developing in France. She articulated and expanded her radical anarchist feminist pedagogy in New Caledonia and then continued it in England and Algeria. Recognizing Kanak culture and ways of knowing, while abjuring accepted European pedagogical approaches, Michel's goal of what would today be termed "decolonizing the curriculum" entailed both teaching and learning from the Kanak.

Despite her advocacy for the Kanak and self-identification as an anti-imperialist, Michel remained imbricated in the rhetoric of empire. She often described the Kanak as unspoiled, childlike, and "natural" in ways intended to praise aspects of their lives and culture. Michel's tacit acceptance of the dominant European evolutionary hierarchy, although reemployed as an intended critique of those norms, exemplified the pervasiveness of the era's discourses of empire and race. Yet her experience in the South Pacific led her to a political stance deeply at odds with that of her compatriot prisoners.

As the previous chapter showed, Michel's engagement with everyday aspects of New Caledonia—the prison colony, Kanak oral culture, and the ideas and practices of civilizational rankings—shaped her opposition to colonialism and reinforced her anarchist feminism. Her activism, in turn, influenced each context. Alongside the everyday, Michel also used universalism as a strategy against colonialism. Her longstanding attention to questions of language, education, and revolution highlights structures and institutions linked to universalism—not the accepted nineteenth-century French universalism, but rather a radically democratic and inclusive idea of unity. Through these frameworks, Michel worked toward eradicating global divisions and overcoming imperial dominations. Discovering and creating human bridges, Michel refuted the widely accepted idea that essential differences existed between genders, religions, and races. In seeking the universal, she endeavored to excavate connections between peoples, bonds that she argued lay buried beneath artificial divisions created by linguistic, ideological, and political differences.

Michel strove to revolutionize and decolonize language, erasing international and class barriers to communication and expression; to revolutionize and decolonize education, destabilizing conventional forms and hierarchies of learning and knowledge; and to (literally) revolutionize and decolonize specifically France, New Caledonia, and Algeria, but more broadly and ambitiously, the capitalist and imperialist worlds. To achieve these ends, Michel advocated new ways to speak, to teach, and to revolt against capital and empire—connecting the New Caledonian milieu with her experiences in England, Algeria, and France in a commitment to the universality of human experience and justice.

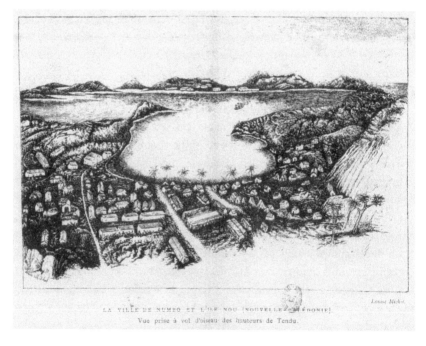

5.1. Drawing by Louise Michel: "The City of Numbo and Nou Island (New Caledonia). Bird's eye view from the heights of Tendu." Includes a portion of the prison complex. 1870s. Bibliothèque Nationale de France.

Unifying Languages

The New Caledonian Kanak have twenty-eight languages (not including dialects), which are specifically connected to individual islands and to particular valleys in the mountainous Grand Terre, the largest island in the archipelago. Each language represents a strong historical and spiritual link to place and forms an elemental aspect of Kanak identity.[3] In addition to these languages, the Kanak have long utilized Bichelamar, a pidgin composed of English, French, and Polynesian and Southeast Asian dialects, as well as various Kanak languages. Originating before colonization but after contact with Europeans, Bichelamar ("Bislama" in English) emerged as a trading language and evolved over the centuries. Coincident with the initial appearance of Esperanto, widely touted as an international tongue to transcend nationalist divisions and promote global peace, Bichelamar, in Michel's view, was already an entrenched, living universal language. For the Kanak, Bichelamar allowed the perpetuation of their local languages and identities while engaging in both internal and international trade. For Michel, their development and utilization of Bichelamar represented an inclusive and transformative example for Europeans to emulate.

The roots and history of Bichelamar, as a primarily oral language, remain murky. Its name likely comes either from the Portuguese *bicho de mar*, the term for sea cucumber (dried sea cucumber was valued as an aphrodisiac in China), or from a combination of the English word "beach" and the Portuguese *mar*, or sea.[4] Originally a pidgin English, a French-based version developed around the New Caledonian capital Nouméa after France took possession of the archipelago in 1853. The two pidgins coexisted for about fifteen years, but the French-based Bichelamar overtook the English-rooted dialect by the time of Michel's deportation.[5] French engineer and author Jules Garnier, writing of his first voyage to New Caledonia, explained, "It is a language . . . spoken on all of the coasts and allows communication between the Kanak, and occasionally between the whites themselves when they are from different nations."[6] Garnier pragmatically described the purpose and uses of Bichelamar in a strictly regional register. When Michel encountered the language, she saw a tool for furthering her universal, unifying goals.

In her memoir of her time in New Caledonia, Michel negatively compared Europe's fragmentation to Kanak cohesion. She wrote: "Right now in New Caledonia, they have taken the first step toward peace between peoples, the universal language, composed simply of common terms from each nation. . . . Bichelamar already includes French, English, and Chinese words. Who knows what strange and rich constructions will naturally form from these diverse elements. The civilized nations should be able to follow the example of the savages."[7] From her perspective, the existence of Bichelamar underscored the absurdity of Europeans calling themselves "civilized" and the Kanak "savage"; here she used the terms ironically, employing the era's accepted labels while clearly making a counterargument. Unlike the Europeans, the Kanak had already undertaken measures toward linguistic unity—which Michel designated "the first step toward peace."[8]

Addressing "European Friends" in the 1885 introduction to the second edition of *Légendes et chants de gestes Kanak*, Michel wrote: "Your philosophers discuss the possibility of a universal language chosen from among the dead languages, our people of the Stone Age use and *live* this language, taken from the English, French, Spanish, Chinese, from the sea cucumber fishermen, their everyday language. . . . This bizarre dialect, is called 'Bichelamar' ('deer of the sea'), another name for the sea cucumber, an object of coastal commerce."[9] Michel lauded the Kanak's development and use of this hybrid vernacular, which, she contended, "will become a language as all others . . . once it has its storytellers and poets."[10] Michel identified revolutionary potential in language. She considered Bichelamar a unifying force, a living creation rooted in multiple tongues. While linguistically a pidgin (based on both its rootedness in one language and its functioning almost exclusively as a second language), Bichelamar appeared to Michel as closer to what Édouard Glissant would later define as a creole. "As long as a creole language continues to combine the forms of two (or more) linguistic traditions, the product of this synthesis is a new kind of expression, a supplement to the two (or more) original roots, or series of roots, from which this creole language was born."[11] Seeing in Bichelamar the amalgamation of multiple linguistic traditions, Michel imagined that "strange and rich constructions will naturally form from these diverse elements."[12] The result of such a synthesis, the new creation from the melding of cultures and languages—what Glissant termed "creolization"—held both unifying and revolutionary possibilities.[13]

In the quotation above "To European Friends," Michel aligned herself with the Kanak, calling them "our people," in contrast to "your [European] philosophers." Yet she referred to the Kanak as "Stone Age," again demonstrating complicity with empire despite her commitment to anti-imperialism. Profoundly critical of imperial theory and practice—condemning "the White men, there [in New Caledonia] to exploit the 'natural' as they do the mines"— she nonetheless applied a European measure to the Kanak, finding the native population lacking.[14] For Michel, the civilizational hierarchy was neither clear nor absolute, but she did not fully transcend it. Lauding Kanak linguistic systems, she could not escape her era's hierarchical rhetoric that justified empire.

Michel's reference to "a universal language" emerged from the late-nineteenth-century European interest in international constructed languages, perceived as potential steps toward world peace. In addition to Esperanto, the best known and most successful universally intended tongues included Volapük, the second-most widespread, about which Michel spoke, and which boasted 283 clubs world-wide within ten years of its 1879 creation by the German Catholic priest Johann Martin Schleyer.[15] Universalglot, the earliest of these vernaculars, was created in 1868; Spokil in 1890; and Bollak in 1899. Esperanto was developed in the early 1880s by Ludwig Lazarus Zamenhof, a Jew trained as an ophthalmologist living in Bialystok, Poland (then part of the Russian Empire). Zamenhof explained, "In Białystok the inhabitants were divided into four distinct elements: Russians, Poles, Germans and Jews; each of these spoke their own language and looked on all the others as enemies. . . . [One feels] the misery caused by language division and sees at every step that the diversity of languages is the first, or at least the most influential, basis for the separation of the human family into groups of enemies."[16] Zamenhof created Esperanto in response. Labeling language as "the most influential" cause of social fragmentation, Zamenhof attributed profound power to it. In doing so, he built on Enlightenment-era contentions, asserted by Descartes and Johann Comenius, among others, linking reality to language.[17]

In Zamenof's era, anarchist thinkers and educators in France and England, with whom Michel was closely linked, embraced Esperanto as a means toward breaking down political and cultural barriers.[18] French anarchist geographer and Commune veteran Élisée Reclus explained that none of Esperanto's proponents "hope to replace existing languages, with their long and beautiful literary and philosophical pasts; they propose [Esperanto], their mechanism of common understanding between the nations, as a simple auxiliary of the national vernaculars. . . . A revolution as fundamental as the adoption of a universal language could not occur without bringing peace and a conscious accord to the life of nations."[19] Michel envisioned Bichelamar as such a unifying bridge language, a tongue to coexist with and join together disparate prevailing vernaculars. Like her compatriot Reclus, Michel argued that this would effectively unite peoples once linguistically divided.

A self-taught linguist, Michel sought connections between and among world languages. Exploring language commonalities, she espoused Darwinian conceptions of humans and tongues emerging from a "community of descent."[20] Simultaneously, she refuted the period's dominant philological theories that linked language and race and naturalized, hierarchized, and reified differences among peoples.[21] As part of a larger, never-completed encyclopedia project,

Michel examined and compared vocabularies, literary fragments, pronunciations, letters, and grammars across a broad range of world vernaculars.[22] To facilitate this project, before setting sail for the prison colony, Michel arranged to have a Breton dictionary and Russian and Polish grammar books shipped to her.[23] Consistent with her internationalist and antihierarchical politics, she strove to demonstrate legacies of an originary, singular language.

Michel compiled a nearly two-hundred-page notebook titled "Mélange en divers dialectes" ("Mixing various dialects"). The pages included poems and fragments of novels and stories in a wide variety of languages and dialects, some translated to several languages. Analyzing and comparing aspects of the various vocabularies and alphabets, Michel sought linguistic links. She scrutinized cuneiform and runic characters, emphasizing the importance of understanding them as sources of contemporary alphabets. Underscoring historic intercultural relations, Michel explained that "there are ancient runic characters etched on rocks in Scandinavia. . . . The characters were believed to be brought to Scandinavia by the Phoenicians."[24] The notebook includes charts of Russian, English, and German letters, listing the upper case, lower case, name, and pronunciation of each letter, as well as comparisons between the tongues' vowel and diphthong pronunciations with those of French. Nearly thirty additional pages of charts compare "Grammatical Notes" and other linguistic elements of Russian, English, and German. Structuring these frames contributed to both Michel's politically rooted linguistic and pedagogical theorizations. She affirmed that "the human language composed of all of the languages, broken down, condensed, gathered into harmonious and strong language, is capable where ours lack."[25]

The notebook begins with songs in "Patois Lorraine Champagne," German, and Basque; a Basque proverb; extracts of Don Quixote (in Spanish and French) and of Lermontov (in Russian and French). The large "General Notes" section includes vocabulary fragments grouped by language families and by region. Looking, for example, at the Ural-Altaic languages,[26] Michel examined Turkic, Mongolic, Tungusic, Koreanic, and Japonic tongues. Within these, she listed "vocabulary fragments" including Samoyed, Magyar, Mongol, Mordvine, Ostyak,[27] and "Greenland Eskimo," noting that the Ural-Altaic group "includes current dialects spoken in remote parts of Asia, Arctic Polar Regions, America, Africa, and the South Pacific Islands."[28] Michel sought not only to find associations between contemporary vernaculars, but also to understand "how modern languages connect to their sources."[29] She investigated relationships between Icelandic and Swedish with their linguistic predecessors Gothic and Anglo-Saxon. Aryaque intrigued her, as the theoretical philological root of all

"Aryan" (Indo-European) languages, thus the fount of Old and Middle German, which in turn were the ancestral languages of German, Flemish, Dutch, and English. In a section titled "Vocabulary Fragments of the peoples of Africa and America" Michel wrote, "The American Indian dialects evidently derive from Sanskrit, preceded not less evidently by a primitive language." She followed this claim with brief comparative word lists from Canadian tribes including Blackfeet, Saulteaux, Sioux, and Cree.[30] By positioning Native American dialects as descending from Sanskrit, Michel placed them within the Indo-European language family, effectively challenging the distinction of the Algonquin language group. Locating Native American vernaculars within the Indo-European group denied the linguistic and cultural barriers recently asserted by nineteenth-century philologists. Endeavoring to substantiate transnational and transcultural connections, Michel engaged the era's comparative linguistic debates regarding both languages and their speakers.

The field of comparative linguistics emerged in the mid-nineteenth century, growing from the work of German philologist Franz Bopp, whose six-part work *Vergleichende Grammatik des Sanskrit, Zend, Griechischen, Lateinischen, Litthauischen, Altslawischen, Gotischen, und Deutschen* (*Comparative Grammar of Sanskrit, Zend, Greek, Latin, Lithuanian, Old Slavic, Gothic, and German*) established a framework for comparing the histories and grammars of languages.[31] Bopp, his Danish contemporary Rasmus Kristian Rask, and later August Schleicher proposed a romantic, "scientific" model of languages as organisms, as literal organic bodies that would grow, develop, and ultimately die in accord with internal laws. Their work built on the British Orientalist and jurist William Jones's discovery of the Indo-European language family in the late eighteenth century, a profoundly influential event that spurred a broad and growing interest in the connections between language and race.[32] Comparative linguistics (or philology)—considered a natural science during this period—rose in concert with ideas of race.[33] As postcolonial scholar Bill Ashcroft has argued, the link between philology and ethnology provided a powerful foundation for the marriage of linguistic hegemony and racial marginalization that came to be fundamental to imperial discourse.[34]

By the 1870s, Darwinian evolutionary models took hold in comparative linguistics, superseding the theories that posited languages as individual living organisms.[35] But this change merely shifted debates regarding the relationship between language and race. Darwin altered his own position between the 1859 publication of *Origin of Species* and 1871's *Descent of Man*. According to Stephen Alter, Darwin initially coupled the development of languages and races, but subsequently contended that they had evolved separately and at different rates.[36]

Michel clearly adhered to the latter. Informed by and engaged in the debates surrounding language and race, she referred to linguists such as Heinrich Gottfried Ollendorff, a grammarian and language pedagogue, and Frédéric Gustave Eichhoff, who wrote on parallels between European and Indian languages.[37]

Michel made a serious comparative study of linguistic structures and histories. Writing of Kanak language, she posited, "The vocabulary of a people, is it not its customs, its history, its physiognomy?"[38] Michel did not reject Esperanto, but considered Bichelamar preferable as a natural, living language, a creole-like tongue that had emerged organically through intercultural engagements. (Antonio Gramsci, among others, would later criticize Esperanto as artificial.[39]) The Kanak's creation of Bichelamar exemplified what Michel considered their natural tendencies toward openness and universality, as well as their cultural development. An 1886 article in *Le temps* reported on Michel's lecture to a group of writers involved in the Decadent movement. "Imitate the Kanak," she advised, "who are less educated than us, but who are also less barbaric. They have taken words from Chinese, from French, from English, from all languages, and they have made one language. . . . All the languages must one day melt into one universal language."[40] Michel championed the Kanak creation of a creole as a unifying success. It brought together vernacular elements while simultaneously breaking down cultural and political divisions. She also countered France's denigration of Kanak languages, which they saw as inferior to tongues spoken by Polynesians, in line with dominant French racialized constructions of the Polynesians as more civilized than the Melanesian Kanak.[41] Valorizing Bichelamar and the Kanak exemplified Michel's challenges to the era's philological ties between language and race and her efforts to subvert the dominant imperial discourse. Her inability to fully extract herself from the latter underscores its iniquitousness.

Anthropolitically embracing Bichelamar dovetailed with Michel's interest in the politics of language. Among her many literary and political works, she published three novels between 1886–1890 that centered language as a revolutionary force.[42] Received with a combination of hostility and bewilderment, the novels appeared as radical interventions, both ideologically and literarily. Politically, she issued them on the one hundredth anniversary of the French Revolution and the enormous 1889 Universal Exposition. As Claude Rétat and Stéphane Zékian explain in their 2013 introduction to the trilogy, during this period "the socialist press, especially the anarchists challenged the confiscation of the Revolution by bourgeois authorities (commemorations) and the confiscation of the product of labor by the capitalist powers (exposition)."[43] The final novel, *Le claque-dents*, engages these contestations.[44] More broadly, the anarchist-rooted trilogy denigrates elections and parliamentarism as reformist and lauds the general strike and anti-imperial insurgencies—including contemporary anticolonial uprisings by both the Zulu and the Irish against British rule.[45] It does so, however, in an avant-garde literary style that rejected formal grammar, embraced slang and orality, and sought to reclaim the French language for the revolution.

In the first two novels, *Les microbes humains* and *Le monde nouveau*, Michel acclaimed a universal language. Building toward a new, cohesive world, *Les microbes humains* suggests that since "dialects of principal languages fade away, soon perhaps these languages themselves will be absorbed in that of humanity," which will lead to the ideal of one human language.[46] Continuing the advocacy for universal language that she had begun with the New Caledonian Bichelamar, Michel again privileged "naturally" evolving languages over the era's constructed languages such as Esperanto and Volapük.

Further valorizing a bottom-up organic rather than top-down structure, Michel integrated oral forms and *l'argot* (slang) into these novels, including taking the title of the third novel, *Le claque-dents*, from *l'argot* of the period. Stéphane Zékian contends that her use of orality "sometimes pushed to the limits of readability."[47] While some writers of the era, including Emile Zola, included oral phrasing to convey authenticity (particularly in dialogue), Michel integrated orality more thoroughly and with a political intent.[48] Affirming the links between the peasant women storytellers at the *écrègnes* of her Haut-Marne childhood and the oral tales of the New Caledonian Kanak, Michel sought to wrest control of the French language from elites. Her extensive inclusion of *l'argot*, a primarily oral vocabulary of the popular classes, radicalized her writing in a particularly politicized, ideological direction. Anthropologists and criminologists of the period considered the use of *l'argot* as evidence of criminality, of a biologically predisposed marginal "type," and of participation in the underworld. *L'argot* revealed deviance, a category into which political radicals fell.[49] As criminal anthropologists César Lombrosse and Rodolfo Laschi argued in 1892, "It is precisely by this language of *l'argot* that the character, or at least the criminal penchant, of a great number of Communards manifests itself."[50]

Accustomed to accusations of unlawfulness and deviance, Michel also faced ongoing denigration of her literary work. While she was disparaged by avant-garde writers of her era and undercut by sexist critics who attacked her specifically as a woman, even her otherwise sympathetic twentieth-century biographer Edith Thomas declared Michel's novels "absolutely unreadable."[51] Michel manipulated French to appropriate it for nonelites and to revolutionary universalist ends. As Édouard Glissant's translator Betsy Wing wrote of Glissant, "He repeatedly destabilizes 'standard' French in order to decategorize understandings and establish new relations, so that the constant transformation always at work in any living symbolic system . . . can form the vibrant grounds for a full and productive participation among world cultures."[52] Michel's destabilization of standard French similarly worked to reorder assumptions of meaning and categories of acceptability and authority. She rejected fixed linguistic rules to allow for the incorporation of nonelite spoken language onto the page—moving the more rapid and "incorrect" linguistic changes that occur in the oral into the realm of the written. She also brought in popular vernacular that would otherwise remain marginalized and ephemeral. Loosening the boundaries of a language could also allow for greater permeability of elements of other languages and cultures and lead toward her ultimate goal of linguistic, and human, universalism.

This democratization of language dovetailed with Michel's extolling of the power and value of literature, art, and music created by the unschooled or "primitives." In a 1902 letter to the Federation Feministe des Arts et Métiers (Feminist Federation of Arts and Trades) lauding the organization for its local and international work, Michel affirmed,

> There are popular groups of poets, having never learned the rudiments of their language, who suddenly amaze with a magnificent thought expressed in a strange rhyme; painters who, knowing nothing of the elements of design or color, create haunting effects; inexperienced voices finding magical melodies. They don't know, they don't copy, they are the love of beauty, the dream of art.[53]

She also commended the working women who continued their education and those who taught, writing that "their work brings together the labor of all, like . . . coral building the archipelagos that punctuate the great ocean."[54] Recalling the intricate and enormous coral reef of New Caledonia—the longest barrier reef in the world—Michel highlighted the global and connected nature of their work. Turning to language, Michel addressed the Federation Feministe's upcoming International Exposition, underscoring how "the multiple dialects of the earth . . . will fall, one after the other . . . and a new language will speak of the new arts, dawning perhaps at your exposition."[55] She emphasized the vitality of feminists' roles in overcoming linguistic, national, and human divisions. Ultimately, she continued, "When the horrible mountain of the past, which has for so long been slowly sliding, finally collapses, women will have cleared most of the paths to the future. Yes, you are doing well, the time is now!"[56]

The idea of linguistic concord directly supported Michel's anarchist criticism of state power and aspiration to global unity. Michel's lingual aims demonstrated her efforts to undercut existing power hierarchies while keeping revolution as her primary goal. Addressing a London audience, Michel asked them to "look to the horizon, to the time when between the English and French, Germans or Russians, when there will be no differences beyond the differences between distinct regions within the same country."[57] Moving conceptually beyond language barriers, Michel envisioned the eradication of national borders. She asserted the artificiality of these political frontiers, while recognizing that certain differences between nations did exist and likening them to regional, "natural" variances "within the same country." Her logical extension of this border destruction, with acknowledged local dissimilarities, was geographic unity, an accord that would also undermine language barriers and end imperial reach. Michel promoted a United States of Europe. "The day is not far when, on a starred flag, we will read the three letters 'EUE' [États-Unis d'Europe] across from that of USA."[58]

The idea of a United States of Europe had circulated in leftist circles for several decades prior to Michel's statements. Victor Hugo, with whom Michel had long corresponded and whom she revered—once writing to him that "believing neither in the devil or god, I believe in you"—promoted an evolving vision of a United States of Europe.[59] Initially proposing the idea at an 1849 Peace Conference in Paris, in the wake of the European Revolutions of 1848, Hugo became increasingly interested in a united Europe; the concept held growing importance in both his political and literary work.[60] The Italian revolutionary and nationalist Giuseppe Mazzini considered a United States of Europe his long-term goal.[61] Perry Anderson, in *The New Old World*, catalogues the genealogy of nineteenth-century leftist advocates of a United States of Europe, from Victor Considérant, who hoped to avoid war, to Leon Trotsky, who hoped to expedite the unity of the working class. But Anderson neglects Michel and her anti-imperial goal.[62] As Michel wrote. "How many times have I been to meetings where women are excluded!"[63]

Michel envisioned a distinct version of a United States of Europe. Rather than suggesting the destruction of political borders on only the European continent, as did other nineteenth-century thinkers, she conceptualized the European union as only one component of the "Great natural divisions of the globe."[64] In notes for a 1900–1901 series of conferences about New Caledonia, Michel elaborated the idea of multiple united states as a way of hypothesizing the "future of the human races." While arguing for the inevitability of the United States of Europe, she made clear that it would not be the first of such entities: "The United States of Africa has begun, justly by the South African War."[65] As she so often did, Michel underscored Europe's status as one among many, rather than above or beyond other continents. By proposing the contemporary Second Boer War as the impetus for the first (non–North American) United States, she claimed an anti-imperial conflict as the source of the union.

In addition to Europe and Africa, Michel anticipated a United States of Asia, a United States of Australia, and a United States of the United Archipelago Islands (which would include New Caledonia). These geographically limited, primarily continentally based sets of United States not only erased political lines between existing states, but also physically circumscribed the political units. Michel's regionally defined strategy therefore precluded intercontinental imperialism. But in the long run she insisted that "the great continental unions," though vital steps away from existing oppressive systems, constituted merely temporary answers, "while awaiting the one true union of humanity on earth."[66]

Teaching Radically

Education played a central role in Michel's revolutionary universalism. Her revolutionary, anarchistic, anticlerical, feminist vision of Western education aimed toward liberation, "uplift," and a way to break down barriers to unity. In Europe, she focused on elementary education and literature; in Algeria and New Caledonia she targeted subjugated peoples. Michel's pedagogical theories explain why she equated the development of children with the liberation of a culture and thus inadvertently centered imperialist Western forms. Yet she also simultaneously challenged not only those forms, but also Western ways of knowing and definitions of what constituted knowledge. Nearly 150 years before the concept of "decolonizing the curriculum" emerged, Michel took steps toward democratizing and decolonizing education.

Trained in the liberal Enlightenment tradition, Michel became a teacher. In 1852, at the age of twenty-two, she opened a girls' school in her home village of Audeloncourt, beginning a life-long scholastic commitment.[67] Four years later, she moved to Paris, where she taught and became increasingly involved with socialism. By 1865, Michel had established a girls' school in Montmartre, one whose curriculum held the seeds of anarchist feminist instruction. During the 1871 Paris Commune, she created a radically egalitarian instructional program, but the seventy-two-day duration of the revolution prevented its fruition. Embracing revolutionary anarchism in the wake of the Commune, her new politics intersected with her feminism and anticlericalism and infused both her instructional theory and practice. Deported to New Caledonia after the Commune, she established a school for the children of French deportees and a Sunday school for adult Kanak.

Michel's New Caledonian experience further radicalized her, expanding her pedagogical vision—and her broader ideology—to include anti-imperialism. Interacting with, teaching, and learning from the Kanak led Michel to challenge Western civilizational and racial hierarchies; observing the processes of colonial occupation illuminated for her their inequities. Continuing to center education, she thereafter theorized and enacted a revolutionary instructional and literary pedagogy intended to undermine state and church power, patriarchy, and imperialism. In the 1890s, living in London to escape French police harassment, she founded and ran an international anarchist school; finally, on a 1904 propaganda speaking tour of Algeria, she promoted radical teachers' role in instigating anti-imperial revolt.

Michel's revolutionary anarchism was rooted in Enlightenment positivism. She believed in science, reason, and progress. In 1875 she wrote from New Caledonia that "science is a torch in the hands of the enlighteners; the further it is carried forward, the further darkness retreats."[68] From Michel's perspective, the light of science would eradicate the darkness of religion and superstition, which she saw as identical to one another. Writing in an Algerian anarchist newspaper nearly thirty years later, Michel announced that "mysticism is dead, it is now the love of the unknown, of discoveries, of genius, the arts, science, a new stage *en route* to a new age of humanity."[69] Embracing a humanistic positivism, she promoted the power of free thinking, spreading it through the written word, the classroom, and the orator's pulpit. In Algeria, thirty years after her time in New Caledonia and in a colonial milieu over 10,000 miles away, Michel continued to proclaim education's optimistic vision. She had called it "the sole refuge against all of today's poverty and dissensions" in a 1900 interview in the newspaper *Le petit sou*.[70] Although both New Caledonia and Algeria remained under French rule in 1904, Michel saw hope for "a new age of humanity" in the revolutionary seeds of knowledge and education. Her anti-imperialist plans relied on both radical European and Indigenous ideas to overthrow European power.

Michel's feminist pedagogical activism in the decade before the Paris Commune included both her schools and the organization La Société du Droit des Femmes (The Society for Women's Rights). Established with the socialist feminists Mink and André Léo (during the period when Michel identified as socialist), the society advocated secular primary education for girls, rejecting the strong role that the Catholic Church played in girls' public instruction in France, while also promoting women's labor and marriage reform.[71] Léo, a well-known novelist and journalist, had long campaigned against France's clerically based, gender-segregated, hierarchical educational system and condemned its role in maintaining the subjugation of both women and the working class.[72] Months before the advent of the Commune, Léo wrote, "The partisans of women's equality . . . have come to understand this truth. Their primary objective is the free school, the school of reason and liberty. This will be a girls' school."[73] With the 1871 inauguration of the Commune, in which Paris declared itself an independent revolutionary city, Michel and her compatriots worked to implement their radical pedagogical models in the absence of existing institutional state and religious strictures. They outlined a secular, egalitarian, and moral instructional program in which "no reward or punishment can exist apart from the feeling of having done one's duty or having acted badly."[74] By advocating a free, nongendered, nonpunitive education, Michel sought to counter the repressive and disciplinary school culture and allow the "natural" moral development of the students—something she saw as stunted by France's traditional, religiously based, hierarchical educational approach. Reflecting on the sexism in the era's dominant pedagogies, she wrote, "I have never understood why one sex sought to atrophy the intelligence of the other, as if there was already too much [intelligence] in the human race."[75]

After the Commune, in New Caledonia, Michel encountered racism regarding Indigenous education. While most of the Communard deportees remained uninterested in the Kanak, three of Michel's comrades, Augustin Verdure, Charles Amouroux, and Henri Place, supported educating them. Verdure, a teacher, member of the International Working Men's Association, and close friend of Michel, held views similar to hers regarding the Kanak, but died within a year of arriving in New Caledonia.[76] Amouroux and Place had distinctly different perspectives. While Michel understood the Kanak as merely less historically developed than white Europeans, Amouroux and Place saw a more fundamental biological difference and termed them "a decadent race" with "underdeveloped brains." Writing in 1881, immediately following the French government's 1880 General Amnesty of the Communards, Amouroux and Place stated that "the colonists should not forget that morally, the Kanak is inferior; thus he must be made to feel this and be treated as a child. . . . Each French colonist is an active member of a republican country that has proclaimed the abolition of slavery and the equality of races, each is thus a natural guardian of the Kanak until the day he is emancipated by education."[77] Amouroux and Place, unlike the French colonial authority, implied potential for progress among the Indigenous people. Yet they denigrated and infantilized the Kanak, prescribing their subjugation. Indeed, Amouroux was among the Communards to join the French military in their fight to crush the Kanak's 1878 uprising.[78] Referring to the emancipatory and egalitarian qualities of the republic, Amouroux and Place placed French colonists in the role of moral guardian, awaiting the unnamed future "day" when the Kanak would be "emancipated by education." In taking a more progressive and even relatively humanitarian position, these former Communards nonetheless expressed a deep racism, one indicative, as Alice Bullard has argued, of the particular humanitarian ideology undergirding much of the nineteenth century's colonialism.[79] This stance differs distinctly from Michel's educational undertakings in New Caledonia, as well as her rejection of France's 1870s Third Republic as neither just nor liberatory. Unlike Amouroux and Place, she made no claims of a race-based moral or biological superiority. Rather, she advocated instruction in literacy, numbers, politics, social relations, agriculture, and languages. She simultaneously studied and learned Kanak language, music, culture, and tales.

Michel recalled her fellow deportees' laughter at her decision to establish a Kanak school: "a school for the savages . . . they will not come."[80] But they did. Michel explained, "Every Sunday I met with twenty of the Blacks. I have never before had more disciplined, more attentive students. The Kanak is curious and intelligent. His perseverance is great."[81] Michel advocated an anarchist pedagogical approach to help guide the autochthones to what she saw as intellectual and cultural maturity. While privileging aspects of European ideas and intellectual life, she concurrently valorized Kanak culture and viewed Kanak people with optimism and hope.

While Michel asserted the Kanak's intelligence and their intellectual promise, she often spoke of them as children and idealized them as living in an unspoiled "natural state."[82] She believed that their pristine condition, their "uncultivated brains," allowed greater intellectual receptivity, that "new things are deeply engraved, better perhaps than in ours, which are all confused with doctrines and all stained with erasures."[83] The German anarchist Rudolf Rocker, Michel's associate and ally during her London years, later explained that "her eyes lit up when she spoke about the Kanak of New Caledonia. She sang their praises, their simplicity, their natural intelligence, their complete readiness to help others. She did not overlook the disappearance of these fine native qualities through the inroads of white civilization."[84] Rocker, employing the infantilizing language typical of the era, made clear that Michel recognized the dangers of white contact. Her proposed educational approach would need to navigate between elevation and imposition, a difficult terrain. But, for Michel, it constituted a territory comparable to instructing European children. From her perspective, radical, progressive education could unfetter and advance the Kanak without destroying their cultural core, in the same way that emancipatory and egalitarian pedagogy could facilitate a French or British child's free development. A reimagined and redeployed curriculum would be liberatory.

Here again, while challenging the dominant discourse of Kanak—and Black—inferiority, Michel remained entangled in the edges of imperialist and racist rhetoric. Embracing the archetype of the Kanak as child-like, she artic- ulated a Rousseauian romanticism, asserting the importance of protecting the Indigenous people's unspoiled and uncorrupted nature. Her decades of peda- gogical activism and experience, rooted in both her feminism and anarchism, combined with her belief in Western intellectual superiority to give her con- fidence that she could deliver such an education.

The penal colony's administrators opposed Michel's teaching the Indigenous population. Although education was considered a "natural" role for European women in both metropole and colonies, and the government allowed her to teach the children of French deportees and colonial functionaries in a school in Nouméa, they feared the potential results of Michel instructing the Kanak. The colonial authorities demanded she close her school.[85] During this period, France had no Kanak schools. They initiated a formal Indigenous education program only in 1885, and between 1885 and 1946 (when Kanak gained French citizenship), instruction was limited to three years of primary education. Un- like most French colonies, New Caledonia had no elite educational program to create Indigenous professionals to work in colonial administration.[86] As ethnographer Alban Bensa contends, because of the French certainty of the Kanak's immanent extinction, "It was evident [to the French] that the Kanak would not contribute in any manner to 'the colonial project.'"[87] France's racialized conceptualization of the Kanak as savage and inferior categorized them as uneducable—or not worthy of education, or possibly too threaten- ing to educate.

When pressed to close her Kanak school, Michel defended her curriculum, using the language of French universalism to argue for the values "of human- ity, of justice, of emancipation." The prison administrator replied that "it is not necessary to speak of emancipation to these people. One day or another this could become dangerous"—an observation foreshadowing the 1878 in- surrection.[88] Michel ignored the command, shifting her classroom from an old hut to a remote outdoor spot in an effort to avoid detection. A prison guard ultimately discovered her giving lessons in a shady wood. Declaring "you have been forbidden from holding class for these idiots," the guard grabbed her arm violently. A Kanak student intervened, picked up the guard "and threw him several meters, into a bramble thicket."[89] Michel faced serious consequences both for ignoring the administration's prohibition against instructing the Kanak and for refusing to reveal the name of the person responsible for injuring the prison guard. The penal colony's governor announced her banishment to iso- lation as an "incorrigible," but Michel challenged both his authority to take such action and the basis for his charges. Relying on her status as "not an or- dinary convict . . . as well as being a woman," she defended her right to teach and she challenged the colonial governor, who would have rarely faced such contestations from prisoners, especially from women. Michel recognized the politics involved in the governor's position and responded in kind. Aware that he could face reprimand if he altered the terms of her imprisonment without his superiors' authorization, Michel was also cognizant of the gendered parameters of the penal context. As on her initial arrival in the archipelago, Michel's legal knowledge and defiance protected her and prevented her separation from her comrades.[90]

In a retrospective 1888 Parisian lecture entitled "À travers l'océan," Michel overtly presented the educator as the revolutionary agent. Reflecting on her time in New Caledonia working with the Kanak, she stated with a mix of levity and seriousness, "If events don't move more rapidly in France, and if there is no need of revolutionaries here, perhaps I would be better off going there [New Caledonia] to educate those people who still do not know much about civilization."[91] Michel gently "threatened" her audience that unless they pushed more aggressively toward overthrowing the republic, she, a true agent of change, would shift her radicalizing educational labor (and herself) to New Caledonia.

Michel never returned to New Caledonia, despite many, and more serious, assertions that she had hoped to do so.[92] In 1890, she fled to England, where she spent several years avoiding the relentless political pressure and police harassment she faced in France. Immersing herself in London's international anarchist community, Michel established an anarchist school, the International School, for the children of French and other political exiles.[93] She felt comfortable in Britain, which she considered less politically oppressive than France, explaining, "Yes, I admit it, I love this England where my banished friends are always welcome. This old England is a more liberal place, even in the shadow of the gallows-tree, than the home of all those bourgeois so-called 'Republicans,' whether they think so or not."[94] With the International School, Michel put her decades of radical educational activism, theory, and practical experience into action. Building on feminist and anarchist critiques of existing educational approaches, as well as her own experiences in France and New Caledonia, Michel implemented an *éducation intégrale*—an "integral education" that recognized and promoted the many facets of each student's intellectual, physical, and moral selves in a coeducational context, bridging theory and praxis, and employing science and reason to bring about change.[95]

The International School drew on the radically egalitarian educational proposals of the anarchists Pyotr Kropotkin, Mikhail Bakunin, and Paul Robin and of her fellow Paris Commune veterans Mink and Léo. The institution's genealogy thus combined the culmination of Michel's intersectional radical pedagogy with the tenets of contemporary anarchist thinkers, many of whom she had influenced. Utopian socialist Charles Fourier had introduced the term *éducation intégrale* in 1829, promoting a universal, egalitarian, intellectual, physical, and practical educational program.[96] Forty years later Bakunin employed the same phrase, arguing that "education must be equal for everyone in all respects, consequently it must be integral—it should prepare every child of both sexes for the life of thought as well as for the life of labor so that all are equally able to become complete men [*hommes*]."[97] Kropotkin, who sat on the International School's guiding committee, also theorized an integral education, positing the promotion of a cooperative and harmonious existence both among people and between people and their environment.[98] And Robin, who significantly influenced Michel's approach, emphasized the productive over the theoretical, promoting the needs of the laborer rather than those of state or church, while working to integrate the individual into the requirements and goals of the collective. He also advocated coeducational instruction.[99] Rejection of the era's typically dis-integrated education—segregated in terms of gender and class, intensely individuated, enveloped in religion, and alienated from both reason and human emotion—spread among the period's libertarian thinkers. Michel, however, was one of the first to put theory into action.

The International School operated for three years in London's Fitzroy Square, offering classes including music, geography, needlework, gymnastics, technical skills, and language.[100] They taught in English, French, and German—three of the four languages Michel had comparatively analyzed in her black linguistic notebook two decades earlier.[101] She had also written on the Ollendorff Method, which promoted the simultaneous teaching of related tongues, contending "it is easier to learn a group of languages than one isolated language." In a series of lectures on education in 1887, Michel advocated teaching children multiple languages, "affirming that her system was very simple; it was sufficient for learning the most ancient languages. In addition," she observed, "the diverse dialects of peoples have a striking concordance."[102] Drawing on her earliest research into linguistic continuities and her ongoing development of pedagogical methods, Michel promoted educational approaches to demonstrating human commonalities in language.

The International School implemented these theories. Emphasizing the utility of learning foreign tongues, the school's promotional brochure avowed: "He who learns one or more foreign languages thereby acquires a capital of which he may never be deprived and which, at all times, guarantees him a more certain and profitable income than any other employment."[103] The focus on foreign language reflected not only the institution's internationalism, but also its sophisticated approach to acquiring practical skills. Making clear the school's political position, the pamphlet further explained that the institution provided an alternative to "the religiously oriented state schools which, consciously or unconsciously, teach that the people are to be sacrificed to the power of the State and the profit of the privileged classes."[104] The brochure cover had an elaborate illustration of "a woman wearing a Liberty Cap and lighting her lamp from the sun of Truth with one hand, while feeding children the fruits of knowledge with the other."[105] Referencing the French Revolution with the representation of the Liberty Cap, Enlightenment rationality with the sun of Truth, and the classical world with the fruits of knowledge, the International School promoted a historically rooted rational, yet revolutionary, image. The school intended to revolutionize education. Walter Crane, the well-known artist, illustrator, and socialist, created the design, and William Morris—a member of the school's guiding committee—paid the engraving costs.[106] In addition to making the promotional pamphlet available in London, the organizing committee also sent one thousand copies to Paris's Bourse de Travail, a labor exchange bureau established by trade unions.[107]

In an article discussing the newly opened school's progress, the London anarchist newspaper *Freedom* noted that, "Walter Crane has also sent a large number of his beautifully illustrated books for the use of the children; C. Walkden has sent flowers and fruit from the country, besides giving a liberal donation. . . . It is hoped by the committee that they will be able to make the day school a free one, and to this end ask all who are interested to give as freely towards the expenses as their means will allow."[108] The school relied on, and received, financial and in-kind support from London's local and international anarchist and socialist communities. *Freedom* reported that "P. Kropotkine lectures on its behalf August 31st, at the Athenaeum Hall, Tottenham Court Road, on 'Brain Work and Manual Work' . . . and Dr. J. Barker Smith has offered to give a course of six lectures on Botany." While the day school was for children, the International School also offered evening classes, such as Dr. Barker Smith's botany course, for adults.[109] Michel and her comrades conceived of the school as a center of free, radical, and expansive learning, combining new progressive approaches with traditional socialist ideas of night schools and continuing education.

The pedagogical program itself minimized discipline and structure and instead emphasized children's individual interests and liberty. While teachers offered a broad range of classes, there were no specific requirements, and they encouraged students to suggest topics or areas to be studied. Rejecting any idea of original sin, Michel believed that children were naturally good and that their innate instincts and desires should direct their intellectual path. Teachers acted as guides. They taught courses as small discussion groups, avoiding lecture and formal hierarchy. As a result, the International School differed profoundly from most typical educational institutions during this period.[110] As in her New Caledonian Kanak school, Michel altered usual pedagogical approaches and topics, creating what she considered a liberated and liberatory curriculum. She attracted supporters and advocates who lauded her unconventional pedagogy, while critics decried the institution's unruliness and disorder. Even some anarchists questioned her instructional approach. As W.C. Hart wrote, "While in one part of the room the teachers tried to attract their pupils to lessons of arithmetic, Louise herself gave them lessons in piano playing, the children surrounding her, climbing on chairs, and even on her shoulders; the general noise being so great that nobody could be heard at all by either teachers or pupils."[111]

The International School came to a dramatic close when a police raid "discovered" bombs in the building's basement. Auguste Coulon, a French refugee deeply involved in teaching and running the school, had been working as an *agent provocateur* and planted the devices to incriminate Michel and her comrades.[112] Profoundly dismayed, Michel wrote, "I went back to East Dulwich [where she lived] in a most troubled frame of mind. There is nothing so terrible as to feel oneself surrounded by enemies, without being able to guess either their identity or their purpose."[113] Michel escaped prosecution by proving her innocence under questioning. Several of her comrades were imprisoned. Although her London educational experiment ended, it came to hold an important place in the history and development of anarchist pedagogy.[114]

More than two decades later, Emma Goldman, writing in 1917 on the Modern School, an outgrowth of *éducation intégrale*, stated that "its originator, though on a small scale, was our own sweet spirit Louise Michel . . . [who] felt long ago that the future belongs to the young generation; that unless the young be rescued from that mind- and soul-destroying institution, the bourgeois school, social evils will continue to exist."[115]

Michel took revolutionary pedagogical approaches in the classroom, in her public lectures, and in her writing. Her educationally themed novel (ultimately unpublished), "Les filles de la Galoubette," tells a feminist story of the five daughters of a Restoration-era prostitute.[116] Children of different fathers, the girls follow starkly differing paths and possess sharply contrasting natures. Anita, the daughter of an Italian revolutionary, is the only one of her siblings to receive a substantial and progressive education (the other fathers include a painter, a merchant, and an "old debauched man."). Anita becomes a teacher and a feminist. Demonstrating the combined influence of nature (heredity) and environment (her education), Michel describes Anita as having "a rich and powerful nature."[117] Opening several girls' schools, Anita develops an innovative and engaging pedagogy in which "geography is presented in the form of voyages, history lives through dramatic tales . . . mathematical formulas were applied . . . in such amusing ways that the little girls were thrilled to study them."[118] A rather autobiographical character for Michel, as Juliette Parnell-Smith argues, Anita fights for "free and mandatory education for all, equal salaries, and the abolition of inheritance."[119] Michel presents the successful woman as a deeply progressive teacher, struggling for a more egalitarian world.

Radical education held a central place in Michel's ideology and activism throughout her career. Teaching and learning, breaking down cultural and linguistic barriers, developing and accepting new forms of knowledge and communication, Michel understood pedagogy as a key revolutionary tool. When she traveled to Algeria at the end of her life, she promoted equal and secular education as key to the colony's liberation from French imperial oppression, and she stressed the teacher's central role in fostering that anticolonial revolution.

Three Revolutions

In 1904, at the age of seventy-four and in ill health, Michel embarked on an antimilitarism, antireligion, and anticolonial speaking and propaganda tour of Algeria. Traveling to the colony fulfilled a promise she had made to her fellow political exiles, satisfying a decades-long desire to demonstrate her solidarity with the Algerian Kabyle insurrectionists she had encountered in New Caledonia. She hoped her visit would inspire an anti-imperial uprising, one of at least the magnitude of the Paris Commune, the Kabyle insurgency, and the Kanak insurrection.

Michel considered revolution to be fundamental to the larger universal process toward human equality. The synchrony of the Paris Commune with the 1871 Kabyle revolt, followed by the 1878 Kanak uprising—combined with the instability of the conservative Third Republic throughout the 1870s—signaled both France's vulnerability and the readiness of subjugated groups to rise up.[120] These three revolutions shaped Michel's politics and worldview. Expanding her perspective outward, while simultaneously underscoring the commonalities of the oppressed, Michel recognized fundamental intersections of imperial and class oppression

Two days before the 1871 Paris Commune began, Algerian Kabyles and Arabs revolted against the French imperial authority.[121] A confluence of factors sparked the revolt, including resentment toward French colonists, whose power had increased following France's 1870 shift from military to civilian authority

5.2. "The Life of Louise Michel: Propaganda for Children, Good Culture Brings A Good Harvest, Education & Revolution." Fifteen frames show and tell the highlights of Michel's life, emphasizing her revolutionary devotion, selflessness, and bravery. Published shortly after her death. Bibliothèque Nationale de France.

in Algeria; a period of famine and economic crisis; and France's perceived weakness after its 1870 loss to Prussia. Led by the Kabyle aristocracy, the insurrection resulted in the first alliance of Algerian Kabyle and Arabs against the French.[122] The rebellion ultimately faced a brutal repression. Retribution included the appropriation of extensive territories, which France subsequently opened to colonization; sweeping punishments of both involved and uninvolved tribes; and the trial and exile of 121 Kabyle leaders to New Caledonia, alongside the Parisian Communards.[123] When the Kanak revolted seven years later, France treated this new anticolonial action in similar ways, by seizing lands, penalizing both involved and uninvolved clans, and exiling Indigenous people—this time without trial.[124] These attempts to throw off colonial rule faced reprisals that intensified and extended that rule.

Many of the Communard deportees expressed solidarity and affinity with the Algerians (sentiments they pointedly did not extend to the Kanak). The exiled Communard Jean Allemane explained his initial encounter with "the Arabs," as the French labeled all Algerian insurgents, in the Toulon prison, where both the French and Algerians were held before deportation to New Caledonia. Allemane compared the Kabyles' experience with that of his comrades: "I learned that the new arrivals were, like me, the defeated, and they were treated in the same fashion: the Algerian Councils of War rivaled the zeal of those of Versailles."[125] Like Allemane, Charles Malato, a young anarchist Communard and friend of Michel, looked for links between his comrades and the Algerians. Malato, whose parents were also deported to New Caledonia, developed friendships with the Algerians. In his memoirs, he lauded the language skills of "their great chief, [Boumezrag] Mokrani, who spoke excellent French, nearly like a Parisian."[126] Perhaps explaining this Kabyle's French fluency, Malato suggested that Mokrani "descended on his mother's side, we seriously believe, from the aristocratic family Montmorency, and his Arab name is only a corruption of his French name."[127] In language and lineage, Malato directly connected Mokrani with the French, to the point of asserting his aristocratic French pedigree. Surprisingly the anarchist and former Communard said nothing negative about Mokrani's possible aristocratic connections, focusing instead on the romantic nature of the possible link. With their shared experiences of French repression and the eradication of physical distance brought about by deportation, Allemane, Malato, and other Commune veterans worked to diminish the cultural—and civilizational—divisions between themselves and the Kabyle insurgents.

And yet the French exiles did not fundamentally identify with the Algerians. While articulating both concrete and romantic connections to the Kabyle, the Communards also exoticized their fellow deportees. After inferring Mokrani's

European familial and cultural connections, Malato described in flattering and effusive language how Mokrani and many of his compatriots "possessed the physical characteristics of a race for which one would search in vain among the stout descendants of our seigneurs: white teeth, fine form, slender fingers with pink nails that would cause all the duchesses of a noble quarter to die of spite."[128] Malato's description dramatically depicted Mokrani's and other "Arabs'" physical characteristics in positive terms, but using language that crossed gendered boundaries, attributing to them decidedly feminine characteristics.

Remarking approvingly again on the men's physical qualities, Malato portrayed "another Ahmed, handsome as a prince of *A Thousand and One Nights*."[129] His reference to the widely known Persian, Arabic, and Indian collection reflected the Orientalist cultural context from which his perceptions and understandings of the "Arabs" emerged. As Michel later described, "the Arab deportees" arrived in New Caledonia "in their great white *burnous*," long, flowing, hooded cloaks. The exotic image of the "men of the dessert," prevalent in France during this period, shaped the Communards' reception of the Kabyle.[130] This sentimental Orientalism, enabled by the North Africans' recognizable elite status and bearing, created space for an acceptable, feminized masculinity, a gender construction appropriate only within the narrow race and class parameters of the deported Kabyle. The French deportees' romantic preconceptions intersected with their solidarity to provide a framework within which to place fellow displaced victims of French oppression. The Communards thus sympathized with the Algerians' experience of repression and deportation. But they did not recognize it as a product of imperialism; nor did they identify imperialism as problematic.

Like her comrades, Michel felt a sense of connection and allegiance with the Algerian Kabyle, which emerged based on common experiences: both parties had attempted to overthrow French governmental authority, both movements had suffered brutal defeat, and both groups had faced severe reprisals, including exile. When France passed a General Amnesty for political prisoners in 1880, it freed the Communard deportees but not the Algerians. The liberated Communards demanded their co-detainees' release. Henri Rochefort, a politician, journalist, former Communard deportee, and Michel's decades-long benefactor and ally, had established friendships with some of the Kabyle.[131] Following the General Amnesty, Rochefort published articles and a propaganda brochure asserting the illegality of the Algerians' exclusion from the amnesty. Rochefort also organized an assembly of 1,500 former Communards, of which Michel was an honorary president, to plan means of pressing the government to free the Algerians. Petitions and protests ultimately led the government in 1887 to admit the illegality of continuing to hold the Algerians, finding them covered by the General Amnesty, but the penal authorities took no action, and the insurgents remained interned. Technically freed, the Kabyle were nonetheless barred from leaving the archipelago.

In a July 1889 Chamber of Deputies discussion of the government's Amnesty Commission's report—a debate so heated that it led to a duel between two deputies—Interior Minister Ernest Constans expressed the government's fear of the Kabyle's disruptive power, declaring, "These Algerians have organized the most perilous of insurrections; their return to Algeria would present the gravest of dangers."[132] The professed anticolonial deputy Camille Pelletan retorted, "These alarms are exaggerated. The Chamber must not forget that these Algerians have fought for France in New Caledonia. We have promised them amnesty, we must grant it."[133] Approximately forty of the Algerian deportees, had, indeed, fought with the French (alongside Tahitians, whom the French considered "faithful subjects, good soldiers . . . for contributing to the work of 'pacification.'"[134]) against the Kanak in their 1878 uprising.[135] The Kabyle had been guaranteed their freedom for their efforts. Despite these assurances, the ongoing pressure from former Communards, and the Kabyle deportees' petitions to the Chamber of Deputies, France prevented the Algerian insurgents from leaving New Caledonia until February 1, 1895.[136]

Looking back on the Kabyle's arrival in New Caledonia, Michel wrote in 1898, "The Arabs were deported for having risen against oppression. These Orientals, imprisoned far from their tents and their tribes, were simple and good and just."[137] Michel used the Rousseauian language of the innocence of the pre-civilized, characterizing the Kabyle in the same way she had described the Kanak years earlier. In a letter to her fellow deportee Henri Bauer, written during their exile, Michel addressed these feelings, stating, "Bauer, while you do not share my affections for the Kanak, you do share it for the Arabs, and I believe that we will see them again with great pleasure."[138] Although Michel identified with both the Kabyles and the Kanak in their desire to cast off French imperial power, most of her comrades empathized only with the North Africans.

Like many Communard exiles, Michel romanticized and exoticized the deported Algerians, characterizing them as guileless and righteous "Orientals."[139] More pointedly, in her writings she made no mention of the Kabyle volunteering and fighting against the Kanak, and alongside the French, in 1878—actions that would have directly contradicted her portrayal. For Michel, the Kanak anti-imperial uprising held great significance and value. As the only Communard deportee to consistently support the Indigenous people, she found her co-detainees' lack of solidarity incomprehensible, especially given their recent experiences of violent repression and exile at the hands of the French government. Michel held particular antipathy for those who not only supported the French, but also volunteered and fought at their side. Years later, conveying her feelings regarding the deportees who allied with the imperial authority and against the colonized Kanak, Michel explained that "I have great esteem for them [Communard deportees], but at that point, they disgusted me."[140] Her abhorrence at the oppressed siding with the oppressor casts in particular relief her silence regarding the Kabyle fighting with the French.

Choosing to stay quiet about the Kabyle's actions, Michel ignored the same engagements for which she denigrated the fraternizing Communard deportees. This enabled her to maintain a fiction of the Algerians' anti-imperial purity in order to preserve her romantic political affinity with them. As she did in her translations and transcriptions of Kanak tales, narratives she shaped and edited to present the Kanak in ways she considered most palatable to Europeans, Michel quietly elided what she would otherwise consider traitorous acts: colonized people fighting against another colonized group on the side of their mutual colonizer.

Of the multitude of prison memoirs published after the General Amnesty, only one other Communard veteran—an anonymous deportee—defended the Kanak. The unknown author of *Mes sept ans de bagne, par un forçat* (My seven years in the prison colony, by a convict) declared, "I must reveal all the iniquities, all of the crimes committed against the unhappy Kanak. Not only were they stripped of their land . . . but this free savage was forced to work eight to ten hours per day for the colonial administration . . . whose employees pocketed the Kanak's money." Accusing the French government of enserfing the Kanak, the author questioned, "I ask how we French, who cry out against the Khedive of Egypt for forcing his subjects into unpaid labor, can impose the same burden on our Kanak subjects?"[141] Indicting his compatriots for hypocrisy, he continued: "Not one convict moved, helped, or wished the triumph of the Kanak during the insurrection."[142] We know nothing of the author's actions during the uprising, and while he expressed solidarity with the Kanak in the aftermath, he did so without revealing his identity and thus openly taking a stand. The fact that the lone Communard beside Michel to publicly support the Kanak revolt did so undercover underscores the uniqueness of Michel's stance and highlights the distinctiveness of both her racial and anti-imperial politics.

The unnamed deportee lauded Michel, calling her "a saint." Portraying Michel as a selfless, de-sexed martyr—"She never even thought that she was a woman"—he implied that she thus managed to supersede her biological destiny. Yet the author mentioned nothing of her support for the Kanak.[143] Rather than recognizing her political engagement or actual undertakings, he instead characterized her as a secular savior of fallen women (who, for him, included all female prisoners).[144] "I know nothing more touching," he expressed, "than the devotion so complete, so simple, so pure, of Louise Michel, moralizing and instructing so many unhappy women at the women's camp."[145] Subsequently launching into a discourse on "women's virtue, which is made up of much dignity, reserve, and timidity; woman is extremely delicate,"[146] he argued that most *femmes bagnardes* (women prisoners) had lost these characteristics and that Louise Michel had worked to restore them.

The author's sexist assumptions shaped his misperception of Michel and prevented him from identifying her political, revolutionary activism.[147] Michel did not live in the women's camp, but remained in the main deportee prison on the Ducos Penninsula, many miles away. The anonymous critic so narrowly defined women's capacity that, because Michel operated beyond those parameters while still remaining a "saint" in his view, she had to be seen as something other than a woman. In reality, Michel did no gendered moral uplift work. The author distorted and intensely feminized Michel's reputation as self-sacrificing (she did refuse to accept amnesty before all Communards received it, and she did consistently give away her belongings), while erasing the radical actions that she actually did undertake, including supporting the Kanak revolt—a position that he shared.

Most of the other prisoners had either taken no interest in the Indigenous community, or they feared the Kanak in light of tales of cannibalism and savagery. Few had any concern with the broader colonial question or the realities of colonial dispossession or subjugation.[148]

Some deportees did, however, have cordial relationships with some Kanak. Communard veteran Théodore Ozéré recounted in 1874: "In order to distract ourselves, we paid a visit to our Kanak suppliers. These savages know very well how to socialize, and since we had invited them to eat with us several times, they had returned the favor."[149] The insurrection of 1878 ended these neighborly relations. It pushed the colonists—both free and incarcerated—to choose sides, to ally themselves either with France or the Kanak, with whiteness or Blackness, with oppressor or oppressed, with civilization or savagery.

The revolt began on June 25, 1878, when the Kanak clans of La Foa and Boulouparis coordinated attacks on nearby colonial settlements. Within two days they had killed one hundred people, destroyed villages, burned crops, and slaughtered livestock.[150] Historian Bronwen Douglas maintains that assailing local communities of Europeans—people the Kanak worked for or knew—involved "a calculated use of terror."[151] Utilizing unexpected and extreme violence as a political and psychological tool to terrorize the settlers, these Indigenous clans hoped to drive out all of the colonists. The specter of Indigenous violence, rooted in French perceptions of the Kanak as savage cannibals, had played a role in shaping not only settler fears and attitudes toward the

5.3. Kanak Warrior Group, ca. 1880.© Roger-Viollet/Roger-Viollet.

autochthones, but also colonial policy.[152] Refusing to acknowledge the Kanak as martial opponents with political goals, the French government characterized the insurgency as base savagery and took what Isabelle Merle has termed a "scorched-earth" policy—the approach they had employed earlier to crush smaller conflicts in regions across the Grand Terre between 1856 and 1870.[153]

European colonists allied with the French, defending "their" property— from the people from whom it had been recently usurped. Nearly half of the Algerian Kabyles, exiled to the New Caledonian penal colony following their 1871 anti-imperial uprising against the French, joined forces with that same imperial power to quash the Kanak revolt. Possibly the hope of reduced sentences as compensation (which they did not receive) or a sense of racial and cultural superiority to the Kanak led them to align with the French—despite profound political differences.[154] Even some Kanak clans—particularly the Canala—seized the opportunity to strike traditional adversaries by taking up arms and siding with the French.[155]

On the first day of the uprising, a group of thirty-six deportees formed a French fighting unit, under the command of the former Communard Malherbe, and battled the Kanak at La Foa. On the second day of conflict, eighty-four more former Communards volunteered and took arms. The governor general of New Caledonia demonstrated gratitude to the French deportees by requesting the abrogation of their sentences—in contrast to ignoring similar requests by Kabyle fighters. By December, Malherbe and five others received pardons and returned to the metropole. The French valued the Kayble more than they did the Kanak, but not as much as they valued fellow Frenchmen.[156]

Simon Mayer, a Communard veteran and former commandant of the Parisian National Guard (the Commune's citizen army that fought the French national military in 1871), wrote, "On the Ducos Peninsula," where Louise Michel was also interned "we believed that because of the Kanak insurrection, it was our duty to not lull ourselves into a coward's sleep, and to defend the French government."[157] Only seven years after the brutal repression of their attempted revolution, for these prisoners to feel a "duty . . . to defend the French government"—the French government that had slaughtered their comrades, friends, and in some cases family, and had deported them to the South Pacific prison colony—required an enormous psychic shift. It necessitated a profound alteration in their self-identities as revolutionaries and oppositional forces, as well as their conception of the state as enemy and oppressor.[158] Racial, cultural, and "civilizational" solidarity trumped all. The former Communards claimed no allegiance or association with the Kanak, despite suffering under the same systemic yoke.

A short-lived weekly New Caledonian newspaper, Le parisien, edited by the Commune veteran L. Barzon, exemplified the disconnection most French exiles felt toward the Kanak. Published in 1878, the year of the revolt, the journal mentioned the ongoing conflict only once, to "sadly announce the deaths of four deportees . . . who have been assassinated . . . by the Indigenes."[159] Explaining that "our unfortunate comrades were attacked by a band of Kanak," the front page, black-box article described how three Frenchmen died following "an energetic fight," a fourth perished from his wounds shortly afterward, and a fifth "escaped massacre, thanks to his courage"—in hand-to-hand battle, he was ultimately able to reach and then use his gun. The piece concluded, "We await the details of this scene of savagery."[160]

As political deportees, most of the French prisoners kept their eyes and minds on France, biding their time until their longed-for return home. New Caledonia was their prison, the Kanak wild characters peopling the landscape, one part of the foreign and hostile island terrain. Few Communards had a larger critique of empire or saw the Indigenous people as fully human beings, worthy of connection or understanding. Few could—or wanted to—think beyond the penal confines to explore or appreciate the broader physical and cultural environment into which they had been exiled.

Isolated, traumatized, homesick, uncertain of when or even if they would return to France, the anti-imperial rupture pressed the Commune veterans to choose a side. Henri Berthier, a Communard deportee, expressed this sense of racial solidarity, declaring that "the . . . [Kanak] chiefs . . . began a war of extermination against the whites."[161] Placing Communards and the colonial authority—prisoners and jailers—under the same umbrella of whiteness, the former insurgents stood with their oppressors and against the new insurgents. Embracing political solidarity would have meant forsaking whiteness for Blackness; even for these radical revolutionaries, it would have meant forsaking Frenchness. After five grueling years of clinging to their European and urban identities in the rural South Pacific archipelago, their racial—and perceived civilizational—affiliation remained paramount.

In the years after their repatriation, some deportees expressed remorse at their lack of solidarity with the Kanak. Charles Malato wrote in 1894 that these "men, although cannibals, were fighting for their liberty," lamenting that the Communards had made a "race war"; in 1888 Maxime Lisbonne termed the Kanak "the Communards of New Caledonia"; and Simon Meyer portrayed the Kanak as "having had their land stolen" and suffering under "a bad approach to colonizing."[162] These former revolutionaries articulated their regrets with the distance of time. But they also expressed these sentiments only after anti-imperial ideas had begun to spread among the French left, more than a decade after Michel had first asserted her anti-colonial critique.

Michel was unique. She recognized an alliance, professed her support, and persisted as the only Communard of whom we have evidence openly and consistently siding with the Kanak. She likened the Indigenous uprising to that of 1871 Paris, comparing imperial and class dominations: "They also struggled for their independence, for their life, for their liberty. I am with them, as I was with the people of revolutionary Paris, crushed, defeated!" In public lectures two decades later in Paris, reflecting on her publication of the Kanak tales and her experiences in New Caledonia, Michel recalled how she had "retraced the life and legends of these Kanak that our hypocritical civilization has murdered."[163] An October 1900 police report related her claim that "at the moment of the revolt against the whites, she advised them to cut the telegraph wires."[164]

Michel understood that the Indigenous insurrection had resulted from years of French colonial assaults on Kanak property, people, sacrality, and culture.[165] Carefully planned and executed, the initial Kanak anti-colonial incursions manifested the consequence of decades of subjugation and efforts at erasure by colonizers who did not recognize the Kanak as having politics, culture, or full humanity. As historian Roselène Dousset-Leenhardt explains, while the French characterized the uprising as reactive savagery, the "insurrection of 1878 presented itself . . . as a realization of a people intending to defend the highest values of their civilization."[166]

Between 1847 and the late 1860s, Kanak clans had repeatedly attacked colonists and members of the colonial authority, in reaction to their dispossession and to other colonial oppressions, which included forced labor, kidnapping and raping Indigenous women, and profaning sacred sites.[167] The French brutally repressed each uprising, thereby increasingly decimating the Kanak population and its morale.[168] After 1869, the raids and assaults dropped dramatically. According to both Dousset-Leenhardt and ethnographer Alban Bensa, the Kanak used these years to plan, coordinate, and prepare for the 1878 multiclan, anticolonial uprising against the French.[169] Geographer Alain Saussol has argued that the unique size, intensity, and coordination of the 1878 revolt occurred in reaction to the Europeans' substantial expansion of their settlement frontier.[170] But the imperial power never termed conflict with the Kanak "war"; nor did they admit the Kanak capacity for any sort of strategic or sophisticated combat. They refused to recognize the Kanak as an equal adversary.[171]

In 1881, Henri Rivière, the head of the French military repression of the 1878 uprising, wrote, "The major cause of the insurrection, perhaps the only one, is the antagonism that one always sees between the conquering and conquered peoples. The latter must be absorbed by the former or it will disappear. The black or copper races of America or Oceana are unable to be absorbed. They differ too much from the white race."[172] Rivière, like many of his contemporaries, believed that the Kanak, like the American Indians, were destined to extinction. Considered incapable of assimilation—what Rivière termed "absorption"—the Kanak no longer had a space for existence and survival, once the French took possession of their land. The geographer Austin Bernard reiterated Rivière's contention in 1894: "Without a doubt, the indigenes of New Caledonia are beginning to disappear, and we will soon be speaking of them in the past. . . . The withering, then the extinction of the savages . . . when they find themselves in the presence of the white man, is a fact on which much as been written. The civilized life and the savage life seem incompatible on the same soil."[173] Bensa underscores that while the French held this belief about Indigenous people in all of their colonies, nowhere did they hold it with such absolute certainty as in New Caledonia.[174]

Michel understood this extinction theory as a rationalization of the effects of colonial programs through which the Kanak were, indeed, being pushed toward cultural and physical destruction. The fierce repression of the uprising, she contended, only further annihilated them. She declared, "The Kanak insurrection was drowned in blood, the rebel tribes decimated; they are in the process of being wiped out."[175] Rather than a natural or inevitable byproduct of empire, the disappearance of the Indigenous people resulted from France's active and systematic efforts to advance their extinction and to replace them with both free and convict colonists. This move toward removal was fundamental to settler colonialism, as anthropologist Patrick Wolfe explains: "Settler colonizers come to stay. . . . Invasion is a structure, not an event," a framework built on a "logic of elimination."[176]

In late September 1878, the minister of the Marine and Colonies commissioned General Arthur-Ernest Comte de Trentinian, the inspector general of the armies, to investigate and report on the uprising's causes. To the surprise and disappointment of his superiors, Trentinian issued a document blaming colonial abuses (expropriating land, exploiting labor, kidnapping women, destroying crops with grazing animals) for pushing the Kanak to revolt.[177] His position sharply contradicted that of most of his contemporaries. Ignored, then buried, the Trentinian Report remained essentially absent from the historical record until Dousset-Leenhardt rediscovered and published it in 1970. The report's author, a young and highly successful general, paid for his honest and thorough investigative efforts with his career; all subsequent advancement was stymied.[178]

Trentinian challenged the dominant colonial narrative that denied both Kanak agency and French culpability. As Bensa convincingly argues, France's theory of Kanak extinction utilized "social Darwinism as an explanatory general model, in perfect accord with the conquering interests of the epoch. This ideology of Melanesian extinction defined a very particular form of racism . . . a *racism of annihilation* which had never envisaged the Kanak as anything other than nonentities."[179] Refusing to recognize not only Kanak culture, Kanak social and political organization, Kanak sovereignty, Kanak land tenure, and Kanak military competence, but also Kanak humanity and right to life allowed the French to employ a policy of slow genocide. Effectively categorizing these New Caledonians as outside of the human and destined to extinction, the French used political, military, and legal means to facilitate what they asserted to be the Kanak's natural dissolution.

On September 1, members of the Kanak Canala clan ambushed and beheaded the renowned Ataï, chief from the La Foa region and one of the insurgency's primary leaders. Decrying this treachery in her *Mémoires*, Michel wrote that "Ataï was struck down by a traitor . . . Noudo, a chief sold to the whites."[180] The colonial governor Jean-Baptiste Léon Olry shipped Ataï's head to Paris, where it was examined, dissected, and exhibited.[181] By the end of 1878, the rebellion, too, was dead.

Toward Decolonizing

In her *Mémoires*, Michel stated that "the task of teachers, these obscure soldiers of civilization, is to give people an intellectual means to revolt."[182] Traveling to Algeria in 1904, as she had promised the exiled Kabyle insurgents she had encountered in the New Caledonia prison colony decades earlier, Michel strove to foment an anti-imperial uprising. She lectured to audiences of four hundred to five hundred people per night, a significant number of whom were educators. Anarchist Ernest Girault, with whom Michel traveled and spoke, wrote that "as in all of Algeria, the corps of teachers stood out, with enthusiasm, its spirit truly secular and antimilitarist."[183] Again and again, reports specifically mention the attendance of teachers and their fervor. Engaging crowds with what one newspaper described as an "incontestable eloquence," Michel brought together the central elements of her universal vision: language, education, and revolution.[184] Mixed crowds, including those in traditional Kabyle clothing "in the middle of the *toilettes européennes*," came to hear the renowned orator and revolutionary. "Each will aid the other," Michel professed, "and humanity will march in the steps of giants. . . . Each will speak a piece of the universal language, that of humanity."[185]

Michel understood education, language, and revolution as interwoven. Words and ideas together could spark liberatory action, they could bring peoples together, and they could overturn repression. In Paris in the 1860s and during the Commune, Michel developed and practiced feminist, equitable pedagogies. In New Caledonia in the 1870s, she introduced egalitarian and anarchist Western ideas, carefully chosen and transmitted, to educate and "advance" the Kanak, while simultaneously promoting Kanak knowledge and language to improve Europeans. Following her return from New Caledonian exile, Michel spent decades traveling across France, as well as through Belgium, the Netherlands, and Spain, rousing audiences with impassioned oratory, relating histories of oppressions and uprisings, illuminating injustices, and striving to stir revolt. In the 1880s, she worked to appropriate the French language through a set of novels, stripping the language of elite sanction and radically democratizing it to reflect its oral creolization in the hands of the working class. In London in the 1890s, she used anarchist instruction to help shape enlightened, multilingual, and liberated European children as a means of advancing global solidarity. Finally, in Algeria in 1904, she promoted education and free thought as a means to uniting Algerians and Europeans in anticolonial liberation. Linguistic unity, anarchist feminism, and anti-imperialism ultimately interconnected all of these. Highlighting the intersection of capitalism and imperialism, she queried in a volume of her memoirs, "What purpose do the colonies serve if they do not produce fortunes for their exploiters?"[186] She blamed patriarchy for "the etiolation inflicted on women's intelligence"—for blocking the light of knowledge from women and thus stunting their intellectual growth.[187]

For Michel, as for many other progressive activists of the final two decades of the nineteenth century, imperialism meant the political and socioeconomic domination of a people by another, more powerful nation. She saw parallel power relations between women and men. Michel would not have recognized her approaches to either Algeria or New Caledonia as imperialist and would likely have argued vociferously against such a contention. In her efforts to empower and liberate Indigenous groups living under colonial rule, Michel took a parental stand toward what she considered more childlike, less developed peoples, employing the same pedagogical philosophies and methods that she did with European children. Yet she not only taught, but also studied and learned from the Kanak, especially investigating their ideas about the relationships between people and nature, the transmission of histories, and death and the dead. Michel rethought and redesigned the content and delivery of education. She embraced a humanistic, positivistic belief that progress in rational thought would enable teachers to successfully deliver revolutionary empowerment to those who might not attain it on their own. In radically reworking instructional theory and praxis, she took steps toward decolonizing and democratizing not just the curriculum, but the entire educational—and ultimately communication—process.

Speaking about the Kanak years later at a rally commemorating the anniversary of the Commune, Michel testified that "these savages were the true patriots defending their country against barbarians who wanted to civilize them with cannon balls."[188] Still using the condescending (if ironic) language of savagery to describe the Kanak, she simultaneously characterized them as "true patriots" in contrast to the French, whom she termed "barbarians," and by implication, false patriots. Michel described the Kanak uprising as a national defense, a rational and legitimate political action. Inverting the international playing field, she designated France's actions as barbaric, as illegitimate, as irrational violence. How could civilization rationally be brought by cannonballs?

The French colonial authority had constructed the Kanak as savages—as base, cultureless, less-than-human beings. France could thus ignore native claims to property ownership, refuse to recognize them as legitimate military opponents, and insist that their very existence was naturally and logically coming to an end. This settler colonial vision of the unavoidable disappearance of the Indigenous Kanak, akin to the North American myth of the "disappearing Indian," constituted a self-serving positivism that the French colonial authorities advocated for their own ends. Against this racialized imperial pessimism, Michel instead championed a universalism for humanity, a future available to all peoples in all places.

Michel's positivism supported her perception that humanity was naturally progressing but doing so unevenly and inconsistently. In an essay about the earth, its human and animal inhabitants, and geologic time, Michel wrote,

"The same attraction which makes the planets revolve around our sun in a harmonic order attracts the human societies toward the ideal of justice and intelligence which constitute progress."[189] Her anarchist feminism, radical pedagogy, and revolutionary anticolonialism provided the theory and praxis to help her advance the forward movement as she analyzed gender, race, and class hierarchies in multiple contexts. Living in New Caledonia profoundly shaped all of these politics. And yet it did not enable her to extract herself from a European framework.

Michel's politics and experience underscore the impossibility of a clear dichotomy between imperialism and anti-imperialism in this period. Even the most fervent European anti-imperialists drew on a hierarchy of development so normalized as to be made invisible. In the face of this, Michel saw education as neutral, not recognizing its imperial and totalizing components. She recognized only its radical possibilities, missing the ways in which her presumptions that the Kanak needed to be educated occluded Indigenous capacities and denigrated their culture.

Language, education, and revolution formed the core of the worldview Michel wrought in New Caledonia, underpinning a universalism that was both potentially liberatory and potentially imperialist. She saw the pidgin Bichelamar as evidence of the Kanak's ability to overcome fragmentation by surmounting linguistic barriers, and she considered the language itself as a universal tongue, which brought together multiple cultures and could be theoretically viable around the world. Participating in the era's search for a unifying vernacular as a means to overcome political divisions, she posited Bichelamar, pointedly rejecting France's characterization of Kanak languages as intrinsically inferior tongues. When faced with revolution—in the form of the 1878 Kanak uprising—she stood alone among the French exiles in supporting the Indigenous people. A deeply engaged intellectual, she wielded theoretical tools that she shaped and honed in the successive crucibles of revolution and exile to a penal colony. Those tools helped to undermine European hegemonic power and promote international unity. Michel's project contested metropolitan-centered epistemologies and frameworks and refocused on the intersections of aspects of those with Indigenous, peasant, and other marginalized peoples' forms of knowledge. Consistent with her steps toward decolonized, democratic, and feminist education, she introduced the beginnings of a revolutionary postcolonial universalism. Analogizing the aggressive powers to an ancient and precarious paperbark tree in New Caledonia, Michel wrote, "A dull thud, a cloud of dust, and it was finished; the great tree became a little heap of dust. . . . Thus will disappear this society where might makes right."[190]

CHAPTER 6

Familiar Stranger

The Figure of "The Jew"

Crossing Russia by train in the mid-1860s, Olympe Audouard wrote, "The Jews made my trip intolerable."[1] Casual antisemitism wound through Audouard's work as she described and critiqued the societies she encountered on her travels through Turkey, Egypt, Russia, Palestine, and Lebanon. In the world of empire, other French feminists also wrote of encounters with Jews, discussed conceptions of the place of Jews in society, made passing remarks regarding Jews, or merely used the figure of "The Jew"—or Jewish difference—as a point of reference. Jews embodied a foreignness at home and thus became a "familiar stranger" abroad. For these feminists, the recognizable alterity of Jewish individuals and cultures provided an international touchstone around or against which arguments concerning empire and citizenship could be made and points regarding religion and identity proven and disproven. "The Jew" defied the perceived dichotomy of colony versus metropole by bridging ideas of citizenship, belonging, authenticity, and otherness along a wide range of conceptual references.[2]

The figure of "The Jew" (and "The Jewess") pervaded French intellectual, cultural, and social life, weaving in and out of political discourses throughout the nineteenth century. These representations shifted over time, emerging as socially constructed and historically specific, existing in tension with the multiple realities of Jewish lives. Writers, orators, politicians, and artists used the figure of the Jew not only to promote antisemitism, but also to support tangentially related arguments and positions concerning gender, race, imperialism, and civilization.[3]

Audouard, Auclert, and Michel each employed the figure of the Jew to support their particular and often conflicting political agendas. Audouard demonstrated and promoted a gendered, Orientalized antisemitism. She denigrated Jews she encountered on her travels, retold and wielded gendered cultural and Catholic stereotypical tales and images, and utilized both real Jews and the idea of the Jew to exemplify an absence of civilization. Auclert, for her part, instrumentalized the figure of the Jew to promote women's suffrage. She easily equated Jews with the capitalist class and—in the colonial context—with the French imperial authority, both groups that she perceived to be exploitative and that she actively opposed. Repeatedly publishing pro–women's suffrage articles in the virulently antisemitic newspaper *La libre parole*, Auclert tacitly accepted the journal's profoundly discriminatory stance by using it as a political platform, while elsewhere decrying antisemitism. Michel took a third approach. Declaring religion irrelevant, she criticized bourgeois Jews as she did any member of the bourgeoisie, and she considered working-class Jews as subjugated as any member of the working-class. She saw the figure of the Jew as a pernicious result of capitalist pressures. Michel engaged this idea of the Jew to expose its illegitimacy, as well as the divisiveness of religion, the aberrance of capitalism, and the corrupt nature of antisemitism. In wielding stereotypes in order to debunk them, she reproduced those prejudicial characterizations. For each feminist, the figure of the Jew comported with a political order of a world being remade through France's imperial undertakings and ambitions.

Audouard, Auclert, and Michel all used "the Jew" to make gendered claims regarding race and civilization. They based these assertions primarily on their encounters in imperial contexts, while also connecting these ideas to the metropole. Predominant attitudes toward Jews and conceptions of Jews both influenced and intersected the emergent feminist understandings of race and empire; these stances were fashioned, in turn, by politics of class and religion. The figure of the Jew emerged as a historically specific familiar stranger, an other saturated with both persistent and contemporaneous prejudices and stereotypes, in implicit or explicit opposition to the dominant ideals of gendered and racialized Frenchness.

The three women each stood at a temporal and intellectual junction of imperial and Jewish engagement, both literal and metaphorical, across the span of feminist politics. They shared four commonalities. First, as the previous chapters have explored, they were among the earliest nineteenth-century French feminists not only to consider questions of empire, but also to travel and live beyond the metropole. Their varied experiences across continents internationalized and globalized the three women's gendered and racialized perspectives and influenced their particular politics. Political theorist Roxanne Euben writes that voyages involve a "dialectical process of acquiring and producing knowledge about others and about one's own cultural and political world."[4] Encountering Jews beyond the metropole remolded or reified the women's existing comprehensions and categorizations of Jews—a known other in France, now confronted among unknown others in radically new contexts. The multi-local presence of Jews muddied metropole/colony oppositions and clouded definitions of French and Other.

Second, they wrote about Jews in a global imperial context as well as in metropolitan France. Each woman moved within France's colonies; Michel lived in the British metropole; and Audouard voyaged through the Russian and Ottoman Empires and the North American West. All three travelers thus experienced the gendered social and economic realities of imperialism and colonialism from several perspectives, and they all encountered Jews in these various milieux. Each feminist discussed actual Jewish people and communities, yet they also used the figure of the Jew, and its concomitant complex set of stereotypes, to assert or support closely or tangentially related issues. Examining the scope of their attitudes toward Jews and the "Jewish Question," in both metropole and empires, reveals the ways in which their individual approaches to race and religion more broadly relate to their racialized and gendered conceptions of Jews.

Feminisms constituted their third commonality, with each woman holding a distinct position on the spectrum of feminist politics, spanning from Michel's revolutionary anarchist feminism on the far Left, through Auclert's republican socialist feminism, to Audouard's liberal feminism in the center.[5] Their particular stances reflected each woman's class politics, perspectives that filtered their experiences of otherness, their adherence to the status quo, and their interpretations of inequity.

And finally, in differing ways, the three feminists rhetorically and politically employed Jewish difference to bolster their specific, and often conflicting, ideological stances and political programs. They exemplify the ways in which Jewish difference was used to foster broader, and often disparate, agendas.

Overall, the three women's work provides a chromatic window into the ways in which the figure of the Jew influenced and shaped the era's gendered and racialized political thought. Their words and actions elucidate the powerful presence of "Jewish difference," revealing how not only French feminists but also thinkers and activists across the political spectrum engaged and employed these ideas in metropolitan and colonial worlds.

As defined by Lisa Silverman, the analytic of "Jewish difference" constitutes "the relationship between the constructed, hierarchical ideals of the Jew and the non-Jew."[6] Silverman explains it as conceptual category—comparable to gender—both socially constructed and performative. (The relationship between sexism and gender is analogous to the relationship of antisemitism and Jewish difference.) The figure of the Jew and the non-Jew are mutually constitutive, historically and culturally specific, and deeply gendered.[7]

Audouard, Auclert, and Michel's encounters with Jews were mediated by their distinct understandings of Jewish difference, perspectives that manifested the complex intersections involved in any individual politics. Each drew upon the ideas of Jewish difference that permeated mid- to late-nineteenth-century French culture and society providing an ideological tool to advance or stymie a wide range of political agendas; each relied upon and employed the presumption of Jewish difference to articulate her ideal vision of both metropole and empire. Because of Jews' diasporic presence and long-term marginalization, they constituted a bridge between metropole and colony, between French and Other, between Occident and Orient. Ivan Davidson Kalmar and Derek Penslar state that "historically, Jews have been seen in the Western world variably and often concurrently as occidental *and* oriental."[8] Jewish people in France presented many French Christians with their original encounter with otherness, whether through literal or metaphorical interactions. As recognizable and somewhat familiar "foreigners," they occupied a unique cultural, social, physical, and imaginary place.[9] Audouard, Auclert, and Michel each held particular conceptualizations of Jews as a certain kind of alien—a known other, against whom they could measure and evaluate the new peoples they encountered while in empire.

As this book has shown, each feminist sought change both within and beyond France. They shared a basic critique of existing late-nineteenth-century Western gender relations, one fueled, augmented, and shaped by their time outside of Western Europe. These experiences motivated their condemnations of contemporary imperial practices and the anti-imperialist positions that they articulated using languages of race and class, as well as gender. Audouard, Auclert, and Michel each examined dominant hierarchies and stereotypes involving the people they encountered. In their respective assessments—analyzing questions of race (based on scientific hierarchy), of class difference (based on politics and economics), or of gender relations (based on their particular feminism)—each suggested a model for civilization and a particular definition of Frenchness. Their considerations of Jews and utilizations of the idea of Jews reflected and supported these politics.

The Liberal

As Olympe Audouard journeyed through Algeria, Egypt, Turkey, Russia, the Middle East, and the United States, observing, analyzing, and describing life in these global imperial spaces, she established a hierarchy of cultures based on a combination of preconceived conceptualizations and literary impressions, religion and ideology, personal engagements and observations. She placed Jews in the lowest stratum.

In her travel writing, Audouard used a profoundly racialized and gendered version of the figure of the Jew to advance her antisemitic, Catholic-based politics. The intensity of this ideology shaped her discussions and descriptions of Jews and Jewish life to such an extent that it supplanted her feminism in these contexts. Her antisemitism also interwove with her liberalism and her elite class politics. Jews repeatedly reappeared in her interpretations of these travels.

Audouard extolled many aspects of Turkish life in her first book, *Les mystères du sérail et des harems turcs: Lois, mœurs, usages, anecdotes* (Mysteries of the seraglio and of Turkish harems: laws, customs, manners, anecdotes), published in 1863. She particularly challenged the widespread European conceptions of Turkish women's circumscribed and exploited position, and she bolstered her argument with her first-hand experiences. Audouard claimed that "I have seen with my own eyes that all that has been written about Turkish women's lives, their customs, their position . . . was completely wrong."[10] Schooled in the romance and exoticism of the Orient, she traveled to Turkey with her father for a spur-of-the-moment adventure. On her arrival she began comparing the myth to the reality she experienced.[11]

Audouard commended Turkish women's lives based on her experience visiting elite Turkish families. She placed enormous value on the comforts of wealth.[12] In Constantinople, the lack of gas lighting and of cleanliness appalled her. Audouard's class privilege and expectations left her ill-equipped to see the realities of poor peoples' lives. Thus, her entrenched antisemitism filtered her perceptions of impoverished Jews and their environments. She wrote: "Between all the unclean quarters of Constantinople, the Jewish Quarter distinguishes itself by its revolting filth. When approaching this quarter, a nauseating odor fills one's throat. Their homes, their streets, their persons, all ooze with dirtiness."[13] Audouard brought not only romanticized, exotic conceptions of Turkish life to her travels, but also preexisting class and racialized religious prejudices. She repeatedly employed the antisemitic slur of the dirty and inferior Jew. Fixated on uncleanliness, she made no mention of the associated poverty of the neighborhoods. Her reports supported the common libel that all Jews

6.1. Olympe Audouard, ca. 1870s. © Paris Musées/Musée Carnavalet—Histoire de Paris.

had wealth, but that their naturally miserly character led many to live as apparent paupers. While Audouard Orientalized Turks and Jews, her conceptualization of the two peoples contrasted starkly: she romanticized and idealized Turks, while perceiving Jews as abject and common.

Audouard came of age in the wake of the 1840 Damascus Affair (also known as the "Damascus Blood Libel"), in which the disappearance of a Capuchin monk and his assistant in Damascus resulted in the city's Jewish population facing accusations of ritual murder. The Damascus Affair attracted significant and lasting attention in France. When French Jews—shocked at the French press's willingness to legitimate such an egregious lie—came to the defense of their Syrian co-religionists, metropolitan antisemitism spiked as journalists questioned where French Jews' loyalty lay.[14] The Syrian context of the blood-libel charges fed the French population's fascination with the "Orient" and its particular, deeply gendered, conceptions of "Oriental" Jews. Linking French Jews with those of Syria categorized all Jews as other and foreign, as beyond the bounds of true Frenchness. The Damascus Affair and its repercussions significantly affected French ideas of Jews and Jewishness, contributing to popular conceptions of Jews upon which Audouard drew.[15]

Audouard's antisemitism, birthed in this context, spanned gender and class boundaries. Class superseded race for Audouard—as evinced by her strong defense of elite Turkish life—but her antisemitism fully shaped her views of Jews of all classes. It also underscored her gendered perceptions of both Jewish women and men. In many of her works, Audouard denigrated Jews' physical environment and their bodies. She wrote of her train journey from Warsaw to Vienna ("the dirtiest and most uncomfortable that I have seen, except in Italy"), in which she encountered Polish Jews living under the Russian Empire.

> Certainly I am very tolerant and I have nothing against the Jews, in terms of their religion, but in terms of their physical appearance, that is another thing. The Polish Jews are disgustingly dirty. They wear long robes, so shiny and worn that one can no longer tell its original color; their long beards are filthy; two long, frizzy curls fall from each side of their faces. . . . One can tell from the curvature of their spines that they are prone to constant submission. They have a crafty air . . . that makes one fearful of allowing them to approach.[16]

Audouard, after carefully declaring her tolerance of Jewish people and their religion, viciously disparaged aspects of their manners and appearance reflective of beliefs (beards and *peyos*) and of miserliness (the worn robe). Her accusations of craftiness and submissiveness evoked typical antisemitic behavioral stereotypes; the descriptors "frizzy" and "curls" evoked a racialized, Oriental-ized, and feminized image of "Jewish hair."

Antisemitic discourse linking Jews with women stretched back before the Renaissance, but took a more modern form during the Enlightenment, when both women and Jews sought access to citizenship and public inclusion.[17] The era's conservative opposition, reacting against these simultaneous efforts to alter the status quo, propounded a misogynistic antisemitism. Addressing the "coincidence of antisemitism and misogyny," Paula Hyman explains, that by "disputing their subordination and making a claim to equality, both modern Jews and modern women challenged the antisemites' nostalgic and anti-modern vision of a smoothly functioning, non-egalitarian, hierarchical social order, in which subordinate groups (like women and Jews) knew their place."[18] Audouard, a liberal feminist, would not have overtly agreed with the misog-yny in these associations. Yet by describing the Polish Jewish men as having "long frizzy curls fall from each side of their face," she implicitly disparaged them by casting doubt on their masculinity. Though different from the misog-yny of Enlightenment-era conservatives, Adouard's adherence to hierarchies of class and status did reflect her opposition to certain forms of egalitarian-ism and acceptance of particular types of marginalization. She overtly used widely recognized misogynist rhetoric in her efforts to vilify Jews.

Ascribing effeminacy to Jewish men formed a central element in the op-eration of Jewish difference, as well as the positioning of Jews as racialized others. Constructing Jewish men as effeminate, including feminizing the Jew-ish male body, denied them the characteristics that the period's dominant cul-ture defined as properly male, thus barring their inclusion in the European Christian masculine world. Within this world of binary gender construction, Jewish men's alleged absence of essential masculine virility pushed them to the side of inferiority, to the side of the feminine and the homosexual. Their Jewish difference, their very nature, was positioned as transgressing vital gen-der boundaries. This "nature" became part of a set of racialized characteris-tics that shifted understandings of Jews as a religion to one of Jews as a race.[19] And while Enlightenment influence in the nineteenth-century made religious oppression and overt marginalization less acceptable, at least in terms of citi-zenry and universalism, the era's emergent racial characterizations and cate-gorizations (which attained considerable intellectual and popular acceptance) excluded metropolitan Jews from the French mainstream, from being truly French. As Sander Gilman was among the first to argue, Jewish men's alleged effeminacy—due at least in part to their circumcision—formed a central ele-ment and an explanation of the racial differentiation of Jews.[20]

Audouard metonymically translated this lack of virility to social life in Jerusalem under the Ottoman Empire. Describing the four sections of the city—Christian, Armenian, Muslim, and Jewish—Audouard once again (as in Constantinople) portrayed the Jewish quarter as the filthiest and lowest, affirming that "it is the most unhealthy and stifling. . . . The houses are made of mud, and serve as a shelter for swarms of insects who descend upon the five or six families living in each. . . . Topping it off is a cesspool where all of the city's sewers empty . . . leaving a nauseating odor."[21] Having set the dismal scene, Audouard spoke of life in the quarter, where she found "Jewish girls of an admirable beauty, with a biblical air. . . . It makes a painful impression. These girls, beautiful as angels . . . [are] like seeing the most beautiful, fresh, and rare flowers thrown on a dung heap."[22] For Audouard, lovely young women living in particularly Jewish uncleanliness seemed contrary to nature, the luminous squandered on the sordid, the potentially sacred sullied by squalor. But, she contended, "at least these young girls enjoy a security they would not have elsewhere. We profess a contempt so unchristian, that the parents can be nearly certain that no one will make an attempt on the girls' virtue. The man who would be accused of loving a Jewish woman would see himself dishonored."[23] Recognizing anti-Jewish contempt to be so extreme as to be "unchristian," and including herself in the "we" that "professed" it, Audouard underscored the intensity of the prejudice among Jerusalem's non-Jewish residents and visitors. These beautiful young Jewish women therefore remained safe from any "attempt on [their] virtue" because of the shame any man would face by seducing them. Her category "man" meant non-Jewish men—real men in her estimation. Jewish men, with their "long frizzy curls" and curved spines, lacked the virility to pose a threat to these appealing women.[24] For Audouard, Jewish men fell outside of the category "man" and beyond the bounds of masculinity.

Such characterizations of Jewish men as effeminate dovetailed with similar conceptions of racialized other men as lacking masculinity. Ascribing femininity to Indigenous men emerged as a tool among colonizers who consistently ascribed masculinity to themselves as they worked to reify colonial hierarchies. Assigning femininity to the racialized other preserved manliness for the imperialist, under the assumption of a clearly ranked gendered dichotomy. The socially constructed nature of the categories of masculine and feminine provided colonial powers with flexible tools to continue to redefine this gendered hierarchy as colonial circumstances and contexts evolved over time.[25]

Audouard also used gendered and sexualized stereotypes in describing Jewish women. Extolling their "admirable beauty," Audouard deployed the trope of *la belle juive*, the exoticized, eroticized, Orientalized Jewish woman. As Julie Kalman has argued, "The Jewess lived in the Orient and yet she was an approachable subject because she also existed in French society. At the same time, she was still very much a symbol of alterity."²⁶ *La belle juive* transcended place in her embodiment of the triply othered subject: Oriental, Jew, and woman.²⁷

The figure of the Orientalized *la belle juive* permeated mid-nineteenth-century French culture. A somewhat contradictory and shifting character, *la belle juive* could represent either victimized or predatory beauty. Works such as Honoré de Balzac's *Splendeurs et misères des courtisanes*, Eugene Sue's *Le Juif errant*, and Fromental Halévy's opera *La Juive* presented audiences with the exotic, often good-hearted, yet morally questionable Jewish woman.²⁸ But *la belle juive* could also embody a dangerous, threatening character, evoking biblical *femmes fatales* who seduced and killed.

Audouard also located these Jewish women in the historic past, imbuing them "with a biblical air." Akin to Michel's portrayal of the New Caledonian Kanak and like her own judgement of Native Americans, Audouard temporally distanced these Orientalized Jews, denying them coevalness with the nineteenth-century world. Writing about Jews in Jerusalem, then under Ottoman rule, but a city under successive empires reaching back millennia, Audouard described an ancient Eastern people, living in a less-civilized time.

For Audouard, a self-described "good Catholic," visiting Jerusalem resembled a religious pilgrimage.²⁹ Kalman has explained how Christian pilgrims consistently described Jerusalem's Jewish quarter as the filthiest and most impoverished and the Jews living there as deeply debased. From the pilgrims' perspective, these Jews were paying for both their ancestors' crime of Christ-killing, in the very place of that act, and their own ongoing heresy of denying Jesus's divinity.³⁰ Audouard's portrayal of "the most unhealthy and stifling" quarter, swarming with insects and stinking of a cesspool, clearly replicated pilgrims' characterizations. The majority of the Jerusalem section of Audouard's book *L'Orient et ses peuplades* (The Orient and its peoples) addressed Christian pilgrimages and the Church of the Holy Sepulcher. She gave a long, emotional, and highly detailed description of that church—a pilgrimage destination that includes the sites of Jesus's crucifixion, the empty tomb signifying burial and resurrection, and the final four Stations of the Cross. Its hallowed magnificence was such, she proclaimed, that "if the Jews, who deny Jesus Christ, enter this sanctuary, it seems impossible to me that the veil that covers their eyes would not be ripped away, and that they would not be able to resist recognizing, with the Christians, the divinity of Our Father."³¹ Characterizing the spiritual power of the Holy Sepulcher as sufficient to remove violently—to "rip away"—the nearly two-millennia-old obstruction preventing Jews from seeing "the divinity of Our Father," Audouard extolled the holiness of this pilgrimage site, while simultaneously denigrating Jews for their repudiation and blindness.

Audouard addressed her audience as one sharing her religious beliefs, as a group who knew "the divinity of *Our* Father."[32] Jews, in contrast, occupied an external space, outside of the "we" implied in those who share "Our Father." This "we," for Audouard, defined Frenchness in the metropole and civilization in global empire. The Oriental Jew, rejecting Christ, mired in filth and degradation, existed for Audouard as a trans-spatial other against which the identity of "we"—of Catholic Frenchness—was constructed and measured.[33]

In another section of *L'Orient et ses peuplades*, Audouard reported her additional encounters with Polish Jews living under the Russian Empire. Her account of why "the Jews are not loved in Poland" employed not only stereotypes of usury, which she termed "the most honest" of Jewish trades, but also of the dangerous Jewess seductress. Her use of gendered rhetoric extended to the feminization of threat. She explained that in the fourteenth century, Poland's King Casimir the Great, "wise and enlightened, with an ardent and tender heart," met "a Jewess with big, flame-throwing eyes . . . who seized the heart of this sensible monarch; she became his mistress and . . . convinced him to grant monopolies on all of the lucrative trades, and of money-changing, to the men of her race. From this moment, this foreign race set about sucking all of the money from Poland."[34] Audouard perpetuated a far-fetched tale rooted in interwoven sexist and racialized antisemitic narratives. This story undoubtedly emerged from the "Esterke" legend—both a Polish and Jewish folk tale—in which a beautiful Jewish woman seduces King Casimir and he in turn grants favors to the Jewish people. (This tale reworks and reimagines the biblical story of Queen Esther. It typified portrayals of the Jewess, likening her to powerful, Orientalized female biblical characters, who were coterminous with a distant, less civilized past.[35]) In attempting to reconcile the Polish Jews' contemporary oppressed and marginalized status in spite of having "maintained all the monopolies over several centuries," the story continued: in 1818, Polish laws terminated the monopolies, forced Jews out of the lucrative trades, and ghettoized them. Yet, contrary to this "history" and to the apparent socioeconomic reality of the Polish Jews she encountered, Audouard asked, "How could anyone take pity on people with caves full of gold? On people who have a hatred of soap and water which can only be compared to their love of gold?"[36] Again employing the anti-Semitic trope of the wealthy Jew feigning poverty, she alleged that although ostracized, oppressed, and ghettoized, Jews still maintained secret stores of wealth.[37]

For Audouard, Jewish men embodied greed, dissimulation, dirtiness, and effeminate weakness. In contrast, she portrayed the "Jewess" as beautiful, seductive, manipulative, and treacherous: the stereotype of *la belle juive*. Her characterizations reflected the contrasting, yet not quite dichotomous, mid-nineteenth-century stereotypes of Jewish men and women.[38] These images of "the Jew" and "the Jewess" emerged as profoundly gendered constructions, wrought by the era's dominant ideals of gender, enmeshed with long-standing antisemitic conventions.[39] They exemplified the period's popular conceptions of Jewish difference. Audouard's feminism did not extend to Jewish women.

Assessing and narrating her extensive travels and engagements, Audouard ranked societies based primarily on the status of their women. She instrumentalized this information to demonstrate France's lack of civilization, taking a more pointed version of the widely used European metric of women's status reflecting a culture's level of civilization. In different contexts, Audouard had turned this Eurocentric measure on its head, arguing that France scored poorly regarding women's customary and legal positions relative to Turkey, Syria, Russia, and others.[40] In contrast, Audouard did not address Jewish women's standing within their communities. She chose not to evaluate contemporary Jewish culture under the same temporal terms she assessed other peoples she encountered. Instead, she presented a deeply critical appraisal of Jewish gender roles and relations in the biblical period, a period to which antisemitic stereotypes consistently consigned Jewish women. Denying them coevalness with the nineteenth-century world, Audouard relegated Jewish women to the ancient, Oriental past.[41]

In her 1873 book, *Gynécologie: La femme depuis six mille ans* (Gynecology [the study of women]: Six thousand years of women), Audouard argued that women in antiquity and the biblical era suffered under brutally unjust patriarchies.[42] The text examined the history of women over millennia, ranging from Hindustan and Persia, through Greece, Rome, "Biblical Times," and finally "the Christian World."[43] Audouard grouped all pre-Christian periods together, terming them times of "pagan and impure beliefs," which saw the "degradation of women."[44] But, then came "the divine religion, the pure and moral holiness of Christ!" She proclaimed that with the dawn of Christianity, "we will see woman shake off her soiled robe with joy; her soul will awaken after its long slumber. . . . With Christianity, woman has proudly lifted her head once again; she has become conscious of her moral value, which the laws of men had made slumber, and she has shown that the feminine soul is not at all inferior to the masculine."[45] Audouard believed that Christianity allowed women's true, innate moral position to reemerge after millennia of subjugation, including the time of the Hebrew Bible. She considered the Jews, the "people of whom the Bible speaks" to be completely ignorant of "justice, equity, and moral purity," qualities taught to men by Jesus.[46] She asserted, "If the heroes and heroines of the Bible returned to the world as they were then, they would not receive a tip of the hat from an honest man today."[47]

Audouard explained that she undertook writing this volume to determine whether woman was truly inferior to man. She avowed that while conducting her research, "more than one time I believed that I would be forced to recognize her inferiority . . . but Christianity gave me irrefutable proof of the perfect equality between the feminine and masculine soul."[48] Declaring Jesus as the ultimate bringer of truth, Audouard saw Christianity as allowing the revelation of woman's truly superior nature, which had remained hidden and distorted through prior epochs. In her chapter on "Woman in Biblical Times," she detailed a number of female Jewish heroes and martyrs, all of whom, she wrote, employed trickery or immoral sexuality to attain their goals. She compared the biblical Judith, who saved her people through "seduction . . . ruse and treason," to "our Joan of Arc, who saved France, but without compromising her honor and feminine dignity. . . . Joan of Arc is the symbol of the purest Christian virtue. Judith is the symbol of biblical virtue, which is always tinged with shamelessness."[49] Shamelessness clung to all Jewish heroines. Although valiant, Judith was a prostitute, a dangerously sexual being, and willing to use deceit to save the Jews. Her Oriental, threatening, and immoral seductiveness contrasted sharply with Joan of Arc's true French virginal purity and innocence.[50] Judith and Joan of Arc represented the perfect gendered characterizations and sharp contrasts of Judaism and Christianity, of Other and French.

Castigating Judaism and its adherents, Audouard simultaneously lauded Islam. In *L'Orient et ses peuplades* (The Orient and its peoples), she wrote that if she had not "the good fortune of being a good Christian . . . I would like to be a Muslim."[51] She specifically admired Mohammed, professing that his religion brought a much-needed monotheism, humanitarianism, and justice to those who followed him. Yet her esteem had its limits. She affirmed that "one must not forget that Mohammed was the son of an idolater, and an idolater himself. . . . Certainly, if he had known the admirable religion that the Son of God made man had come to give, if . . . he had been a Christian living among Christians, and he would have made and imposed a new religion, he would have been very guilty."[52] Because Mohammed emerged from a pagan context, Audouard maintained that he did not actually reject Christianity. He, his professions, and his actions, therefore remained blameless. This contrasted sharply with Jews, who denied Jesus as the son of god and Christianity as the true religion, both of which made them "very guilty" in Audouard's eyes.[53] This perceived betrayal likely informed her antisemitism. The Jewish women and men she encountered in her travels, living lives she would have considered more primitive and closer to the biblical than the Jews of France, underscored the linkage to the corrupt ancient era.

The Republican Socialist

In her writings on empire, Hubertine Auclert also made antisemitic references, but she did so with much less frequency and vehemence than Audouard. While Audouard used the figure of the Jew to promote her racially based antisemitic politics, Auclert, in contrast, instrumentalized antisemitic stereotypes and concepts of Jewish difference in the service of her opposition to the existing French imperial project, her anti-capitalist class politics, and, most dramatically, her commitment to women's suffrage. While occasionally denouncing antisemitism, Auclert simultaneously played to right-wing xenophobia and plied Jewish stereotypes. Attempting to garner support from an unlikely camp, she readily denigrated the figure of the Jew to assert French women's suffrage as both a bulwark against foreign influence and a means to further the civilizing mission.

Whereas Audouard's engagements beyond France were as a traveler, Auclert lived and worked in Algeria from 1888 to 1892, an experience that significantly shaped her feminist politics. An active opponent of the French colonial authority in Algeria, as we have seen, Auclert did not oppose the imagined uplift of colonialism, but instead advocated a feminist imperialism, initiated by French feminists, to emancipate Algerian women.[54]

In Auclert's limited writing about Algerian Jews she likened them to the exploitative French imperial authority. While living in Algeria, she periodically contributed articles to the newspaper *L'intransigeant illustré*, examining aspects of life in the colony. Explaining an ill-fated encounter between an Algerian Jewish moneylender and a Parisian man working as a postmaster in Ghardaia, Algeria, Auclert claimed, "In Algeria, when a functionary requests a loan, it is very rare that it does not fall on the ears of a Jew. For the Algerian Jews, functionaries are like the inexhaustible gold mines of Peru."[55] As a republican socialist, Auclert criticized capitalists and the processes of capitalism, but here she employed an economic antisemitism, presenting the idea of the Jew exploiting the Christian in order to boost her arguments (with the underlying assumption that only Christians would be French colonial functionaries).[56] Correspondingly, in contending that Algerian Jews viewed Christian functionaries as "inexhaustible gold mines of Peru," filled with endless, extractable resources, Auclert likened the Jews to an abusive imperial power, while simultaneously playing on Orientalist Jewish tropes. Like Audouard, Auclert conjured the stereotypical link between Jews and gold.

Continuing the postmaster's story, Auclert explained that the man had agreed to pay usurious rates to the Jewish moneylender, and when the debt came due, the postmaster was unable to meet it. Employing classically clichéd images of Jewish men, Auclert depicted the lender as having a "long and hooked nose and a shifty look."[57] She quoted the two men's exchange, narrating "proper" French for the functionary, and a pidgin, broken French for the moneylender. Linguistically distancing him from her audience, his poor French underscored both his lack of civilization and his non-Frenchness. Ultimately, like Shakespeare's Shylock, the lender shows no mercy; the postmaster is arrested, and in his shame, he swallows glass and dies a slow and painful death.[58]

Auclert published the postmaster's dramatic tale more than a decade after France passed the highly contested and controversial Crémieux decree in 1870, which gave Algerian Jews French citizenship.[59] Critics assailed the decree for emancipating only Algerian Jews and not Muslims, arguing that the law unjustly privileged one "foreign" group over another. Some opponents of the decree insisted that Algerian Jews would be unable to comprehend the electoral workings of the republic, and so they would merely vote as the rabbinic leadership told them; others asserted that Jewish family law and practice fundamentally conflicted with precepts of French citizenship; yet others posited that Algerian Jews were more Arab than French.[60] The well-known antisemitic journalist, writer, and politician Édouard Drumont attacked Adolphe Crémieux, the French-Jewish lawyer and politician who promoted the decree. Writing in his high-profile antisemitic newspaper *La libre parole*, Drumont alleged that Crémieux intended to advance the Jewish people at the expense of France.[61] As Dorian Bell argues, Drumont's vitriol toward Crémieux and the eponymous decree illustrate the antisemitic vision of Jews' conspiratorial transmetropolitan/colonial reach. Bell explains: "To Drumont, the Crémieux decree represented [a] . . . Jewish power grab. . . . Catapulted to the highest ranks of power by the war, a Jew had symbolically opened the doors of the nation to the hordes of his coreligionists in the south."[62] Drumont's ongoing and multipronged criticism of the decree accused French Jews of loyalty to their coreligionists over the best interest of both colony and nation. It exemplified the antisemitic allegation of Jewish global power and machination.

In her widely reviewed book, *Les femmes arabes en Algérie*, Auclert condemned the French government for emancipating Algerian Jews while denying Algerian Arabs representation and citizenship. She stated, "In lieu of reversing the Crémieux decree, it is necessary to appeal to the Arabs to exercise their political rights and to aid them in gaining influence to counterbalance the excessive in-fluence of the Jews."[63] Auclert linked Algerian Jews with the French colonial authority, whose policies and approach to imperial rule she reviled. Yet at the time of emancipation, a significant portion of Algerian Jews strongly resisted French citizenship and rejected civil marriage. They recognized the measure's intent to assimilate them by cutting them off from their traditional law and custom, contrary to allegations that they had successfully pressed for natural-ization ahead of their Muslim compatriots.[64] Five years earlier, an 1865 law had offered citizenship to both Algerian Jews and Muslims if they surrendered the personal status that allowed them "special customs" under rabbinic and Qur'anic law, respectively. Virtually no one of either group chose to do so. The Crémieux decree made the shift mandatory for Jews. Seen by the liberal wing of the French government as more assimilable than Muslims, Algerian Jews served to exem-plify the Third Republic's universal republicanism. Simultaneously, however, the decree further othered Algerian Muslims in excluding them from such manda-tory citizenship.[65]

Auclert used the representation of Algerian Jews as deceptively powerful to further her broader argument against economic and imperial oppression. She propounded, "If the Arabs were made equal to their Algerian and Jewish ex-ploiters, conflict would immediately cease. . . . [Arabs'] political exclusion so-cially debases them and economically crushes them."[66] For Auclert, Algerian Jews coordinated with and reinforced the oppressive capitalist and imperialist apparatus.

During this period, Algeria experienced the emergence of an extreme anti-Jewish movement. Having begun as early as 1871, the year the first Algerian antisemitic society was founded, *antijuif* rhetoric and violence mounted through the 1880s. As Nathan Godley explains, the movement specifically self-identified as *antijuif* rather than *antisémite* (the term used in the metropole) to make clear their opposition to Jews only and not to the indigenous Muslims (who were also considered Semitic). Rooted in racialized conceptions of Jews' inferiority and essential foreignness, this colonial anti-Judaism thrived in a pro-republican milieu. French and other European colonists in Algeria (who re-ceived naturalization in 1889) questioned Jews' electoral and citizenship fitness. They underscored linguistic, cultural, racial, and (of course) religious differ-ence and criticized the ways in which Jews had exercised their citizenship rights in the years since the 1870 Crémieux decree.[67] The other colonists considered the Jews unwanted competition. The *antijuif* movement peaked in the 1890s, when, Sophie B. Roberts contends, "antisemitism became deeply engrained within Algerian colonial society."[68] Roberts utilizes postcolonial scholar Homi Bhabha's idea of the colonial other to convincingly argue that despite Jews' citizenship and their efforts at assimilation and integration, they remained permanently inassimilable. "Jews' status competitors," Roberts posits, "emphasized Jewish difference as a way of questioning their Frenchness."[69]

Within this climate, Auclert used antisemitic tropes to promote her imperialist and republican feminist politics. During her Algerian years, Auclert published an article in her feminist newspaper, *La citoyenne*, which addressed the plight of Eastern European Jews. Examining Jews in another imperial context— under Russian rule—Auclert took a distinctly different tone from that of her *L'intransigeant illustré* and *Les femmes arabes* writings. Here she sympathized with Jews' oppression. Auclert condemned the "hypocritical people who abuse them . . . under the pretext of religion . . . in order to dispossess them." She stated that Russia persecuted Jews under its rule not because of their religion, but rather to appropriate their wealth. Reiterating the stereotype of universal wealth among Jews (reminiscent of Audouard's accusations of "caves full of gold"[70]), but couching it in somewhat sympathetic language, Auclert described Jews as "the people whose labor and intelligence have made them the wealthiest in the world, and to whom this wealth was worth being periodically plundered and robbed."[71] Like Audouard, Auclert attributed vast fortunes to a deeply impoverished and subjugated population. Yet unlike Audouard, she also echoed the stereotype of native Jewish intelligence, something absent from Audouard's more denigrating portrayals.

From this point of relative empathy, Auclert proposed a means to stop what she termed the "cowardice" of acquisitive acts like those of the Russians, and with it other social injustices. She reasoned that "there is more to do than just platonically proclaim the equality of humans regardless of color or belief, one must positively decree that this equality is rationally based in the equality of the sexes."[72] Auclert declared that ending racial or religious injustice—here specifically the Russian persecution of Jews, but more broadly all such injustice— rested in attaining the equality of the sexes. She asserted gender equity as a prerequisite for all religious and racial justice. Softening her accusations of avarice, but retaining the implication in her assumption of riches, Auclert attempted to link the subjugation of women and Jews. Correspondingly, she tied Jewish emancipation to that of women and called on Jewish women to "each sacrifice a little time and a little money." She continued, "Jewish women, whose beauty and fortune make them queens, and who nonetheless suffer because of their religion and their sex, are well placed to lead their race, indeed to lead the world in a general movement for feminine and Semitic emancipation."[73] Evoking the *belle juive* stereotype, Auclert appealed to Jewish women to spearhead the fight for female liberation, suggesting that they were well placed socially, economically, and historically. She called on all women, "Jewish women, Christian women, free-thinking women, and atheist women," to work for their own liberation—but she proposed Jewish women lead the fight.[74] Seeking allies in her battle for women's liberation, Auclert turned to and included Jewish women based on chauvinistic preconceptions that she believed would both advance her cause and ameliorate their conditions. Her politics here fell in the interstices between antisemitism and philosemitism, professing a gendered Orientalism that both idealized and stereotyped, a "middle space," as Kalman terms it, "where contact, interchange, idealization, hatred, and even ambivalence could play out," a space "between the concrete and the imagined."[75] This was the space constituting the "figure of the Jew," through and against whom political claims could be made.

Like Audouard, Auclert linked Jewish women to the biblical heroine Judith. Rather than using the tale to condemn and judge Jewish women as both a historical and contemporary group, however, she employed it to flatter and inspire. Auclert wrote:

> Today's Jewish women can be proclaimed the *rédemptrices* of humanity; they can be the modern Judiths, definitively delivering their race and their sex, not by killing the men who usurped their rights, as the heroine of Israel killed Holhofernes, but by putting them where they could no longer do harm, creating on their destroyed privileges the equality of sex which will be the true human equality, without distinction of race nor religion.[76]

Consistent with her greater regard for Christian women than Christian (or secular) men, Auclert held Jewish women in higher esteem than she did Jewish men. She nonetheless viewed both sexes through prejudicial veils. Her assumptions of their universal wealth extended to men and women, but her portrayal of female Jews emphasized the more "positive" stereotypes of beauty and intelligence. From Auclert's gendered perspective, Jewish women possessed wealth but were not guilty of the crimes involved in its procurement. That belonged in the already exploitative and repressive male realm.

In 1894, the year of the Jewish army captain Alfred Dreyfus's arrest and conviction for treason—events that led to a groundswell of popular antisemitism in metropolitan France and Algeria and led to a decade-long crisis that divided the nation[77]—Auclert wrote a series of twelve articles for Drumont's profoundly anti-Jewish newspaper *La libre parole*. Eight years earlier, Drumont had published the antisemitic tome *La France juive*. A widely popular book that saw two hundred printings, it combined aspects of racial, economic, and traditional Catholic anti-Jewish prejudices.[78] Drumont spearheaded the development of the era's political antisemitism, founding the Ligue Antisémitique de

France in 1889. Decrying Jewish immigration to France, Drumont had written, "Jews, vomited from the ghettoes of Europe, are now installed as the masters of the historic houses that evoke the most glorious memories of ancient France."[79] Drumont, France's leading anti-Jewish journalist, along with his newspaper which was distributed through both France and Algeria, played a central role in the growing anti-Dreyfusard movement.[80] His notoriety resulted in his election on an antisemitic platform to France's Chamber of Deputies representing Algiers in 1889.

At the time Auclert published in Drumont's newspaper, he and his paper were notorious for their antisemitism. Aggressively anti-Jewish politics dominated in Algeria, coming from both the Left and the Right, fed by anti-Dreyfusard journalists and politicians, and stoked by blood libel rumors of Jews drinking the blood of Christian children. A series of violent and deadly antisemitic riots ensued. For the anti-Jewish French settler colonists in Algeria, the Dreyfus Affair served as a useful vehicle to drive their politics of resentment.[81]

Auclert did not consider herself an antisemite. She specifically criticized "Algerian antisemites" who wanted to terminate Jews' civil rights, as well as publicly reproving Russian antisemitism and lauding Jewish women.[82] Her *La libre parole* articles, entitled "Les droits de la femme," addressed topics including women's status under the Napoleonic Code, the inadequacy of girls' professional schools, and women's unequal and inadequate pay. The pieces expressed minimal blatant bigotry. They did, nonetheless, engage and employ Jewish difference and antisemitic rhetoric and images, exploiting the era's political antisemitism to promote her agenda.[83]

Auclert's first article for *La libre parole*, in 1894, opened by lauding the periodical, pronouncing that it had "charged itself with the courageous task of denouncing current infamies. . . . [Thus it] cannot remain indifferent to the legal oppression to which women have been subjected since the Revolution."[84] The specific "current infamies" to which she referred remain indeterminate, but there existed no question of the newspaper's antisemitic stances. Continuing her appeal, Auclert challenged *La libre parole* readers to support her fight for women's rights, "a cause on which the life of *this race* exists."[85] In a forum that made frequent reference to the "Jewish race," she again attempted to establish a solidarity with the readers. Auclert then extended these presumptions beyond the metropole and Europe, avowing, "We bring the savages our emancipating flag, yet there is a slave to liberate among us!"[86] Again referring to race—in terms of the "we" and "our emancipating flag"—Auclert reaffirmed her commonality with Drumont's readership. Propounding imperialism's emancipatory benefits to subject peoples, she simultaneously condemned

France's willingness to free "savages" while keeping a portion of "us"—white Christian women—enslaved. She pandered to Drumont's racist and xenophobic readers, hoping to bring them to support French women's liberation.

Auclert wielded her most unabashedly prejudicial language in her May 17 article opposing the Napoleonic Code's barring women from acting as civil witnesses. "Is it not a shame that a German Jewish man . . . is able to obtain all the rights of a Frenchman, of citizenship, and that women, French by race, by origin, the sisters of Joan of Arc, are bereft of these rights?"[87] Although clearly decrying France's inequitably gendered naturalization laws, Auclert's exemplification of a specifically Jewish German man, in juxtaposition to an implicitly Catholic ("sisters of Joan of Arc") French woman, belies the appearance of a merely legal critique. Auclert appealed to Drumont's antisemitic audience, playing on particularly nationalist forms of prejudice, while invoking the iconic and purely Catholic image of French womanhood.[88] The Napoleonic Code not only allowed foreign Jewish men access to the rights of citizenship denied Catholic French women, but also, by implication, recognized the word of those men as holding greater value than that of French women. Once a German Jewish man held French citizenship, he could be a civil witness, a right denied all French women.

Auclert wrote this article in the wake of the 1892 papal encyclical known as the *Ralliement*, in which Pope Leo XIII urged French Catholics to support the republican form of government; this marked a sea change from the Church's historical position championing the restoration of monarchy. Many French Catholics took this as a call not to support the existing government, but rather to engage in the republic to eradicate perceived anticlerical measures and rid it of its Jewish and Freemason influence. As the priest and politician Abbé Hippolyte Gayraud proclaimed, "The sympathies of Christian democracy go out to the Republic, not to the Masonic and Jewish Republic, but to a Republic that we will infuse with Christian blood."[89] Attempting to appeal to both ultraconservative monarchist *Libre parole* readers, who completely rejected the republican system, and to its right-wing antisemitic republican Catholic audience, who hoped to revise aspects of the law, Auclert used antisemitic xenophobia to gain allies in her efforts to alter the Napoleonic Code.

In the same article, Auclert pointed out that prior to the French Revolution women had possessed the right to give legal civil testimony. "Before the Revolution, when the Church controlled the registers of birth, marriages, and deaths, a woman possessed the same right as a man to witness legally both public and private acts."[90] Here Auclert exploited *La libre parole* readership's nostalgia for the pre-revolutionary, pre-Jewish emancipation, Church-dominated world. On the opening page of his book *La France juive*, Drumont had written, "The only one who benefited from the Revolution was the Jew."[91] Instrumentalizing the right-wing contention that the Jews both caused and profited from the fall of the ancien regime, Auclert idealized the pre-revolutionary era here and in three other articles in the series. She claimed that the Revolution had brought inequality to half of the nation (in enfranchising only men),[92] that women had more rights prior to 1789,[93] and that during the Crusades women could become judges under particular circumstances.[94]

In each example, Auclert utilized reactionary ideas to further progressive goals. An avowed republican socialist, she nonetheless pandered to antirepublicans and antisemites, hoping that their common opposition to revolutionary results—although each contested a different set of those revolutionary outcomes, would bring support to her fight to change the Napoleonic Code.[95] Auclert had attempted to make links with socialist groups and activists earlier in her career. Briefly involved in the socialist Parti Ouvrier in 1879, internecine battles led to her ouster within a year. Her efforts to ally with the mostly revolutionary French socialist women's leadership—including Mink and Michel— in the 1870s and early 1880s also failed, as both spurned her reformism.[96] Frustrated by a lack of support on the Left, Auclert took her suffrage campaign to the Right.

In the years immediately following Auclert's *La libre parole* articles, the era's feminists (like much of the rest of France) split over the Dreyfus case. Without proclaiming allegiance to either camp, Auclert differentiated herself from Dreyfus supporters. Writing in the strongly Dreyfusard feminist newspaper *La fronde* in 1897, at the height of the affair, Auclert avowed, "People pity the fate of a man who may have been unjustly condemned, while they remain indifferent to the noise of the chains of millions of galley slaves, women, who are absolutely innocent, civically degraded and condemned to social slavery even before they are born."[97] Referring to those who pity Dreyfus and simultaneously questioning his innocence, Auclert established a comparison similar to the one she proposed in *La libre parole* regarding civil witnesses. Dreyfus, implicitly a foreign and possibly seditious man, enjoyed rights denied all French women.[98]

Auclert's declaration dovetailed with that of the newly emergent right wing of French feminism, led by Marie Maugeret. The founder of Christian feminism and an avowed antisemite, she took an unsurprisingly unambiguous anti-Dreyfus stand. Maugeret had originally allied with *La fronde*. She owned a printing house that initially printed the newspaper, she published an article in it, and her newspaper *La féminisme chrétien* and *La fronde* had reciprocally promoted each other. Maugeret broke with *La fronde* and its editor Marguerite

Durand by early 1898, once Durand and the paper became vocally Dreyfusard. Their long-standing differences regarding issues such as divorce and birth control could be overlooked, but the Dreyfus divide could not.[99] Ultimately articulating her anti-Dreyfusard position as ethnic nationalism, Maugeret intensified and expanded the sort of xenophobia Auclert articulated. In 1898, Maugeret founded the organization L'Union Nationaliste des Femmes Françaises, also known as L'Union Nationale Jeanne d'Arc (she later held an annual Congrès Jeanne d'Arc), to promote these politics. Like both Audouard (who died before the Dreyfus Affair) and Auclert, Maugeret employed the image and idea of Jeanne d'Arc as the ideal, true, Catholic French woman.[100] Implying a *mission civilisatrice*, Maugeret stated, "As France is the elder sister of humanity . . . she owes it to those younger than her to be an example, helper, and protector."[101] Maugeret thus fostered a nationalist, implicitly imperialist, antisemitic, anti-Dreyfusard position, one that created an increasingly insurmountable division between her and other French feminists of the period. She spearheaded a distinct right-wing feminism.[102]

Like Maugeret's, Audouard's Christian feminism had an antisemitic core. Auclert's did not. She considered Jews and Jewish difference a useful political tool. Auclert's intense drive and passion for women's suffrage led her to accept prejudices and politics she would otherwise reject; her specific feminist agenda overrode all else. Writing in an era of mounting anti-Jewish bigotry, Auclert appealed to that audience, wielding words and images of Jewish difference intended to sway antisemites toward supporting women's suffrage. In contrast, Audouard felt it necessary to deny her antisemitism, as this blatant prejudice was less acceptable in France during the 1860s, 1870s, and 1880s than in the subsequent decade. While disavowing her antisemitism, however, she concurrently disparaged and denigrated Jews and wielded ideas of Jewish difference.

Auclert's willingness to swim in chauvinistic waters arose from the absolutism of her drive for women's political equality. Whether using Jewish difference to critique capital and the imperial state or to advance women's rights in France and its colonies, Auclert willingly accepted and employed antisemitic stereotypes and bigotry. Although she engaged a range of issues, women's suffrage superseded all. Devoting her time, energy, and resources to this end, Auclert pursued support in realms far removed from her usual political milieux and instrumentalized positions that appeared contradictory to her republican socialist feminism. Her pragmatic, narrowly focused agenda allowed her to imply support for both an anti-republicanism she did not espouse and a clericalism in which she did not believe.

6.2. Four "types" in traditional nineteenth-century attire: "1. Berber. 2. Black Woman. 3. and 4. Jewish Man and Jewish Woman of Algeria." Musée d'Art et d'Histoire du Judaïsme, Paris.

The Revolutionary

Louise Michel espoused the most radical politics of the three women, advocating a thorough break with capitalism and the overthrow of the republic. She sought a fundamental overturning of inequitable regimes. Capitalism, for Michel, underlay institutional injustice and oppression, while also causing individual inhumanity, venality, and immorality. Taking a historicized perspective, Michel contended that capitalism had (mis)shaped social and political relations and that empire had, in turn, spread and reproduced these systems. As a result, Michel repudiated the era's naturalized linkage between Jews and exploitative wealth. She did not, however, dispute the idea of the contemporary Jew as acquisitive and venal.

Asserting the socially constructed nature of these stereotypical characteristics, Michel argued that rather than being an essential part of Jews, these negative qualities had emerged from the corrupt circumstances of capitalism: the capitalist era, and its concomitant oppressions, created the Jew. Yet, she affirmed in an 1890 article in *L'égalité*, "It is wrong to use the word 'Jew' to mean capitalist. . . . Capital is a religion shared by all the vultures on earth, whether Hebrews, Muslims, or Christians; they are the universal Shylocks."[103] Michel wrote this in a climate in which the identification of Jew with capital had become pervasive; in which Drumont's *La France juive*—a central theme of which alleged Jews' control of capital—had seen two hundred printings; and in which earlier that year the antisemitic nationalist Maurice Barrès had written in *Le Figaro*, "Jew is an adjective labeling usurers, monopolizers, stockbrokers, those that abuse money."[104] Removing the Jew from the capitalist definition and redefining "Shylock" as a capitalist of any religion, Michel endeavored to counter a widespread antisemitic trope by reworking it in an alternative political vein.

Michel held a complex position regarding Jews. As an anarchist, she disavowed religions as merely divisive social constructions. Throughout her voluminous analyses and critiques, she rarely spoke specifically of Jews, thereby creating a meaningful absence and demonstrating her sense of religion as neither defining nor significant. Yet a notable exception, her 1890 novel *Le claque-dents*, portrayed Jews playing leading roles in the destruction of capitalism and the birth of the new, egalitarian world.[105] Its title, a slang term for "death rattle," likely referred to capitalism's demise.[106] The work challenged antisemitic contentions and acts, but it did so by employing particular Jewish stereotypes in an effort to expose and refute them. For Michel, antisemitism not only defamed and damaged Jews, but also masked one of capitalism's core evils: the moral deformation of peoples.

Consistent with her history and egalitarian principles, Michel challenged anti-Jewish bigotry where she encountered it. In 1895, she expressed opposition to the presumption that "Jew" equaled "usurer," maintaining that "people claim that the Jews are the exploiters of the proletariat, that all the great Jewish financiers are guilty, but it is wrong to accuse them thus. In matters of finance, there is no religious distinction. . . . Moreover, for us, religion should not exist. This is why we do not distinguish between Jewish and Christian financiers."[107] For Michel, all financiers—Jewish or Christian[108]—exploited the proletariat. Rather than viewing Jews as a race, as did most of her contemporaries, Michel recognized Judaism as a religion: a social rather than a bodily identity. In sharp contrast to Audouard, she considered all forms of religion irrelevant and divisive; only class mattered. Denouncing financiers made sense to her, while censuring Jews did not. She therefore overtly contested the essentialist conception of the money-grubbing Jew.

Michel wrote this piece in the immediate wake of Alfred Dreyfus's arrest, condemnation, and court-martial for treason. Edith Thomas, one of Michel's earliest biographers, asserted that Michel faced a profound conflict during the Dreyfus Affair. Henri Rochefort, her decades-long benefactor, close comrade, and fellow Communard deportee to New Caledonia, was a prominent antisemitic leader of the anti-Dreyfusard movement. While supporters of Dreyfus insisted on his innocence and called for his release from imprisonment on Devil's

Island, France's notorious penal colony in Guiana, Rochefort, like Drumont and the other anti-Dreyfusards, employed stereotypes of Jews' fundamental foreignness and disloyalty to enforce popular views of his guilt. Thomas suggests that Michel actively avoided offending Rochefort by never explicitly stating her support for Dreyfus—an allegation reiterated by literary scholar Julie Sabiani.[109] Michel's silence and unwillingness to denounce Rochefort led to conflict with many of her comrades, including Mink.

Mink vociferously defended Dreyfus. She signed the Dreyfussard *Manifeste des intellectuels* (Manifesto of the intellectuals) and spoke publicly in favor of the unjustly convicted army captain—including censuring both Rochefort and Drumont for their anti-Dreyfus positions in a March 1898 public meeting.[110] At another such meeting in June of that year, a police spy reported that Mink shouted "Down with Rochefort!" as Michel spoke.[111] A subsequent police statement claimed that "Louise Michel, having refused to side with Zola against Rochefort and the antisemites, has angered all of the anarchist and revolutionary groups. It is likely that she will not return to France for a long time."[112]

Despite her disinclination to break with Rochefort, Michel supported Dreyfus. Writing of her regular visits to Rochefort (a fellow self-exile) in London during a period that overlapped the Dreyfus Affair, Michel recognized that "at times we did not agree on certain points, but our discussions were always absolutely courteous."[113] In the portion of her memoirs written in London and published the year before her 1905 death, Michel wrote that after Dreyfus's conviction and exile to Devil's Island, she had considered organizing an escape for him. She developed a plot with "our brave friends in London, and a group of Parisian students . . . to take Dreyfus from Devil's Island and free him."[114] Undoubtedly a far-fetched scheme—few prisoners escaped Devil's Island—Michel's own exile to the New Caledonia penal colony, from which Rochefort did escape, may have inspired her proposal. They halted the plan, however, when "Dreyfus's family, when consulted by one of our friends, responded that they did not want an escape, but rather a trial in which his innocence would finally be recognized!"[115] Lamenting the abandonment of their rescue scheme, Michel saw it as a missed opportunity to have prevented the antisemitic explosion fed by the affair. She contended that liberating Dreyfus "would have prevented the reactionaries from escalating the question [of Dreyfus's alleged treason] to sow hatred."[116] She said nothing of the role that Rochefort and other antisemitic leftists played in the propagation of such hatred.

In addition to her rescue plan, Michel gave a pro-Dreyfus public lecture in London in December of 1897, and the following year she co-published a pamphlet with fellow anarchist Constant Martin titled "Inquisition and Anti-Semitism, Review of Jewish History, Commentaries on the Anti-Semitic

Movement," in which Martin wrote the text and Michel penned a long poem titled *Le rêve* (The dream).[117] In *Le rêve*, a man has a strange dream in which he finds himself shouting "Death to the Jews! to all, without mercy." When he awakens he recognizes his city of Algiers. Michel continued;

> It was indeed the city, but dead. He looked in each door and saw people with their throats slit. Also, those who had been dragged in the shadow: the old, small children, under knives they fell without number. What have they done? He said "They are Jews! Have you not said that all of the race must perish without leaving a trace?" We are the passive killers.[118]

The poem reviled the recent violent assaults on Jews in 1890s Algeria.[119] Michel both accepted and attributed culpability for the brutal incidents. On one level, she condemned the acts of Algerian Arabs, a group with whom she had a particular affinity. Since their time as prison-mates in New Caledonia, Michel had considered Algerian Arabs her comrades and often expressed solidarity with their anticolonial resistance. Yet she did not hesitate to assail French Algerian antisemitic brutality in her poem. Her censure extended beyond the specific perpetrators of the violence to France: the "we" in "We are the passive killers" included all French.[120]

She clarified the capitalist roots of the hatred and brutality, lamenting "Arabs and Jews, oh misery! Your blood fills the gutters. . . . Oh poor oppressed multitude! . . . The light of time will reveal the true perpetrators . . . the kings of finance."[121] Michel ultimately blamed capitalists for the anti-Jewish Algerian violence, charging them with a divide-and-conquer approach that pitted Algerian Arabs and Jews against each other. She ended her long poem with a sympathetic portrayal of the Algerian Arabs. Romanticizing "the men of the tents," she described them as "proud, naïve, and brave, and no longer wanting to be slaves."[122] Writing during a period of intense anti-Jewish politics and violence in Algeria, Michel determinedly denounced the brutal attacks and placed culpability squarely on the shoulders of the financial class. Significantly, Michel made no connection between those elites and the victimized Jews. In line with her earlier positions, she denied the stereotypical link between exploitative capitalists and Jews. Michel saw Jews as shaped and trapped by historical circumstances. "If the Jews symbolize the love of possession," she declared, "is it not the result of the avidity with which lords, high barons, and kings robbed them during the Middle Ages?"[123] Pointing to Jews as *symbolizing* the "love of possession," rather than embodying it as part of their nature, Michel blamed a history of elite antisemitism for the Jewish condition.

In her 1890 novel *Le claque-dents*, Michel described how capitalist society and antisemitism together produced the contemporary Jew. Published before the

Dreyfus Affair, but in the milieu of the enormous success of Édouard Drumont's deeply antisemitic work *La France juive*, Michel examined the historical roots of the prejudicial, pervasive connections between Jews and wealth through a tale of anarchism's triumph over capitalism. The novel centers on Baron Eléazer, a widowed Jewish financier, who, in his grief, is duped into marrying the conniving and avaricious Gertrude Nathan. Under her sway, his commercial interests become progressively dubious and exploitative, and he—a poet in his youth—personally grows increasingly callous, weak, and passive. Utilizing the stereotype of the emasculated Jewish man, Michel wrote, "The servants say: it is Madame who is Monsieur le Baron, and they are right."[124] Throughout *Le claque-dents*, as it traces the brutal decline and fall of capitalist society and, by novel's end, the triumph of a global Social Republic, Michel maintained that social relations and hierarchies, not essential flaws, had deformed the Jewish character. Antisemitic clichés and references pervade the tale; Michel deployed them to reveal the structural factors and cultural conventions from which they emerged.

Reiterating how Jewish acquisitiveness had developed as a survival tactic, Michel explained that "Jews had been badly burned before they began to peck at human flesh."[125] Her use of strong language and imagery, meant to remove blame, simultaneously exploited the Shylock allusion while teetering on vilification of present-day Jews. Intending to explain the immense negative pressures that malformed Jewish character, she nonetheless affirmed that the contemporary Jewish character was, indeed, malformed. Michel presented Jews as cannibals—and thus outside of ethical human behavior.

Michel wrote *Le claque-dents* in the years following her return from exile and imprisonment in New Caledonia. Just as she had characterized the New Caledonian Kanak as savage and childlike while simultaneously supporting them, Michel also proved unable to escape the language of religio-racial stereotypes of Jewish life and oppression—even while purposefully countering those stereotypes. Her defense of both Jews and Kanak remained enmeshed in the era's nearly pervasive images and language, even when she saw no essential racial inferiority in either Kanak or Jews. Intending to rehabilitate and validate both groups, she turned to and appropriated the available discourses of otherness in ways that reflected their deep and ubiquitous nature.

Employing history to explain and debunk essentialist understandings of Jewish greed and miserliness, Michel utilized the language of evolution. An advocate of Darwinian theory, Michel articulated the Jewish experience in terms of survival, clarifying that "the sense of acquisitiveness evolved because they had to pay with either all of their blood or with gold."[126] Their lives depended on embracing avarice. In *Le claque-dents*, Michel conveyed these sociocultural and economic factors through the person of Baron Eléazar, using the then-common idea that ontogeny recapitulates phylogeny. Eléazar embodies his entire people, transforming from a young and pure poet to a hard and rapacious old man, just as the Jews—once poets, Michel contended—adapted to a hostile context in order to survive.[127] Eléazar ultimately endures through further evolution, renouncing his extremely covetous ways and embracing the new, egalitarian world brought about by revolution.[128] Removed from the pernicious pressures of capitalism, Michel suggested, Jewish people could revert (and thus progress) to their decent, undistorted selves.

Eléazar's survival rests on his recognizing and embracing the supreme importance of cooperation and the overall good. Likely drawing on Peter Kropotkin's ideas of mutual aid as a key evolutionary factor, Michel illustrated capitalism's multifaceted destructive forces.[129] Not only did it turn Jews vicious—as both individuals and a group—but it also hindered human evolution by limiting cooperation. Michel gave Kropotkin a small but key role in *Le claque-dents*: a little book falls from Eléazar's daughter Esther's pocket midway through the novel. Fearing his daughter has fallen under the influence of "some religious intrigue," he picks up the book, opens it, "then felt the wind which transformed beings and changed the face of the world, the Revolution! It was *Words of a Rebel* by Peter Kropotkine."[130] Eléazar laughs and sneers at the text, but Esther cries out, "Read it, read it, Father!"[131] The reader never learns if he does, but the moment marks Eléazar's awakening to his daughter's radical politics and Michel's demonstration of the significance of Kropotkin's thought.

Michel presented the baron's children from his first marriage, Marius and Esther, both "of pure Jewish race," in an exceptionally positive light. They have "a proud beauty and immense ambition—made even more immense because it extended globally, they wanted *la vie large* for all, liberty for the world. . . . They were good, as they were beautiful."[132] Underscoring the nonessential nature of Jews' negative characteristics, Michel drew Esther and Marius as integrally involved in the revolutionary movement and thus cleansed of capitalism's taint. They represent not only the hope for the future, but also the saviors of the world. The siblings appear as equals in the tale, participating in revolutionary activism without gendered distinctions. Marius and his companions treat his sister as a comrade and a peer; in their struggle for an egalitarian world, they have rejected gendered inequities. Esther and Marius battle side by side; Marius falls, a martyr to the cause, and Esther joins those ushering in "the Social Republic of the world."[133]

Michel thus showed a progressive perspective on the family—an escape from the historically limited equation of Jews with usury and capitalism to a future of liberatory and revolutionary consciousness. As she did with the

Kanak, Michel trapped the fictional Eléazar and his family in a teleological, generative timeline, locating them in a position where a vital growth would enable their full flowering. She placed Jews evolutionarily ahead of the "Stone Age" Kanak, yet imbued both groups with similar potentiality. Michel had supported the Kanak in their anti-imperial uprising against the French colonial authority in New Caledonia, vehemently disputed French claims of Kanak barbarity and cannibalism, and averred that their civilization surpassed France's in many ways. Although she evoked images of contemporary Jews as cannibals and vultures, she did so in order to counter such stereotypes. Michel contended that anarchist thought had begun to elevate Jews to insurrectionary leadership roles. Indeed, her novel posits Jews as the saviors of humanity.

Just as Michel had characterized the exiled Algerian insurgents as naïve seekers of freedom, her representation of both Kanak and Jews reflected her desire to demonstrate the potential equality of each "tribe." Unlike antisemites, who saw fundamental ontological and racial difference, Michel perceived temporal disparities. Time and the implementation of liberatory ideas could free Jews, Algerians, and Kanak from the distortions and oppressions of capital and empire.

Familiar Foreignness and Foreign Familiarity

Audouard, Auclert, and Michel each employed antisemitism and Jewish difference to advance political goals. As the women traveled, wrote, and engaged in debates about empire, religion, and race, they also represented Jews as emblematic precursors to the questions of otherness raised by imperialism. For all three feminists, Jews and Jewishness constituted a concrete and theoretical presence, a historical and contemporary idea of a people who stood for something separate and other, bridging both metropole and empire. Yet this meant something distinctly different to each of them. Their individual understandings and interactions with Jews—real and imagined—both within and outside of France, engaged with the era's ideas of Jewish difference and exemplified the wide-ranging and mutable impact that this idea of the Jew had on feminist and political thought.

Jewish difference emerged in historically and culturally specific forms. It comprised the often-antithetical relationship between a society's hierarchical, gendered ideals of non-Jews and of Jews. In this context, Jewish difference developed as the reversal of nineteenth-century French cultural ideals: the Jewish man was effeminate, weak, conniving, and uncivilized; the Jewish woman was sexualized, manipulative, domineering, and dangerously seductive. Deeply gendered, Jewish difference operated on a register of oppositions, all of which defined civilization.

While progressive politics in terms of gender, or race, or class cannot presume progressivism in any other area—examples of sexist revolutionaries or racist feminists abound—in the cases of Audouard, Auclert, and Michel, the spectrum of their class-based ideologies directly corresponded with the range of their antisemitisms. The liberal Audouard displayed an often rabid antisemitism; the republican socialist Auclert instrumentalized and strategically employed Jewish stereotypes; and the revolutionary anarchist Michel iterated prejudicial characterizations in an effort to debunk them, sympathetically identifying Jews as an oppressed people. In these examples, a fealty to liberalism linked closely to antisemitism: the greater the author's opposition to the existing class hierarchy, the greater her opposition to antisemitism. And although their approaches to the "Jewish Question" and their employment of Jewish difference profoundly diverged, they all understood Jewishness as problematic and other, as a distinction or inequity best erased.

Using a gendered, Orientalized figure of the Jew, Audouard promoted an antisemitic politics that spanned metropole and global empires. Her racialized construction of Jewish men and women as temporally stunted and uncivilized easily meshed with contemporary anthropologic characterizations of colonized people. Jews and Jewishness constituted a distinct category for Audouard, however, one that drew a dramatic version of her ire. She saw Jews as a degenerative threat. Audouard employed racialized religious characterizations to denigrate male and female Jews based on antisemitic physical, social, economic, and sexual stereotypes. The era's dominant idea of the Jew and Jewish difference dovetailed with Audouard's belief in Jews as deniers of Christ. Defending the supremacy of Christianity and extant constructions of civilizational hierarchies, Audouard—in line with her liberal feminism and Catholic identification—also defended the hierarchical class status quo. She displayed her reification of class in recognizing and praising non-Western, elite practices and in simultaneously disparaging the poor. Unlike her other critiques, however, Audouard's antisemitism superseded class, alleging that all Jews possessed wealth but lived in squalor due to their degenerate miserliness. Antisemitism also wrought Audouard's feminism. Her liberal feminism allowed the exclusion of Jewish women, whom she relegated to an ancient and barbaric, pre-Christian world. The intensity of her antisemitic politics pushed Audouard's portrayals to the misogynistic. Constructing Jews as an uncivilized people of an inferior past era, she represented them as a corrupt, corrosive social force spanning metropole and global empires. Audouard's figure of the Jew served to gender antisemitic politics.

Auclert took a more paradoxical and complex position. She saw the Jew as emblematic of everything wrong with the French imperial project. Alternatively denouncing, tolerating, or manipulating prejudiced tropes of Jewish difference, she employed the figure of the Jew to promote her imperial feminist political aims. Focusing especially on Algeria, Auclert played on stereotypes of avarice, linking Jews to what she considered the wealth and power of the colonial authority, which she aggressively opposed. She portrayed Algerian Jews as particularly privileged, pointing especially to the Crémieux decree that granted them, but not Muslims, citizenship. In a period of mounting anti-Jewish sentiment in France and Algeria, Auclert both overtly and subtly worked to gain antisemites as allies in supporting women's suffrage and relatedly for her argument for a feminist imperialism.

Ultimately considering Jewishness a category to overcome, she nonetheless used Jewish difference to support her politics both through efforts at flattery to Jewish women, and—more frequently—by utilizing the Jewish threat to appeal to xenophobes and antisemites. Auclert viewed the French republic as perfectible, but only once women attained equality through suffrage. Envisioning social and economic transformation to a just and egalitarian system, one ushered in through her version of republican socialism and republican socialist feminism, Auclert advocated feminist-influenced, evolutionary, parliamentary change to bring about gender and class equity in both France and Algeria. Her figure of the Jew was comparable to the capitalist and imperialist exploiter: in the imperial context, all three victimized Algerian Arabs. Yet she maintained that the social republic had the power to civilize these groups, alleviating class and race-based oppressions in France and the colony. Auclert drove passionately toward this aim for decades. She saw antisemitism, via the manipulation of the figure of the Jew, as facilitating her goals of women's full citizenship, the demise of the existing French imperial authority, and the ascendency of feminist imperialism.

Michel saw the Jew as a product of society—a character formed at the intersection of the divisive nature of religion and the pernicious pressures of capitalism. She did not deny the contemporary existence of the prejudicial Jewish "type"; rather she insisted on its artificial, externally imposed character. Michel employed these stereotypes in the service of destabilizing them, by exposing the historical and cultural forces that created the figure of "the Jew." In Les claques-dents, she not only maintained that the eradication of capitalism would remove deleterious characteristics from Jews, but she also suggested that radically enlightened Jews—female or male—could lead this fight. Rejecting the validity of Jewish difference, she concurrently recognized and acknowledged its presence and destructive power. Michel's figure of the Jew served to castigate the antisemitism that resulted from these French, French imperial, and Algerian social constructions.

Michel viewed Judaism as primarily a religious rather than a racial identity, and as a revolutionary anarchist feminist, she opposed all religions. For her, the category Jew had no essential meaning: poor Jews suffered as did all other impoverished peoples, and capitalist Jews posed the same problems as did capitalist Christians. When addressing the oppressions and exploitations of empire, Michel squarely blamed the "kings of finance"—be they Christian or Jewish. She also attributed to capitalists the Dreyfus-era antisemitic violence in Algeria, alleging that they pitted Arabs against Jews. Capitalism, for Michel, created the injustices of antisemitism and the inequities of empire.

As Audouard, Auclert, and Michel turned their attention to empire, each read differing relationships between the civilized and the uncivilized, the oppressors and the oppressed, and the Occident and the Orient. Their cognizance of Jewish difference, developed at home, evolved as they moved beyond the metropole, and became an additional locale in which their political visions became clarified.

Each woman had a particular political goal for which she used the figure of the Jew: Audouard to promote antisemitism; Auclert to advance women's legal equality; and Michel to condemn capitalism and religion. Operating through metropole and colony, antisemitism—while long present in France—took historically specific forms. Recent scholarship by Julie Kalman, Ethan Katz, Lisa Leff, Maud Mandel, Dorian Bell, and others has addressed important connections between antisemitism and colonialism, yet none has recognized feminism's interplay in this milieu.[134] Beyond the shared goal of altered gender hierarchies, feminisms diverged regarding other power relations. The Jewish Question—the debate over whether Jews could be integrated and assimilated into society—intersected with categories of class, religion, race, and gender, while the presence of both actual Jews and the figure of the Jew arced across metropole and colony. The availability of the idea of the Jew, its foreign, trans-spatial familiarity, and its easily recognized significance, made it a useful and comprehensible political tool.

Feminists' imperial entanglements simultaneously utilized the figuration of Jews. Just as the political projects and ideological commitments supporting these women's stances on empire involved an array of complex relationships to liberalism, universalism, rights, and gender equality, so too did their formulations of Jewishness. Feminists thought empire through Jews engaging them more as ideas than as people. Jews constituted recognizable points of alterity, around which these feminists mapped newly engaged others. The question of the Jew represented the question at the heart of France's empire: who already was, who could become, and who would always be excluded from true Frenchness?

Conclusion

Feminists, by definition, oppose gender hierarchies. Across the nineteenth century, French feminisms challenged various aspects of patriarchal law, traditions, politics, and other power structures. With the rise of France's modern empire, these activists began to encounter aspects of imperialism within a culture already replete with images and ideas of exoticism and the Orient. For feminists intellectually nourished on rhetorics of republicanism, equality, and an idealized "Frenchness," the realities of the French imperial project flew in the face of these principles. The recognition of these global hypocrisies dovetailed with their existing enmities toward national and cultural gender inequities, particularly those based in the pretense of republican universalism.

Rooted in the Napoleonic Code, this "universalism" marginalized the entire female population. As the French Empire reached increasingly beyond Europe, the exclusions to universalism included nonwhite races, non-Christian religions (although this long existed for metropolitan Jews), and non-French ethnicities and nations. Gender remained fundamentally interlaced through these segregations— something apparent to the feminists who first engaged imperialist operations, whether initially in print or in person, within the French Empire, in other global imperial spaces, or the colonial imaginary. These experiences led Audouard, Auclert, Rouzade, Mink, and Michel to become among the era's first critics to condemn the injustices of empire.

While not using the term "gender," these feminists focused on women's status, hierarchies of power between women and men, women's roles in society, and women's legal rights. These attunements informed each political engagement. They investigated gendered hierarchies and institutions in terms of both their structures and the ways in which they shaped women's and men's lives. Observing the world's nearly ubiquitous patriarchies, feminists laid bare the normalization of the universal male—initially in the metropole and subsequently as they encountered female marginalization in sites across the globe. In law and in custom, men were the assumed citizen and subject, women the special and aberrant case. French imperialism and colonialism perpetuated this framework. Coming from dissimilar social, regional, and political backgrounds and embracing divergent class politics, Audouard, Auclert, Rouzade, Mink, and Michel nonetheless all identified and contested the gendered nature of imperial relations. Beyond that, however, their evaluations and analyses diverged.

Imperial contexts caused a positional shift for French feminists. Even a French woman of relative privilege, in an era of growing feminist visibility with expanding forums for women's voices, could not escape political disenfranchisement and political exclusion. Despite the inclusive promises of republican universalism, citizenship remained gendered male, a category that unequivocally omitted women. Feminists argued that universalism, by definition, demanded the inclusion of women, yet France's republican universalism rested on "natural" sexual differences. Joan Scott has contended that French feminists (the female ones—she did not address male feminists) embodied paradox, as they demanded the republican individual rights due them, but they did so as women, and thus as the "natural" opposite of citizens. As Scott states, "The history of feminism can be understood as an interplay between a repetitive pattern of exclusion and a changing articulation of subjects."[1] French feminists from across the political spectrum recognized an internal/external structure in imperialism, similar to the one that marginalized both their embodied selves and their gender politics in the metropole. Imperialism's and colonialism's gendered and sexualized racial hierarchies established categories of inclusion versus exclusion rooted in both universalism and the language of "nature." Native people living under colonization, like metropolitan women, faced theoretical yet impossible paths to integration and enfranchisement under the ideals and rhetorics of Third Republic France.

While feminists (along with all French women) remained disenfranchised throughout this period, extra-metropolitan travel transformed their standing. In the world of empire, they bore the cachet of white skin, Europeanness, and Frenchness. This bestowed a rarified status that allowed immediate entree to elite realms and a privileged social passport to observe and to interact with people living their lives. They were thus both alienated from, but also central to, French citizenship.

Such advantage sat easily with Audouard and Auclert. Both women felt comfortable with affluence and, to differing degrees, hierarchy. They presumed access and license because of both their Europeanness and their class positions. Audouard assumed a right to travel and observe a wide variety of global imperial contexts, while Auclert expected to live in and critique France's primary colony. Mink and Michel, in contrast, each held antagonistic positions toward governmental power and elite status, yet their racial and national identities assured their separateness from the Algerian and New Caledonian populations they encountered. Michel did not go to New Caledonia of her own will, but both she and Mink traveled to Algeria, each confident that she could move and speak freely there and be easily able to engage and observe multiple populations.

The Algerian feminist Marnia Lazreg wrote in 1988,

> It is true that a feminist engaged in the act of representing women who belong to a different culture, ethnic group, race, or social class wields a form of power over them; a power of interpretation. However, this power is a peculiar one. It is borrowed from the society at large which is male-centered. It is borrowed power that gives academic feminists engaged in interpreting difference status and credibility.[2]

This also held true for nineteenth-century feminist writers and activists. The power to study or to see, to interpret or translate, to assess, and ultimately to characterize and represent was available to men, specifically European men, born of white masculine privilege. In the world of empire, white European women's elevated status conferred on them certain prerogatives. Imperial milieux amplified the command of their racial, national, and class ranks.

Although disparaging of European imperial undertakings and censorious of multiple forms of hierarchy, feminists remained imbricated in these relationships. In differing ways, each appropriated imperial concepts—including racialization, sexualization, and ethnographic categorization—to advance their political programs. The general experience of French feminists traveling into imperial locations intersected with the particular, embodied, and contextualized engagement of each woman. And, critically, politics mediated these points of convergence, influencing each individual's reception of and reaction to imperial spaces.

As each woman's experience was affected by her feminist ideology, so, too, was that ideology simultaneously altered and shaped by her imperial or colonial encounter. The range and diversity of these feminisms reveals the ways in which variances in gender politics encouraged disparate approaches to empire. What were (or are) the relationships between feminisms and imperialisms? What about feminisms fostered anti-imperialisms?

Audouard's Empire

Olympe Audouard began her travel earlier and voyaged more widely than the other women. The most conservative of the activists, she was a liberal feminist who identified not only as a monarchist, but also as both a republican and a democrat. Her politics thus requires the most detangling and explication.

Audouard explained her own incongruous position in her 1871 *À travers l'Amérique: North-America*, published in the wake of the Franco-Prussian War and the subsequent Paris Commune. She affirmed, "I remain a republican, but wish, for the love of my country, that not for another thousand years do we again attempt a republic in France."[3] Audouard termed "shameful" France's post-1789 republican endeavors and particularly the recent Paris Commune (government by "la canaille," the rabble). Expressing her support for a republic in theory but not in practice in France, Audouard advocated for a royal restoration. In discussing the pool of possible monarchs who might rule France at that turbulent historical juncture, she ultimately expressed her support for the Orleans family, who she "hoped would promptly take the French throne." Her monarchical advocacy rested on an opposition to authoritarianism, a stance she shared with conservative thinkers (including Edmund Burke). Characterizing the French version of the republic as mob rule, Audouard professed that she "loves independence, true and healthy freedom, too much to patiently support the arbitrary and excess authority of what France calls a Republic."[4]

In the first of the two-volumes of *À travers l'Amérique*, the volume subtitled *Le Far West*, Audouard clarified that before her thirteen-month trip across the United States, she was a republican. She had traveled to the United States with an idealized vision of a republic, a land she believed to be "synonymous with liberty for all, with work and well-being, with little place for abuse and arbitrariness, where finally all of the great humanitarian and egalitarian sentiments were put in practice." Instead, she found—"Quelle error!"—a nation where money reigned supreme and where egalitarianism, "under the name of democrats," was replaced with "intolerant and proud *aristos*," who devalued and denigrated those without wealth.[5] "In the Far West," she wrote, "you find true savagery."[6] Audouard consistently referred to white Europeans in the American West as *colons*, settlers, and to the areas under their control as colonies (*colonies*). Writing of settlers "taking possession" of territories, ignoring or denying the legitimate presence of Native peoples on their own lands, lamenting "unpopulated states suffering Indian attacks," discussing the "savage tribes of Louisiana" in a letter to her friend Victor Hugo, and dehumanizing and desexualizing Indians in her book on *Le Far West*, Audouard easily employed the language of empire.[7] This imperial world, like those of her African and Asian voyages, shaped her politics.

Audouard's romantic vision of republicanism gave way under her empirical observations of an undemocratic world of unfettered capitalism. Like her predecessor Alexis de Tocqueville, she clearly felt more comfortable with those she would have understood as "true" aristocrats, the blood-line French version, than with the gloves-off American economic elites (although she continued to idealize "Yankees"). In terms of class, monarchist affiliation presupposes an absence of confidence in the population's ability either to select its leadership or to govern itself. She argued that in France, "The crowd does not know liberty, only license."[8] Her assessment of France's most recent republican effort, the Paris Commune, demonstrated her disdain toward popular rule. Audouard declared, "In making the republic, her majesty The Rabble has shown us that she was of the school of Nero, of Caligula, and of Soulouque. The students had surpassed their masters. But, I repeat, I saw neither republic nor republicans."[9] Audouard labeled the Communards as disciples of three notorious emperors and accused the 1871 insurgents of being even less republican than those undemocratic leaders. In evoking Faustin Soulouque, the black, slave-born Haitian military leader and veteran of the Haitian Revolution, Audouard equated the French working class with a racialized, indigenous savagery; soon after being elected president of the Haitian Republic in 1847, the controversial Soulouque purged elites from power, replaced them with his followers, and declared himself Emperor Faustin I.

Audouard's politics never strayed far from her Catholicism. An opposition to free thinkers—who, she wrote, "merit the title of tyrannical-thinkers"—and republican anticlericalism more generally deeply affected her stance.[10] Further distancing her own position from authoritarianism, she linked Christianity with democracy. Asserting that Jesus was the first democrat, in word and in practice, she contended that "as a Christian, thus, I am a democrat," an identity she professed to maintain despite the challenges presented by its misuse by "certain red newspapers."[11] While acknowledging that democracy had radical leftist linkages, Audouard superseded that claim by fundamentally connecting it to the Christian origin story. This, in turn, supported her definition of free thinkers as tyrannical—the antithesis of democratic. Following the logic of Jesus as the source of democracy meant that those who denied Christ—Jews, Muslims, and free thinkers—would correspondingly reject democracy.

While Audouard understood peoples and nations as possessing essential characteristics, she saw among them a range of possibilities for change and progress. In *La femme dans le mariage, la separation et le divorce*, Audouard lauded the United States for fighting a civil war so that "the word *homme* [man] includes the Black as well as the white race."[12] Simultaneously, she condemned the United States' ongoing marginalization of women, who are "not included in the word *homme*, which designates the human race."[13] This feminist stance—a disputation of the universal male—formed the core of her politics. Audouard's concurrent identification as a monarchist, republican, and democrat shared the common thread of her conception of freedom: an absence of slavery and coercion. She did not challenge hierarchies of class, she embraced those of religion, and she contested those of race only to the extent of opposing bondage, but she consistently vilified hierarchies of gender.

Audouard placed great value on law codes, both as a way to understand imperial contexts and as the prime focus for change. She studied her destinations' legal systems in advance of her travels. Once arrived, she observed gendered social structures and relations, analyzing them in light of their legal frameworks and comparing them to the Napoleonic Code. Audouard used these assessments in her push for legal amelioration in France and to support her categorization of France's imperial project as illegitimate. Her anti-imperialism emerged from her liberal feminist critique of French gender relations.

Audouard articulated a vision of a new Frenchness, expressed in her widely read, contentious works. *Les mystères du sérail et des harems turcs* (Mysteries of the seraglio and of Turkish harems), for example, went through four editions (the final in 1884) and garnered notable attention, including reviews (mostly negative or hostile) in a number of French and British journals. Audouard's high-profile, controversial positions paved the way for subsequent feminist challenges to France's patriarchal civilizing mission, while simultaneously reifying racial and religious stereotypes. Working to amend the existing legal and political framework, accepting of most hierarchies except gender, hers was a liberal feminist anti-imperialism, established on the eve and fostered through the dawn of the Third Republic.

Auclert's Empire

Like Audouard, Hubertine Auclert contested the validity of French republicanism. While the former viewed the republican form positively in theory, yet opposed its actual reintroduction in France because of its specific national evolution, the latter saw the French republic as potentially perfectible. Witnessing it from differing historical moments—they overlapped temporally for a decade, as Audouard was active from the mid-1860s through the 1880s and Auclert from

the late 1870s to 1914—they also examined the republic through divergent political optics. Although Audouard fell closest to Auclert on the ideological spectrum
of this group of feminists, Audouard remained an outlier due to her monarchism, clericalism, and acceptance of nearly all nongendered status quos. Nonetheless, the two women's politics also coincided at points. Both were feminists
who supported evolutionary and lawful change within the current state framework; both were among the first French feminists not only to advocate women's
suffrage but also to engage with empire. They shared elite socioeconomic status,
which they did not reject, as well as a sense that they were entitled to live and
move in imperial spaces, including (for both) Algeria. Finally, significant portions
of the two feminists' work focused on imperial worlds.

Their differences both rested in and grew from the soil of ideology. As a
republican socialist, Auclert promoted a social republic, one that integrally addressed questions of social, economic, and political equity. Although she
challenged class-based hierarchies, she did not seek the overthrow of existing
economic or political systems. Rather, she championed change through parliamentary socialism, the success of which she understood as being reliant on
female enfranchisement. This comprised her primary goal. In her 1908 *Le vote
des femmes*, Auclert argued, as she had for nearly thirty years, that women's
suffrage "would enable the modification of society and the realization of the
Republic."[14] She used her substantial personal wealth to fund the suffrage
struggle, her commitment to which extended to allying with the rabidly antisemitic Édouard Drumont in hopes of garnering support for her cause.

France's imperial project, for Auclert, contributed to the flawed state of the
republic, particularly in its Algerian engagements. A sharp critic of the Napoleonic Code, she nonetheless condemned France's hypocrisy in allowing and
fostering separate legal systems on territory considered part of greater France,
particularly because those codes allowed polygamy and child marriage. Interested especially in the gendered structures and forces that shaped Algerian
women, Auclert viewed imperialism as a tool to improve their lives. She reproached France for failing to live up to what she saw as the republican and
imperial promise behind the *mission civilisatrice*.

From 1896 to 1909, Auclert wrote a regular Sunday column entitled "Le
Féminisme" in the newspaper *Le radical*, in which she discussed and analyzed a
broad range of feminist issues. In her December 2, 1901, column, subtitled "No
more pillaging!," Auclert vehemently attacked France for its treatment of Algeria and Algerians. "We have pillaged in Algeria as in China. At the same time
that we take the great gold and silver earrings from Muslim ears, we block the
instruction of the feminine sex in order to insure, by keeping women ignorant,
the degeneration of the Arab race, which will make it easier to plunder. Today,

civilized France seems to desire a return to the wrongdoings of barbaric France."[15] Equating economic and social imperialism with pillage, Auclert linked France's termination of Algerian girls' education to its theft of Algerian wealth and resources: both robbed Algeria of a rich future. The French colonial authorities had closed girls' schools with the complicity of Algerian elites; Auclert accused France of barbaric behavior in intentionally "keeping women ignorant" by refusing to reintroduce girls' education in Algeria. Because she considered women central to civilizational advancement, Auclert saw girls' education as vital not only to improving the status of Algerian women but also to elevating Algerian society as a whole.

Consistently frustrated with the inaction of the French state regarding Algerian girls' education, as well as its acceptance of polygamy and child-marriage, Auclert prioritized French women's suffrage as the means to reform and elevate both republic and colony. She identified the status of metropolitan and Algerian women as vitally interlinked, but she did not see them as contemporaneously equal. For Auclert, French women's enfranchisement was an essential precursor to improving Algerian women's (and men's) conditions, which she took seriously as France's colonizing duty. Men had failed; once full citizens, women would not. Auclert's essentialist understanding of women as naturally more just and compassionate than men assured her that women would use their vote to end practices that she saw as fundamentally wrong and, indeed, against nature. Imperialism, she believed, required feminism to succeed.

More than any of the other activists, Auclert heartily embraced imperialism for what she understood as its liberatory potential. She did so while actively opposing France's specific imperial project. Working for women's emancipation first in metropole and then in colony, she saw no contradiction in concurrently and interdependently advocating feminism and imperialism or in simultaneously espousing targeted anti-imperial and pro-imperial positions. Auclert's political stance was one of a "white savior": she believed that French women, armed with the vote, could rescue Algerian women (and men) from their subjugated status. Denying them agency to liberate themselves, Auclert maintained that only feminist imperialism could free them.

Rouzade's Empire

Léonie Rouzade's involvement with empire was conceptual rather than experiential. Her use of imperial and Orientalist tropes to make a socialist feminist argument in her 1872 novel *Le monde renversé* places her at the chronological forefront of the era's earliest feminists to engage empire. A republican social-ist like Auclert, Rouzade advocated a legislative route to socialism and de-manded women's full incorporation. While she supported women's suffrage and stood for the twelfth *arrondissement* seat in the 1881 Paris Municipal Coun-cil elections, she prioritized questions of class, poverty, and maternity. More politically radical than Auclert, Rouzade supported the redistribution of wealth (via legislative, not insurrectionary means) and called for the exaltation and state support of motherhood.[16] Although she wrote *Le monde renversé* before she became involved with organized socialist or feminist politics in the later 1870s, the book envisions the sort of radically egalitarian realm she would later work toward. It presents a utopian version of a world that would answer the question she posed in an interview forty-five years after the novel's publica-tion: "What is necessary to found the true human family?"[17]

Using exaggeration, satire, and the utopian genre, the novel suggests that a European feminist could introduce egalitarianism in an exotic Muslim place where male privilege and female subjugation and marginalization had been the norm. The Orientalized setting assured her readers' comprehension of these stereotypical gender relations. Initially imposing an absolute inversion in gender power to make clear the absurdity of one sex ruling over another, the feminist character Célestine ultimately establishes a republican system (and then dramatically exists the scene). Recognizing the intractability of en-trenched power relations, Rouzade proposed that feminist input—either fan-tastically via shipwreck, or pragmatically via women's enfranchisement—could overturn deeply entrenched hierarchies, including patriarchy and capitalism, in empire and metropole. Like Auclert, Rouzade asserted a feminist imperi-alism: one brought by a French woman to save and redeem other cultures.

Mink's Empire

Mink's socialism went further, embracing and promoting revolution across the latter third of the century. Although once an anarchist and a leader in the grass-roots radical political club movement during the Commune, the disorder and brutal suppression of the revolution led her to shift away from bottom-up, popu-lar activism. In the Commune's wake, she turned to the conspiratorial, top-down revolutionary socialism of Auguste Blanqui. Actively against women's suffrage, she considered it a mollifier, distracting women from seeking the one thing that would truly liberate them: socialist revolution.[18] Diverging sharply from Audouard, Auclert, and Rouzade's belief in the republic's potential for redemption, Mink fundamentally opposed the state and saw its overthrow as vital to bringing freedom and equity to women and the working class.

Imperialism played a relatively small part in Mink's writing and speaking—which was typical of her era's revolutionary socialists. Yet it distinctly shaped her politics. In 1884, she traveled to Algeria to promote anti-imperialism, anticlericalism, and anticapitalism. Lecturing on the eve of her departure, Mink castigated the republican leaders for sacrificing French money and blood in pursuit of empire and accused them of having no concern for "the interest of the people and the dignity of France."[19] After her propaganda tour of Algeria, she continued to protest France's imperial military actions. In 1885 in Marseilles, Mink called the war in Tonkin—an attempt to solidify French control of what is now northern Vietnam—"shameful" and "the fruit of underhanded infamy."[20] A decade later, a police report (the Paris Prefecture of Police continued to follow and monitor Mink from when she returned to France from post-Commune exile in 1880 until her 1901 death) recounted Mink's October 1895 oration condemning French intervention in Madagascar and empathizing with French mothers "who protest when their children are sent there to die for no reason."[21]

Mink's Algerian experience did not alter her opposition to French imperial militarist undertakings; she remained constant in connecting empire to other forms of oppression. It did, however, have two notable effects. First, it shifted her estimation of the role of empire, and second, it influenced her feminism.

Algerian patriarchal culture deeply disturbed Mink. Her racialized gendered observations described an Indigenous culture that both brutalized and marginalized women. Rather than question the possible role that colonization had in women's oppression, Mink implied that France might have a civilizing influence on Algerian Arab men. In a dramatic departure from her decades-long vilification of the French state, she acknowledged that it had introduced "ideas of liberty and of dignity" to men among whom those concepts were foreign.[22] Although Mink opposed empire as an expansion of exploitative state power, and patriarchal culture as oppressing women and deforming society, she did not conjoin the two. Instead, like Auclert, she argued that France had the responsibility to intervene in Algerian Muslim gender relations to ameliorate women's oppression at the hands of men.

Akin to Auclert's condemnation of polygamy and child marriage, Mink's censure highlighted Arab gender relations as well as gender roles. Both women asserted a larger critique of Arab masculinity and patriarchy. However, while Auclert recognized particular advantageous aspects to Algerian women's lives, as in marriage law and custom, Mink reported nothing favorable. In the colonial milieu, her feminist concern with women's roles and lives intersected with racialized French stereotypes of Algerian Arab men and resulted in a political assessment inconsistent with her revolutionary anti-statist stance. Mink did not overtly advocate imperialism, yet, in this context, her feminism and her belief in French cultural superiority mitigated her otherwise uniformly aggressive anti-imperialist position.

In addition to altering her conception of the role of empire, traveling to Algeria also affected Mink's feminism. Late in life, she shifted away from her absolute and vociferous opposition to women's electoral participation and agreed to an offer from the socialist feminist organization Solidarité des Femmes to stand as a candidate in the 1893 Parisian municipal elections.[23] Mink announced and explained her candidacy (which was not legal for a woman under the Napoleonic Code) in an acceptance letter published in numerous socialist newspapers. She declared her run as a demonstration of her allegiance to the socialist workers' party, the Parti Ouvrier Français (POF), claiming that her candidacy would fulfill the party's commitment to "the economic, civil, and political equality of women."[24] In reality, the POF leader, Jules Guesde, had long paid only lip service to issues of gender equality, an issue over which not only Mink, but also Auclert and Rouzade had fallen out with him over the previous fifteen years. The POF ignored her candidacy, both due to her sex and because she ran as a revolutionary socialist, a position the reformist Guesde and his party had abandoned.[25] Mink's claim to be demonstrating party loyalty via her candidacy should be understood as a highly public broadside against Guesde and the POF—for both their ongoing sexist politics and their desertion of revolutionary socialism—rather than an exhibition of loyalty.

Mink never wavered from her conviction that only socialist revolution could emancipate women. Affirming this position in an article titled "Why I Have Posed My Candidacy," published during the election, Mink wrote: "Claiming women's political and civil rights will not be sufficient to emancipate them and to end their suffering. I do not at all believe . . . that granting women the vote will annihilate all of the abuses. . . . That is why . . . all the women who seek rights and justice for all . . . must become socialist."[26] Yet she saw sufficient value in women's electoral engagement to enter the contest, something she had not only refused to do fewer than ten years earlier but also against which she had overtly argued. Mink's acknowledgment of the possible value of rights-based feminism in the wake of her colonial encounter reflected a significant alteration in her feminist politics. Never relinquishing revolutionary socialism, she nonetheless could accept ameliorative endeavors as constructive measures rather than harmful diversions. Imperialism altered Mink's feminism, just as her feminism shaped her anti-imperialism.

Michel's Empire

Louise Michel, like Mink, opposed the state, rejected parliamentary change, and saw revolution as the single route to universal emancipation. In contrast to Mink, who left anarchism and embraced Blanquist revolutionary socialism in the aftermath of the Commune, Michel attributed the defeat of the insurgency at least in part to flaws inherent to hierarchy and leadership as modes of organizing politically. As Mink turned away from anarchism, Michel turned to it in the Commune's aftermath. She subsequently developed her relationship to the ideology and adapted it to her feminism during her imprisonment in New Caledonia.

Michel's anarchist feminism evolved along universalist lines, but her universalism differed notably from that of French republicanism.[27] Radically democratic and global in scope, Michel's universalism developed with roots in place-based, material particulars of New Caledonia. Already attuned to concerns of class and gender when she arrived in the archipelago, she directly encountered racial ranking there, as well as the quotidian experiences of imperial hierarchy.[28] As a female prisoner in a nearly exclusively male carceral colonial world, she experienced the deeply gendered nature of the penal colony. Simultaneously, she observed the interactions between the European prisoners and jailers and the Kanak concessionaires and local population—contacts fraught with racialized and civilizational presumptions that intensified acutely during the 1878 Kanak uprising. Permitted significant physical mobility during her incarceration, especially during the final years when she received authorization to live in the capital, Michel undertook ethnographic fieldwork, political observations, botanical studies, and academic investigations. These experiences influenced her ideologically and politically, as well as intellectually.

Michel mined structures and institutions seeking universal links and theoretical and activist paths to liberation. In language, she searched for the common roots of international tongues to underscore global human connections. She also promoted the idea of developing a universal language, finding in the Kanak's Bichelamar a living, organic, potentially global idiom. Underscoring the importance of a worldwide vernacular for her universal revolutionary vision, Michel avowed that

> the human beast who, through the ages, has ascended from family, to tribe, to hoard, to nation, ascended, and ascended again, always ascending; and the family becomes the entire race. Languages, which have evolved following human vicissitudes, adopt similar words for their new needs, because all people experience the same need: Revolution. And

revolutions in science, the arts, and industry make more and more necessary this universal language which is already forming and which will
be the corollary of the great rebirth.[29]

Seeing human and linguistic evolution as intrinsically interwoven, Michel asserted an anarchist, positivist, universal progression toward revolution. She
posited that the human family's shared goal of revolution—what she termed
"the great rebirth"—would generate the need for new words across languages
and cultures. Each would experience the demand for similar words, a need generated by their common revolutionary aim, leading to a singular human
tongue. This universal language, "already forming," would play a fundamental role in the emergence of postrevolutionary society.

To advance this process, Michel worked to democratize the French language, appropriating it from its elite gatekeepers. In several novels and her
Mémoires, she destabilized its structure and rules. For example, she inserted a
chapter on women's subjugation in her memoirs, concluding it by stating:
"This chapter is hardly a digression. As a woman I have the right to speak about
women."[30] Juliette Parnell-Smith analyzes Michel's unconventional composi-
tion, with its "plurality of narrative voices, a multiplicity and variety of tex-
tual structures" and contends that "Louise Michel deliberately plays on all
registers, when she simultaneously uses all of the verbal tenses: simple past,
imperfect, and present. She also employs different levels of language like prison
slang, patois, and Kanak."[31] Replacing the formal with the "improper," Michel
introduced elements of popular argot, regional and Indigenous vocabularies,
and orality, intending to revolutionize French. As with her valorization of the
orality of both Kanak tales and French peasant women's stories, Michel claimed
language for the popular classes. She also, Parnell-Smith argues, "destabilized
official masculine discourse, which she mocked mercilessly."[32] Her feminism
subverted the pillars of French linguistic power and propriety.

In undercutting the linguistic parameters and hierarchical aspects of French,
Michel made porous its boundaries, introducing marginalized and subversive
elements while allowing influence from other languages and cultures. As part of
her larger universalist goals, the importance of linguistic commonalities also infused Michel's anarchist feminist pedagogical theorization and practice. Identifying teachers as agents of revolutionary change, Michel developed and promoted
egalitarian education in her schools in France, England, and New Caledonia. In
Algeria, she combined education and revolution with anti-imperialism, challenging Algerian teachers to lead the way in anticolonial uprisings. And in New
Caledonia, she both taught and learned from the Kanak. Instructing them in
Western thought, Michel undertook a parental, imperialist practice, infantilizing

them, presuming the superiority of European ideas, and believing that her teaching would "uplift" the Indigenous people. Yet she saw the educational process and her interactions with the Kanak as a two-way relationship, one that also valorized Kanak culture, from which she learned. Michel exemplified the impossibility of an absolute anti-imperialist stance during this period. Even an activist committed to antiracist, anti-imperial, and antisexist activism could not fully separate herself from aspects of the supremacism of white European intellectual culture.

Acutely conscious of exploitation, Michel analyzed Kanak women's place and their relationship to Kanak men, while simultaneously condemning the white/Black, colonizer/colonized dichotomous hierarchy on the islands. She developed a critique of both Indigenous gender and colonial race relations based on her first-hand experience, on stories from her Kanak informant Daoumi, and on traditional tales; all intersected with her developing anarchism.

An anthropomorphic Kanak legend about the male thunder, Théama, wooing the "beautiful unknown woman," the moon, Moinouk, served as an exemplary narrative for Michel to address both the specificity and the universality of women's plight. She emphasized that this "legend is the same as those of India." Just as she sought common roots to global languages, Michel highlighted the transcultural nature of stories, as a way both to minimize differences between peoples and to stress the shared human experiences that led to the creation of universal tales. Relating this thunder/moon legend, Michel described how even the moon was "charged as other women" with preparing "the tools for fishing, war, and for turning the earth; and the children."[33] She underscored the ways in which women, regardless of their culture, "succumb under the burden" of these tasks.[34] Contesting widely held European assumptions regarding their own supremacy over and fundamental difference from colonized people in general, and Melanesians in particular, Michel continued, "Are these morals not nearly similar, except for this transparent gauze that Europeans call civilization? We all must work in harmony. Since we still have kings and monks as in the time of King Solomon, there is nothing shocking about these women . . . suffering under the same laws."[35] Likening the concept of civilization to a sheer, flimsy cover—an insubstantial and insignificant cloak—and disputing arguments regarding European advancement by reminding her readers of Europe's millennia-old, entrenched political and religious hierarchies, Michel disdained the extant civilizational and evolutionary rationales for imperialism. In countering notions of fundamental differences and essential superiorities and inferiorities and in challenging French professions of a *mission civilisatrice*, Michel made clear her own observations as to the colonizer's motivations and rationale: "The White," she declared, "is there in order to exploit not only the mines, but also the native."[36] Her work to decolonize and democratize language and education and to contest empire affected not only radical politics in France and Europe but also anthropological and pedagogical theorization and scholarship.

In 1880, Michel left New Caledonia, following France's General Amnesty of all imprisoned and exiled Communards. Writing of her departure, Michel described how her work had also made human connections. She told how some Kanak men "presented me with small wooden sculptures that they had made with infinite care. Others gave me unusual ornaments: bracelets, copper rings, wrought iron earrings. Women brought me fruits, and they insisted on travelling away with me. I had all the trouble in the world to make them understand that it was impossible."[37]

Finally arriving in Paris on November 9, her train was welcomed by nearly ten thousand people, including Auclert, crowding in and around the Gare St. Lazare.[38] Less than two weeks later, Michel presided over her first post-exile public meeting. The newspaper *L'électeur* used the language of the French Revolution to report her reception with "applause and enthusiastic cries. . . . *Citoyennes* and *citoyens* came forward and brought bouquets to the *citoyenne* Louise Michel. . . . She stood and emotionally thanked the *citoyennes* and *citoyens* present at the meeting." Michel then spoke of New Caledonia and remembered all who were deported there. "The enthusiasm," the journalist recounted, "was indescribable."[39] Ten days, and several public events later, Michel appeared with Mink and Rouzade. *L'électeur* recounted that Mink "rose energetically against the social order that condemned workers to poverty"; Rouzade "likened the miners and factory workers to the Blacks, who cannot earn enough to survive, while their exploiters live lavishly"; and Michel "traced woman's roles since distant times, showing that in the mid-nineteenth century, she struggled between hunger and shame." "Woman must aid man," Michel proclaimed, "and man must aid woman. That is the route to complete emancipation."[40] Reflective of their sense of solidarity and political commitment— as well as their ideological intersections—these three activists began the first of many speaking engagements and tours, together and separately, immediately after Michel's return.

Continuing her commitments to both revolutionism and universalism, Michel consistently supported and published regularly in the newspaper *L'égalité*, which strove to unite all socialists and anarchists under a revolutionary banner. Three of her books first appeared serially in the periodical, including *Le claque-dents*, her 1890 novel that used antisemitic tropes and stereotypes in an effort to refute them and particularly to disprove cultural assumptions equating Jews with capitalist exploitation and greed.[41] Selecting *L'égalité* to publish this work signaled Michel's interest in fighting the antisemitism present within the radical French Left by demonstrating that capitalist avarice was class-based and transcended religion. In the wake of her years in New Caledonia and of the more recent enormous success of Drumont's *La France juive*, Michel's defense of Jews, as both internal and external others, clearly interlaced with her larger politics of class, race, and religion.

Religion

Like Michel, Audouard and Auclert used the figure of the Jew as an ideological weapon. They, however, employed the associated stereotypes with no intention of challenging them. All three of these women relied on cultural understandings of Jewish difference, on the availability of tropes related to the figure of the Jew. Yet their comprehension and manipulation of these tropes differed fundamentally. Languages of Jewish difference and of antisemitism existed clearly and legibly: Jewish difference constituted the socially constructed and performative analytical category, and antisemitism named the prejudice against and enmity toward Jews, yet both were (and remain) temporally and spatially specific, and ideologically dependent.[42] Thus the meaning of the idea of the Jew, the meaning of Jewish difference, arose at the intersection of time, place, and ideology. Sandrine Sanos has convincingly argued against antisemitism's ahistoricity, refuting assertions of it as an ideology always and everywhere the same. Correspondingly, Sanos has underscored the need for scholars to interrogate the "embedded," constitutive nature of the development of antisemitism and colonial racism.[43] Just as feminisms and imperialisms influenced each other's evolution in specific metropolitan and colonial contexts, with ideologically dependent outcomes, so, too, did antisemitism enter this integrative and formative crucible, shaping and being shaped by particular feminisms and racialized imperialisms.

Religion played a notable role in defining feminists' imperial encounters. In addition to Judaism, Catholicism, Islam, Kanak animisms, and Mormonism filtered activists' perceptions of and responses to aspects of empire. Religion operated as belief, stereotype, symbol, and ideal. French Catholicism constituted a primarily conservative metropolitan force, absent the separation between church and state prior to 1905, and was at sharp odds with most leftist and feminist positions. The sole religiously identified of these feminists, Audouard, viewed the imperial milieux, and Muslims and Jews more specifically, through a deeply gendered and racialized Catholicism. Auclert, a nonbeliever, used Catholicism as a political tool, deploying its antisemitic tropes to advance her specific feminist agenda in both France and Algeria.

Kanak animisms, Mormonism, Coptic Christianity, and Islam appeared to these feminists as foreign and exotic creeds. Michel alone experienced Kanak animism, to which the otherwise anticlerical anarchist showed respect and even idealized, emphasizing its nonhierarchical, nonindividualist aspects. Her admiration became particularly clear in her translation and transcription of Kanak oral tales, even as she sanitized those tales for European consumption. In contrast, Audouard's long and detailed recounting of an Egyptian Coptic Christian wedding reflected her deep discomfort with the gendered and sexualized aspects of their nuptial traditions, which she characterized as barbaric and indicative of a people living in archaic ways. Audouard was also the only one among the feminists to observe Mormonism as she crossed the Western United States. Somewhat tongue-in-cheek, but promoting a serious point, Audouard contrasted Mormon polygamy positively with French conjugal traditions, in which men marry one woman but conduct multiple other unsanctioned sexual relationships with women who receive neither recognition nor support.

All five of the women encountered Islam beyond France. Audouard ranked it below Catholicism but above Judaism, which she actively denigrated. Auclert, who wrote the most extensively about Muslims, held a more complex and nuanced position. Both she and Mink viewed Islam as primarily responsible for Arab women's subjection to polygamy and child marriage. But while Mink judged the religion barbaric for its gender hierarchies, Auclert applauded elements of Muslim marriage that allowed women greater economic, legal, and symbolic independence than did the French institution. Rouzade interpreted Islam as despotic and the antithesis of republicanism. And Michel opposed Islam as she did all other organized religions. All of these women developed perspectives on Islam that reflected their own religious and political positions enmeshed with their individual racialized and gendered understandings of each particular cultural context.

Ideological Reconstitutions: Feminist Encounters with Empire

As political theorist Uday Singh Mehta argues, nineteenth-century liberals used the "uplift" of races to justify empire and conquest (in contrast to conservative thinkers who tended to view non-European people as unworthy of such "aid").[44] Each of the five feminists espoused complex politics that held something of this idea of imperialism as a form of assistance, couched within emerging conceptions of racial and cultural equality. Even Michel, who unwaveringly condemned empire, perceived non-Europeans as infantile or lagging in historical time and promoted a particular kind of aid to native people. Elements of imperialism permeated even self-consciously erected anti-imperialist ideological walls.

While Michel presumed that the Kanak would benefit from Western knowledge, she did not envision herself a "white savior." In addition to her Kanak school, Michel undertook multiple projects to ameliorate their colonial conditions and to alter what she understood as their denigrated, racist, colonially constructed global image. She did not contend that the Kanak *needed* either European ideas or her ventures. Michel saw the Kanak's efforts to throw off French imperial occupation as the soundest route to their survival: she buoyed their own endeavors to save themselves. Her contestation of the colonial, respect for Kanak lifeways, and support for their 1878 anti-imperial insurgency, in concert with her ideas and efforts toward global unity, developed as the beginnings of a revolutionary, postcolonial universalism. Imbricated in the colonial as a white French woman and an ethnographer, she concurrently strove to remove the French presence and championed the Kanak's fight for self-determination.

As with the broad range of feminist politics, differing understandings of gender equality emerged in particular attitudes toward empire. Michel asked about women, "Could one . . . uniformly portray the beings who make up half of the human species?" To which she answered, "No, because there is an entire abyss between one woman and another. . . . While recognizing these incredible differences, one can classify those that make up this sex according to the various milieux into which society throws them, or instead according to their own nature."[45] She rejected the idea of the category "woman" as something monolithic and consistent. Arguing that such a heterogeneous group could be classified by socially assigned categories—which for her could have meant class, religion, or race—or by what she termed their "own nature," their true selves, Michel made clear her insistence upon the latter. Denying the validity of constructed categories typified her anarchist feminism. Audouard, Auclert, Rouzade, and Mink would each agree with Michel's insistence on the manifold nature of womanhood. In contrast, they would each embrace as legitimate or useful certain of the socially produced classifications Michel disavowed. Class, religion, and/or race served as organizational and analytical categories for the other four feminists. The more radical the person's politics, the fewer socially constructed categories she accepted.

Individuals' experiences in global empire reconstituted their ideological commitments. Feminist attitudes toward imperialism arose at the deeply gendered intersections of ideologies with embodied experiences; religious, cultural, and class identifications and assumptions; racial constructions; imperial and national contexts; and temporal locations. To differing degrees, the resultant positions bridged imperial advocacy and imperial opposition rather than falling absolutely to one side or the other. The accepted categorization of activists, writers, and thinkers into "pro-" and "anti-"imperialist camps proves too simplistic, too inattentive, too dichotomous.

Examining the array of ideological positions of the five feminists shows, instead, intricate and deeply intertwined understandings of political power. It also illuminates historical and spatial locatedness, and gender, race, and class hierarchies. Women's lives and statuses, the gendered nature of law codes and justice, the import of language, the role of education, the meaning and validity of religion, the weight of sexuality and embodiment, the significance of love and emotions: if all or most of these factors come to bear on the modeling of either "pro-" or "anti-" imperial stances—and they do—the impossibility of establishing definitive binary camps becomes clear.

French feminists' potent interest in redefining Frenchness contributed to this permeability between pro-imperial and anti-imperial positions. From the empire itself to the nation's universalist principles, the particularities of France oriented their thinking about politics and the justness of imperialism. The Enlightenment legacy of reason and progress infused feminist thought in differing ways, with the concomitant understanding that this epistemology stood at the vanguard of human development and progress. Similarly, the race-based republican ideology of empire, interlaced with the period's constructions of Jewish difference and antisemitism, influenced and in turn was influenced by multiple feminisms. Working to reconceptualize Frenchness, feminists investigated multiple and intersecting alterities in imperial contexts. Yet Western imperial rhetoric and concepts dominated with such intensity that even highly politically astute thinkers and activists could not escape stereotypes and tropes of their era.

A universal feminism did not—and cannot—exist. The fantasy of such a politics erases the reality of multiple and often conflicting positions extant at a given time and place, shaped by particular factors, and driven by specific motivations. Feminisms have always been located. They arise from discrete histories, entangled in their own ways with the various power relations transfusing their particular location. Their emergence cannot be unitary or monolithic. Whether engaging with states or cultures, struggles for gender equity are born within, and ultimately grapple or ally with, competing forms of power and modes of ideological formation. Feminisms develop and operate at distinct gendered and politicized conjunctions of space, time, and ideology.

Within this specific spectrum of gender-based activism, the more radical a person's feminist politics, the more open she was to experiencing difference and the more she vocally opposed cultural, social, or political imperialism. Those most critical of social structures and hierarchies of power had the greatest ability to see the world through others' eyes. Thus, where the revolutionary anarchist Michel supported the New Caledonian Kanak in their revolt against French imperial rule, the republican socialist Auclert advocated a French feminist imperialism to "elevate" Algerian women through cultural assimilation, and the liberal monarchist Audouard demonstrated a deeply gendered, Orientalized antisemitism when describing Jews she encountered in Constantinople and Jerusalem. The left-to-right location of the intersecting ideology that each woman modified with her feminism—Michel's revolutionary anarchism, Mink's revolutionary socialism, Rouzade and Auclert's republican socialisms, and Audouard's liberal monarchism—corresponded to their intensity of opposition to the French imperial project. This correlation cannot be coincidental.

Yet each of the five strongly decried existing imperialisms. Feminisms encouraged a critique of empire unlike any other politics. The feminist perspective and central focus on gendered questions sparked the era's anti-imperialisms rooted in egalitarianism and justice. In contrast to other ideologies, feminisms attuned people to lived and embodied inequities. Liberalism, socialisms, and anarchism addressed the socioeconomic and the political. Feminisms not only engaged the junctures between gender and society, economics, and politics but also investigated the personal, intimate, sexual, and physical. The recognition that the many aspects of personal life were shaped by multiple, layered institutions and hierarchies transformed feminists' political thinking. Although the phrase would not be coined for another hundred years, they recognized that "the personal is political." This insight facilitated their identification and condemnations of injustices that remained invisible or irrelevant to other activists and thinkers of their era. Thus when these five feminists encountered imperialism, they identified it as an institution being practiced unjustly—although only Mink and Michel considered it intrinsically oppressive. Obviously opposing prevailing imperialisms did not guarantee that these activists would equally contest other power inequities. A feminist stance did not ensure that its adherents would be conscious of and challenge other repressive hierarchies—that depended upon the individual's intersecting ideologies. Yet a feminist consciousness brought the five women to various forms of anti-imperialism.

Diversity among feminisms encompassed political activities and critiques on subjects often seen as having little or nothing to do with feminisms. Understanding the contextualized feminisms of the period illustrates the dense, gendered junctions of these politics and ideologies and sheds new light on perceptions of imperialisms and their elaborately enmeshed ideological, political, social, cultural, and economic undercurrents. Imperialisms pervasively influenced the latter part of the nineteenth century as global political, cultural, and conceptual forms. They did so, however, in spatially and temporally located ways. Even more particularly, imperial concepts—the rhetorical and social products and tools of empire, including racialization, sexualization, and ethnographic categorization—developed in concert with certain ideologies within distinct metropolitan and colonial contexts. Feminists appropriated and adapted these instruments of empire. Whether contesting existing forms of colonialism, attacking or embracing imperialism as an idea, or endorsing new imperial approaches, they used the languages and practices of empire, redeploying them in ways that reshaped both feminisms and imperialisms. The divergent empires that Audouard, Auclert, Rouzade, Mink, and Michel imagined traveled tensely hand-in-hand with the French imperial project that each of them attacked, seeking multiple routes to equality and liberation. What kind of equality and whose liberation were questions that continued to drive, and to this day still propel, both anti-imperialisms and feminisms.

NOTES

Introduction

1. Michel 1898, 385. Unless otherwise noted, all translations are mine.

2. Michel's ally and fellow deportee Nathalie Lemel was, like Michel, an anarchist feminist, but we have no evidence of her supporting the Kanak revolt.

3. For the 1890s emergence of Third Republican anti-imperialism, see, among others, Liauzu 2007; Merle 2003; and the classic works, Ageron 1973; and Girardet 1972.

4. "Liberal feminism" pursues gender equity within the existing socioeconomic and political framework; liberalism as a political theory focuses on individualism, personal freedom, and legal categories. "Republican socialist feminism" seeks both gender and economic equity through reformist, legal political change within the extant political form. "Revolutionary socialist feminism" works toward gender and class equity through the radical overthrow of existing class relations and governmental structures. And "revolutionary anarchist feminism" strives for gender and class equity by replacing the present political system with no new governmentalism, by simultaneously overturning capitalism, church, and state.

5. Voices raised against Algerian conquest gained no traction. See Pitts 2006, 13, 159–177; Liauzu 2007; Sankar 2003; and Ageron 1973.

6. Michel's long-time ally and friend, the anarchist feminist geographer Élisée Reclus, was an exception: his 1877–1878 newspaper, *Le travailleur*, censured France's imperial project, and his anarchist feminist politics set him apart from other leftist thinkers, as did his anti-imperialism (Ferretti 2016, 68–88). Nicholls (2019) addresses Reclus's writings on empire, but not his feminism. She focuses almost exclusively on male revolutionaries.

7. By the 1880s, Audouard's Spiritist commitments increasingly led her away from feminist circles. Spiritist affiliation could also explain her relative absence from the feminist historiography. Olympe Audouard, public conferences, May 30, 1873, April 7, 1887, and October 8, 1887, BA 941, APP. Archives designated by abbreviations are listed at the beginning of Works Cited.

8. In the wake of Napoleon III's 1868 liberalization of freedoms of speech and assembly, republicans, socialists, and feminists organized public meetings attracting as many as seventy thousand people in one night at locations across the city (Dalotel, Faure, and Freiermuth 1980, 123–126; Eichner 2004, 44–46).

9. Audouard 1871, i–ii.

10. Translated from Arabic into French as *Les mille et une nuits, contes arabes traduits en français*, this multi-volume collection of ancient Middle Eastern tales garnered enormous popularity (Marzolph, 2007, ix–xi).

11. See chap. 6.

12. Hause 2007, 22–27; Taïeb 2006, 271–272.

13. Hause 1987, 68–86; Sarazin 2008.

14. Hause 2007, 52–53.

15. Hause 1987, 68–86; Blacher 2017, 30–34.

16. Sowerwine 1982, 29–31.

17. She is recognized as a science fiction writer today.

18. This year-long, unexplained archival gap alerted me to Mink's absence from France. Neither the English nor French-language historiographies address Mink's Algerian experience or her involvement with empire.

19. A vast literature exists on Michel's role in the Commune, and much less on her time in New Caledonia.

20. Although not all feminists were women.

21. French women remained excluded from suffrage and thus full citizenship until 1944 (Scott 1996, 1–18; Pateman 1988).

22. Liauzu 2007; Merle 2003; Ageron 1973.

23. Clément 2013, 51–81; Singaravélou 2008, 135–148; Ageron 1973.

24. Stoler 2002, xvi.

25. Lorcin 2004, 45–46.

26. Scott 1994; Eichner 2004; Moses 1984.

27. Bush 2016; Burton 2009; Murphy 2009. In Britain, the all-male, free-trade Cobdenites were the era's earliest anti-imperialists (Sexton and Hoganson 2020, 166–168).

28. This holds equally true for both the French and the English-language historiographies.

29. Although not addressing empire, some scholars have investigated French feminisms in transnational contexts; See especially Carlier 2012; Cova 2010.

30. While the nation-state paradigm persists among many historians of France, most contemporary scholars of empire now reject this binary. Among the first to do so were Cooper and Stoler 1997, 1–4.

31. Camiscioli 2013, 139.

32. Sessions 2016.

33. One exception is Steven Hause's (1987) biography of Hubertine Auclert, which includes a chapter on her experience of living in Algeria and the ways in which it influenced her feminism.

34. See, among others, Midgley 1998; Pierson, Chaudhuri, and McAuley 1998; Burton 1994; Wilson 2004.

35. Levine 2004, 1.

36. Clancy-Smith 1998, 154–174.

37. Hugon 2004, 8; Camiscioli 2013, 139–140; Robert-Guiard 2009, 5–7; Barthélémy, Capdevila, and Zancarini-Fournel 2011, 7–22; Rogers 2016, 124–133.

38. For utopian socialist feminisms, see Schlick 2012; Foley 2004; Veauvy 2011; Champion 2002. One exception was midcentury pro-colonial feminist Eugénie Luce; see Rogers 2013a.

39. Women's travel writing has drawn significant attention from both historians and literary scholars since the early 2000s, but only Bénédicte Monicat (1996), Isabelle Ernot (2011), Rachel Nuñez (2006), and Renée Champion (2002) have focused on late-

nineteenth century feminists. (Both Nuñez's and Champion's dissertations remain unpublished.)

40. Clancy-Smith 1998, 154–174; Ernot 2011; Nuñez 2012, 23–45; Nuñez 2006; Monicat 1996.

41. Monicat's book (1996) focuses more broadly on women travel writers. Clancy-Smith 1998, 154–174; Nuñez 2012, 23–45; Nuñez 2006; Taïeb 2006; Hause 1987.

42. For studies of feminism and imperialism in the first half of the twentieth, see the landmark work, Boittin, 2010; see also Kimble 2006; Siegel 2015; Germaine and Larcher 2018.

43. Wilder 2010.

44. Lorcin (2016, 113) contends that scholars increasingly reject the binary and recognize productive overlaps between interrogations of discourse and experience.

45. During the late-nineteenth century, France and its colonies had not yet become what Wilder (2005) terms the "imperial nation state," but were building toward that status.

1. Ideologies and Intimacies of Imperialism

1. Auclert 1900, 100.

2. Auclert 1900, 99–101.

3. Chapter 2 discusses feminist assessments of women's comparative international metropolitan and colonial legal statuses.

4. For intimacy and empire, see especially Stoler 2016; Stoler 2002; Lowe 2015; Ballantyne and Burton 2008.

5. Stoler 2016, 325–329; Stoler 2002, 9–13; Ballantyne and Burton 2008.

6. The same argument holds for the contradictions in republican support of imperialism; Pitts 2006, 16.

7. Both Fortunati (2001, 9) and Monicat (1996, 29) point out the doubled otherness of European women travelers, yet feminist European women voyagers bore an additional layer of politically based difference.

8. For the late-nineteenth century evolution of the concept of race in France, see Conklin 2013.

9. Ernot 2011.

10. Firpo 2011; Boittin 2015.

11. Chapter 2 more fully addresses feminist redefinitions of Frenchness.

12. Chapman and Frader 2004, 1–5.

13. Gobineau 1853; Goldstein 2015; Jugé 2009.

14. Chapman and Frader 2004, 4.

15. Merriman 1996, 988.

16. Both virility and population concerns permeated the Third Republic. For population, see Offen 1984; Andersen 2015. For virility and masculinity, see Forth 2006; Miller 2018; Nye 1994.

17. Stovall 2015, 207–216.

18. Liauzu 1992, 41–72.

19. Vergès 2003, 194–196; Blanchard and Lemaire 2003, 23–26, 31–32; Conklin 1997.

20. English 2006.

21. Blanchard et al. 2013, 3–8; Girardet 1972, 3–23.

22. Cooper and Stoler 1997, 1–4.

23. Clément 2012, 6.

24. Liauzu 2007, 14. In the final years of the Second Republic, a few male socialists condemned colonialism in passing, including Altin Vertet and Paulet in Paris's public meeting movement, and Communard Benoît Malon in *Le Troisième défait du prolétariat* (Dalotel and Freiermuth 1988, 267; Malon 1871, 2).

25. Nicholls 2019, 249–253. Nicholls does not recognize Reclus's feminism.

26. Clemenceau moved consistently to the right over subsequent years. Liauzu 2007, 72; Cohen 1980, 261.

27. Liauzu 2007, 70–72; Bondi 1992, 23–27.

28. Manceron 2003, 2007; Liauzu 2007, 70–72.

29. Offen 2000, 19.

30. Dossier Michel, Ba 1183; Dossier Mink, October 2, 1880, Ba 1178, APP.

31. See, for example, January 8, 1881, Ba 1184, and December 20, 1895, Ba 1886, APP; see also Verhaeghe 2019, 83–85.

32. Rapport de Hilaire, December 3, 1880, APP.

33. Where she became deeply involved in the international anarchist community, opened an anarchist school, and continued her activism.

34. Michel, who never married or had children, periodically aided her comrade Mink, including holding a fundraising lecture to help support Mink's children during one of Mink's imprisonments. Paule Mink to Louise Michel, copy, Marseilles, June 5, 1881, Ba 1178, APP.

35. *Le matin*, March 9, 1889.

36. Hause 1987, 63.

37. Rapport, March 11, 1880, Ba 1178, APP.

38. "Chronique," *XIXe siècle*, March 12, 1880; Paul Ginisty, "Conférence de la salle Oberkampf," Gil Blas, March 12, 1880. Auguste Blanqui participated in this meeting at Auclert's invitation. In his final years, Blanqui significantly moderated his politics to support the Third Republic and women's suffrage. While most self-identified Blanquists—such as the post-Commune Mink—allied with revolutionism, Auclert aligned with less-recognized, late-life republicanism. Hause 1987, 51–52, 62–63.

39. Sowerwine 1982, 29–42. Sowerwine conflates Mink's opposition to women's rights with an acceptance of the gendered status quo. Rather, Mink espoused a difference feminism, valuing women's embodied dissimilarities from men, while simultaneously accepting essentialist, gender-based characteristics. She viewed political rights for women as meaningless under the existing system, and even counterproductive in placating women. For her, only socialist revolution could bring true fundamental change.

40. Michel 1983, 388.

41. Hause 1987, 47–68.

42. She shared this position with most of the male French Left, who retained it into the mid-twentieth century. April 20, 1884, Ba 1178, APP.

43. *La citoyenne*, August 14, 1885.

44. "Chronique méridionale," *Progrès du midi*, October 1883; "Le droit de femmes: Conference de Hubertine Auclert," *Nîmes*, October 1883.

45. Fonds Hubertine Auclert, box 2, BHVP.

46. Conklin 1997, 2.

47. Fonds Auclert, BHVP.

48. Raymond 2018.

49. Sowerwine 1982, 37–41.

50. Dalotel, Faure, and Freiermuth, 1980, 123–126; Moses 1984, 178–179; Eichner 2004, 44–46.

51. French and British imperialists asserted levels of scientific and technological advancement as another measure of civilization; see Adas 2015.

52. Clancy-Smith 1998, 154–156.

53. Audouard 1869, 149.

54. Audouard 1869, 149.

55. Audouard 1869, 150.

56. Audouard 1869, 150.

57. Brantlinger 2003, 2–5. The French asserted an extinction narrative regarding native populations in several of their colonies, including the Kanak of New Caledonia. This is further discussed in chapter 4.

58. Fabian 2002, 31–32; Mignolo 1998, 32–53.

59. Cook-Lynn 2001.

60. Audouard 1869, 166.

61. Audouard 1869, 166.

62. Audouard 1869, 166.

63. Audouard 1869, 167.

64. Audouard 1869, 167

65. Audouard 1869, 231.

66. Audouard 1869, 231.

67. Audouard 1863b, 233.

68. Mink 1886.

69. Evidence of Mink's Algerian trip, where she apparently drew significant and enthusiastic crowds, is limited to a few newspaper accounts and reports by observers. The existing English and French-language scholarship makes virtually no mention of her time in the colony, but primary source material clearly outlines parts of her journey. Leaving Europe and experiencing North Africa first hand affected Mink's intellectual trajectory; the place of the Algerian people and France's relationship to its colonies thus comprise an as-yet unacknowledged component in her feminist and radical politics. *L'indépendent de Mascara*, May 7, 1885; *La citoyenne*, August 14, 1885; *Le cri du peuple*, August 14, 1885; *Le coup de feu*, no. 5, January 1886; *Le cri du peuple*, February 19, 1888; Beguin and Peigneaux 1888, 60–61.

70. Mink 1886.

71. Mink 1886.

72. Mink 1886.

73. *Le coup de feu* no. 5 (January 1886).

74. Paule Mink, Ba 1178, APP. *Cochinchine* was the southern part of present-day Viet Nam, and *Tonkin* was the northern section; the central portion was known as *Annam*.

75. Mink 1886.

76. In the 1860s, during the late Second Empire, Mink had advocated rights-based feminism. She changed her position in the wake of the 1871 Paris Commune, but then became open to it again in the 1890s. Eichner 2004.

77. Mink 1886.

78. Eichner 2004, 49–51.

79. Eichner 2004, 49–51.

80. Beguin and Peigneaux 1888, 60.

81. Beguin and Peigneaux 1888, vii.

82. Beguin and Peigneaux 1888, 60.

83. Beguin and Peigneaux 1888, 60.

84. *Le cri du peuple*, February 19, 1888.

85. Auclert 1900, 30–36, 138–146; Clancy-Smith 1998, 169–170.

86. Eichner 2004, 198–200. Mink had refused a candidacy offer a decade earlier, while traveling in Algeria. In a letter dated August 14, 1885, and reprinted in Auclert's newspaper, *La citoyenne*, and in the socialist *Le cri du peuple*, Mink wrote to the Fédération Socialiste des Femmes à Paris to refuse their proposal to slate her as a candidate for the upcoming municipal elections. Explaining her opposition to women's electoral participation, she asserted that only revolution, the "social transformation of the old world," would ameliorate women's condition. Mink thanked the organization for thinking of her, as "far from Paris, in Algeria for nearly a year, I had thought I might have been forgotten." *La citoyenne*, August 14, 1885; *Le cri du people*, August 14, 1885.

87. Audouard 1863a, 194.

88. Audouard 1863a, 195; ellipses in the original.

89. Audouard 1863a, 195.

90. Audouard 1863a, 195.

91. Audouard 1863a, 195.

92. Audouard 1863a, 195.

93. Audouard 1863a, 195.

94. Audouard 1863a, 196.

95. Audouard 1866, 423.

96. Audouard 1866, 423

97. Audouard 1866, 424.

98. Audouard 1866, 378.

99. Audouard 1866, 380.

100. Audouard 1866, 381–382.

101. Audouard 1866, 382.

102. Audouard 1866, 382.

103. Audouard 1866, 390.

104. Audouard 1866, 391; ellipses in the original.

105. Audouard 1866, 391.

106. Audouard 1866, 391–392; ellipses in the original.

107. Audouard 1866, 393.

108. Audouard 1873.

109. Audouard 1866, 41.

110. Audouard 1866, 41.

111. Audouard 1866, 41.

112. Bird 2012, 94.

113. Audouard 1866.

2. Sex, Love, and the Law

1. Audouard 1871, 317.

2. Audouard 1884, 2.

3. For questions of Frenchness, see Hajjat 2012; Saada 2012; Brubaker 1992; Boittin and Stoval 2010.

4. Surkis 2019, 11–12.

5. Rouzade is the lone exception.

6. Monicat 1996, 29; Perrot 2002, 468.

7. For scholarship on French women's travel writing, see Monicat 1994, 1995, 1996; Rogers and Thébaud 2008b; Pellegrin 2011a; Pellegrin 2011b; Bourguinat 2008a; Mellman 2008; Champion 2002.

8. Ernot 2011, 2.

9. See especially, Barthelemy, Capdevila, and Zancarini-Fournelt 2011; Rogers and Thébaud 2008a; Loth 2009; Champion 2002; Bourguinat 2008a.

10. Bourguinat 2008b, 7–18.

11. As noted above, while many female travelers focused on aspects of these issues, particularly as they related to women's lives, feminists differed in their activist goals—aimed at both metropole and colonies.

12. Auclert 1900, 52.

13. Auclert 1900, 56–57.

14. Auclert 1900, 56–57.

15. Auclert 1900, 56–57.

16. For the family as a model of larger political structures and operations, see Ferguson 2012, chap. 2.

17. Mainardi 2003, vii.

18. Desan 2004, 3.

19. Desan 2004, 15.

20. Pateman 1988, 2.

21. de Gouges 1791; Desan 2004, 15–16, 23–24; Mainardi 2003, 8–9.

22. Mesch and Belenky 2008, 1–6; Desan 2004, 18–20, 49.

23. Robcis 2013, 22–23.

24. Mainardi 2003, 12–18; Mesch and Belenky 2008, 2; Eichner 2004, 10.

25. Desan 2004, 283–310.

26. *Code civile de Français* 1804.

27. Desan 2004, 310.

28. McBride 1995, 59.

29. de Bonald 1818, 118.

30. Mesch and Belenky 2008, 2.

31. Tristan 1838.

32. Fortescue 1993.

33. Pedersen 2003, 21–22; Eichner 2004, 51–54.

34. Audouard 1863b, 143–144.

35. Nuñez 2012, 27–28; Monicat 1996, 58–59.

36. Audouard 1863b, 143–144.

37. Audouard 1863b, 143.

38. Audouard 1863b, 143.

39. Audouard 1863b, 143.

40. Audouard 1863b, 144.

41. Intended to underscore the absence of male-on-female violence in Turkey, Audouard's emphasis that "not even a man of the people" (1836b, 144) would commit such an act exposed a strong current of elitism that ran through her work.

42. Monicat 1996, 58.

43. Audouard 1863b, 70. Rachel Nuñez (2006) examines Audouard's comparisons of France's level of civilization to that of other nations, often finding it lacking.

44. The speech was subsequently published by Audouard's editor and publisher, E. Dentu. Audouard 1870, 8.

45. Audouard 1871.

46. Audouard 1870, 13–16.

47. Audouard 1870, 18.

48. Audouard 1870, 22.

49. Audouard 1870, 22.

50. Audouard 1870, 22.

51. Moran 2004.

52. What Debra Thompson (2009, 357) terms "anti-miscegenation regimes, encompassing laws, jurisprudence and social norms in a particular jurisdiction."

53. Audouard 1876, 362.

54. Audouard 1871, 357, 386.

55. Audouard 1869, 220.

56. Audouard 1869, 224.

57. Audouard 1870, 26.

58. Audouard 1870, 26.

59. Rouzade 1872.

60. Rouzade 1872, 33.

61. Rouzade 1872, 43.

62. Eustache 1987, 41–44.

63. Rouzade 1872, 156.

64. Rouzade 1872, 173.

65. Rouzade 1872, 173; Eustache 1987. Rouzade foreshadowed by nearly 130 years France's 2000 law on parité, which requires (ultimately) an equal number of women and men in its legislative bodies.

66. Rouzade 1872, 36.

67. Chafer and Sackur 2002, 5.

68. Lehning 2001, 1–11.

69. Conklin 1997. For feminists appropriating the civilizing mission, see Nuñez 2006.

70. Audouard 1870, 28.

71. Audouard 1870, 29.

72. Audouard 1870, 30.

73. Audouard 1870, 30.

74. For a fascinating analysis of France's legislative debates over divorce, see Mansker 2011.

75. Audouard 1884, 73.

76. Audouard 1884, 73.

77. Auclert 1904, 9–10.

78. Audouard 1863b, 117.

79. Audouard 1863b, 70–71.

80. Fuchs 2008, 60.

81. Fuchs 2008, 75.

82. Fuchs 2008, 60–61.

83. Fuchs 2008, 61.

84. Audouard 1863b, 201.

85. Audouard 1871, 358–359.

86. Grossberg 1998, 215.

87. Grossberg 1998, 216.

88. Audouard 1871, 346.

89. Audouard 1871, 347.

90. Audouard 1871, 345–346.

91. Audouard 1863b, 121–123.

92. Audouard 1863b, 129, 123.

93. Beginning in 1896, Auclert published over four hundred columns in *Le radical* over a thirteen-year period. For a comprehensive list of her columns (and her other publications), see Hause 1987, app. 1, 227–236.

94. Fuchs 2008, 109.

95. Auclert, "Le féminisme: Matriarcat," *Le radical*, July 6, 1897. *L'état civil* refers to the official status—including marital and birth—of French citizens and subjects.

96. Auclert, "Le féminisme: Matriarcat."

97. Auclert, "Le féminisme: Matriarcat."

98. Earlier feminists to appropriate the matriarchy argument include Friedrich Engels, August Bebel, Elizabeth Cady Stanton, and Matilda Joslyn Gage. Eller 2006; Eller 2005, 2–5.

99. Auclert, "Le féminisme: Matriarcat."

100. See Hause 1987.

101. Auclert 1908, 1.

102. France's treatment of Polynesian Tahiti differed markedly from that of its Melanesian colonies, particularly New Caledonia. Of the two regional, racialized Pacific categories created by France, Polynesians had lighter skin, and thus the French considered them to be more evolved than the darker-skinned Melanesians.

103. Saada 2006.

104. Saada 2006, 189.

105. Rouzade 1872, 193.

106. Rouzade 1872, 172.

107. Auclert 1900, 42–43.

108. Auclert 1900, 43.

109. Auclert 1900, 48.

110. Auclert 1900, 48.

111. Auclert 1900, 48–49.
112. Surkis 2019, 119–124.
113. Surkis 2019, 49.
114. Audouard 1863b, 111.
115. Audouard 1836b, 112.
116. Audouard 1836b, 112
117. Matsuda 2005, 173.
118. Matsuda 2005, 173.
119. Matsuda 2005, 117–118.
120. Mink 1886.
121. Mink 1886.
122. Karandashev 2017, 113–118; Ikuenobe 2018.
123. Auclert 1900, 65.
124. Auclert 1900, 67–68.
125. Auclert 1900, 67–68.
126. Auclert 1900, 66.
127. Rachel Nuñez argues that Auclert focused almost exclusively on Arab sexual practices, particularly polygamy, in an effort to underscore Arab difference. Motivated by her desire to demonstrate French women's relatively higher level of civilization, Auclert, Nuñez contends, unintentionally simultaneously undermined her argument regarding the possibility of Algerian Arab assimilation. For Nuñez, Auclert's denigration of Jews and foreigners, along with her Oriental othering of Arabs, emerged as part of her move toward right-wing nationalism, in her efforts to bolster French women's relative status. See Nuñez 2006, 249–280.
128. Nuñez 2006, 249–280.
129. This was consistent with the dominant Western critique of polygamy in this period. See, for example, the widely read Finck 1891.
130. Auclert 1900, 58.
131. Auclert 1900, 70.
132. Although effectively local Arab and Berber leaders ruled much of the country beyond the cities of Algiers, Constantine, and Oran.
133. Saada 2012, 95–101; Saada 2003, 15–17; Brett 1988, 441–442.
134. "Special customs," including polygamy and divorce, had been abolished for metropolitan Jews in 1807, but they were allowed to Algerian Jews, because they did not have French citizenship until the 1870 Crémieux Decree. Surkis 2010, 27–32; Saada 2003, 15–17
135. Surkis 2010, 32–33.
136. Richard in Surkis 2010, 32–33.
137. Surkis 2010, 32–33.
138. Surkis 2010, 31–34; Lorcin 1995, 63–67.
139. Lorcin 1995, 7.
140. Abi-Mershed 2010, 1–4.
141. Hubertine Auclert, "Arabophobes. Arabophiles," *Le radical*, March 15, 1891.
142. This contrasts with Isabelle Ernot's assessment that in European women travelers' writings about Indigenous women, including those of Audouard and Auclert, "the other civilization is rarely understood in its diversity and complexity but more

often in a negative and caricatural alterity" (2011, 54). This does reflect the majority of the cases. Yet, it is important to examine the ways in which some women—in these cases feminists—did positively regard and present Indigenous women.

143. Auclert 1900, 58.

3. La Citoyenne

1. Hubertine Auclert, *La citoyenne*, February 12, 1881. Portions of this chapter appeared previously as *"La citoyenne* in the World: Hubertine Auclert and Feminist Imperialism," *French Historical Studies* 32, no. 1 (Winter 2009): 63–84.

2. Clancy-Smith 1998, 154–174; Clancy-Smith 1996; Nuñez 2012, 23–45; Taïeb 2006, 271–272; Eichner 2009, 63–84.

3. Conklin and Clancy-Smith 2004, 504–505.

4. "Protestation des femmes," *La citoyenne*, May 8, 1881.

5. Bidelman 1982, 111–112.

6. Roberts 1999, 307; Sullerot 1996.

7. Hause 1987, 91–93.

8. Bidelman 1982, 111–112; Hause 1987, 89.

9. Hause 1987, 89.

10. Bidelman 1982, 112; Hause 1987, 91.

11. Impugning women's sanity was widely used to undermine their credibility. Paule Mink also faced similar attacks. See, for example, Eichner 2004, 192–193.

12. For the reception of *La citoyenne*, see, for example, Hubertine Auclert, "Arabophobes. Arabophiles," *La citoyenne*, April 1, 1891; Felicien Champsaur, "Hubertine Auclerc [sic]," *Les contemporains. Journal hebdomodaire* (includes cover caricature), n.d, Dossier Hubertine Auclert, BMD; Blacher 2017, 47–50; and Hause 1987, 95–96.

13. Lys de Pac, February 25, 1891, quoted in Wiart 1997, 28; Blacher 2017, 46–49.

14. Auclert, "Arabophobes. Arabophiles"; Blacher 2017, 49.

15. *La citoyenne*, February 12, 1881.

16. These articles focusing beyond France appeared an average of six per year. Taïeb 2006, 35–36; Bidelman 1982, 111–112; Hause 1987, 89.

17. The organization's name translates as "The Society for Claiming the Political and Social Rights of Women." Henry Fouquier, "Chronique," July 30, 1880 (no journal name), BMD; Dossier Hubertine Auclert, Ba/885, APP; Hause 1987, 87–88, 96.

18. Blacher 2017; Taraud 2008.

19. Auclert 1900.

20. Lorcin 2004, 45–61.

21. Clancy-Smith 1998, 154.

22. Clancy-Smith 1998, 154.

23. Surkis 2019, 6.

24. "Instructions anthropologiques," in *La grande encyclopédie* (Paris, 1885), quoted in Wiart 1997.

25. For Fabian's conception of the "denial of coevalness," see Chapter 1.

26. Mignolo 1998, 32–53; Fabian 2002, 31–32.

27. Haggis 1998, 63–64.

28. Scott 1996, 90–99.

29. Hubertine Auclert, "L'avis des Musulmanes," *La citoyenne*, May 1, 1891.

30. Wiart 1997, 56–59, 93. A classic text on assimilationism is Betts 1961.

31. Auclert, "L'avis des Musulmanes." Auclert wrote a number of other articles on assimilation. The absence of Algerian women's voices in Auclert's work strongly suggests that her arguments regarding Arab women's desire for assimilation rested primarily on her own assumptions and projections. Her writings on assimiliation include: "Arabophobes. Arabophiles"; "Françisons l'Algérie," *La citoyenne*, April 15, 1891; Auclert 1900, 9–17, 20–26, and 30–36; "Le féminisme: La femme et l'Algerie," *Le radical*, November 22, 1896. See also Hause 1987, 141.

32. Auclert, "Françisons l'Algérie." Michel took a similar approach, locating the Kanak in France's historical past. Yet she did not propose assimilation as their route to advancement. See chapters 4 and 5.

33. Auclert, "Françisons l'Algérie."

34. Auclert, "Françisons l'Algérie."

35. Auclert, "Françisons l'Algérie"; emphasis added. Auclert continued to write and publish arguments against polygamy for the rest of her life. See especially her weekly Sunday column, "Le féminisme," in *Le radical* between 1896 and 1909.

36. Taïeb 2006, 276–277.

37. Unknown author, unnamed newspaper clipping, 1891, Fonds Hubertine Auclert, Archives Marie-Louise Bouglé, BHVP.

38. Burton 1992, 137–138; Rupp 1996, 8–10.

39. Auclert 1900, 16; Clancy-Smith 1998, 170.

40. Clancy-Smith 1998, 163.

41. Auclert 1900, 247.

42. Auclert 1900, 3.

43. For further discussion of Auclert's position on Jews, see chapter 6. Chapman and Frader 2004, 4–5; Schreier 2007, 99–103; Lorcin 1995, 8.

44. Hubertine Auclert, "Préjugé de race et de sexe," in *Affaires Algériennes*, n.d., Fonds Hubertine Auclert, BHVP.

45. Known as the July Revolution, the Revolution of 1830 ended the reign of the Bourbon kings, introduced a constitutional monarchy, and brought Louis Phillippe Orleans to the throne.

46. Andrews 2006, xx–xi, 26–31;

47. Andrews 2006, 29.

48. During the Revolution of 1848, they shifted their approach to focus more on political rights. Andrews 2006, xx–xi, 26–31; Moses and Rabine 1993, 20–22.

49. Schlick 2012, 120–121.

50. Anne-Caroline Sieffert points out the rarity of any female journalists publishing travel narratives in the nineteenth century. Sieffert 2008, 110–111.

51. Eichner 2014.

52. Andrews 2006, vii–viii; Moses 1984, 52–63; Eichner 2014, 663.

53. Eichner 2014, 664–665; Sullerot 1966, 143–162.

54. The newspaper changed names several times, including *La femme libre* (The free woman), *Apostolat des femmes* (Apostolate of women), and *La femme de l'avenir* (The woman of the future). Eichner 2014, 664.

55. Ragan 2000, 91.

56. Veauvy 2011, 222; Moussa 2002, 225.

57. Pilbeam 2013, 107.

58. Voilquin 1865.

59. Voilquin 1865, 299–301.

60. Voilquin 1865.

61. Champion 2002, 157–158; Voilquin 1865, 368.

62. Champion 2002, 159.

63. Ernot 2011, 6.

64. Foley 2004, 216–221.

65. Conklin 1997, 1–2.

66. Among their projects, the Saint-Simonians were centrally involved in planning the Suez Canal. Pilbeam 2013, 125–126.

67. Hubertine Auclert, "Industries des femmes arabes," *Le petite république*, May 28, 1892.

68. Eugénie Allix to Prefect of Algiers, November 1, 1850, quoted in Rogers 2013a, 3.

69. Rogers 2013b, 160; Rogers 2013a, 3.

70. Rogers 2009, 48–53.

71. Auclert petitioned the Ministry of the Interior in 1891, the Senate in 1892, and the Chamber of Deputies in 1893. She addressed the issue in her *Le radical* column, including "M. Jonnart et les mauresques," October 25, 1900; "Réponse du gouverneur général du Algérie," December 18, 1900; and "On attend l'avis de la Chambre," April 2, 1901. See also Clancy-Smith 1998, 169–170; and correspondence and manuscripts, Fonds Hubertine Auclert, BHVP.

72. Michel advocated a radical form of Western education for the New Caledonian Kanak. See chapter 5.

73. "Protestation des femmes."

74. "Protestation des femmes."

75. Draigu, "Les eunuques blancs," *La citoyenne*, June 12, 1881.

76. Draigu, "Les eunuques blancs."

77. *La citoyenne*, April 1884.

78. *La citoyenne*, April 1884. Divorce was first made legal in France during the Revolution, in 1792. It was subsequently abolished in 1816 and reinstated only in 1884.

79. Hubertine Auclert, "Le mariage arabe," *La citoyenne*, no. 144, May 1889. For the purchase of brides and the issue of child marriage, see Auclert, "Voile et viol," *La citoyenne*, January 1889.

80. Auclert, "Le mariage arabe."

81. Auclert, "Le mariage arabe."

82. *La citoyenne*, April 2–May 6, 1883.

83. Une Voyageuse, "La Reine de Madagascar," *La citoyenne*, March 1884.

84. Une Voyageuse, "La Reine de Madagascar."

85. Lorcin 1995, 1–3, 53–62.

86. "La femme en Kabyle," *La citoyenne*, May 16, 1881.

87. Auclert, *Le radical*, January 1899.

88. Auclert, *Le radical*, January 1899.

89. Boulle 2003, 11–13.

90. Burton 1994, 1–19.

91. Burton 1994, 1–19; Offen 2000, 154; Moses 1984, 215–221; Eichner 2004, 196–197.

92. Burton 1994; Midgley 2007; Hall 1992, 208.

93. Tabili 2003, 125–130; Ware 1992.

94. "X," *La citoyenne*, 1884.

95. "La femme arabe, IV," *La citoyenne*, May 1884.

96. "La femme arabe, IV."

97. Interestingly, Auclert did not clarify that it was the French colonial authorities, with the complicity of local Muslim officials, who closed existing Muslim girls' schools in the capital, Algers.

98. For ideas of degeneration in the colonial context, see Mantena 2010, 56–88; Edwards 1998. For the metropolitan context see Karen Offen's (1984) germinal article.

99. Camille, "La France africaine," *La citoyenne*, 1886.

100. For an examination of citizenship, Algeria, and empire, see Sessions 2011.

101. Wiart 1997, 49–51.

102. Dzeh-Djeh 1934.

103. Auclert did not include Judaism in her anticlerical critique. For her complicated relationship to Judaism and her political uses of the mythical figure of "The Jew," see chapter 6, "Familiar Stranger: The Figure of the Jew."

4. Imprisoned, Colonized

1. Portions of this chapter previously appeared as "Language of Imperialism, Language of Liberation: Louise Michel and the Kanak-French Colonial Encounter," *Feminist Studies* 45, no. 2 (2019), 377–408.

2. Michel 1999a, 310.

3. Michel 1999b, 202.

4. Michel 1999b, 202.

5. Louise Michel to Victor Hugo, July 14, 1876, in Michel 1999b, 237–238.

6. Louise Michel, "Chers concitoyens," reprinted in *Citoyen*, August 27, 1881.

7. Michel, "Chers concitoyens."

8. Audouard 1869, 150; Brantlinger 2003, 2–5.

9. Multiple documents in Ba 1184, Dossier Louise Michel, APP. For the Egypt quote, see Rapports, July 30 and August 23, 1882.

10. Dossier Louise Michel, ANC; Pain 1880, 500–558.

11. Michel 1998, 199–211; Michel 1999a, 304–311; Mailhé 1994, 258–265; Dauphiné 2006, 12–23; Baronnet and Chalou 1987, 104–122.

12. Report of the *médecin-major* of the *Virginie*, Nouméa, Dec. 7, 1873, FM, H//30, ANOM.

13. Henry Messager quoted in Barronnet and Chalou 1987, 107.

14. Michel 1999a, 310.

15. Girault 2007, 61–62.

16. Michel 1998, 209.

17. The Guanches are the earliest known inhabitants of the Canary Islands. Michel 19986a, 210.

18. The Communards were the first political prisoners, or *déportés*, sent to New Caledonia. The majority of prisoners were *transportés*, common criminals; after 1885

France condemned recidivists to *relégation*, perpetual internment in the colony. Barbançon 2006.

19. Barbançon 2003, 330–331; Barronnet and Chalou 1987, 135–136.

20. Dépêche ministerial, January 9, 1870, quoted in Barbançon 2003, 330–331.

21. Krakovitch 1990, 13, 155–198.

22. Letter from Gaultier de la Richerie, August 30, 1872, quoted in Barbançon 2003, 332.

23. Michel 1999a, 311.

24. The March 23, 1872, law decreed that all Communard deportees with a first-degree conviction, *la déportation en enceinte fortifiée*, be imprisoned on the Presqu'île Ducos (Ducos Penninsula); Barbançon 2006.

25. Michel 1983, 43–44.

26. Waldman 1973.

27. Madame Hagen, "La femme au bagne," *La fronde*, October, 24–26,1898.

28. Governor Galtier de la Richerie to Vice-Admiral Dompierre d'Hornoy, December 13, 1873, NCL, box 56, ANOM.

29. Michel 1983, 46.

30. Caton 1986, 251.

31. Caton 1986, 251; Pierre Malzieux to André Léo, January 2, 1874, Descave Collection, IISH; Pain 1880, 513–514.

32. Père Montrouzier to Père Poupinel, December 26, 1873, quoted in Dauphiné 2006, 28.

33. Père Montrouzier to Père Poupinel, December 26, 1873, quoted in Dauphiné 2006, 28; Eichner 2004, 110.

34. Père Montrouzier to Gabriel Montrouzier, December 8, 1873, quoted in Dauphiné 2006, 28.

35. Dauphiné 2006, 30.

36. Briot to Ministère de Guerre, LY7, SHD.

37. Eichner 2004, 110–111.

38. Merle 1997b, 23.

39. Bullard 2000a, 3–4.

40. Toth 2006, xiii.

41. Matsuda 2005, 119–124.

42. Lemire 1884, 298. Emphasis in original.

43. Conklin and Clancy-Smith 2004, 500.

44. Conklin and Clancy-Smith 2004, 500.

45. Bullard 2000a, 5–10, 72–73.

46. Bullard 2000a, 297–298.

47. Kafka 1995, 166–174

48. Kafka 1995, 175.

49. Lemire 1884, 297–298.

50. Political theorist Margaret Kohn's 2005 assertion that "In the Penal Colony" had rarely been examined within the literal colonial context of the story still holds true. Rather, it has most often been studied and interpreted as a morality tale, a legal critique, or an existential or psychoanalytic piece. Kohn 2005, 1–2, 8.

51. Kohn 2005, 6.

52. Kohn 2005, 6.; Bennett 1994, 650–670.

53. Lowy 2004.

54. Mirbeau 1899; McClintock 2004.

55. Louise Michel to Administration Pénitentiaire, 1 D 21, item 8, Louise Michel Dossier, ANC.

56. Foucault 1995, 302–303.

57. Foucault 1995, 231.

58. Louise Michel to Georges Périn, February 2, 1881, Ba 1184, Louise Michel Dossier, APP; Michel 1983, 57

59. Michel 1885, 72.

60. Angleviel 2005a, 71–81; Thomas 2000, 298–302.

61. "Virginie," FM, H/30, Dossier Louise Michel, ANOM.

62. Michel 1983, 43–44.

63. Michel 1983, 53.

64. Michel à Victor Hugo, June 18, 1876, in Michel 1999b, 237–238.

65. See chapter 5 for Michel's pedagogical theory and practice. Michel 1983, 69–73.

66. Michel 1998, 213.

67. Michel 1998, 213.

68. Michel 2006, 56. This is from the 1875 version of "Aux amis d'Europe," which differs from the 1885 version of the "Aux amis d'Europe" published in *Légendes et chants de gestes canaques.*

69. Urbain Grandier was a seventeenth-century French Catholic priest convicted of witchcraft and burned at the stake. Michel 1885, 110.

70. Bogliolo 1997, 156–158.

71. McClintock 1995, 40–41.

72. Fabian 2002, 31–32, 153–4.

73. Ramsay 2014, 144.

74. Michel 1998, 251.

75. Gauthier 2000, 51–52.

76. An experienced teacher, Michel had created an egalitarian educational program for the Paris Commune government. She subsequently developed these ideas into an anarchist pedagogy, ultimately establishing an International Anarchist School in London in the 1890s. See chapter 5.

77. Michel 1976, 204–205.

78. Rapport d'Augny, 1887, Dossier Louise Michel, Ba 1187, APP.

79. Dossier Louise Michel, Ba 1185, APP.

80. Rogers and Thébaud 2008, 13.

81. Pons-Ribot 1989, 22; Mohamed-Gaillard 2003, 171–173.

82. Le Meur 2013, 130–146; Merle and Muckle 2019, 107–109; Dousset-Leenhardt 1976, 27–38; Pons-Ribot 1989, 23; Mohamed-Gaillard 2003, 171–173

83. Déclaration de Bouzet, January 20, 1855, in Merle 1995, 99.

84. Le Meur 2013, 130–146; Dousset-Leenhardt 1976, 27–38; Pons-Ribot 1989, 23; Mohamed-Gaillard 2003, 171–173.

85. Pons-Ribot 1989, 23; Dousset-Leenhardt 1976, 27–38; Berman 2006, 24.

86. Rochas 1862, 165–166.

87. Rochas 1862, 166.

88. Taiaiake 2009.

89. Michel, "Chers concitoyens."

90. Michel 2006 (1875), 57.

91. Andersen 2015, 42–43.

92. Glissant 2008, 81–89.

93. For the idea of *métissage* and the French state's developing conceptualization and regulation of *métis* status from the late nineteenth to the early twentieth century, see Saada 2012.

94. Brantlinger 2003, 2–5.

95. Ihage 1992, 12.

96. Vernaudon 2009, 77–88.

97. Garnier's 1864 discovery of nickel led to widespread mining and extraction, bringing wealth to the French mining enterprises that exploited Kanak labor and serious environmental degradation to the Grand Terre. Filer and Le Meur 2017, 1–4; Ramsay 2014, 140–141; Bogliolo 1994.

98. Ramsay 2014, 140–141; Bogliolo 2006, 31.

99. Soula 2014, 38.

100. Gehrmann 2005, 157–180.

101. Ogden 2005.

102. Fabian 2002, 108–110; Clifford 1986, 11–12.

103. Michel 1875a.

104. Michel 1886, 22–39; Hart 2004, 144–149; Hart 2001, 107–114.

105. Michel 1886, 39.

106. Boyer 1927, 40–47.

107. Michel 1886, 52.

108. The 1880s, when Michel wrote her memoirs, was a period of folk revival. Michel 1886, 52, 225–226; Hart 2004, 147–148; Retat 2019, 12.

109. Michel 2006 (1875), 72–73.

110. Ramsay 2011, 17.

111. Gehrmann 2005, 160.

112. Michel 1983, 56.

113. Ramsay 2014, 141–143.

114. A note on the terms used to label stories. Michel titled her collections *Légendes* (legends) and *chants de geste* (epic tales), but she did not differentiate between the two types of stories. According to Kanak sociolinguist Weniko Ihage, ethnographers' efforts at differentiating between legends, tales, and myths tend to reflect the ethnographer's understanding of those categories rather than those of the Kanak. He explains that "there is no direct correspondence between the western classifications and the Melanesian categorizations of literary tales" (1992, 29–30). Additionally, the anthropologist Alban Bensa, a specialist in Kanak and New Caledonian culture, and Jean-Claude Rivierre, a scholar of Oceanic and New Caledonian linguistics, underscore Western miscategorizations as they examine "the study of formalized and coded narrations that we improperly call "tales" or "myths" (Bensa and Rivierre 1988, 263–295, 289). I make no attempt to categorize Kanak narratives in this work. Rather, I interchangeably use the terms "tale," "legend," and "story." I avoid the word "myth," unless it is specifically used in a text, because it can imply fabrication.

115. Bogliolo 2005, 84.

116. Michel translated and transcribed fifteen of the tales; her fellow Communard deportee Charles Malato translated and transcribed one. Michel 1885; Angleviel 2005b, 297–298.

117. Hardison, Preminger, and Warnke 2014, 257; Delmaire 2014, 95.

118. Michel 2006 (1875), 56.

119. Michel 2006 (1875), 56.

120. Michel 2006 (1875), 56–57.

121. Boulay 2000, 14–21; Bullard 2000a, 30–38.

122. Michel 1983, 57.

123. Daoumi's brother, whose name we never learn, knew virtually no French and dressed traditionally when Michel first met him. Michel 1886, 296–297.

124. Michel never wrote about the specific processes through which she received the tales, so we have no access to that information.

125. Bogliolo 2006, 32.

126. Bogliolo 2006, 32.

127. Ramsay 2014, 134–135.

128. Ramsay 2011, 17.

129. Fabian 2002, 17, 88.

130. Clifford 1986, 2–3.

131. Leonardo 1991, 27.

132. Clifford 1986, 7.

133. Michel 2006.

134. Michel 2006 (1885), 98.

135. Michel 1983, 56.

136. Michel 2015, 113; Louise Michel, "Souvenirs de Calédonie," Louise Michel Collection, #802, IISH.

137. Michel 2015, 113.

138. Michel 2015, 113; Michel, "Souvenirs de Calédonie."

139. Hart 2001, 107–20.

140. In the original manuscript, Idara was initially called Poëma throughout the text; the name was crossed off and changed to Idara only in the title. Louise Michel Papers, IISH.

141. Michel 2006 (1885), 111. Hart 2001, 117–118.

142. Michel 2006 (1875), 77–78.

143. Michel 2006 (1875), 77–78.

144. Michel 2006 (1875), 58–59.

145. Michel 2006 (1875), 58–59.

146. Porcher-Wiart 2015, 410–411.

147. "Déluge canaque" (1875) appears as "La légende des cyclones" in the 1885 version of *Légendes et chants*. Michel 1875, 55–58; Michel 2006 (1875), 65–68; Michel 2006 (1885), 51–55.

148. Michel 2006 (1875), 59–60. The tale remains unchanged in *Légendes et chants de gestes Canaques* (1885).

149. Leenhardt 1979, 39.

150. Leenhardt 1979, 36–40.

151. Despite having titled the second volume of her memoirs as a book, during her life the memoirs were only published serially in the newspaper *L'égalité* between 1886 and 1890, well before her 1904 death. Rétat 2015.

152. Michel 1886, 47.

153. "Dans le grand silence dans l'ombre, à travers les espaces et le temp, ò morts repris par la nuit tombe, Pour moi vous êtes là vivante" (Louise Michel, "Aux morts," 1 D 21 pièce 4, Louise Michel Dossier, Collection Scheler, ANC).

154. Michel 1886, 39. She frequently invoked supernatural images, as in her May 1871 poem, "Les spêctres," written in the Versailles prison in the immediate wake of the Commune. Dedicated "To my brothers," (*A mes frères*), she proclaimed, "We will come, we will take the roads, avenging specters emerging form the shadows" (*Nous viendrons partons les chemins, Spectres vengeurs sortent de l'ombre*); (1 D 21 pièce 5, Louise Michel Dossier, ANC).

155. Michel 2006 (1875), 64–65.

156. Michel 2006 (1875), 64–65.

157. Michel 2006 (1875), 64–65; Michel 2006 (1885), 117–118.

158. Ramsay 2011, 66–68.

159. Ramsay 2014, 148–149. As discussed above, Michel did write about distinctly less flattering aspects of Kanak life and culture in her unpublished work and her memoirs. She intended her publications of the somewhat sanitized tales for a wider audience, one whom she hoped to convince of Kanak civilization.

160. Porcher-Wiart 2015, 405–430

161. Porcher-Wiart 2015, 405–430.

162. Klein 2000, 130.

163. Porcher-Wiart 2015, 410; Leenhardt 1979, 22–23; Bullard 2000, 53.

164. Lemire 1884, 95; Faessel 2004, 178–179.

165. Vengefully feeding a blinded person their cooked eyes occurs in a number of tales.

166. Guiart 1957, 14–15.

167. Guiart 1957, 17–18.

168. Guiart 1957, 17–18.

169. In the Kanak language Drehu, one of the most serious insults for a woman is to say she is married to her brother. Moyse-Faurie 2004, 45.

170. Guiart 1957, 19–20. Birth order has great importance in Kanak culture. Leenhardt 1979, 21.

171. Guiart 1957, 19–20. The Kanak incest taboo is so strong that it prohibits a brother from sitting next to, or speaking the name of, his sister. Patouillard, Greley, and Lary 2008, 37.

172. Letourneau 1894, 42–50.

173. I thank Bastien Craipain for this reference.

174. *La revue socialiste* 1 (January–June 1885): 189–190.

175. Demanches 1886, 166–170.

176. "Bibliographie des traditions et de la littérature populaire en orale de France d'Outremer," *Revue de linguistique et de philologie comparée* (1886): 1.

177. Papin 1898, 116.

178. Sébillot 1892, 452.

179. Sébillot 1892, 452.

180. *Englische studien* 1889, 158–159.
181. Michel 1998, 251.
182. Michel 2006 (1885), 139.
183. Michel 2006 (1885), 141.
184. Gould 1985.
185. Gould 1985, 143.
186. Newman 1999, 173–174.
187. Newman 1999, 159.
188. As part of a transition to autonomy guaranteed by the 1998 Nouméa Accords (established in the wake of a 1980s civil war), in 2018 and 2020 New Caledonians narrowly voted to remain French, with the votes favoring independence increasing by 3.5 percent in the second poll. A third failed independence referendum, held in December 2021, was boycotted by most Kanak, who had unsuccessfully called for postponement to respect the mourning period for COVID-19 deaths. Its legitimacy is thus widely questioned.
189. "Un dossier" 2005.
190. Tjibaou 2006, 9.
191. Tjibaou 2006, 9.

5. Universal Language, Universal Education, Universal Revolution

1. Michel 1998, 214.
2. The generally accepted difference between pidgin and creole is that pidgin is usually a second language, while a creole has native speakers. Pidgins often evolve into creoles. Muysken and Smith 1994, 3; "Definitions of Different Language Varieties," 2020.
3. Rano 2009.
4. Darot 1997, 12–13.
5. Tryon and Charpentier 2004, 107–109, 154–155, 199–205; Hollyman 1964, 57–58.
6. Garnier 1871, 162.
7. Michel, "Souvenirs de Calédonie," 21, IISH.
8. Michel, "Souvenirs de Calédonie," 21, IISH.
9. Emphasis in original. Michel 1885, 3–4.
10. Michel 1885, 3–4.
11. Glissant 2008, 83.
12. Michel, "Souvenirs de Calédonie," 21, IISH.
13. Michel, "Souvenirs de Calédonie," 82–83, IISH.
14. Michel 2015, 113.
15. Sprague 1888; "Rapport," March 2, 1887, Préfecture de la Police, Dossier Louise Michel, Ba 1187, APP.
16. Ludwig Lazarus Zamenhof to Nikolai Borovko, quoted in Matthias 2002, 23.
17. Esperanto Museum, Austrian National Library, Vienna.
18. Thomas 2004, 421; Levy 2011, 272–273.
19. Reclus 1908, 468.
20. Alter 2008.
21. Ashcroft 2001, 311–328; Simonet 1866.

22. The unpublished drafts, which include sections on topics including evolution, geography, mathematics, astronomy, history, and the arts, are in the Louise Michel Papers, Descaves Collection, IISH.

23. M. de Fleurville to Louise Michel, August 2, 1873, in Michel 1999a, 202.

24. Michel, "Mélange en divers dialectes," Louise Michel Papers, #869, IISH.

25. "Mélange en divers dialectes."

26. A Eurasian language group now disputed, but fully accepted in the nineteenth century.

27. Former name used to identify several Siberian peoples and languages.

28. Michel, "Mélange en divers dialectes."

29. Michel, "Mélange en divers dialectes."

30. Michel, "Mélange en divers dialectes."

31. Bopp's work was published beginning in 1833 and translated into French during the 1850s. Pedersen 1972, 241–243; Alter 1999, 2–6.

32. Newmeyer 1986, 19–26; Ashcroft 2001, 316–319.

33. Ashcroft 2001, 316–319

34. Ashcroft 2001, 311.

35. Newmeyer 1986, 19–26.

36. Alter (2008, 357–358) contends that Darwin made this shift based on the widespread acceptance of the idea of "deep time" in the 1860s.

37. Eichhoff 1836.

38. Michel, 2006 (1875), 57.

39. Levy 2011, 272–273.

40. "Louise Michel et les décadents," *Le temps*, October 22, 1886, 3. A December 16, 1878, letter to Michel from an unknown correspondent suggests that she was compiling a Kanak dictionary. Michel 1999a, 245–246.

41. Moyse-Faurie 2004, 32.

42. During this enormously productive period, she also published a volume of memoirs, two plays, a book of poetry, an additional novel, a scholarly treatise, two brochures, and multiple journalistic pieces. See Rétat and Zékian 2013, 8.

43. Rétat and Zékian 2013, 12.

44. The term *claque-dents* means something like death rattle. In the nineteenth century it had multiple slang meanings, including vagabonds, the broken-down places in which impoverished people lived, and houses of prostitution. The novel *Le claque-dents* is discussed in Chapter 6.

45. Rétat and Zékian 2013, 12–13; Michel, *Les microbes humains*, in Michel 2013a, 156–157; Michel, *Le monde nouveau* in Michel 2013b, 320. Michel challenges the legitimacy of representation and the value of the vote throughout much of her career. See especially her anarchist pamphlet (Michel 1890c).

46. Michel, *Les microbes humains*, in Michel 2013a, 48.

47. Zékian 2015, 108.

48. Zékian 2015, 114–117; Rétat and Zékian 2013, 32–33. A brief example of her written orality is the phrase "très zumble," correctly spelled as "très humble." Spoken French uses "liaison," the sliding together of the final consonant of one word with the first sound of the subsequent word. Thus articulated, "très humble" sounds like "très zumble." Michel 2013b, 165.

49. Zékian 2015, 118–120.
50. Lombroso and Laschi 1892, 126.
51. Thomas 1971, 302; Zékian 2015, 107–109.
52. Wing 1997, 12.
53. Michel 1999a, 689–690.
54. Michel 1999a, 689–690.
55. Michel 1999a, 689–690.
56. Michel 1999a, 689–690.
57. Michel, "Souvenirs de Calédonie," 20, IISH.
58. Louise Michel, "Dans la revue des revues," n.d., Dossier Louise Michel, IISH.
59. Michel 2005, 50. Hugo dedicated the poem "Viro Major" to Michel.
60. Ousselin 2005–2006, 35.
61. Mazzini 1850.
62. Anderson 2011, 481–484.
63. Parnell-Smith 1997a, 76.
64. Louise Michel, "Série de conférences sur la Calédonie," 1900, 1901, LM 893, IISH.
65. Michel, "Série de conférences."
66. Michel, "Série de conférences."
67. Thomas 1980, 14–15, 31–33.
68. Michel 1885, 1.
69. Louise Michel, in *La pensée libre*, October 23, 1904, quoted in Chauvin 2007, 72.
70. Its title, "Louise Michel: Une conversation avec la vièrge rouge," ("Louise Michel: A conversation with the Red Virgin"), uses the epithet "Red Virgin" given to the already mythical Michel. Still used today, this sexist label defined her by presuming her sexual relationships (or lack thereof) with men. It implied her "pure" love for revolution, while allowing imaginings of her as a lesbian. Michel lived with Charlotte Vauvelle for the final fifteen years of her life.
71. Eichner 2004, 61.
72. Eichner 2004, 58–62. An 1870 report on Parisian schools made clear the institutional disregard for girls' education: "The women teachers' . . . knowledge and teaching ability leave something to be desired, but they are morally superior, more tactful, and more devoted [than the male teachers]" (quoted in Hunt 1971, 419–420).
73. André Léo, *Le siècle* (Paris), July 16, 1870. Like Michel—with whom both she and Mink would ally during the Commune—Léo's gender equity and language of "free school . . . school of reason and liberty" foreshadowed anarchist *éducation intégrale*. Many of Léo's novels, published between 1865 and her 1900 death, addressed ideas of free and republican education. See Eichner 2004; and Beach 2008.
74. Louise Michel, quoted in Thomas 1966, 114.
75. Michel 1886, 42.
76. Michel 1983, 49–51.
77. Amouroux and Place 1881, 7–8, 161, 163–164, quoted and translated in Bullard 2000b, 92–93.
78. Pannoux, 202.
79. Amouroux and Place 1881, 7–8, 161, 163–164.
80. Michel 1983, 57.
81. Michel 1983, 57.
82. Michel 1885, 139.

83. Michel 1983, 57.

84. Rocker 2005, 19.

85. Rogers and Thébaud 2008, 10.

86. Salaun 2010, 60–61.

87. Bensa 1995, 115.

88. Michel 1983, 57.

89. Michel 1983, 57–59.

90. Michel 1983, 57–59.

91. "Louise Michel à la salle des Capucines," *Cri du progress*,1888.

92. In an 1885 letter to the Minister of the Interior, written shortly following her mother's death, Michel requested that she be sent back to New Caledonia to open a school for the Kanak in lieu of finishing her prison sentence in France. F7 12 / 505, AN.

93. Thomas 2005, 78–79; Bantman 2006, 962, 970–974; Bantman 2017b, 994–995; Aprile 2010.

94. Louise Michel, *Mémoires*, quoted in Thomas 1980, 320.

95. Thomas 2005, 78–79; Esbjörn-Hargens, Reams, Gunnlaugson 2010.

96. Molz and Hampson 2010, 35–36.

97. Mikhail Bakunin, "L'Iistruction intégrale," in *L'égalité* no. 31 (August 1869). The contradictory nature of calling children of both sexes "men," of course, went unnoticed in this era.

98. Sonn 1992, 33–41.

99. McLaren 1981, 320; Fidler 1989, 40; Demeulenaere-Douyère 2003, 125.

100. Fidler 1989, 40.

101. Russian was the fourth language. "Mélange en divers dialectes."

102. "Rapport," March 2, 1887, Préfecture de la Police, Dossier Louise Michel, Ba 1187, APP.

103. Prospectus de l'école de Louise Michel, quoted in Thomas 1980, 318.

104. Prospectus de l'école de Louise Michel, quoted in Thomas 1980, 318.

105. Thomas 1980, 318.

106. *Freedom*, September, 1891.

107. Thomas 1980, 319.

108. *Freedom*, September 1891.

109. *Freedom*, September 1891.

110. Thomas 2004, 415–417, 429; Thomas 1980, 318–319.

111. Michel also composed music. Michel 1998, 77–81; Hart 1906, 21, in Thomas 2005, 80.

112. Bantman 2014, 53; Thomas 1980, 319–320.

113. Michel 1983; E. Thomas quote from Boyer 1927, 233.

114. Thomas 2004, 413–414, 417.

115. Goldman (1969, 148–149) referred specifically to Michel's Montmartre girls' school, the one established in 1865, prior to the Paris Commune. Michel later extolled this school in her *Mémoires*, exclaiming, "Science and liberty! . . . These things breathed under the Empire in this little lost corner of Paris!" (1998, 104).

116. The manuscript includes no date. Juliette Parnell-Smith (1997b, 48–49) argues that Michel wrote it in New Caledonia.

117. Louise Michel, "Les filles de la Galoubette," n.d., 54, Dossier Louise Michel, Descaves Collection, IISH.

118. Michel, "Les filles de la Galoubette," 36.

119. Michel, "Les filles de la Galoubette," 113; Parnell-Smith 1997b, 53–54.

120. Inspired by the Paris Commune, colonists in Algeria, most of them exiled from France following the Revolution of 1848, formed a Commune in March 1871. These white colonists neither opposed imperialism, nor supported the Kabyle uprising. Plaetzer 2021.

121. The Kabyle are the predominant Berber people, living primarily in the Atlas Mountains to the east of Algiers.

122. Scholars long attributed the rebellion to an anti-Semitic reaction to the 1870 Crémieux Decree, which gave Algerian Jews—but not Muslims—French citizenship. Antisemites, and later anti-Dreyfusards including Communard Henri Rochefort, blamed the Crémieux Decree for the insurrection. Historian Nathan Godley (2006, 190) argues against Crémieux's role, asserting instead Algerian Muslim's perception of France as vulnerable after the Prussian defeat. See also Rochefort 1896–1898, 169; Ouennoughi 2005, 88, 95–97; Lallaoui 1994, 9, 13–15; Aldrich and Connell 1992, 46–48; Clair 1994.

123. Additionally, over 2,100 Algerian common criminals and recidivists were exiled to New Caledonia between 1864 and 1897 (Barbançon 2011). Unlike the French convicts, the Algerians were prohibited from having their spouses and families join them in exile. Ouennoughi 2005 153–157; Chauvin 2007, 17–21, 31; Lallaoui 1994, 32–33; Meynier and Thobie, 11–13.

124. Bensa (2013, 14, 19) explains that while contemporary Kanak still tell the story of 1878, it has yet to be systematically transcribed or published.

125. Lallaoui 1994, 42.

126. Malato 1894, 47.

127. Malato 1894, 47.

128. Malato 1894, 47.

129. Malato 1894, 48.

130. Michel 1999a, 332.

131. And later, renowned antisemite.

132. L'est républican, July 13, 1889.

133. L'est républican, July 13, 1889.

134. Merle and Muckle 2019, 110–111.

135. Mailhé 1994, 359–360; Lallaoui 1994, 93; Latham 1978, 73–75; Duparc 2003, 187.

136. Forsdick 2018, 250–251.

137. Michel 1999a, 332.

138. Quoted in Lallaoui 1994, 84.

139. Michel 1999a, 332.

140. Louise Michel to Ernest Girault, quoted in Thomas 1970, 46–67.

141. Mes sept ans de bagne, par un forçat 1880, 203. The author refers to the French government's 1871 introduction of a "corvée," forced labor for the state and for white colonists, for which the state paid the Kanak either one half or one quarter what a non-Kanak would receive for the same work. Bensa 1995, 118–119.

142. Mes sept ans 1880, 214.

143. Mes sept ans 1880, 249.

144. He considered these debauched women to be poor material for colonial development.

145. Mes sept ans 1880, 249.

146. *Mes sept ans* 1880, 250.

147. Constance Bantman has shown that "masculinist bias" has similarly distorted assessments of Michel's political engagements during her London exile. Bantman 2017a.

148. Merle 1997a, 81–93; Reynolds 1985

149. Quoted in Cornet 1999, 150.

150. Merle 1995.

151. Douglas 1998, 199.

152. Muckle 2002, 25–44.

153. Merle 1995, 112. The historiography of the 1878 insurgency, like much of the broader historiography of New Caledonia, remains conflicted and politicized. See Veracini 2003, 331–352; Merle 1995, 93–94, 110–112; Bullard 2000b, 85–86.

154. Mailhé 1994, 359–360.

155. Latham 1978, 59. According to historian Alain Saussol (2013), the Canala's position remains somewhat unclear. They ultimately sided with the French, but Saussol argues that they may have been involved with the other Kanak clans in the initial planning of the uprising, but then pragmatically switched sides and supported the colonizer.

156. Bierman 1990–1991, 528.

157. Simon Meyer, "70 déportés demandent à être armés,. ANC.

158. Meyer, "70 déportés.".

159. *Le parisien* no. 2 (September 14, 1878), 1. ANC.

160. *Le parisien*, 1.

161. Henri Berthier, "Texte du bagnard déporté Berthier," ANC.

162. Malato, 1894, 194; Pannoux, 2020, 1189–1190. My thanks to Michel Cordillot and Laure Godineau for drawing my attention to the Pannoux essay.

163. *L'Aurore*, n.d. (likely 1899 or 1900).

164. Dossier Paule Mink, October 21, 1900, Ba 1178, APP.

165. Pons-Ribot 1989, 22–24; Berman 2006, 25.

166. Dousset 1970, 112; Cormier 1993.

167. Dousset-Leenhardt 1976, 37–38; Pons-Ribot 1989, 23–24; Arthur de Trentinian, "Rapport sur les causes de l'insurrection Kanak en 1878," Fonds ministerial, Série géographique, NCL/43, ANOM.

168. Dousset-Leenhardt 1976, 39.

169. Bensa 1995, 104–107; Dousset-Leenhardt 1970, 110–112.

170. Saussol 1979, 195–202.

171. The Kanak prepared elaborately for war, with dances, rituals, speeches, and body painting. Bensa (2013, 22) explains that the Kanak who fought alongside the French expressed shock at the French lack of pre-battle psychological preparation. See also Merle 1995, 93; Bensa 1988, 189.

172. Rivière 1881, 281.

173. Bernard 1894, 295, 297.

174. Bensa 1995, 113–114.

175. Michel 1999a, 332.

176. Wolfe 2006, 388.

177. Trentinian, "Rapport."

178. Dousset-Leenhardt 1976, 62–65, 127–159.

179. Bensa 1988, 191. Emphasis in original.

180. Michel 1998, 249.
181. France would not return his skull to New Caledonia for proper interment until 2014.
182. Louise Michel, *Mémoires*, quoted without page number in Chauvin 2007, 119.
183. Girault 1905, 83.
184. *Le réveil de sétif*, November 13, 1904.
185. *La pensée libre*, November 6, 1904.
186. Michel 2015, 113.
187. Michel, "Les filles de la Galoubette," 1.
188. Louise Michel, "Anniversaire de la Commune," Ba 1186, APP.
189. Black notebook, p. 3, Dossier Louise Michel, Descaves Collection, IISH.
190. Michel 1890a, 2.

6. Familiar Stranger

1. Audouard 1867, 95.
2. Ann Laura Stoler's (2002) argument that European women often formed a barrier between colonizer and colonized suggests an interesting opposition. European women in empire also constituted a "familiar other," but one rather different from Jews. While European women created barriers as familiar others, the Jew in the form of familiar other established links back to a recognizable metropolitan alterity.
3. Hammerschlag 2007, 25–31; Kalman 2017, 8–9; Cheyette and Valman 2003, 5, 8–9; Hallman 2002, 254–257.
4. Euben 2003.
5. Right-wing, or Christian, feminism, did not emerge until the 1890s.
6. Silverman 2011.
7. Though Silverman (2011) develops this theory to examine and explain early twentieth-century Central Europe, its application stretches farther both geographically and temporally.
8. Kalmar and Derek Penslar 2005, xiii; emphasis in original.
9. Katz, Leff, and Mandel 2017, 10–11; Kalman 2017, 6–7.
10. Audouard 1863b, 11. This successful book went through four editions and was reviewed in a number of widely recognized English-language journals, including the *Westminster Review* 88 (October 1, 1867); the *Cornhill Magazine* (edited by William Makepeace Thackaray) 13 (1866); and the *Saturday Review of Politics, Literature, Science, and Art* 15 (1863): 576–578.
11. Audouard 1863b, 5.
12. Monicat 1996, 98–100.
13. Monicat 1996, 237.
14. Frankel 1997.
15. Kalman 2007, 35–37, 51–52; Kalman 2017, 8–9.
16. Audouard 1867, 94–95.
17. Mary Louise Roberts (2002, 5) demonstrates how, later in the century, this continued and intensified as French "nationalist, antisemitic ideology relied on tropes of gender and linked stereotypes of the New Woman and the Jew." See also Brown 2004; Birnbaum 1992, 147–149; Hyman 1995, 136–142; Pellegrini 1996, 112–114.

18. Hyman 1995, 137.

19. Gilman 1991; Birnbaum 1988; Schuler-Springorum 2018, 1214–1215; Geller 1992, 21–48; Pellegrini 1996, 109–110.

20. Gilman 1991; Brunotte 2015, 196–198.

21. Audouard 1867, 462–463.

22. Audouard 1867, 464.

23. Audouard 1867, 464.

24. Audouard 1867, 94–95.

25. Sinha 1995,

26. Audouard 1867, 38–39.

27. For the formation and impact of *la belle juive*, see Fournier 2012.

28. Guenoun 2015, 8.

29. Audouard 1867, 484.

30. Kalman 2017, 26–28.

31. Audouard 1867, 470–471.

32. Audouard 1867, 470–471; emphasis added.

33. Kalman 2017, 8–9.

34. Audouard 1867, 95.

35. My thanks to Joel Berkowitz for pointing out the connection with the biblical story of Esther. Bar-Itzhak 2008.

36. Audouard 1867, 95

37. Audouard 1867, 95.

38. Ockman 1991, 524–525.

39. Brunotte, Ludewig, and Stähler 2015, 14–15.

40. As discussed in chapter 2. Audouard, public conferences, May 30, 1873, April 7, 1887, and October 8, 1887, Ba 941, APP; Audouard 1863b; Audouard 1867; Monicat 1995, 26–27, 35; Nuñez 2012, 23–24.

41. Kalmar and Penslar 2005, xiii; Kalman 2017, 61

42. Audouard 1873.

43. Ernot 2009. Ernot convincingly argues that Audouard was among the first authors to undertake a history of women in France.

44. Audouard 1873, 309.

45. Audouard 1873, 309–310.

46. Audouard 1873, 289.

47. Audouard 1873, 289.

48. Audouard 1873, 331.

49. Audouard 1873, 293–294.

50. Birnbaum 1992, 147–148; Garb 1995, 26–27.

51. Audouard 1867, 240.

52. Audouard 1867, 240–242.

53. Audouard 1867, 240–242.

54. Eichner 2009; Hause, 2007, 22–27; Taieb 2006, 271–72.

55. Hubertine Auclert, *L'intransigeant illustré*, n.d., Fonds Marie-Louise Bouglé, BMD.

56. Winock 1998, 88–91; Birnbaum 1992, 89–91.

57. Auclert, *L'intransigeant illustré*.

58. Auclert, *L'intransigeant illustré.*

59. Shurkin 2010, 258–280.

60. Friedman 1998, 9–13; Schreier 2010, 8–11.

61. Birnbaum 1992, 279.

62. Bell 2018, 97–98.

63. Auclert 1900, 14–16.

64. Schreir 2010, 3; Friedman 1998, 8–13.

65. Shepard 2013; Surkis 2010, 27–32.

66. Auclert 1900, 14–16.

67. As Nathan Godley (2006, 269) explains, "Despite the rapid decline of the anti-Jewish movement as a single-issue interest group, the odd colonial combination of racism and republicanism that formed its basis remained a core ideological and rhetorical trope of Algerian settler politics. A significant anti-Jewish undercurrent also persisted, with occasional popular and electoral outbursts." See also Dermenjian 1986; Leff 2006, 207–218.

68. Roberts 2017, 3.

69. Roberts 2017, 4.

70. Audouard 1867, 95.

71. Hubertine Auclert, "Les Judiths modernes," *La citoyenne,* June 2, 1882.

72. Auclert, "Les Judiths modernes."

73. Auclert, "Les Judiths modernes."

74. Auclert, "Les Judiths modernes."

75. Kalman 2017, 9–10, 119–121.

76. Auclert, "Les Judiths modernes."

77. Hyman 1998, 91–103; Cole 2019, 38–42.

78. Drumont 1886; Hammerschlag 2007, 36.

79. Édouard Drumont, quoted in Lindemann 1997, 206.

80. Kaplan 2009, 98–100; Almog 1990, 44–47; Wilson 1982.

81. Cole 2019, 38–42.

82. Hubertine Auclert, "Le féminisme," *Le rappel,* January 5, 1899; Auclert, "Les Judiths modernes."

83. Bergmann and Wyrwa 2012.

84. Auclert, *La libre parole,* March 24, 1894.

85. Auclert, *La libre parole,* March 24, 1894; emphasis added.

86. Auclert *La libre parole,* May 3, 1894; Nuñez 2012, 35–36.

87. Hubertine Auclert, "Les droits de la femme," *La libre parole,* May 17, 1894.

88. Nuñez 2006, 261–269.

89. Caron 2009, 309–310; Laplanche 1996, 271.

90. Laplanche 1996, 271; Auclert, "Les droits de la femme.".

91. Drumont 1886, 1.

92. Drumont, *La libre parole,* August 22, 1894.

93. Auclert, *La libre parole,* March 24, 1894.

94. Auclert, *La libre parole,* September 10, 1894.

95. Nuñez 2012, 34–35; Hause 1987, 47–68, 156–158; Eichner 2009, 64–66.

96. Hause 1987, 47–68; Eichner 2009, 66.

97. Hubertine Auclert, *La fronde,* December 13, 1897.

98. Auclert, *La fronde*, December 13, 1897; Auclert, *La libre parole*, May 17, 1894.

99. Everton 2011, 391–400.

100. Everton 2011, 401, 451.

101. Marie Maugeret, "A bâtons rompus," *l'écho littéraire de France*, February 1897, 2, quoted in Everton 2011, 401.

102. Everton 2011, 401.

103. Michel 1890b.

104. Hammerschlag 2007, 36–38; Barrès 1890.

105. *Le claque-dents* (1890) was the third novel of a trilogy; the first two books were *Les microbes humains* (1886) and *Le monde nouveau* (1888). Recently reissued in one collection, *Trois Romans* includes an excellent introduction by editors Claude Rétat and Stéphane Zékian (Michel 2013c).

106. *Claque-dents* carried multiple additional meanings in the nineteenth century. See Chapter 5, note 44.

107. Louise Michel, "L'agiotage et les pots de vin," December 1895, Ba 1186, APP.

108. Or Muslim, as quoted above in Michel 1890b.

109. Thomas 1980, 354–359; Sabiani 1983, 200–206.

110. Blum 1998, 98; Rapport, March 11, 1898, Ba 1187, Dossier Louise Michel, APP.

111. Quoted in Bantman 2017, 179.

112. Bantman 2017, 179. Michel traveled often between Paris and London, while living primarily in London, during these years.

113. Michel 1983, 189.

114. Michel 2000, 160.

115. Michel 2000, 160.

116. Michel also expressed disappointment in the cancelation of the rescue because she had hoped that Dreyfus would go immediately from Devil's Island to Cuba to join their independence struggle. Recognizing that "this could appear to be a dream, it could appear to be impossible, but is it not the impossible that happens most often" (Michel 2000, 161).

117. Thomas 1980, 354–359.

118. Michel 2004, 225–229.

119. Godley 2006.

120. Michel 2004, 225–229.

121. Michel 2004, 225–229

122. Michel 2004, 225–229

123. Michel 1890b.

124. Michel 1890a, 129.

125. Michel 1890a, 181.

126. Louise Michel Papers, Descaves Collection, IISH; Michel 1890a, 181.

127. Rétat and Zékian, 2013, 36.

128. Michel 1890a, 316–319.

129. While Kropotkin's *Mutual Aid: A Factor of Evolution* was not published until 1902, the first chapter appeared in the British literary journal *Nineteenth Century* in 1890. Michel avidly followed and corresponded with Kropotkin.

130. Michel 1890a, 126.

131. Michel 1890a, 126.

132. Michel 1890a, 183.

133. Michel 1890a, 319.

134. Kalman 2017; Katz, Leff, and Mandel 2017; Bell 2018.

Conclusion

1. Scott 1996, 1.

2. Lazreg 1988, 96–97.

3. Audouard 1871, vii. This was the second of her two-volume series about her trip to the United States, the first of which was *À travers l'Amérique: Le Far West*, published in 1869. Publication of the second volume was delayed by the 1870–1871 conflicts.

4. Audouard 1871, x–xi.

5. Audouard 1869, 15

6. Audouard 1869, 14, In contrast to those in the American West, Audouard idealized "Yankees"; see chapter 1.

7. Audouard 1869, 102; Olympe Audouard to Victor Hugo, Paris, December 7, 1867.

8. Audouard 1871, v.

9. Audouard 1871, iv–v.

10. Audouard 1871, v–vi.

11. Audouard 1871, 7–8

12. Audaourd 1870, 7.

13. Audaourd 1870, 8.

14. Auclert 1908, 1.

15. Hubertine Auclert, "Le féminisme," *Le radical*, December 2, 1901.

16. Rouzade 1895, 24.

17. Léonie Rouzade, "Idées," *Revue de France*, 1917.

18. Eichner 2004.

19. Dossier Paule Mink, "Rapport," June 24, 1884, 1178, APP.

20. "Une réunion socialiste," *Le matin*, March 9, 1885.

21. Dossier Paule Mink, October 22, 1895, Ba 1178, APP.

22. Mink, "La femme en Algérie," *Le coup de feu*, January 1886.

23. They had also invited Rouzade, the liberal feminist Maria Deraimes, and the journalist Séverine, all of whom—except Mink—declined. Eichner 2004, 198.

24. *Germinal*, April 7, 1893.

25. Eichner 2004, 198–200.

26. *L'éclair*, May 1, 1893.

27. Verhaeghe 2019, 81–82, 97–98.

28. The Black population in metropolitan France remained small prior to World War I. During and after the war, a significant number of Black colonial migrants arrived in France. Boittin 2009.

29. Michel 2014, 19.

30. Michel 1998, 89.

31. Parnell-Smith 1997a, 70.

32. Parnelle-Smith 1997a, 70–71.

33. Michel 2015, 105.

34. Michel 2015, 105.

35. Michel 2015, 105.

36. Michel 2015, 105, 112–113.

37. Michel 1983, 75.

38. Michel's biographer Edith Thomas (1980, 167) included Audouard among those welcoming Michel at the train station, but I have seen no other evidence of this, and it would be inconsistent with Audouard's politics and actions.

39. "Salle de L'Elysée-Montmartre," *L'électeur*, November 23, 1880.

40. "Salle Rivoli," *L'électeur*, December 4, 1880.

41. Michel 1890a.

42. Silverman 2011, 27–45.

43. Sanos 2014, 252–254.

44. Mehta 1999, 1–45.

45. Michel, "Les filles de la Galoubette," 1, IISH.

WORKS CITED

Archives

Archives de la Nouvelle-Calédonie (ANC), Nouméa, New Caledonia.
Archives de la Préfecture de la Police (APP), Paris.
Archives Nationales (France) (AN), Paris.
Archives Nationales d'Outre Mer (ANOM), Aix-en-Provence, France.
Bibliothèque Historique de la Ville de Paris (BHVP), Paris.
Bibliothèque Marguerite Durand (BMD), Paris.
Bibliothèque Nationale (BN), Paris.
Esperanto Museum, Austrian National Library (EM), Vienna.
International Institute of Social History (IISH), Amsterdam.
Service Historique de la Défense (SHD), Vincennes, Paris.

Primary Sources

Amouroux, Charles, and Henri Place. 1881. *L'Administration et les Maristes en Nouvelle Calédonie, Insurrection des Kanaks en 1878–79*, 2nd ed. Paris: Imprimerie P. Worms.
Auclert, Hubertine. 1900. *Les femmes Arabes en Algérie*. Paris: Societé d'Éditions Littéraires.
Auclert, Hubertine. 1904. *l'argent de la femme*. Paris: Pédonne.
Auclert, Hubertine. 1908. *Le vote des femmes*. Paris: V. Giard & E. Brière.
Audouard, Olympe. 1863a. "Alger." *Le papillon* 61 (March 29): 194–196.
Audouard, Olympe. 1863b. *Les mystères du sérail et des harems turcs: Lois, mœurs, usages, anecdotes*. Paris: E. Dentu.
Audouard, Olympe. 1866. *Les mystères de l'Égypte dévoilés*. Paris: E Dentu.
Audouard, Olympe. 1867. *L'Orient et ses peuplades*. Paris: E. Dentu.
Audouard, Olympe. 1869. *À travers l'Amérique: Le Far-West*. Paris: E. Dentu.
Audouard, Olympe. 1870. *La femme dans le mariage, la séparation et le divorce*. Paris: E. Dentu.
Audouard, Olympe. 1871. *À travers l'Amérique: North-America, États-Unis, constitution, mœurs, usages, lois, institutions, sectes religieuses*. Paris: E. Dentu.
Audouard, Olympe. 1873. *Gynécologie: La femme depuis six mille ans*. Paris: E. Dentu.
Audouard, Olympe. 1876. *Les nuits russes*. Paris: E. Dentu.
Audouard, Olympe. 1884. *Voyage à travers mes souvenirs: Ceux que j'ai connus, ce que j'ai vu*. Paris: E. Dentu.
Bakunin, Mikhail. 1869. "L'instruction intégrale." *l'égalité*, July 31–August 21, 1869.

Barrès, Maurice. 1890. "La formule antijuive." *Le Figaro*, February 22.

Beguin, A., and B. Peigneaux. 1888. *En zizag du Maroc à Malte. À travers l'Algèrie, la Tunisie, et les États Barbaresque*. Lyons: X. Jevan.

Bernard, Augustin. 1894. *L'archipel de la Nouvelle-Calédonie*. Paris: Hachette et Cie.

"Bibliographie des traditions et de la littérature populaire en orale de France d'Outremer." 1886. *Revue de linguistique et de philologie comparée* 19.

de Bonald, Louis Ambroise, vicomte. 1818. *Du divorce: considéré au XIXe siècle*. Paris: d'A. le Clere.

Caton, Joannès. 1986. *Journal d'un déporté de la Commune à l'île des Pins*. Paris: Éditions France-Empire.

"Chronique Méridionale." 1883. *Progrès du midi* (October).

Clemenceau, Georges. 1907. *La mêlée sociale*. Paris: Bibliothèque Charpentier.

Code civile des Français. 1804. Paris: L'Imprimerie de la République.

Demanches, Georges. 1886. "Correspondances et nouvelles: Légendes Canaques." *Revue française de l'étranger et des colonies*, vol. 2. Paris: Imprimerie centrale du chemins des fer.

"Un dossier: Les déportations politiques en Nouvelle-Calédonie, un supplément couleurs sur l'expositions 'Paris-Nouméa, Les communards en Nouvelle-Calédonie,'" 2005. *Mwà Véé*, no. 51.

"Le droit de femmes: Conférence d'Hubertine Auclert." 1883. *Nîmes* (October).

Drumont, Édouard. 1886. *La France Juive*. Paris: Marpon & Flammarion.

Duriez, M. 2001 (1863). "Eloge d'*Un Mariage scandaleux*." *Le siècle*, September 4. Reprinted in Gastadello, Fernanda. *André Leó: Femme écrivain du XIXe siècle*. Paris: Publi Chauvinoi.

Eichhoff, Frédéric Gustave. 1836. *Parallèle des langues de l'Europe et de l'Inde*. Paris: Imprimerie Royale.

Englische studien: Organ für englische philologie unter mitberücksichtigung des englischen unterrichts auf höheren schulen. 1889. Gebr. Henninger.

Finck, Henry T. 1891. *Romantic Love and Personal Beauty: Their Development, Casual Relations, Historic and National Peculiarities*, 5th ed. London: MacMillan.

Garnier, Jules. 1871. *Le voyage autour du monde: La Nouvelle-Calédonie*. Paris: Plon.

Girault, Ernest. 1905. *Une colonie d'enfer*. Alforville: Librarie internationalist.

de Gobineau, Arthur. 1853. *Essai sur l'inégalité des races humaines*. Paris: Librairie de Firmin Didot.

Goldman, Emma. 1969. "Francisco Ferrer: The Modern School." In *Anarchism and Other Essays*. NY: Dover.

de Gouges, Olympe. 1791. *Les droits de la femme. A la Reine*. Paris.

Hart, W. C. 1906. *Confessions of an Anarchist*. London: E. Grant Richards.

Kafka, Franz. 1995. *The Complete Stories*. New York: Schocken Books.

Lemire, Charles. 1884. *Voyage à pied en Nouvelle-Calédonie et description des Nouvelles Hébrides*. Paris: Challamel aine.

Letourneau, Charles. 1894. *L'évolution littéraire dans les diverses races humaines*. Paris: Ancienne Maison Delahaye.

Lombroso, César, and Rodolfo Laschi. 1892. *Le crime politique et les révolutions par rapport au droit, à l'anthropologie criminelle et à la science du gouvernement*, vol. 2. Translated by A. Bouchard. Paris: Félix Alcan.

"Louise Michel et les décadents." 1886. *Le temps*, October 22, 3.

Malato, Charles. 1894. *De la Commune à l'anarchie*. Paris: Stock.

Malon, Benoît. 1871. *Le troisième défait du prolétariat*. Neuchâtel: Guillaume Fils.

Mazzini, Guiseppe. 1850. "From a Revolutionary Alliance to the United States of Europe," In *A Cosmopolitanism of Nations: Guiseppe Mazzini's Writings on Democracy, Nation Building, and International Relations,* edited by Stefano Recchia and Nadia Urbaniti, 132–135. Princeton: Princeton University Press.

Mes sept ans de bagne, par un forçat. 1880. Paris: Administration des Publications Républicains.

Michel, Louise. 1875a. "Aux amis d'Europe." Petites affiches de la Nouvelle-Calédonie, November 24.

Michel, Louise. 1875b. *Légendes et chansons de gestes canaques*. Louise Michel Papers, IISH.

Michel, Louise. 1885. *Légendes et chants de gestes canaques*. Paris: Kéva.

Michel, Louise. 1886. *Mémoires de Louise Michel, écrits par elle-même*. Paris: F. Roy.

Michel, Louise. 1890a. *Le claque-dents*. Paris: E. Dentu.

Michel, Louise. 1890b. "Les mémoires de Louise Michel." *L'égalité*, June 26.

Michel, Louise. 1890c. *Le prise de possession*. Paris: Groupe Anarchiste de Saint-Denis.

Michel, Louise. 1898. *La Commune: Histoire et souvenirs*. Paris: Stock.

Michel, Louise. 1976. *Mémoires de Louise Michel, écrits par elle-même*. Paris: F. Maspero.

Michel, Louise. 1983. *Souvenirs et aventures de ma vie*. Edited by Daniel Armogathe. Paris: La Découverte/Maspero.

Michel, Louise. 1998. *Mémoires de Louise Michel, écrits par elle-même*. Arles: Éditions Sulliver.

Michel, Louise. 1999a. *La Commune: Histoire et souvenirs*. Paris: La Découverte.

Michel, Louise 1999b. *Je vous écris dans ma nuit. Correspondance générale de Louise Michel—1850–1904*. Edited by Xavière Gauthier. Paris: Éditions de Paris.

Michel, Louise. 2000. *Histoire de ma vie: seconde et troisième parties: Londres 1904*. Lyon: Presses Universitaires de Lyons.

Michel, Louise. 2004. "*Le rêve.*" In *Louise Michel (1830–1905)*, edited by Gérald Dittmar, 225–229. Paris: Éditions Dittmar.

Michel, Louise. 2005. *Lettres à Victor Hugo: 1850–1879*. Edited by Xavière Gauthier. Paris: Mercure de France.

Michel, Louise. 2006. *Légendes et chansons de gestes canaques (1875) suivi de Légendes et chants de gestes canaques (1885) et de Civilisation*. Edited by François Bogliolo. Lyon: Presses Universitaire de Lyon.

Michel, Louise. 2013a (1886). *Les microbes humains*. In *Trois romans: Les microbes humains, Le monde nouveau, Le claque-dents*, edited by Claude Retat and Stéphane Zékian. Lyon: Presses Universitaires de Lyon.

Michel, Louise. 2013b (1888). *Le monde nouveau*. In *Trois romans: Les microbes humains, Le monde nouveau, Le claque-dents*, edited by Claude Retat and Stéphane Zékian. Lyon: Presses Universitaires de Lyon.

Michel, Louise. 2013c. *Trois romans: Les microbes humains, Le monde nouveau, Le claque-dents*. Edited by Claude Rétat and Stéphane Zékian. Lyon: Presses Universitaires de Lyon.

Michel, Louise. 2014 (1887). *L'ère nouvelle*. Paris: Éditions d'Ores et Déjà.

Michel, Louise. 2015. *À travers la mort. Mémoires inédits, 1886–1890.* Paris: La Découverte.

Mink, Paule. 1886. "La femme en Algérie." *Le coup de feu* 5 (January).

Mirbeau, Octave. 1899. *Le jardin des supplices.* Paris: Charpentier-Fasquelle.

Pain, Olivier. 1880. *Henri Rochefort: Paris, Nouméa, Genève.* Paris: Périnet.

Papin, Henri. 1898. *Les étapes de la chanson: Histoire pittoresque de la chanson à travers les âges.* Vol. 1. Paris: Henry Lachize.

Reclus, Élisée. 1908. *L'homme et la terre.* Paris: Librarie Universelle.

Rivière, Henri L. 1881. *Souvenirs de la Nouvelle-Calédonie. L'insurrection Canaque.* Paris: Calmann-Lévy.

Rochas, Victor. 1862. *La Nouvelle-Calédonie et ses habitants, productions, mœurs, cannibalisme.* Paris: Ferdinand Sartorious.

Rochefort, Henri. 1896–1898. *Les aventures de ma vie.* Vol. 3. Paris: P. Dupont.

Rocker, Rudolf. 2005. (1956) *The London Years.* London: AK Press. Rouzade, Léonie. 1872. *Le monde renversé.* Paris: Lachaud Editeur.

Rouzade, Léonie. 1895. *Petit catéchisme de morale laïque et socialiste.* Meudon: chez l'auteur.

Sébillot, Paul. 1892. "Les femmes et les traditions populaires: La section des traditions populaires à l'Exposition des Arts de la Femme." *Revue des traditions populaires* 7, nos. 8–9 (August–September).

Simonet, J. 1866. *Eléments de philologie ou histoire comparée des langues.* Paris: Librarie Classique de André-Guèdon.

Sprague, Charles E. 1888. *A History of Volapük.* New York: The Office Company.

Tristan, Flora. 1838. *Pétition pour le rétablissement du divorce à Messieurs les députés, le 20 décembre 1837.* Paris: Imprimerie de Mme Huzzard.

Voilquin, Suzanne. 1865. *Souvenirs d'une fille du peuple, ou, La saint-simonienne en Égypte.* Paris: E. Sauzet.

Newspapers

L'aurore, 1897–1900.

Bulletin de la Société d'Acclimatation. 1873–1874. Paris: Au Siège du Société.

Citoyen, 1881–1884.

La citoyenne, 1881–1891

Le coup de feu, 1885–1888.

Le cri du peuple, 1885–1888.

Cri du progrès, 1888.

L'éclair, 1893.

L'égalité, 1869–1890.

L'électeur, 1880.

L'est républicain, 1889.

Freedom, 1891.

La fronde, 1897–1898.

Germinal, 1893.

L'indépendent de Mascara, 1884–1885.

Liberté belge, October, 1871.

La libre parole, 1892.

Le matin, 1885.

Le papillon, 1861–1863.
Le parisien, 1878.
Le petite république, 1892.
Les petites affiches de la Nouvelle-Calédonie, 1875.
Le petit sou, 1890–1900.
Le radical, 1891–1909.
Le rappel, 1899.
Revue de France, 1917.
La revue socialiste, 1885.
Le réveil de sétif, 1904.
Le siècle (Paris), 1870.
Le temps, 1886.

Secondary Sources

Abi-Mershed, Osama W. 2010. *Apostles of Modernity: Saint-Simonians and the Civilizing Mission in Algeria*. Stanford: Stanford University Press.
Adas, Michael. 2015. *Machines as the Measure of Men: Science, Technology, and Ideologies of Western Dominance*. Ithaca, NY: Cornell University Press.
Ageron, Charles-Robert. 1973. *L'anticolonialisme en France de 1871 à 1914*. Paris: Presses Universitaires de France.
Aldrich, Robert, and John Connell. 1992. *France's Overseas Frontier: Départements et territoires d'outre-mer*. Cambridge: Cambridge University Press.
Almog, Shmuel. 1990. *Nationalism and Antisemitism in Modern Europe 1815–1945*. New York: Pergamon.
Alter, Stephen G. 1999. *Darwinism and the Linguistic Image: Language, Race, and Natural Theology in the Nineteenth Century*. Baltimore, MD: Johns Hopkins University Press.
Alter, Stephen G. 2008. "'Curiously Parallel': Analogies of Language and Race in Darwin's *Descent of Man*. A Reply to Gregory Radick." *Studies in History and Philosophy of Biological and Biomedical Sciences* 39: 355–358.
Andersen, Margaret Cook. 2015. *Regeneration through Empire: French Pronatalists and Colonial Settlement in the Third Republic*. Lincoln: University of Nebraska Press.
Anderson, Perry. 2011. *The New Old World*. London: Verso.
Andrews, Naomi. 2006. *Socialism's Muse: Gender in the Intellectual Landscape of French Romantic Socialism*. Lanham, MD: Lexington.
Angleviel, Frédéric. 2005a. *Histoire de la Nouvelle-Calédonie: nouvelles approches, nouveaux objets*. Paris: L'Harmattan.
Angleviel, Frédéric. 2005b. "Historical colonial literature and New Caledonia, 1853–1945 or how a settlement colony generates hagiographic writings." *International Journal of Francophone Studies* 8, no. 3: 289–394.
Aprile, Sylvie. 2010. *Le siècle des exiles. De 1789 à la Commune*. Paris: CNRS Éditions.
Ashcroft, Bill. 2001. "Language and Race." *Social Identities* 7 (3): 311–328.
Ballantyne, Tony, and Antoinette M. Burton. 2008. "Introduction: The Politics of Intimacy in an Age of Empire." In *Moving Subjects: Gender, Mobility, and Intimacy in an Age of Global Empire*, edited by Tony Ballantyne and Antoinette M. Burton, 1–30. Urbana: University of Illinois Press.

Bantman, Constance. 2006. "Internationalism without an International: Cross-Chanel Anarchist Networks, 1880–1914." *Revue belge de philologie et d'histoire* 84, no. 4: 961–981.

Bantman, Constance. 2017a. "The Dangerous Liaisons of Belle Epoque Anarchists: Internationalism, Transnationalism, and Nationalism in the French Anarchist Movement (1880–1914)." In *Reassessing the Transnational Turn: Scales of Analysis in Anarchist and Syndicalist Studies,* edited by Constance Bantman and Bert Altena. Oakland, CA: PM Press.

Bantman, Constance. 2017b. "Louise Michel's London years: A political reassessment (1890–1905)." *Women's History Review* 26, n.6: 994–1012.

Barbançon, Louis-José. 2003. *L'archipel des forçats: Histoire du bagne de Nouvelle-Calédonie (1863–1931).* Paris: Presses Universitaires Septentrion.

Barbançon, Louis-José. 2006. "Déportation, transportation et relégation française." Criminocorpus. July 7. https://criminocorpus.org/en/criminocorpus/authors/barbancon/.

Bar-Itzhak, Haya. 2008. "Esterke." In *The YIVO Encyclopedia of Jews in Eastern Europe,* edited by Gershon David Hundert. New Haven, CT: Yale University Press. http://www.yivoencyclopedia.org/article.aspx/Esterke.

Baronnet, Jean, and Jean Chalou. 1987. *Communards en Nouvelle-Calédonie: Histoire de la déportation.* Paris: Mercure de France.

Barthelémy, Pascale, Luc Capdevila, and Michelle Zancarini-Fournel. 2011. "Femmes genre et colonisations," *Clio. Femmes, genre, histoire* 33: 7–22. https://doi.org/10.4000/clio.9994.

Beach, Cecilia. 2008. *"Savoir c'est pouvoir:* Integral Education in the Novels of André Léo." *Nineteenth Century French Studies* 36, nos. 3 & 4 (Spring–Summer): 270–285.

Bell, Dorian. 2018. *Globalizing Race: Antisemitism and Empire in French and European Culture.* Evanston, IL: Northwestern University Press.

Bennett, Jane. 1994. "Kafka, Genealogy, and the Spiritualization of Politics." *Journal of Politics* 56, no. 3 (August): 650–670.

Bensa, Alban. 1988. "Colonialisme, racisme et ethnologie en Nouvelle-Calédonie." *Ethnologie française* 18, no. 2: 188–197.

Bensa, Alban. 1995. *Chroniques Kanak: L'ethnologie en marche.* Paris: Peuples Autochtones et Développement.

Bensa, Alba. 2013. "Presentation." In *1878: Carnets de campagne en Nouvelle-Calédonie,* by Michel Millet, 3–4. Toulouse: Anacharsis.

Bensa, Alban, and Jean-Claude Rivierre. 1988. "De l'histoire des mythes: Narrations et polémiques autour du rocher Até (Nouvelle-Calédonie)." *L'homme* 38, nos. 2–3 (April–September): 263–295.

Bergmann, Werner, and Ulrich Wyrwa. 2012. "Introduction." In *The Making of Antisemitism as a Political Movement. Political History as Cultural History (1879–1914),* edited by Werner Bergmann and Ulrich Wyrwa. *Quest. Issues in Contemporary Jewish History. Journal of Fondazione CDEC,* no. 3 (July).

Berman, Alan. 2006. "Kanak Women and the Colonial Process." *International Journal of Law in Context* 2 (1): 11–36.

Betts, Raymond. 1961. *Assimilation and Association in French Colonial Theory, 1890–1914.* New York: Columbia University Press.

Bidelman, Patrick Kay. 1982. *Pariahs Stand Up! The Founding of the Liberal Feminist Movement in France, 1858–1889.* Westport, CT: Praeger.

Bierman, Guy. 1990–1991. "Le recrutement extraordinaire en Nouvelle-Calédonie pendant la Grande Révolte Canaque de 1878." *African Economic History* 19: 517–531.

Bird, Dúnlaith. 2012. *Travelling in Different Skins: Gender Identity in European Women's Oriental Travelogues, 1850–1950.* Oxford: Oxford University Press.

Birnbaum, Pierre. 1988. *Un mythe politique: La "république juive,"* De Léon Blum à Pierre Mendès-France. Paris: Librairie Arthème Fayard.

Birnbaum, Pierre. 1992. *Anti-Semitism in France: A Political History from Léon Blum to the Present.* Translated by Miriam Kochan. Oxford: Blackwell.

Blacher, Clara. 2017. "Féminisme et colonialisme: Les paradoxes de l'universalisme, À travers l'exemple d'Hubertine Auclert." MA thesis, Université de Lyon.

Blanchard, Pascal, and Sandrine Lemaire. 2003. "Avant propos. La constitution d'une culture coloniale en France." In *Culture coloniale. La France conquise par son empire, 1871–1931,* edited by Pascal Blanchard and Sandrine Lemaire, 5–39. Paris: Éditions Autrement.

Blanchard, Pascal, Sandrine Lemaire, Nicolas Bancel, and Dominic R. Thomas, eds. 2013. *Colonial Culture in France since the Revolution.* Bloomington: Indiana University Press.

Blum, Françoise. 1998. "Itinéraires féministes à la lumière de l'Affaire." In *La Postérité de l'affaire Dreyfus,* edited by Michel Leymarie, 93–101. Paris: Presses Universitaires du Septentrion.

Bogliolo, François. 1994. *Paroles et écritures: Anthologie de la littérature néo-calédonienne.* Nouméa: Les Éditions du Cajou.

Bogliolo, François. 1997. "Parabole et silence dans la littérature néo-calédonienne." In *Parole, communication, et symbole en Océanie,* edited by Frédéric Angleviel, 156–158. Paris: Harmattan.

Bogliolo, François. 2005. "Notre edition." In *Aux amis d'Europe: Légendes et chansons de gestes canaques,* by Louise Michel. Edited by François Bogliolo. Nouméa: Éditions Grain de Sable.

Bogliolo, François. 2006. "Présentation: La Pétroleuse et le Kanak." In *Légendes et chansons de gestes canaques (1875) suivi de Légendes et chants de gestes canaques (1885) et de Civilisation,* by Louise Michel, 13–46. Lyon: Presses Universitaire de Lyon.

Boittin, Jennifer Anne. 2009. "Black in France: The Language and Politics of Race in the Late Third Republic." *French Politics, Culture & Society* 27, no. 2 (Summer): 23–46.

Boittin, Jennifer Anne. 2010. *Colonial Metropolis: The Urban Grounds of Anti-Imperialism and Feminism in Interwar Paris.* Lincoln: University of Nebraska Press.

Boittin, Jennifer Anne. 2015. "'Are You Trying to Play a White Woman?' La Mère Patrie and the Female Body in French West Africa." *Signs: Journal of Women in Culture and Society* 40, no. 4: 841–864.

Boittin, Jennifer, and Tylver Stoval, eds. 2010. "Who Is French?" Special Issue. *French Historical Studies* 33, no. 3.

Bondi, Jean-Pierre. 1992. *Les anticolonialistes (1881–1962).* Paris: Laffont.

Boulay, Roger. 2000. *Kannibals et Vaninés: Imagerie des mers du Sud.* La Tour d'Aigues: Éditions de l'Aube.

Boulle, Pierre H. 2003. "François Bernier and the Origins of the Modern Concept of Race." In *The Color of Liberty: Histories of Race in France,* edited by Sue Peabody and Tyler Stovall, 11–27. Durham, NC: Duke University Press.

Bourguinat, Nicolas, ed. 2008. *Le voyage au féminin: Perspectives historiques et littéraires, XVIIIe-XXe siècles.* Strasbourg: Presses Universitaires de Strasbourg.

Boyer, Irma. 1927. *"La Vierge Rouge": Louise Michel.* Paris: A. Belpeuch.

Brantlinger, Patrick. 2003. *Dark Vanishings: Discourse on the Extinction of Primitive Races, 1800–1930.* Ithaca, NY: Cornell University.

Brett, Michael. 1988. "Legislating for Inequality in Algeria: The Senatus-Consulte of 14 July 1865." *Bulletin of the School of Oriental and African Studies, University of London* 51, no. 3: 440–461.

Brown, Wendy. 2004. "Tolerance and/or Equality? The 'Jewish Question' and the 'Woman Question.'" *Differences: A Journal of Feminist Cultural Studies* 15, no. 2: 1–31.

Brubaker, Rogers. 1992. *Citizenship and Nationhood in France and Germany.* Cambridge, MA: Harvard University Press.

Brunotte, Ulrike. 2015. "'All Jews Are Womanly, but No Women Are Jews': The 'Femininity' Game of Deception: Female Jew, Femme Fatale Orientale, and Belle Juive." In *Orientalism, Gender, and the Jews: Literary and Artistic Transformations of European National Discourses,* edited by Ulrike Brunotte, Anna-Dorothea Ludewig, and Axel Stähler, 195–220. Berlin: DeGruyter.

Brunotte, Ulrike, Anna-Dorothea Ludewig, and Axel Stähler. 2015. "Orientalism, Gender, and the Jews: Literary and Artistic Transformations of European National Discourses." In *Orientalism, Gender, and the Jews: Literary and Artistic Transformations of European National Discourses,* edited by Ulrike Brunotte, Anna-Dorothea Ludewig, and Axel Stähler, 1–16. Berlin: DeGruyter.

Bullard, Alice. 2000a. *Exile to Paradise: Savagery and Civilization in Paris and the South Pacific, 1790–1900.* Stanford, CA: Stanford University Press.

Bullard, Alice. 2000b. "Paris 1871/New Caledonia 1871: Human Rights and the Managerial State." In *Human Rights and Revolutions,* edited by Jeffrey N. Wasserstrom, Lynn Hunt, and Marilyn B. Young, 79–98. Lanham, MD: Rowman & Littlefield.

Burton, Antoinette. 1992. "The White Woman's Burden: British Feminists and 'the Indian Woman,' 1865–1915." In *Western Women and Imperialism: Complicity and Resistance,* edited by Nupur Chaudhuri and Margaret Strobel, 137–157. Bloomington: Indiana University Press.

Burton, Antoinette. 1994. *Burdens of History: British Feminists, Indian Women, and Imperial Culture,1865–1915.* Chapel Hill: University of North Carolina Press.

Burton, Antoinette. 2009. "Rules of Thumb: British History and 'Imperial Culture' in Nineteenth- and Twentieth-Century Britain." In *The New Imperial Histories Reader,* edited by Steven Howe, 41–54. London: Routledge.

Bush, Barbara. 2016. "Feminising Empire? British Women's Activist Networks in Defending and Challenging Empire from 1918 to Decolonisation." *Women's History Review* 25, no. 4: 499–519.

Camiscioli, Elisa. 2013. "Women, Gender, Intimacy, and Empire." *Journal of Women's History* 25, no. 4 (Winter): 138–148.

Carlier, Julie. 2012. "Rethinking the History of the Belgian Movement for Women's Rights through Transnational Intersections." *Revue belge de philologie et d'histoire* 90, no. 4: 1339–1351.

Caron, Vicki. 2009. "Catholic Political Mobilization and Antisemitic Violence in Fin de Siècle France: The Case of the Union Nationale." *Journal of Modern History* 81, no. 2 (June): 294–346.

Chafer, Tony, and Amanda Sackur, eds. 2002. *Promoting the Colonial Idea: Propaganda and Visions of Empire in France.* New York: Palgrave.

Champion, Renée. 2002. "Représentations des femmes dans les récits de voyageuses d'expression française en Orient au XIXe siècle (1848–1911)." PhD diss., Université Paris–Diderot.

Chapman, Herrick, and Laura L. Frader. 2004. "Introduction: Race in France." In *Race in France: Interdisciplinary Perspectives on the Politics of Difference,* edited by Herrick Chapman and Laura L. Frader, 1–19. New York: Berghahn Books.

Chaudhuri, Nupur, and Margaret Strobel, eds. 1992. *Western Women and Imperialism: Complicity and Resistance.* Bloomington: Indiana University Press.

Chauvin, Clotilde. 2007. *Louise Michel en Algérie.* Toulouse: Les Éditions Libertaires.

Cheyette, Bryan, and Nadia Valman. 2003. "Introduction: Liberalism and Anti-Semitism." *Jewish Culture and History* 6, no. 1: 1–26.

Clair, Sylvie. 1994. "La déportation politique en Nouvelle-Calédonie: Répression ou colonisation?" In *Le peuplement du Pacifique et de la Nouvelle-Calédonie au XIXe siècle: Condamnés, colons, convicts, coolies, Chân Dang,* edited by Paul de Deckker, 133–150. Paris: Éditions L'Harmattan.

Clancy-Smith, Julia. 1996. "La femme arabe: Women and Sexuality in France's North African Empire." In *Women, the Family, and Divorce laws in Islamic History,* edited by Amira El Azhary Sonbol, 52–63. Syracuse, NY: Syracuse University Press.

Clancy-Smith, Julia. 1998. "Islam, Gender, and Identities in the Making of French Algeria, 1830–1962." In *Domesticating the Empire: Race, Gender, and Family Life in French and Dutch Colonialism,* edited by Julia Clancy-Smith and Frances Gouda, 154–174. Charlottesville: University of Virginia Press.

Clément, Alain. 2012. "Libéralisme et anticolonialisme: La pensée économique française et l'effondrement du premier empire colonial (1789–1830)." *Revue économique* 63, no. 1: 5–26.

Clément, Alain. 2013. "L'analyse économique de la question coloniale en France (1870–1914)." *Revue d'économie politiques* 123 (1): 51–81.

Clifford, James. 1986. "Introduction: Partial Truths." In *Writing Culture: The Poetics and Politics of Ethnography,* edited by James Clifford and George E. Marcuse, 1–26. Berkeley: University of California Press.

Cohen, William B. 1980. *The French Encounter with Africans.* Bloomington: Indiana University Press.

Cole, Joshua. 2019. *Lethal Provocation: The Constantine Murders and the Politics of French Algeria.* Ithaca, NY: Cornell University Press.

Conklin, Alice. L. 1997. *A Mission to Civilize: The Republican Idea of Empire in France and West Africa, 1895–1930.* Stanford, CA: Stanford University Press.

Conklin, Alice. L. 2013. *In the Museum of Man: Race, Anthropology, and Empire in France, 1850–1950*. Ithaca, NY: Cornell University Press.

Conklin, Alice, and Julia Clancy-Smith. 2004. "Introduction: Writing Colonial Histories." In "Writing French Colonial Histories," edited by Conklin and Clancy-Smith. Special issue, *French Historical Studies* 27 (3): 497–505.

Cook-Lynn, Elizabeth. 2001. *Anti-Indianism in Modern America: A Voice from Tatekeya's Earth*. Urbana: University of Illinois Press.

Cooper, Frederick, and Anne Laura Stoler. 1997. "Between Metropole and Colony: Rethinking a Research Agenda." In *Tensions of Empire: Colonial Cultures in a Bourgeois World*, edited by Frederick Cooper and Ann Laura Stoler, 1–40. Berkeley: University of California Press.

Cormier, Manuel. 1993. *La colonisation pénale*. Nouméa: Centre Territorial de Recherche et de Documentation.

Cornet, Claude. 1999. *Communards, puis Calédoniens: La vie et la descendance des déportés politiques en Nouvelle-Calédonie*. Nouméa, New Caledonia: Éditions Boudeuse.

Cova, Anne. 2010. "International Feminisms in Historical Comparative Perspective: France, Italy and Portugal, 1880s–1930s." *Women's History Review* 19, no. 4: 595–612.

Dalotel, Alain, Alain Faure, and Jean-Claude Freiermuth. 1980. *Aux origines de la Commune: Le mouvement des réunions publiques à Paris 1868–1870*. Paris: François Maspero.

Dalotel, Alain, and Jean-Claude Freiermuth. 1988. "Socialism and Revolution." In *Voices of the People: The Politics and Life of "La Sociale" at the End of the Second Empire*, edited by Adrian Rifkin and Roger Thomas, translated by John Moore. New York: Routledge & Kegan Paul.

Darot, Mireille. 1997. "Calédonie, Kanaky ou Caillou? Implicites identitaires dans la désignation de la Nouvelle-Calédonie." *Mots* 53 (December): 8–25.

Dauphiné, Joël. 2006. *La déportation de Louise Michel*. Paris: Les Indes Savantes.

"Definitions of Different Language Varieties." 2020. Language Varieties website. University of Hawai'i. https://www.hawaii.edu/satocenter/langnet/definitions/index.html.

Delmaire, Dominique. 2014. "From Bard to Boor: The Critical Reception of Robert Burns in France." In *The Reception of Robert Burns in Europe*, edited by Murray Pittock, 67–114. London: A & C Black.

Demeulenaere-Douyère, Christiane. 2003. "Un précurseur de la mixité: Paul Robin et le coéducation des sexes." *Clio. Histoire, femmes et sociétés* 18: 125–132.

Dermenjian, Geneviève. 1986. *La crise anti-juive oranaise (1895–1905): L'antisémitisme dans l'Algérie colonial*. Paris: L'Harmattan.

Desan, Suzanne. 2004. *The Family on Trial in Revolutionary France*. Berkeley: University of California Press.

Douglas, Bronwen. 1998. *Across the Great Divide: Journeys in History and Anthropology*. Amsterdam: Routledge.

Dousset, Roselène. 1970. *Colonialisme et contradictions: Étude sur les causes socio-historiques de l'insurrection de 1878 en Nouvelle-Calédonie*. Paris: Mouton.

Dousset-Leenhardt, Roselène. 1976. *Terre natale, terre d'exil*. Paris: G.-P. Maisonneuve & Larose.

Duparc, Hélène. 2003. *De Paris à Nouméa: L'histoire des communards de la Commune de Paris déportés en Nouvelle-Calédonie*. Saint-Denis, La Réunion: Éditions Orphie.

Dzeh-Djeh, Li. 1934. *La presse féministe en France de 1869 à 1914*. Paris: Librairie L. Rodstein.

Eichner, Carolyn J. 2004. *Surmounting the Barricades: Women in the Paris Commune*. Bloomington: Indiana University Press.

Eichner, Carolyn J. 2009. "*La Citoyenne* in the World: Hubertine Auclert and Feminist Imperialism." *French Historical Studies* 32, no. 1 (Winter): 63–84.

Eichner, Carolyn J. 2014. "In the Name of the Mother: Feminist Opposition to the Patronym in Nineteenth-Century France." *Signs: Journal of Women in Culture and Society* 39, no. 3: 659–683.

Eller, Cynthia. 2005. "The Feminist Appropriation of Matriarchal Myth in the 19th and 20th Centuries." *History Compass* 3: 1–10.

Eller, Cynthia. 2006. "Sons of the Mother: Victorian Anthropologists and the Myth of Matriarchal Prehistory." *Gender & History* 18, no. 2 (August): 285–310.

English, Jim. 2006. "Empire Day in Britain, 1904–1958." *Historical Journal* 49, no. 1 (March): 247–276.

Ernot, Isabelle. 2009. "Des femmes écrivent l'histoire des femmes au milieu du XIXe siècle: Représentations, interprétations," *Genre & histoire: La revue de l'Association Mnémosyne* [Online], 4 (Spring) http://journals.openedition.org/genrehistoire/742.

Ernot, Isabelle. 2011. "Voyageuses occidentales et impérialisme: l'Orient à la croisée des représentations (XIXe siècle)," *Genre & histoire: La revue de l'Association Mnémosyne Online]* 8 (Spring). http://journals.openedition.org/genrehistoire/1272.

Esbjörn-Hargens, Sean, Jonathan Reams, and Olen Gunnlaugson. 2010. *Integral Education: New Directions for Higher Learning*. Albany: State University of New York Press.

Euben, Roxanne L. 2003. "The Comparative Politics of Travel." *Parallax* 9 (4): 18–28.

Eustache, Bernadette. 1987. "Léonie Rouzade, 1839–1916: Biographie d'une féministe socialiste." MA thesis, Université de Paris VII.

Everton, Elizabeth. 2011. "Sisters and Soldiers: The Representation and Participation of Women in the Antidreyfusard Movement." PhD diss., University of California–Los Angeles.

Fabian, Johannes. 2002. *Time and the Other: How Anthropology Makes Its Object*. New York: Columbia University Press.

Faessel, Sonia. 2004. "La Nouvelle-Calédonie, terre de violences au XIXe siècle. Perception du Canaque par les voyageurs." In *Violences océaniennes*, edited by Fréderic Angleviel, 173–188. Paris: L'Harmattan.

Ferguson, Kennan. 2012. *All in the Family: On Community and Incommensurability*. Durham, NC: Duke University Press.

Ferretti, Federico. 2016. "Anarchist Geographers and Feminism in Late 19th-Century France: The Contributions of Élisée and Élie Reclus." *Historical Geography* 44: 68–88.

Fidler, Geoffrey. 1989. "Anarchism and Education: Education Intégrale and the Imperative Towards Fraternité." *History of Education* 18, no. 1: 23–46.

Filer, Colin, and Pierre-Yves Le Meur. 2017. *Large-Scale Mines and Local-Level Politics: Between New Caledonia and Papua New Guinea.* Canberra: Australian National University Press.

Firpo, Christina. 2011. "Shades of Whiteness: Petits-Blancs and the Politics of Military Allocations Distribution in World War I Colonial Cochinchina." *French Historical Studies* 34 (2): 279–297.

Foley, Susan. 2004. "In Search of 'Liberty': Politics of Women's Rights in the Travel Narratives of Flora Tristan and Suzanne Voilquin." *Women's History Review* 13, no. 2: 211–231.

Forsdick, Charles. 2018. "Postcolonizing the *Bagne.*" *French Studies* 22 (2): 237–255.

Fortescue, William. 1993. "Divorce Debated and Deferred: The French Debate on Divorce and the Failure of the Crémieux Divorce Bill in 1848." *French History* 7, no. 2: 137–162.

Forth, Christopher. 2006. *The Dreyfus Affair and the Crisis of French Manhood.* Baltimore, MD: Johns Hopkins University Press.

Fortunati, Vita. 2001. *Travel Writing and the Female Imaginary.* Bologna: Patron.

Foucault, Michel. 1995. *Discipline and Punish: The Birth of the Prison.* Translated by Alan Sheridan. New York: Vintage Books.

Fournier, Eric. 2012. *La "belle Juive" d'Ivanhoé à la Shoah.* Paris: Champ Vallon.

Frankel, Jonathan. 1997. *The Damascus Affair: "Ritual Murder," Politics, and the Jews in 1840.* Cambridge: Cambridge University Press.

Friedman, Elizabeth. 1998. *Colonialism & After: An Algerian Jewish Community.* South Hadley, MA: Bergin & Garvey.

Fuchs, Rachel. 2008. *Contested Paternity: Constructing Families in Modern France.* Baltimore, MD: Johns Hopkins University Press.

Garb, Tamar. 1995. "Introduction: Modernity, Identity, Textuality." In *The Jew in the Text: Modernity and the Construction of Identity,* edited by Linda Nochlin and Tamar Garb, 20–30. London: Thames & Hudson.

Gauthier, Xavière. 2000. Introduction. *Histoire de ma vie, seconde et troisième parties,* by Louise Michel, 7–34. Lyon: Presses Universitaires de Lyon.

Geller, Jay. 1992. "Blood, Sin, and Syphilis and the Construction of Jewish Identity." *Fault Line* 1: 21–48.

Gehrmann, Susanne. 2005. "Written Orature in Senegal, from the Traditionalistic Tales of Birago Diop to the Subversive Novels of Boubacar Boris Diop." In *Interfaces between the Oral and the Written: Versions and Subversions in African Literatures 2nd edition,* Edited by Alain Ricard and Flora Veit–Wild. Amsterdam: Éditions Rodopi.

Germaine, Félix, and Silyane Larcher, eds. 2018. *Black French Women and the Struggle for Equality, 1848–2016.* Lincoln: University of Nebraska Press.

Gilman, Sander. 1991. *The Jew's Body.* New York: Routledge.

Girardet, Raoul. 1972. *L'idée coloniale en France: De 1871 à 1962.* Paris: La Table Ronde.

Girault, Ernest. 2007. *Une colonie d'enfer: Chroniques d'un voyage en Algérie en 1904, lors d'une tournée de conférences avec Louise Michel.* Toulouse: Les Éditions Libertaires.

Glissant, Édouard. 2008. "*Créolization* in the Making of the Americas." *Caribbean Quarterly* 54, nos. 1–2 (March–June): 81–89.

Godley, Nathan. 2006. "Almost Finished Frenchmen: The Jews of Algeria and the Question of French Identity." PhD diss., University of Iowa.

Goldstein, Jan E. 2015. "Toward an Empirical History of Moral Thinking: The Case of Racial Theory in Mid-Nineteenth-Century France." *American Historical Review* 120 (1): 1–27.

Gould, Steven Jay. 1985. *Ontogeny and Phylogeny.* Cambridge, MA: Belknap Press of Harvard University Press.

Grossberg, Michael. 1998. *Governing the Hearth: Law and the Family in Nineteenth-Century America.* Chapel Hill: University of North Carolina Press.

Guenoun, Katherine. 2015. "Between Synagogue and Society: Jewish Women in Nineteenth-Century France." PhD diss., University of Wisconsin–Madison.

Guiart, Jean. 1957. *Contes et légendes de la Grande-Terre.* Nouméa: Éditions des études Mélanésiennes.

Haggis, Jane. 1998. "White Women and Colonialism: Towards a Non-Recuperative History." In *Gender and Imperialism,* edited by Clare Midgley, 45–75. Manchester: Manchester University Press.

Hajjat, Abdellali. 2012. *Les frontières de l'identité nationale: L'injonction à l'assimilation en France métropolitaine et coloniale.* Paris: La Découverte.

Hall, Catherine. 1992. *White, Male, and Middle Class: Explorations in Feminism and History.* , New York: Routledge.

Hallman, Diana R. 2002. *Opera, Liberalism, and Antisemitism in Nineteenth-Century France: The Politics of Halévy's La Juive.* Cambridge: Cambridge University Press.

Hammerschlag, Sarah. 2007. *The Figural Jew: Politics and Identity in Postwar French Thought.* Chicago: University of Chicago Press.

Hardison, O. B., Alex Preminger, and Frank J. Warnke, eds. 2014. *The Princeton Handbook of Poetic Terms.* Princeton, NJ: Princeton University Press.

Hart, Kathleen. 2001. "Oral Culture and Anti-Colonialism in Louise Michel's '*Mémoires*' (1886) and '*Légendes et chants de gestes canaques*' (1885)." *Nineteenth Century French Studies* 30 (1–2): 107–120.

Hart, Kathleen. 2004. *Revolution and Women's Autobiography in Nineteenth-Century France.* Amsterdam: Éditions Rodopi.

Hause, Steven C. 1987. *Hubertine Auclert: The French Suffragette.* New Haven, CT: Yale University Press.

Hause, Steven C. 2007. "Présentation." In *Hubertine Auclert: Pionnière du féminisme,* edited by Steven D. Hause and Geneviève Fraisse, 19–63. Saint-Pourcainsur-Sioule: Bleu Autour.

Hollyman, Jim K. 1964. "L'ancien pidgin français parlé en Nouvelle-Calédonie." *Journal de la Société des Océanistes* 20: 57–64.

Hugon, Anne. 2004. *Histoire des femmes en situation coloniale.* Paris: Éditions Karthala.

Hunt, Persis. 1971. "Feminism and Anti-Clericalism under the Commune." *Massachusetts Review* 12 (Summer): 418–431.

Hyman, Paula E. 1995. *Gender and Assimilation in Modern Jewish History: The Roles and Representation of Women.* Seattle: University of Washington Press.

Hyman, Paula E. 1998. *The Jews of Modern France.* Berkeley: University of California Press.

Ihage, Weniko. 1992. *La Tradition orale à Lifou*. Nouméa: Les Éditions du Niaouli et Agence de Développement de la Culture Kanak.

Ikuenobe, Polycarp. 2018. "The Monogamous Conception of Romantic Love and Western Critiques of Polygamy in African Traditions." *Philosophical Papers* 47, no. 3: 373–401.

Jugé, Tony S. 2009. *Racism in France: The Civilizing Mission of Whiteness*. Riga, Latvia: VDM Verlag.

Kalman, Julie. 2007. "Sensuality, Depravity, and Ritual Murder: The Damascus Blood Libel and Jews in France." *Jewish Social Studies: History, Culture, Society* 13, no. 3 (Spring/Summer): 35–58.

Kalman, Julie. 2017. *Orientalizing the Jew: Religion, Culture, and Imperialism in Nineteenth-Century France*. Bloomington: Indiana University Press.

Kalmar, Ivan Davidson, and Derek Penslar. 2005. "Orientalism and the Jews: An Introduction." In *Orientalism and the Jews*, edited by Ivan Davidson Kalmar and Derek Penslar, xiii–xl. Waltham, MA: Brandeis University Press.

Karandashev, Victor N. 2017. *Romantic Love in Cultural Contexts*. New York: Springer.

Katz, Ethan B., Lisa Moses Leff, and Maud S. Mandel. 2017. "Introduction: Engaging Colonial History and Jewish History." In *Colonialism and the Jews*, edited by Ethan B. Katz, Lisa Moses Leff, and Maud S. Mandel, 1–27. Bloomington: Indiana University Press.

Kimble, Sara. 2006. "Emancipation through Secularization: French Feminist Views of Muslim Women's Condition in Interwar Algeria." *French Colonial History* 7: 109–128.

Klein, Florence. 2000. "La perception du corps." In *Chroniques du pays Kanak*, edited by Orso Filiippi, vol. 2:. Nouméa: Planète Memo.

Kohn, Margaret. 2005. "Kafka's Critique of Colonialism." *Theory & Event* 8 (3): 1–8.

Krakovitch, Odile. 1990. *Les femmes bagnards*. Paris: Olivier Orban.

Lallaoui, Mehdi. 1994. *Algériens du Pacifique: Les déportés de Nouvelle-Calédonie*. Algers: Edition Zyriab.

Laplanche, François, ed. 1996. "Hippolyte Gayraud." In *Les sciences religieuses*, vol. 9 of *Dictionnaire du monde religieux dans la France contemporaine*, edited by Jean-Marie Mayeur et Yves-Marie Hilaire. Paris: Éditions Beauchesne.

Latham, Linda. 1978. *La révolte de 1878: Étude critique des causes de la rébellion de 1878, en Nouvelle-Calédonie*. Translated by Édouard Terzian. Nouméa: Société d'Études Historiques de la Nouvelle-Calédonie.

Lazreg, Marnia. 1988. "Feminism and Difference: The Perils of Writing as a Woman on Women in Algeria." *Feminist Studies* 14, no. 1 (Spring): 81–107.

Leenhardt, Maurice. 1979. *Do Kamo: Person and Myth in the Melanesian World*. Translated by Basia Miller Gulati. Chicago: University of Chicago Press.

Leff, Lisa. 2006. *Sacred Bonds of Solidarity: The Rise of Jewish Internationalism in Nineteenth-Century France*. Stanford, CA: Stanford University Press.

Lehning, James R. 2001. *To Be a Citizen: The Political Culture of the Early French Third Republic*. Ithaca, NY: Cornell University Press.

Le Meur, Pierre-Yves. 2013. "Locality, Mobility and Governmentality in Colonial/Postcolonial New Caledonia: The Case of the Kouare Tribe (Xûâ Xârâgwii), Thio (Cöö)." *Oceana* 83, no. 2: 130–146.

Leonardo, Micaela di. 1991. "Introduction. Gender, Culture, and Political Economy: Feminist Anthropology in Historical Perspective." In *Gender at the Crossroads of Knowledge: Feminist Anthropology in the Postmodern Era*, edited by Micaela di Leonardo, 1–49. Berkeley: University of California Press.

Levine, Philippa. 2004. "Introduction: Why Gender and Empire?" In *Gender and Empire*, edited by Philippa Levine, 1–13. Oxford: Oxford University Press.

Levy, Carl. 2011. "Anarchism and Cosmopolitanism." *Journal of Political Ideologies* 16, no. 3 (October): 265–278.

Liauzu, Claude. 1992. *Race et civilisation: L'autre dans la culture occidentale*. Paris: Syros-Alternative.

Liauzu, Claude. 2007. *Histoire de l'anticolonialisme en France, du xvie siècle à nos jours*. Paris: Armand Colin.

Lindemann, Albert S. 1997. *Esau's Tears: Modern Anti-Semitism and the Rise of the Jews*. Cambridge: Cambridge University Press.

Lorcin, Patricia M. E. 1995. *Imperial Identities: Stereotyping, Prejudice, and Race in Colonial Algeria*. New York: St. Martin's Press.

Lorcin, Patricia M. E. 2004. "Mediating Gender, Mediating Race: Women Writers in Colonial Algeria." *Culture, Theory, and Critique* 45: 45–61.

Lorcin, Patricia M. E. 2016. "Women in France d'Outre-Mer: Pedagogy and Avenues of Research." *Journal of Women's History* 28, no. 4 (Winter): 113–123.

Loth, Laura. 2009. "Journeying Identities: Mid-Nineteenth-Century Women's Travel Writing in French Colonial Algeria." *Symposium: A Quarterly Journal in Modern Literatures* 63 (2): 107–126.

Lowe, Lisa. 2015. *Intimacies of Four Continents*. Durham, NC: Duke University Press.

Lowy, Michael. 2004. *Franz Kafka, rêveur insoumis*. Paris: Éditions Stock.

Mailhé, Germaine. 1994. *Déportations en Nouvelle-Calédonie des Communards et des révoltés de la Grande Kabylie (1872–1876)*. Paris: Éditions L'Harmattan.

Mainardi, Patricia. 2003. *Husbands, Wives, and Lovers: Marriage and Its Discontents in Nineteenth-Century France*. New Haven, CT: Yale University Press.

Manceron, Gilles. 2003. *Marianne et les colonies: Une introduction à l'histoire colonial en France*. Paris: La Decouverte,

Manceron, Gilles. 2007. "Introduction." In *1885: Le Tournant colonial de la République. Jules Ferry contre Georges Clemenceau, et autres affrontements parlementaires sur la conquête coloniale*, edited by Gilles Manceron, 1–26. Paris: La Découverte.

Mansker, Andrea. 2011. *Sex, Honor, and Citizenship in Early Third Republic France*. New York: Palgrave MacMillan.

Mantena, Karuna. 2010. *Alibis of Empire: Henry Maine and the Ends of Liberal Imperialism*. Princeton, NJ: Princeton University Press.

Marzolph, Ulrich. 2007. "Preface." In *The Arabian Nights in Transnational Perspective*, edited by Urich Marzolph, ix–xi. Detroit, MI: Wayne State University Press.

Matsuda, Matt K. 2005. *Empire of Love: Histories of France and the Pacific*. Oxford: Oxford University Press.

Matthias, Ulrich. 2002. *Esperanto—The New Latin for the Church and for Ecumenism*. Translated by Mike and Maire Mullarney. Antwerp: Flandra Esperanto-Ligo.

McBride, Theresa. 1995. "Divorce and the Republican Family." In *Gender and the Politics of Social Reform in France, 1870–1914*, edited by Elinor A. Accamp,

Rachel G. Fuchs, and Mary Lynn Stewart, 59–81. Baltimore, MD: Johns Hopkins University Press.

McClintock, Anne. 1995. *Imperial Leather: Race, Gender and Sexuality in the Colonial Contest.* New York: Routledge.

McClintock, Scott. 2004. "The Penal Colony: Inscription of the Subject in Literature and Law, and Detainees as Legal Non-Persons at Camp X-Ray." *Comparative Literature Studies* 41 (1): 153–167.

McLaren, Angus. 1981. "Revolution and Education in Late Nineteenth-Century France: The Early Career of Paul Robin." *History of Education Quarterly* 21, no. 3 (Autumn): 317–335.

Mehta, Uday Singh. 1999. *Liberalism and Empire: A Study in Nineteenth-Century British Thought.* Chicago: University of Chicago Press.

Melman, Billie. 2008. "Orientations historiographiques: Voyage, genre et colonisation." *Clio. Femmes, genre, histoire* 28: 159–184.

Merle, Isabelle. 1995. *Expériences coloniales: La Nouvelle-Calédonie (1853–1920).* Paris: Belin.

Merle, Isabelle. 1997a. "À propos de l'ouvrage *Expériences coloniales.* La Nouvelle-Calédonie. 1853–1920." In "La Nouvelle-Calédonie après les accords de Matignon. Désignations et identités en Nouvelle-Calédonie," edited by Simone Bonnafous and Jacquline Dahlem. Special issue, *Mots* 53: 81–83.

Merle, Isabelle. 1997b. "Colonial Experiments, Colonial Experiences: The Theory and Practice of Penal Colonisation in New Caledonia." In *France Abroad: Indochina, New Caledonia, Wallis and Futuna, Mayotte: Papers Presented at the Tenth George Rudé Seminar,* edited by Robert Aldrich and Isabelle Merle, 17–33. Sydney: Department of Economic History, University of Sydney.

Merle, Isabelle, and Adrian Muckle. 2019. *L'indigénat: Genèses dans l'empire français pratiques en Nouvelle-Calédonie.* Paris: CNRS Éditions,

Merle, Marcel. 2003. "Anticolonialisme." In *Le Livre noir du colonialisme: XVI à XXI siècle: De l'extermination à la repentance,* edited by Marc Ferro, 815–861. PGS. Paris: Robert Laffont.

Merriman, John. 1996. *From the French Revolution to the Present.* Vol. 2 of *A History of Modern Europe.* New York: Norton.

Mesch, Rachel, and Masha Belenky. 2008. "State of the Union: Marriage in Nineteenth-Century France." *Dix-neuf* 11, no. 1 (November): 1–6.

Mesch, Rachel. 2020. *Before Trans: Three Gender Stories from Nineteenth-Century France.* Stanford: Stanford University Press.

Meynier, Gilbert, and Jacques Thobie, eds. 1996. *L'apogée, 1871.* Vol. 2 of *Histoire de la France coloniale.* Paris: Agora.

Midgley, Clare. 2007. *Feminism and Empire: Women Activists in Imperial Britain, 1790–1865.* London: Routledge.

Midgley, Clare, ed. 1998. *Gender and Imperialism.* Manchester: Manchester University Press.

Mignolo, Walter E. 1998. "Globalization, Civilization Processes, and the Relocation of Languages and Cultures." In *The Cultures of Globalization,* edited by Fredric Jameson and Masao Miyoshi, 32–53. Durham, NC: Duke University Press.

Miller, Randolph. 2018. "A New Brand of Men: Masculinity in French Republican Socialist Rhetoric." PhD Diss., University of Wisconsin–Milwaukee.

Mohamed-Gaillard, Sarah. 2003. "De la prise de possession à l'accord de Nouméa: 150 ans de liens institutionnels et politiques entre la France et la Nouvelle-Calédonie." *Journal de la Société des Océanistes* 117, no. 2: 171–186.

Molz, Markus, and Gary P. Hampson. 2010. "Elements of the Underacknowledged History of Integral Education." In *Integral Education: New Directions for Higher Learning*, edited by Sean Esbjorn-Hargens, Jonathan Reams, Olen Gunnlaugson, 35–46. Albany: State University of New York Press.

Monicat, Bénédicte. 1995. "Ecritures du voyage et féminismes: Olympe Audouard ou le féminin en question." *French Review* 69, no. 1 (October): 24–36.

Monicat, Bénédicte. 1996. *Itinéraires de l'écriture au féminin: Voyageuses du 19ᵉ siècle.* Amsterdam: Éditions Rodopi.

Moran, Rachel F. 2004. "Love with a Proper Stranger: What Anti-Miscegenation Laws Can Tell Us about the Meaning of Race, Sex, and Marriage." *Hofstra Law Review* 34, no. 2: 1663–1679

Moses, Claire Goldberg. 1984. *French Feminism in the Nineteenth Century.* Albany, NY: State University of New York Press.

Moses, Claire Goldberg, and Leslie Wahl Rabine. 1993. *Feminism, Socialism, and French Romanticism.* Bloomington: Indiana University Press.

Moussa, Sarga. 2002. "Les Saint-Simoniens en Égypte: Le cas d'Ismaÿl Urbain." In *La France et l'Égypte à l'époque des vice-rois, 1805–1882*, edited by C. Panzac and A. Raymond, 225–233. Cairo: Institut Français d'archéologie Orientale du Caire.

Moyse-Faurie, Claire. 2004. "Politesse et violence verbale en Océanie." In *Violences océaniennes*, edited by Frédéric Angleviel, 31–46. Paris: L'Harmattan.

Muckle, Adrian. 2002. "Killing the 'Fantôme Canaque': Evoking and Invoking the Possibility of Revolt in New Caledonia (1853–1915)." *Journal of Pacific History* 37 (1): 25–44

Murphy, Erin L. 2009. "Women's Anti-Imperialism, 'The White Man's Burden' and the Philippine-American War: Theorizing Masculinist Ambivalence in Protest." *Gender & Society* 23, no. 3: 244–270.

Muthu, Sankar. 2003. *Enlightenment against Empire.* Princeton, NJ: Princeton University Press.

Muyskin, Pierer, and Norval Smith. 1994. "The Study of Pidgin and Creole Languages." In *Pidgins and Creoles: An Introduction*, edited by Jacques Arends, Pieter Muijsken, and Norval Smith, 3–14. Amsterdam: John Benjamins Publishing.

Newman, Louise Michele. 1999. *White Women's Rights: The Racial Origins of Feminism in the United States.* Oxford: Oxford University Press.

Newmeyer, Frederick J. 1986. *The Politics of Linguistics.* Chicago: University of Chicago Press.

Nicholls, Julia. 2019. *Revolutionary Thought after the Paris Commune, 1871–1885.* Cambridge: Cambridge University Press.

Nochlin, Linda, and Tamar Garb, eds. 1995. *The Jew in the Text: Modernity and the Construction of Identity.* London: Thames & Hudson.

Nuñez, Rachel. 2006. "Between France and the World: The Gender Politics of Cosmopolitanism, 1835–1914." PhD diss., Stanford University.

Nuñez, Rachel. 2012. "Rethinking Universalism: Olympe Audouard, Hubertine Auclert, and the Gender Politics of the Civilizing Mission." *French Politics, Culture & Society* 30, no. 1 (Spring): 23–45.

Nye, Robert. *Masculinity and Male Codes of Honor in Modern France.* Austin: University of Texas Press, 1994.

Ockman, Carol. 1991. "'Two Large Eyebrows à l'Orientale': Ethnic Stereotyping in Ingres's *Baronne de Rothschild.*" *Art History* 14, no. 4 (December): 521–539.

Offen, Karen. 1984. "Depopulation, Nationalism, and Feminism in *Fin-de-Siècle* France." *American Historical Review* 89: 648–676.

Offen, Karen. 2000. *European Feminisms, 1700–1950.* Stanford, CA: Stanford University Press.

Ogden, Daryl. 2005. *The Language of the Eyes: Science, Sexuality, and Female Vision in English Literature and Culture, 1690–1927.* Albany: State University of New York Press.

Ouennoughi, Mélica. 2005. *Les déportés maghrébins en Nouvelle-Calédonie et la culture du palmier dattier: De 1864 à nos jours.* Paris: L'Harmattan.

Ousselin, Edward. 2005–2006. "Victor Hugo's European Utopia." *Nineteenth-Century French Studies* 34, nos. 1–2 (Fall–Winter): 32–43.

Pannoux, Stéphane. "Les déportés de la Commune face à la révolte Kanak de 1871." In *La Commune de Paris 1871: Les acteurs, l'événement, les lieux*, edited by Michel Cordillot, 1186–1190. Paris: Éditions de l'Atelier, 2020.

Parnell-Smith, Juliette. 1997a. "Les mémoires de Louise Michel: Travail de deuil et quête identitaire." *Paroles Gelées* 15, no. 1: 63–81.

Parnell-Smith, Juliette. 1997b. "Les filles de La Galoubette: Un roman naturaliste et feministe de Louise Michel." *Excavatio* 10: 48–56.

Pateman, Carole. 1988. *The Sexual Contract.* Stanford, CA: Stanford University Press.

Patouillard, Victoire, Stany Grelet, and Marion Lary. 2008. "De l'autre côté du mythe. Entretien avec Alban Bensa." *Vacarme* 3 (44): 4–14.

Pedersen, Holger. 1972. *Discovery of Language: Linguistic Science in the 19th Century.* Translated by John Webster Spargo. Bloomington: Indiana University Press.

Pedersen, Jean Elisabeth. 2003. *Legislating the French Family: Feminism, Theater, and Republican Politics, 1870–1920.* New Brunswick, NJ: Rutgers University Press.

Pellegrin, Nicole, ed. 2011a. "Voyageuses et histoire(s)." *Genre et Histoire* 8, Special issue, part 1 (Spring).

Pellegrin, Nicole, ed. 2011b. "Voyageuses et histoire(s)." *Genre et Histoire* 9, Special issue, part 2 (Fall).

Pellegrini, Ann. 1996. "Whiteface Performance: Race, Gender, and Jewish Bodies." In *Jews and Other Differences: The New Jewish Cultural Studies*, edited by Jonathan Boyarin and Daniel Boyarein, 108–149. Minneapolis: University of Minnesota Press.

Perrot, Michelle. 2002. "Sortir." In *Le XIXe siècle*. Vol. 4 of *Histoire des femmes en Occident*, edited by Georges Duby and Michelle Perrott. Paris: Plon.

Pilbeam, Pamela. 2013. *Saint-Simonians in Nineteenth-Century France: From Free Love to Algeria*. New York: Palgrave MacMillan.

Pierson, Ruth Roach, Nupur Chaudhuri, and Beth McAuley, eds. 1998. *Nation, Empire, Colony: Historicizing Gender and Race*. Bloomington: Indiana University Press.

Pitts, Jennifer. 2006. *A Turn to Empire: The Rise of Imperial Liberalism in Britain and France*. Princeton, NJ: Princeton University Press.

Plaetzer, Niklas. 2021. "Decolonizing the 'Universal Republic': The Paris Commune and French Empire." *Nineteenth-Century French Studies* 49, nos. 3 & 4 (Spring–Summer): 585–603.

Pons-Ribot, Géraldine. 1989. "Presentation." In *La guerre en Nouvelle-Calédonie* by Le Vagabond [John Stanley James]. Translated and edited by Géraldine Pons-Ribot. Boulogne, France: Petite Maison.

Porcher-Wiart, Titaua. 2015. "Imagining the Body in Pacific Francophone Literature." *Contemporary Pacific* 27, no. 2: 405–430.

Ragan, John David. 2000. "A Fascination for the Exotic: Suzanne Voilquin, Ismayl Urbain, Jehan d'Ivray and the Saint-Simonians: French Travelers in Egypt on the Margins." PhD diss., New York University.

Ramsay, Raylene. 2011. *Nights of Storytelling: A Cultural History of Kanaky–New Caledonia*. Honolulu: University of Hawai'i Press.

Ramsay, Raylene. 2014. "Translation in New Caledonia: Writing (in) the Language of the Other—The 'Red Virgin,' the Missionary, and the Ethnographer." In *For Better or Worse: Translation as a Tool for Change in the South Pacific*, edited by Sabine Fenton.133–170. New York: Routledge.

Rano, Jonas. 2009. "Kanakitude et créolitude: La langue composante essentielle de la conscience historique d'un people." In *Le rôle, la place et la fonction des académies en contexte plurilingue: Actes du premier colloque de l'Espace Oralité*, edited by Espace Oralité Colloque, Weniko Ihage, Jacqueline de La Fontinelle, and Eric Dell'Erba. 111–134. Nouméa: Académie des Langues Kanak.

Raymond, Justinien. 2018. "Rouzade, Léonie [Née Camusat Louise-Léonie]." Le Maitron, July 22. http://maitron-en-ligne.univ-paris1.fr/spip.php?article85310.

Rétat, Claude. 2015. "Présentation: Louise Michel au bûcher. Les mémoires de 1890 ou les aventures d'un 'second volume." In *À travers la mort. Mémoires inédits, 1886–1890* by Louise Michel. Paris: La Découverte.

Rétat, Claude. 2019. "Présentation: La viellée des armes, ou les contes de la mère Michel, in *La révolution en content: histoires, contes, et légendes de Louise Michel*, edited by Claude Rétat, 7–48. Saint-Fountain-sur-Sioule.

Rétat, Claude, and Stéphane Zékian. 2013. "Présentation." In *Trois romans: Les microbes humains, Le monde nouveau, Le claque-dents* by Louise Michel. Lyon: Presses Universitaires de Lyon.

Reynolds, Siân. 1985. "New Caledonia as a Penal Colony for the Communards, 1872–1880." *Modern & Contemporary France* 21 (March): 15–21.

Robcis, Camille. 2013. *The Law of Kinship: Anthropology, Pschyoanalysis, and the Family in France*. Ithaca, NY: Cornell University Press.

Robert-Guiard, Claudine. 2009. *Des Européennes en situation colonial, Algérie, 1839–1939*. Aix-en-Provence: Publications de l'Université de Provence.

Roberts, Mary Louise. 1999. "Subversive Copy: Feminist Journalism in Fin-de Siècle France." In *Making the News: Modernity and the Mass Press in Nineteenth-Century France*, edited by Jeannene Przyblyski, 302–350. Amhurst: University of Massachusetts Press.

Roberts, Mary Louise. 2002. *Disruptive Acts: The New Woman in Fin-de-Siècle France*. Chicago: University of Chicago Press.

Roberts, Sophie B. 2017. *Citizenship and Antisemitism in French Colonial Algeria, 1870–1962*. Cambridge: Cambridge University Press.

Rogers, Rebecca. 2009. "Telling Stories about the Colonies: British and French Women in Algeria in the Nineteenth Century." *Gender & History* 21, no. 1 (April): 39–59.

Rogers, Rebecca. 2013a. *A Frenchwoman's Imperial Story: Madame Luce in Nineteenth-Century Algeria*. Stanford, CA: Stanford University Press.

Rogers, Rebecca. 2013b. "Relations entre femmes dans l'Alger colonial." *Genre et colonization* 1 (Spring): 144–191.

Rogers, Rebecca. 2016. "'Cherchez la femme': Women and Gender in French Scholarship on the Empire." *Journal of Women's History* 28, no. 4 (Winter): 124–133.

Rogers, Rebecca, and Françoise Thébaud. 2008a. "Editorial." *Clio. Femmes, genre, histoire* 28: 7–16.

Rogers, Rebecca, and Françoise Thébaud, eds. 2008b. *Clio. Femmes, genre, histoire* 28.

Rupp, Leila. 1996. "Challenging Imperialism in International Women's Organizations, 1888–1945." *NWSA Journal* 8: 8–27.

Saada, Emmanuelle. 2003. "Citoyens et sujets de l'empire Français. Les usages du droit en situation coloniale." *Genèses* 53 (December): 4–24.

Saada, Emmanuelle. 2006. "La loi, le droit et l'indigène." *Droits* 43: 179–189.

Saada, Emmanuelle. 2012. *Empire's Children: Race, Filiation, and Citizenship in the French Colonies*. Translated by Arthur Goldhammer. Chicago: University of Chicago Press.

Sabiani, Julie. 1983. "Féminisme et Dreyfusisme." In *Les écrivains et l'affaire Dreyfus: Actes du colloque organisé par l'Université d'Orleans et le Centre Péguy*, edited by Géraldi Leroy, 200–206. Paris: Universités de France.

Salaun, Marie. 2010. "Un colonialisme 'glottophage'? L'enseignement de la langue française dans les écoles indigènes en Nouvelle-Calédonie (1863–1945)." *Histoire de l'éducation* 128 (October–December): 53–198.

Sanos, Sandrine. 2014. *The Aesthetics of Hate: Far-Right Intellectuals, Antisemitism, and Gender in 1930s France*. Stanford, CA: Stanford University Press.

Sarazin, Maurice. 2008. "À Paris, le 3 mai 1908, Hubertine Auclert, la suffragiste bourbonnaise, renversait une urne électorale, puis publiait son livre *Le vote des femmes* . . ." *Les Cahiers Bourbonnais* 204 (Summer): 76–84.

Saussol, Alain. 1979. *L'héritage: Essai sur le problème foncier mélanésien en Nouvelle-Calédonie*. Paris: Musée de l'Homme.

Saussol, Alain. 2013. "En marge de l'insurrection Kanak de 1878: Nos 'fidèles alliés Canala,' mythe ou réalité?" *Journal de la Société des Océanistes*, nos. 136–137, 169–180.

Schlick, Yaël. 2012. *Feminism and the Politics of Travel after the Enlightenment*. Lanham, MD: Bucknell University Press.

Schreier, Joshua. 2007. "Napoléon's Long Shadow: Morality, Civilization, and Jews in France and Algeria, 1808–1870." *French Historical Studies* 30: 77–103.

Schreier, Joshua. 2010. *Arabs of the Jewish Faith: The Civilizing Mission in Colonial Algeria*. New Brunswick, NJ: Rutgers University Press.

Schüler-Springorum, Stefanie. 2018. "Gender and the Politics of Anti-Semitism." *American Historical Review* 123, no. 4 (October): 1210–1222.

Scott, Joan Wallach. 1996. *Only Paradoxes to Offer: French Feminists and the Rights of Man*. Cambridge, MA: Harvard University Press.

Sessions, Jennifer. 2011. *By Sword and Plow: France and the Conquest of Algeria*. Ithaca, NY: Cornell University Press.

Sessions, Jennifer. 2016. "Women and French Empire." *Journal of Women's History* 28, no. 4 (Winter): 186–199.

Sexton, Jay, and Kristin L. Hoganson. 2020. *Taking U.S. History into Transimperial Terrain*. Durham, NC: Duke University Press.

Shepard, Todd. 2013. "Algerian Nationalism, Zionism, and French Laïcité: A History of Ethnoreligious Nationalisms and Decolonization." *International Journal of Middle East Studies* 45, no. 3: 445–467.

Shurkin, Michael. 2010. "French Liberal Governance and the Emancipation of Algeria's Jews." *French Historical Studies* 33, no. 2 (Spring): 258–280.

Sieffert, Anne-Caroline. 2008. "Thérèse Bentzon: Itinéraires d'une française aux États-Unis (1840–1907)." In *Le voyage au féminin: Perspectives historiques et littéraires (XVIIIe-XXe siècles)*, edited by Nicolas Bourguinat, 109–130. Strasbourg: Presses Universitaires de Strasbourg.

Siegel, Mona. 2015. "The Dangers of Feminism in Colonial Indochina." *French Historical Studies* 38, no. 14 (October): 661–689.

Silverman, Lisa. 2011. "Beyond Antisemitism: A Critical Approach to German Jewish Cultural History." *Nexus: The Duke Journal of German Jewish Studies* 1: 27–45.

Singaravélou, Pierre. 2008. "L'empire des économistes: L'enseignement de 'l'économie coloniale' sous la IIIe République." In *L'esprit économique impérial (1830–1970). Groupes de pression & réseaux du patronat colonial en France & dans l'empire*, edited by Hubert Bonin, Catherine Hodeir, and Jean-François Klein, 135–148. Paris: Société Française D'histoire d'Outre-Mer.

Sinha, Mrinalini. 1995. *Colonial Masculinity, the 'Manly Englishman,' and the 'Effeminate Bengali' in the Late Nineteenth Century*. Manchester: Manchester University Press.

Sonn, Richard. 1992. *Anarchism*. New York: Twayne Publishers.

Soula, Virginie. 2014. *Histoire littéraire de la Nouvelle-Calédonie (1853–2005)*. Paris: Éditions Karthala.

Sowerwine, Charles. 1982. *Sisters of Citizens? Women and Socialism in France since 1876*. Cambridge: Cambridge University Press.

Spieler, Miranda. 2012. *Empire and Underworld: Captivity in French Guiana*. Cambridge, MA: Harvard University Press.

Stoler, Ann Laura. 2002. *Carnal Knowledge and Imperial Power: Race and the Intimate in Colonial Rule*. Berkeley: University of California Press.

Stoler, Ann Laura. 2016. *Duress: Imperial Durabilities in Our Times*. Durham, NC: Duke University Press.

Stovall, Tyler. 2015. *Transnational France: The Modern History of a Universal Nation.* Boulder, CO: Westview Press.

Sulerot, Evelyne. 1966. *Histoire de la presse féminine.* Paris: Armand Colin.

Surkis, Judith. 2010. "Propriété, polygamie et statut personnel en Algérie colonial, 1830–1873." *Revue d'histoire du XIXe siècle* 41, no. 2: 27–48.

Surkis, Judith. 2019. *Sex, Law, and Sovereignty in French Algeria, 1830–1930.* Ithaca, NY: Cornell University Press.

Tabili, Laura. 2003. "Race Is a Relationship and Not a Thing." *Journal of Social History* 37: 125–130.

Taiaiake, Alfred. 2009. *Peace, Power, Righteousness: An Indigenous Manifesto,* 2nd ed. New York: Oxford University Press.

Taïeb, Edith. 2006. "Coloniser and Colonised in Hubertine Auclert's Writings on Algeria." In *A "Belle Époque"? Women in French Society and Culture, 1890–1914,* edited by Diana Holmes and Carrie Tarr, 271–282. New York: Berghan Books.

Taraud, Christelle. 2008. "Genre, sexualité et colonisation. La colonisation française au Maghreb." *Sextant* 25: 117–127.

Thomas, Edith. 1966. *The Women Incendiaries.* New York, NY: George Braziller.

Thomas, Edith. 1970. "Louise Michel en Nouvelle-Calédonie." *Nouvelle revue française* 213: 46–67.

Thomas, Edith. 1971. *Louise Michel ou La Velléda de l'anarchie.* Paris: Gallimard.

Thomas, Edith. 1980. *Louise Michel.* Translated by Penelope Williams. Montreal: Black Rose Books.

Thomas, Matthew. 2004. "'No-One Telling Us What to Do': Anarchist Schools in Britain, 1890–1916." *Historical Research* 77, no. 197 (August): 405–436.

Thomas, Matthew. 2005. *Anarchist Ideas and Counter-Cultures in Britain, 1880–1914.* Hampshire: Ashgate.

Thomas, Nicholas. 2000. "Colonial Conversions: Difference, Hierarchy, and History in Early Twentieth-Century Evangelical Propaganda." In *Cultures of Empire: A Reader,* edited by Catherine Hall, 298–328. New York: Routledge.

Thompson, Debra. 2009. "Racial Ideas and Gendered Intimacies: The Regulation of Interracial Intimacies in North America." *Social & Legal Studies* 18, no. 3: 353–371.

Tjibaou, Marie-Claude. 2006. "Avant-propos: Louise Michel, une grande dame dans notre histoire." In *Légendes et chansons de gestes canaques (1875) suivi de Légendes et cants de gestes canaques (1885) et de Civilisation* by Louise Michel, 7–10. Lyon: Presses Universitaire de Lyon.

Toth, Stephen A. 2006. *Beyond Papillon: The French Overseas Penal Colonies, 1854–1952.* Lincoln: University of Nebraska Press.

Tryon, Darrell T., and Jean-Michel Charpentier. 2004. *Pacific Pidgins and Creoles: Origins, Growth and Development.* New York: Bouton de Gruyter.

Vann, Michael. 2017. "Sex and the Colonial City: Mapping Masculinity, Whiteness, and Desire in French Occupied Hanoi." *Journal of World History* 28, nos. 3–4 (December): 395–425.

Veauvy, Christiane. 2011. "Les saint-simoniennes en Égypte. Analyse critique d'un modèle d'émancipation." *Lectora* 17 (February): 221–239.

Veracini, Lorenzo. 2003. "The 'Shadows of the Colonial Period' to 'Times of Sharing': History Writing in and about New Caledonia/Kanaky, 1969–1998." *Journal of Pacific History* 38, no. 3: 331–352.

Vergès, Françoise. 2003. "Coloniser, éduquer, guider: Un devoir républicain." In *Culture coloniale: La France conquise par son empire, 1871–1931*, edited by Pascal Blanchard and Sandrine Lemaire, 191–199 Paris: Éditions Autrement.

Verhaeghe, Sidonie. 2019. "Une pensée politique de la Commune: Louise Michel à travers ses conférences," *Actual Marx* 2, no. 66b: 81–98.

Vernaudon, Jacques. 2009. "De l'oral à l'écrit: les enjeux de la normalisation graphique des langues kanak." In *La rôle, la place et la fonction des académies en contexte plurilingue: Actes du premier colloque de l'Espace Oralité*, edited by Espace Oralité Colloque, Weniko Ihage, Jacqueline de La Fontinelle, and Eric Dell'Erba, 77–88. Nouméa: Académie des Langues Kanak.

Waldman, Martin R. 1973. "The Revolutionary as Criminal in 19th-Century France: A Study of the Communards and Deportees." *Science and Society* 37, no. 1 (September): 31–55.

Ware, Vron. 1992. "Moments of Danger: Race, Gender, and Memories of Empire." *History and Theory* 31 (4): 116–137.

Wiart, Carole. 1997. "Hubertine Auclert. Une feministe en Algérie (1888–1892)." MA thesis. Université Paris 8.

Wilder, Gary. 2005. *The French Imperial Nation-State: Negritude and Colonial Humanism between the Two World Wars*. Chicago: University of Chicago Press.

Wilder, Gary. 2010. "From Optic to Topic: The Foreclosure Effect of Historiographic Turns." *American Historical Review* 117, no. 3 (June): 723–745

Wilson, Kathleen. 2002. *The Island Race: Englishness, Empire and Gender in the Eighteenth Century*. New York: Routledge.

Wilson, Kathleen, ed. 2004. *A New Imperial History: Culture, Identity, and Modernity in Britain and the Empire, 1660–1840*. Cambridge: Cambridge University Press.

Wilson, Stephen. 1982. *Ideology and Experience: Antisemitism in France at the Time of the Dreyfus Affair*. East Brunswick, NJ: Associated University Presses.

Wing, Betsy. 1997. "Translator's Introduction." In *Poetics of Relation*, by Édouard Glissant. Ann Arbor: University of Michigan Press.

Winock, Michel. 1998. *Nationalism, Anti-Semitism, and Fascism*. Translated by Jane Marie Todd. Stanford, CA: Stanford University Press.

Wolfe, Patrick. 2006. "Settler Colonialism and the Elimination of the Native." *Journal of Genocide Research* 8, no. 4: 387–409.

Zékian, Stéphane. 2015. "Roman, oralité, incorrection. Louise Michel et l'écriture de l'insurrection." In *L'insurrection entre histoire et littérature (1789–1914)* edited by Quentin Deluermoz and Anthony Glinoer, 107–124. Paris: Publications de la Sorbonne.

INDEX

Page numbers in *italics* indicate illustrations. Works with known authors may be found under the author's name.

Lightning Source UK Ltd.
Milton Keynes UK
UKHW010918180522
403171UK00003B/319